Between

Two

Trees

Daily Inspiration for the Christian Life

Paul Robinson

ISBN 978-1-7094-0184-8

DEDICATED to my Lord and Savior Jesus Christ. Thank you for thinking so highly of me that You would die in my place.

DEDICATED to my family; my wife Jennifer, who put up with me completing this project. To my children for giving me so much of the material that I used to apply God's Word to our daily adventures.

SPECIAL THANK YOU to Nick Poindexter for the design of the cover for the book.

"Blessed be the God and Father of our Lord Jesus Christ, the Father of mercies and the God of all comfort, who comforts us in all of our afflictions, so that we may be able to comfort those who are in any affliction, with the comfort with which we ourselves are comforted by God." – 2 Corinthians 1:3-4.

A New Birth

A new birth. Every year, on New Year's Day, a bid deal is made in each city about who the first child is born in the new year. Some hospitals and local news agencies give away prizes to the parents of the first child born that particular year. My own sister is a New Year's baby, although nobody gave away any type of prizes back when she was born. Nowadays, families may get a year's supply of diapers or something along those lines. I am sure as you read this first post of the New Year, multiple children were brought into this world on the first day of the New Year. It got me thinking about "new births".

Our new birth as Christians is called being "born again". I have to say that before I became a Christian, that phrase "born again" really through me for a loop. I didn't understand what people were talking about when they said, "you must be born again". What made me feel better was that even a ruler of the Jews in the Bible didn't know what Jesus was talking about when He told him the same thing. "Jesus answered him, 'Truly, truly, I say to you, unless one is born again, he cannot see the kingdom of God.'" Jon 3:3. Nicodemus was quite confused by the response of Christ, questioning how he was going to be able to crawl back into his mother's womb to be born a second time. But that was not the "birth" Jesus was talking about.

"Jesus answered, 'Truly, truly, I say to you, unless one is born of water and the Spirit, he cannot enter the kingdom of God. That which is born of the flesh is flesh, and that which is born of the Spirit is spirit." John 3:5-6. See, just a physical birth (of water) is not enough to get us into the kingdom of God, we must also experience a spiritual birth through the acceptance of Christ as our Savior. When we accept Him, we are indwelt with the Holy Spirit, giving us a spiritual birth.

The Bible is pretty clear that if we are only born once (physically), we will die twice. We will experience a physical death and we will also experience a spiritual death when we stand before Christ and give an account for our lives and be found lacking. However, if we are born twice (physically and spiritually) we will only possibly suffer a physical death if the Lord doesn't return before then.

Have you experienced a second, spiritual birth? We will not gain admittance to Heaven without that second birth. I pray that if you are reading this, that you have accepted Christ as your Savior. If not, there is no better way to start the New Year than with a new birth. Call out to God, confess that you are a sinner in need of a Savior and accept what Jesus Christ did for you on the Cross

Notes:_____
_____
_____
_____
_____
_____

January 2

Riches to Rags Story

Riches to rags. No, you didn't read that wrong, I wrote "riches to rags". We are used to seeing it the other way around, "rags to riches" right? We celebrate those that go from nothing to being on top of the world. Those that pull themselves up by the bootstraps and make something of themselves. But what about the stories of those that have everything and lose it all because of their mistakes or give it all up for something better.

The first riches to rags story we come across in the Bible is the story of Adam and Eve in the Garden of Eden. They had access to all of God's creation and even access to God Himself in a personal face-to-face way. There was nothing God held back from them in the Garden, yet they wanted more, they wanted to be "like" God because of the temptation of Satan. Due to their sin of disobedience, they were kicked out of paradise to live among the thorns and the thistle, having to produce by the sweat of their brows and the work of their hands. The original riches to rags story.

However, the greatest riches to rags story, not associated with being disciplined because of sin, was that of Jesus Christ. He voluntarily left the glory of heaven and the presence of God to be born and take on the form of the creation. The Apostle Paul said it best in his letter to the Philippians, "who, though He was in the form of God, did not count equality with God a thing to be grasped, but emptied Himself, by taking the form of a servant, being born in the likeness of men. And being found in human form, He humbled Himself by becoming obedient to the point of death, even death on a cross."

We celebrate those who make a name for themselves be going from rags to riches, but the Bible teaches the opposite is to be celebrated. Paul continues with the next verse saying, "Therefore God has highly exalted Him and bestowed on Him the name that is above every name, so that at the name of Jesus every knee should bow, in heaven and on earth and under the earth, and every tongue confess that Jesus Christ is Lord, to the glory of God the Father." That is what should be celebrated; the fact that Jesus humbled Himself for our salvation. Do we live with a humble spirit or do we look to exalt ourselves? Be humble and let God exalt you in His time.

Notes:_____
_____
_____
_____
_____
_____
_____
_____
_____

Follow Me

Follow me! That is usually a phrase we only want to hear when someone is bringing us to our table at a restaurant. By nature, we would rather lead than follow. We would rather blaze the trail and get the accolades than just be part of the team coming behind the leader. We want to be the pitcher, the point guard, or the quarterback if we use sports terms. We tell our kids to be leaders and not followers.

We can't truly be leaders until we first become followers. But we also need to be careful who we chose to follow as well as who we chose to lead. When Jesus first called his disciples, his first words to them were "follow me". He didn't ask them to lead Him, He asked them to follow Him. He would ultimately make them fishers of men (leaders), because they would first learn to fish (follow).

It takes a humble spirit to follow someone else and learn the ropes. It takes an even more humble spirit to lead others and teach them the ropes. I've been on both sides of the fence; I've had to be a follower and I've been a leader. In all honesty, I would say a humble spirit is not the words I would use to describe how I followed or how I have led, but I'm learning.

I believe we have to be both a follower and a leader at the same time. There should be someone in our lives that we are leading as a mentor and someone we are following as they mentor us. The Apostle Paul even followed this example. When he started his ministry, he had a mentor on his first journey by the name of Barnabas who vouched for Paul before the church Antioch. By the end of his ministry he was a mentor to Timothy, showing him the way as Timothy lead the church in Ephesus.

Who do you look to at this point in your life as a mentor to help guide you in the right direction as you follow after God? Who are you mentoring to help someone new in the faith along the right path through discipleship? Both are important to your growth.

Notes:_____
_____
_____
_____
_____
_____
_____
_____
_____
_____
_____
_____
_____

January 4

Missed Opportunities

Missed opportunities. Have you ever experienced something in life that was presented to you as an opportunity to change paths? Maybe it was a career changing opportunity or moving to a new state for a job opportunity, and you passed it up because you felt like it may have been too good to be true or it wasn't fitting into your timing. This opportunity may have come and you felt that you may not have been worthy of such an opportunity or maybe in arrogance, you felt that this opportunity didn't fit into your plans for yourself.

This has happened to me (and possibly you as well) and I passed on it because I thought that it wasn't right for me. To be honest, there were some feelings of regret afterwards that I had not taken the chance that God had provided, but life went on and I sort of forgot about it. Well, that same opportunity came back around a second time about nine months later and this time I knew it was what God had planned for me. "For I know the plans I have for you, declares the Lord, plans for welfare and not for evil, to give you a future and a hope" Jeremiah 29:11.

When the opportunity came back a second time, I knew it was a God-given opportunity. I prayed that if this was not of God, that He would close the door and leave me right where I was. There were so many hurdles and obstacles that had to be overcome for this opportunity to come to fruition that I thought it was impossible, but God took care of every one of them without any of them tripping up the path to this new opportunity. That's how I knew this was a "God thing". "In all your ways acknowledge Him, and He will make straight your paths." Proverbs 3:6.

Is there something God is calling you to do? Maybe there is something that He has called you to multiple times and you haven't trusted in Him to see you through the obstacles and hurdles that stand in the way. Pray that if this opportunity is the will of God, that He will remove all obstacles that stand between you and the opportunity He is calling you to. If He wants you there, there will be no stopping Him.

Notes:_____
_____
_____
_____
_____
_____
_____
_____
_____
_____
_____
_____
_____

January 5

Rain, Rain and More Rain

Rain, rain and more rain. I read somewhere that this part of North Carolina had a record setting amount of rain for 2018. I believe it with the remnants of two hurricanes coming through this fall and over a foot of snow in December. The roads show all the effects of the water too with potholes showing up everywhere.

It got me thinking about the story of Noah and the flood found in the book of Genesis. It must have been odd for Noah to hear that God was going to flood the earth because of the wickedness of man with an eventual rain. It had never rained before, so Noah had no understanding of what that meant, he just obeyed God and started building an ark.

It took Noah about 100 years to complete the construction of the ark to the specifications given by God. He endured ridicule from everyone for building such a massive ark while he warned them of the impending storm. His faith in the promises of God helped him to continue even though no one believed him.

Noah had one of the least impactful ministries of all the people in the Bible. One hundred years of warning others that God's judgement would come and only his family listened. Seven other people besides himself were saved from the flood. I think of how hard it must have been for Noah to preach to others for a hundred years and have no one listen to him besides his wife, his three sons and their wives. How did he deal with rejection like that as people probably banged on the doors of the ark after it was too late?

We have the same message as that of Noah; impending doom is coming. We read about the events of the upcoming devastation in the book of Revelation. However, we are to preach the message of Jesus Christ and His salvation through faith in Him and whether people listen and believe or not is not our responsibility; it's theirs. We are just instructed to share the Good News of Jesus Christ. Don't feel rejected because others don't listen, just be faithful to following God's plan. Salvation is of the Lord, not us. We are just messengers.

Notes:_____
_____
_____
_____
_____
_____
_____
_____
_____
_____
_____
_____

January 6

Broken Ankle

That was a broken ankle. Watching the football game last night and the poor receiver for the Dallas Cowboys suffered a serious injury and you could tell his ankle was broken right away. He was in some excruciating pain and it was sickening to watch when it happened. I felt sorry for him, as he played all season to get to the playoffs and now his season is over even though his team won the game.

The good thing for him is that he will be under great medical care by the team physicians and the surgery will probably allow him to heal back to full strength and he will be out on the field at some point next season. That is the great thing amount physical injuries like that. But what about emotional and spiritual injuries? They don't quite heal as fast as physical injuries do.

I'm sure we have all suffered from emotional pain and maybe even some of us are going through that right now. I know some of my friends on here have suffered loss recently because of death. How do you heal from things like that? Unfortunately, I don't have the answers to those types of pains, but I know the One who does. We serve a God who draws close to the broken-hearted.

The LORD is near to the brokenhearted and saves the crushed in spirit. - Psalm 34:18

He heals the brokenhearted and binds up their wounds. - Psalm 147:3

All we can do is pray for those who are going through difficult times. We can be a shoulder to cry on. And we can be an ear for those that just need someone to listen. We don't always need to have the answers to all the questions of life, but it helps to have a relationship with the God of the broken-hearted. I would love to pray for you if you have a need.

Notes:_____
_____
_____
_____
_____
_____
_____
_____
_____
_____
_____
_____

Easily Distracted

Look! Squirrel! We get easily distracted don't we. We have so many things wanting our attention nowadays days that it gets harder and harder to keep our focus on the task. I think it's harder for the younger generation than it is for the older one. They have grown up with the constant stimulation of technology and research shows that the average person's attention span today is significantly shorter than it was thirty years ago.

My post isn't about technology; it's about being distracted from the things of God. Those things that God has specifically appointed us to do. Not that someone else couldn't do them, but it may be a task specifically assigned to us. That thing in our hearts that we know that God has called us and anointed us to do.

It reminded me of the story of Nehemiah and his call to rebuild the walls around Jerusalem after they had been torn down after the exile. He goes back to Jerusalem and starts rebuilding the walls as moved by God to do and some of the religious elite weren't too happy with it. They devise a plan to get Nehemiah to come away from his work and meet them so that they could kill him.

I love Nehemiah's response to their multiple attempts to distract him from his task; "I am doing a great work and I cannot come down. Why should the work stop while I leave it and come down to you?" His task was considered a great work to him because it was something God had placed on his heart to accomplish. He saw no value it stopping his great work to meet with the opposition, and he told them so.

What is it that God has placed on your heart to accomplish for Him? Who or what is working to distract you from completing that great work? Don't let other tasks, other well-meaning people or opposition distract you from completing God's purpose for your life. I don't know what that may be in your life, but I'm sure you do!

Notes:_____
_____
_____
_____
_____
_____
_____
_____
_____
_____
_____
_____
_____
_____

January 8

The Devil Made Me Do It

"The devil made me do it!" Some of you may recognize that line, and the picture, as one of the favorite sayings of Geraldine Jones from the early 70's. (Some of you might have even went back and said that line again in your best Geraldine voice). She was a character of comedian Flip Wilson and many of her sayings became part of our culture still used today. We like to use that line, "the devil made me do it" as an escape for being accountable for our own actions.

To be completely frank, there are a whole lot of people way more important than you and I that the devil is working on. He's not worried about us; his concentration is on those in power in higher office that have a lot more influence than we do. He will use his demons to work on us if we may be advancing God's kingdom too well, but normally we are our own worst enemy.

The Apostle John, in his first epistle, wrote about all of us seeking after "the lusts of the flesh, the lusts of the eyes and the pride of life". These are all worldly things that advertise itself as things we need to be successful. This world system and our own fleshly desires are usually what get us in trouble, not the devil. It's hard to admit that because we want to seek someone or something else to blame for the sin that besets us. We automatically look for a scapegoat to blame so we don't have to be accountable.

This flesh of ours has a need to find pleasure. Our eyes are the windows to our souls and what we let into them has an impact on our thought life. And the pride of being successful or rich or popular in life drives us to do things that do not glorify God. That's why we must take the example of the Apostle Paul and beat our bodies into obedience to God (not literally).

Which one are you struggling with, or maybe it's all three of them? Whatever the situation, understand that "the devil didn't make you do it", it's your own flesh, your own eyes, or your pride that made you do it. Repent and turn back to God.

Notes:_____
_____
_____
_____
_____
_____
_____
_____

Confetti

Confetti. "It's beautiful/what a mess!" Seems like every major event, whether it sports, politics or game shows, have a love affair with shooting off confetti at the end of the event. It's always in celebration of the winner of the event and really looks awesome as it rains down on the players and fans below. But what a mess it is for the people that end up having to clean it up once everyone leaves.

I don't believe I have ever seen where the winning team or the victorious politician or the brand new game show millionaire have to come back out later and clean up all the small pieces of paper that were used to celebrate them. No, it's some group of people standing in the background watching it all come down and knowing they are going to spend hours getting it all up, so the place looks immaculate once again.

Sin is a lot like confetti. It's exciting when it's happening and internally, we may be celebrating but it doesn't last long, and we realize what a mess we have made. Sin of our own doing tends to also must be cleaned up by the sinner. But many times, it's the others in the background, family and friends, that end up having to do most of the cleaning up. Our sins have a ripple effect on the ones we love and are never really contained to just us.

The Bible says that those things that are done in the dark (sin), will at some point be brought into the light. Things we think will be kept secret from others will always be known by God. We may get away with our sin for a while without anyone finding out, but most often it's only a matter of time before it is exposed. We end up having to continue in sin to hide the sins we are trying to keep hidden.

The Apostle Paul told Timothy to "flee youthful passions and pursue righteousness, faith, love, and peace, along with those who call on the Lord from a pure heart." Take every opportunity to flee from sin and you and others will never get caught having to clean up the confetti of your own sins.

Notes:_____
_____
_____
_____
_____
_____
_____
_____
_____
_____
_____
_____

Lukewarm

Lukewarm. If you were to be described as water, what would that definition look like? Would you be hot, cold or just lukewarm? The Christian artist, Lecrae, sings about this in one of his songs. He sings, "with hot water we cook, cold water we drink, but lukewarm does nothing, it just sits, and it looks." The Apostle John records similar words spoken by Jesus in the book of Revelation to the church at Laodicea, "I know your works: you are neither cold nor hot. Would that you were either cold or hot! So, because you are lukewarm, and neither hot nor cold, I will spit you out of my mouth."

We fall into one of these three categories as well, not just as a church, but as individuals. We are either hot for the things of God and people notice that right away or we fall into one of the other two categories. We either having that shock of stepping into a shower where the water is too hot to stand under and we jump and twist trying to reach the faucet handle to cool it down or we don't. Hot Christians give off that feeling of a fire on a cold winter's day that draws others to them to feel the warmth of Christ that radiates from them.

Cold Christians are just that; cold. Their attitude towards their faith pushes people away from wanting to know the love and grace of Christ. Others say, "if that's what it means to be a Christian, I don't want anything to do with that." These are the people that outsiders to Christianity would call hypocrites. Cold Christians do nothing with their salvation to win others to Christ.

But the most dangerous of Christians are those that Jesus called "lukewarm". These are the Christians that if their friends ever found out they went to church they would be totally shocked. How they live Monday through Saturday doesn't match up with the fact that they spend their Sundays at church. They live like the rest of the world does during the week. How they walk and talk at work or at school doesn't match how they walk and talk at church. Jesus would rather have us be either hot or cold than lukewarm. A lukewarm Christian does the most damage to the kingdom of God because he/she portrays Jesus as One who doesn't care how we live our lives in view of the unsaved world.

So, how would you describe your Christian life: hot, cold or lukewarm? If it's not hot, you still have time to turn up the heat and draw others to the love of Christ.

Notes:_____
_____
_____
_____
_____
_____
_____

January 11

Daily Commitments

How are those New Year's resolutions working out for you? Did you resolve this year to join the gym? Or maybe to lose that extra weight you gained during the holidays? Or was it to quit a habit that you have been wanting to quit for years and this was the year you were going to do it? We are now about two weeks into the New Year, how are those commitments working out for you? It's hard to make a commitment and then follow through on them day in and day out, that's why they call it "a commitment". Don't feel bad or be discouraged that you may have already failed on what you planned to do this year, there is nothing special about January 1st that you can't start all over again tomorrow.

I saw a marque sign out in front of a church on my way to and from work the past couple of days that read as follows: "God doesn't want yearly resolutions; He wants daily commitments". Not that there is anything wrong with New Year's resolutions if you make them each year, but God wants you to make just a daily commitment to follow Him and to do His will for your life that particular day. Jesus told His own followers, "If anyone would come after me, let him deny himself and take up his cross daily and follow me." Luke 9:23.

Christ didn't tell His followers that they needed to wait for the New Year to come back around and then make a resolution on the first day of the year to extend over the length of the entire year, He said to follow Him daily, starting with that very day! He wants us to pick up our "cross" every day, day in and day out, and follow Him. When we wake up the following morning, He asks us to do it all over again for that day.

That's hard to do! It's hard for me to do every day and I'm sure that it is hard for you to do every day as well. It's a matter of consistency, to be able to do the same thing day in and day out until it becomes a habit that we do it without even thinking about it. We don't do it in a way that it's done because we "have to", we do it in a way that we "want to" because we know what Christ sacrificed for us.

What is your daily commitment for God? It is something different for each of us. Maybe it's reading our Bibles on a daily basis, or maybe doing a more consistent job of praying, or maybe we make a commitment to God to witness for Him on a daily basis. Whatever it is that you feel that God is calling you to be committed to for His sake, start today as the first day of this new daily commitment.

Notes:_____
_____
_____
_____
_____
_____
_____
_____
_____
_____
_____

Fake News

FAKE NEWS! I don't know what the word of 2018 was, but I would have to say that the phrase "fake news" must be up there among the top choices. It's been used so often that it's hard to know what is true anymore and what is a lie. The phrase has become a punchline among everyday conversation to let the speaker know you don't believe them.

It's nothing new though, we are warned about this "fake news" in the Bible. Jesus even warned His followers not to be alarmed because at the end of the age there will be wars and rumors of wars. But I think the apostle that hit the nail right on the head was Peter. In his second letter he wrote that in the end will come scoffers, those that make fun of what we believe, and they will ask, "where is the promise of His coming?" They will say that they have heard for years that Christ will be returning but they will scoff that it hasn't happened yet and never will.

But Peter promises us that it will happen, that Christ will return as promised. We are instructed to be patient because a day with the Lord is like a thousand years and a thousand years is like a day. Peter says that the reason for His delay is that He is long suffering and that He doesn't want anyone to perish but for all to come to repentance.

If you believe in Christ, take heart, His return is closer today than it was yesterday. If you haven't repented of your sins and accepted Christ as your Savior, He's waiting for you with all His patience because He is long suffering. Today is the day of salvation because He could return tomorrow. Don't believe the fake news that He's not coming back.

Notes:_____

_____

_____

_____

_____

_____

_____

_____

_____

_____

_____

_____

_____

_____

_____

_____

_____

_____

_____

January 13

Mine! Mine! Mine!

Mine! Mine! Mine! If you have kids or grandkids you have probably seen the seagulls from the movie Finding Nemo. This was the only thing they said in the movie every time they saw something that they could possibly eat. We get that way sometimes too when we see things that we either feel we must have or that belong to us. We especially see it in children when they are young, and they believe everything belongs to them and will not share with other kids.

It reminded me of a lesson I did a few weeks ago from 2 Kings chapter 7. There was a group of lepers that were on the verge of starvation because of the famine in Israel. They felt their only hope was to seek refuge in the attacking Syrian camp outside the city. When they arrived, they realized it had been abandoned with all the treasures of the army still in the camp.

They started to eat the food in the first tent they came to and they took the silver and gold and hid it outside the camp to use later. As they were doing the same thing in the second tent they came to, one of the lepers said that what they were doing wasn't right by keeping all these treasures to themselves as others were suffering from the famine. So, they went back to the city to inform the king of the great news and the whole camp was seized thus ending the famine.

Do we as Christians do the same thing that the lepers started out doing? Do we keep this great treasure of salvation to ourselves instead of sharing it with those that are in a great spiritual famine? We need to have that moment like the leper did and tell ourselves "this isn't right" and share the Good News of Jesus Christ with those that are perishing. Salvation is not for us to hoard up with the idea that it's "mine, mine, mine"; but we should be willing to go and share the life changing treasure that has been given to us by God.

Notes:_____

_____
_____
_____
_____
_____
_____
_____
_____
_____
_____
_____
_____
_____
_____

YOU Are Not the Treasure!

YOU are not the treasure! Yesterday's post got me thinking on the word treasure and how many times it is found in the Bible. Let me tell you, it's in there a lot. One place that really caught my eye was in the Apostle Paul's letter to the Corinthians.

In the fourth chapter he tells the Corinthians that we have "this treasure" in jars of clay. "This treasure" that he is referring to is found at the end of the previous verse. The treasure is that God has shown a light into our hearts giving us the knowledge of His glory in the face of Jesus Christ. That, my brothers and sisters, is the treasure: Jesus Christ.

We are not the treasure. We are the vessel that holds that treasure. We are the jars of clay. Jars, in Paul's day, were used for one of three things: as a toilet, to hold documents and to hide valuables, sort of like a safe. Paul was inferring the third meaning when he said we were jars of clays. We are the vessel that contains the valuable things of God.

Being that these jars were made of clay, and not metal, meant that they were disposable. They were meant to be broken when the valuables inside were needed. The value was not in the jar, just like the value is not in ourselves. Jesus Christ is the value and we are the conduit that holds that valuable resource. The Holy Spirit resides in us so that we can transport the glory of God to others.

You, my friend, are an important part of bringing the message of the glory of God to others. But you are not the treasure. That belongs to God Himself in the person of Jesus Christ.

Notes:_____

_____
_____
_____
_____
_____
_____
_____
_____
_____
_____
_____
_____
_____
_____
_____
_____
_____
_____

Give it Away

"Give it away, give it away, give it away now!", as the Red Hot Chili Peppers once sang. I don't remember the song that well to tell you what they were requesting for you to give away, but it goes along with the idea of "treasure" I've been talking about the last two days.

In the gospels of Matthew and Mark, Jesus meets a young man asking what he needed to do to get into heaven. Jesus already knew this young man's heart and what mattered most to him, but He answered his question. Jesus told the young man to follow the commandments of Moses which the young man replied that he had followed all of them to the letter since he was a child. That was a lie.

So Jesus continued straight to the heart of this young man, who was considerably wealthy, telling him to sell all his possessions (treasures) and give the money to the poor. This task was just too hard for the young man to accomplish and he went away sorrowful because the Bible says, "he had great possessions" or treasures.

As Christians, we know that neither following the Ten Commandments nor giving away your possessions will get you into heaven. We don't get to Heaven by works but by grace. The point of the story was giving up the things of this life to surrender our lives to follow Christ just like His twelve disciples had done. This young man's treasure was the stumbling block to the true treasure of knowing the Savior.

What is so important to you that you are unwilling to give it up in order to surrender everything to Christ? Christ wants to know that, in your heart, you are willing to give it all up to be submissive to Him. Just like Abraham and the near sacrifice of his promised son, Isaac. He wants to know that we are willing to let go of what you think matters most. What are you willing to sacrifice to follow Him?

Notes:_____

_____
_____
_____
_____
_____
_____
_____
_____
_____
_____
_____
_____
_____
_____

Treasures in Heaven

Treasures in Heaven. Do you think there are safe deposit boxes in heaven? I don't know why I think of crazy questions like that, but I do. I ask the question because Jesus told us to store up our treasures in heaven instead of here on earth and I just want to make sure my treasures are safe.

Jesus told His disciples not to worry about gaining a whole bunch of treasures here on earth because both moth and rust can destroy them and also because thieves can break in and steal your treasures. All three of these events have taken place in my life. I have taken out a suit to wear that I hadn't worn in a long time and find little holes all in the jacket. My truck is rusting out because of bad design that doesn't let the water drain correctly. And I have had items stolen out of my car before.

I wouldn't really label any of those items' real "treasures", but they were my possessions that I had paid good money for and they would have ultimately been thrown away at some point anyway. Jesus said that we are not to live life to gain possessions just for that very reason; they are all temporary. He told us to store up for ourselves treasures in heaven that moth or rust or thieves cannot get to. These things will be eternal.

But what are those treasures? What do they look like? How do we know what they are and that we have them waiting for us when we get there? The Bible makes it clear what treasures we can attain and make sure they are waiting for us in heaven when we arrive. No safe deposit box needed, and we are going to give them away anyway. We'll look at what those treasures are tomorrow.

Notes:_____

_____

_____

_____

_____

_____

_____

_____

_____

_____

_____

_____

_____

_____

_____

January 17

Crowns

CROWNS! That's a believer's treasure that I spoke about yesterday. Jesus told his followers to "lay up" treasures in heaven. The Apostle Paul said there was a crown of righteousness "laid up" for him. They both used the same phrase for laying up something for future use.

The Bible lists five possible crowns that a believer can have waiting for them when they get to heaven for their actions here on earth. These five crowns are not for our glory but are for us to give back to the Savior. These crowns are conditional, future and temporal.

The first crown found in the Bible is the Incorruptible Crown in 1 Corinthians 9:24-27. This crown is awarded for those that practice self-denial. The whole of chapter 9 deals with the topic of self-denial and liberty.

The second crown is the Crown of Rejoicing found in 1 Thessalonians 2:18-20. The Crown of Rejoicing is also called the soul-winner's crown. It is a crown given to those who win souls for Christ. This seems to be a style of crown that you can win many of.

The third crown is the Crown of Righteousness found in 2 Timothy 4:6-8. This crown should be the easiest of all to receive and everyone should have this one on that day. Everyone who loves the appearing of the Lord will receive this crown.

The fourth crown is the Crown of Life found in James 1:12. This crown is awarded to those who endure trials. Some endure more trials than others and this seems to be a crown that you can receive more than one of as well.

The final crown is the Crown of Glory found in 1 Peter 5:1-4. This crown is also called the Under-shepherd's Crown. This is a crown given to anyone that is an elder or feeds the flock. It is not a crown only for pastors, but it is for anyone that carries out the great commission to make disciples.

"They cast their crowns before the throne" - Revelation 4:10. That is the purpose of our treasure: to give it back to the Lamb of God for what He has done for us. How many crowns will you have to give back to the One who died for you? Kind of humbling when you stop to think about it.

Notes:_____
_____
_____
_____
_____
_____
_____

Friends, Followers, Connections, oh my!

Sometimes we can become enamored by how many "friends" we have on Facebook, or "connections" we have on LinkedIn, or how many "followers" we have on a page we may manage. If we stop and look at how many of those friends, connections and followers we actually know, I bet we would be quite surprised at the low number. If I was in a room with all of my so-called "friends", I bet I wouldn't know all of their names or even recognize who they are or how I know them. Why is it that we have become so engrossed in numbers of "friends" instead of genuine relationships with friends?

We should take our example of our friendships from Jesus. He had the multitudes that followed Him from place to place because He was performing miracles and healing them and feeding them, but He wasn't always among the multitudes. Out of the multitudes, Jesus called a smaller group that He called "disciples" because they were the ones that were actually living out His teachings and not just around for the miracles. We aren't told how many disciples there were but we know it was less than the multitudes. From that group he called twelve which were later called apostles. These were the men that traveled with Christ on a daily basis that He was preparing to take over after His death.

From those twelve, we know that there were three (Peter, James and John) that had an even closer relationship with Christ. These three accompanied Christ on very rare occasions, like the Mount of Transfiguration. These three were allowed to witness things that the others were not. From those three, John calls himself "the one that Jesus loved". John was given the responsibility of looking after the mother of the Savior after His death.

There are things people post on social media that should not be shared with the "masses", they should be thins that we keep within the twelve, or the three or the one person in our lives that we are closest too because they are way to personal to share with everyone. As Christians, there should be things that we do not post on social media for the world to know because they are too private. These things should be shared only within our smaller group. We should not feel the need to post every event of our lives for the whole world to see. Christ kept some of His most private moments for those He held closest to Him. When He was struggling with His own impending death on the Cross, He didn't go to the masses for prayer, He went to the three.

Notes:_____
_____
_____
_____
_____
_____
_____
_____
_____

January 19

Radio

Radio. I admit it, I cried a little last night watching the movie "Radio". If you've never seen it, you must watch it at least once and make sure you have the tissues. It a true story about a man named James Kennedy, nicknamed "Radio" that has a mental handicap. He is befriended by the local high school football coach in Anderson, SC. James Kennedy is played by Cuba Gooding Jr.

It doesn't start out too well for Radio as he is terrorized by the high school star football player named Clay. He, along with some of his other teammates, tape his hands and feet together and lock him in an equipment shed. Later in the movie, Clay tricks Radio into going into the girl's locker room. Radio refuses to name Clay as the one who told him to go into the locker room.

By the end of the movie, Clay finally comes around to seeing what a great person Radio really is and he and his teammates purchase Radio a letterman's jacket.

Radio's unconditional love for all of those around him, especially Clay even when he didn't deserve it, reminded me of the unconditional love of God. We serve a God who knows every detail of our lives, public and private, but still loves us unconditionally anyway. The Bible says, "that even when we were yet sinners, Christ died for us." Even though he knew who we were and what we had done, He loved us so much that He was willing to give up His life in place of our own. That is unconditional love!

Friends, it doesn't matter what you have done in your past, or what you are doing in your present; God love you! He loves you so much He wants to make you part of His family. He wants you to confess your sins, repent from them and accept His free gift of salvation.

It didn't matter what people did to Radio, he loved them unconditionally just like family. We serve a God who loves the same way and He wants us to love others just like Radio did with those that picked on him. It's hard, I know, but that's what God wants from us.

Notes:_____
_____
_____
_____
_____
_____
_____
_____
_____
_____
_____

Warning - Rapture Ahead

WARNING! WARNING! WARNING! There will come a day when people you know might go missing. There will be no sign left by them that they are gone. They will just disappear off the face of the earth with no explanation.

Sounds like something from a science fiction movie, doesn't it? Actually, the event I'm talking about is from the Bible. It's called the Rapture. Even though it's not mentioned by name, the Apostle Paul describes it in his letter to the Thessalonians. It's the next event to happen in the prophetic events of God.

"For this we declare to you by a word from the Lord, that we who are alive, who are left until the coming of the Lord, will not precede those who have fallen asleep. For the Lord himself will descend from heaven with a cry of command, with the voice of an archangel, and with the sound of the trumpet of God. And the dead in Christ will rise first. Then we who are alive, who are left, will be caught up together with them in the clouds to meet the Lord in the air, and so we will always be with the Lord."- 1 Thessalonians 4:15-17

That phrase that Paul uses, "caught up" is the Greek word "rapturo" where we get "rapture" from. Believers in Christ will be snatched away in the twinkling of an eye and will be forever with the Lord.

If you don't know Christ as your Savior, the Bible says you will be left behind when the Rapture happens and the church (believers in Christ) are taken away. You will not want to be left behind for the coming tribulation that will then begin. The time for salvation is now! Do not wait until the Rapture happens!

If these posts suddenly stop one day and millions of people are missing with no explanation, you now know why and what happened. Don't miss out.

Notes_____
_____
_____
_____
_____
_____
_____
_____
_____
_____
_____
_____
_____

January 21

Rapture - Part 2

So, is the Rapture fact or opinion? Well, first off, my opinion doesn't matter! The only way to check if the idea of a future Rapture is true is to check it against what the Bible says about it elsewhere. We can't, as Christians, take certain sections of Scripture and make it fit what we want it to say without checking it against other portions of Scripture to make sure it matches up.

Does the Bible show anywhere else, besides the writings of the Apostle Paul to the Thessalonians, that the Rapture is a factual event? There are two other places in the New Testament that seem to show proof of an event that mirrors the future Rapture.

The first place is in 2 Corinthians chapter 12, where Paul speaks of knowing a man (himself actually) that was "caught up" into the third heaven and heard things he was not allowed to speak of again. That term "caught up", is the same term he used it his letter to the Thessalonians, the Greek word "rapturo". So that is the first cross reference to a Rapture.

The second place where the Rapture of an individual happens is in the Book of Revelation, chapter 4. The Apostle John, in writing the letter to the seven churches in Asia Minor, says that he heard a voice from heaven telling him to "come up here" and immediately he was in the Spirit and was in heaven before the throne of God.

Both of these event show the Rapture of only individual people, but could it be that the events in which they were a part of will be very similar to what will take place during the worldwide Rapture of the church? In Paul's letter to the Thessalonians, the description is almost the same as the two events that happened to Paul and John.

The Rapture will happen as describe in the Word of God. Are you ready to go or will you be left behind?

Notes:_____

_____

_____

_____

_____

_____

_____

_____

_____

_____

_____

_____

_____

_____

When We Get to Heaven

What will we be like when we get to Heaven? Some think we turn into angels and float around on clouds all day with harps. That is so un-Biblical that it's not even worth arguing over. Angels were created beings made before man and have always existed and will continue to exist as angels for eternity, but that's a different post for a different time.

As humans, created by God and in the image of God, we will remain to be humans when we get to heaven. We will shed this human corrupted body and receive a new incorruptible human body just like Christ had when he rose from the dead. He had a body that could be handled, He still got hungry with His new body, but He also had new abilities that He didn't have prior to His resurrection. He was able to show up places whenever He wanted and He was able to walk through locked doors.

In the Apostle John's first letter, he wrote "Beloved, we are God's children now, and what we will be has not yet appeared; but we know that when he appears we shall be like him, because we shall see him as he is." I look forward to being like Him, do you? I look forward to having a body without the aches and pains of getting old. I look forward to having a body that doesn't know sickness or death anymore. And I know people that are blind, deaf or handicapped that look forward to having a totally restored body.

I've heard many commentators say that we will all be around the age of thirty-three in heaven because that was about the age of Christ when He died and rose from the dead. I'm not sure how true that is and it really doesn't matter to me, I just want to be wherever He is for all of eternity.

I think the best thing about heaven, other than being with my Savior and my Heavenly Father, is being able to spend eternity with friends and family that know Christ as their Savior and being able to spend time speaking with the great men and women of the Bible. I can't wait to sit and talk with the Apostle Paul; I have hundreds of questions for him. Who do you look forward to spending eternity with?

Notes:_____
_____
_____
_____
_____
_____
_____
_____
_____
_____
_____

Heaven is Temporary

Heaven is a temporary place. Did that blow your mind? Most people, even Christians, think that we will spend eternity in heaven but that is not Biblically correct. Heaven is a temporary place, but hell is eternal.

Heaven is called by multiple names in the Bible. It's called Abraham's bosom. Jesus even told the thief on the cross that he would be with Him that day in Paradise. However, we will not spend all of eternity there. The Book of Revelation gives us a clue of how things will go.

Christians will all go to heaven at the Rapture of the church. Paul says the dead in Christ will rise first. That is everyone that has already passed away as believers in Christ. Their bodies will come out of the grave and be changed to an incorruptible and immortal body. Right after that, Paul says that those of us that are still alive and remain will be changed in a twinkling of an eye, receiving the same incorruptible and immortal body as the others. We will meet Jesus in the air and go with Him to heaven.

At the end of the Book of Revelation, John writes that we will return with Jesus to the earth for the Battle of Armageddon. When the battle is complete and Jesus has won, He will set up His kingdom here on earth for one thousand years, called the Millennial Reign.

Once that one thousand years comes to an end and Satan is defeated one last time, the current heaven and earth is destroyed and a new heaven and a new earth is created. Out of heaven comes an eternal city called New Jerusalem and that is where we spend all eternity, not in heaven.

Notes:_____

_____

_____

_____

_____

_____

_____

_____

_____

_____

_____

_____

_____

_____

_____

_____

_____

Hell is Real

Hell is Real. Hell is an actual physical place that is an eternal residence for those that don't accept Christ as their Savior. Going to hell has nothing to do with being a bad person; there will be a lot of "good" people in hell. People always ask, "how can a loving God send people to hell?" God doesn't send anyone to hell, people choose hell over God. God gives the way to escape eternity in hell, people just don't accept it.

Jesus spoke more about hell during His ministry than He did about heaven. That's because hell is eternal and heaven is temporary, like I said yesterday. Jesus never spoke of hell as a pleasant place but as a place of torment. Hell wasn't created for humans; it was created for Satan and his demons.

I hear people talk about how much fun they are going to have in hell like it's going to be the ultimate party zone. My heart aches for people who believe that because they have no idea the horror of that place. The Bible calls it by different names: hell, Hades, the pit. It describes it as a place of utter darkness even though there will be flames, a place of unquenchable thirst, a place where there will be wailing and gnashing of teeth because of physical pain.

The Gospels give us two examples of the horrors of hell. The first example was of a rich man that died and went to hell. His only request was for someone to dip their finger in cool water and touch the tip of his tongue because he was in anguish from the flames. The second example was of another man that only wanted to go back and warn his brothers of the horrors so they would not follow him to hell.

Hell is not a joke and definitely not a place you want to spend the rest of your eternity. People that go to hell never have an end of their torment. They do not burn up and cease to exist. They suffer for eternity.

There is an escape from the terror of a place called hell and His name is Jesus Christ. Bow your knee now, humble yourself and accept His Lordship or you will do it when it is too late. You will do it one way or another. Do it now here on earth or do it later before you are sent to hell.

Notes:_____

_____

_____

_____

_____

_____

_____

Upgrade

Upgrade. This word has come up over and over the past couple of weeks and it made me think about upgrading. I have heard it mentioned at work, I've heard it on commercials on the radio and on television and seen it on advertisements on social media. We live in a society that is constantly wanting to upgrade: to the newest phone, the newest car and a bigger and better job or home. We even upgrade the simplest things in life: our food. We "super-size it" or we go for the combo meal instead of just the sandwich by itself. It's what society has trained us to do, even as Christians. Maybe with the new year that just came around, you did some upgrading yourself. There is nothing inherently wrong with upgrading if we aren't doing it for reasons centered around pride.

It's funny how, as I thought about this post and the idea of upgrading, I have done all of these things in the past year myself. I have upgraded my phone, my car, my job and my home. Not for social status or out of pride, but mostly out of necessity. The world tells us that upgrading, especially climbing the corporate ladder at work, somehow automatically puts us in a position of leadership. But the Bible teaches us the exact opposite about leadership.

Jesus taught His disciples that positions of leadership was not about lording their power over those that they lead, but instead being servants to those that were under their protection. "But Jesus called them to Him and said, 'You know the rulers of the Gentiles lord it over them, and their great ones exercise authority over them. It shall not be so among you. But whoever would be great among you must be your servant, and whoever would be first among you must be your slave, even as the Son of Man came not to be served but to serve, and to give His life as a ransom for many." Matthew 20:25-28.

Leadership is shown by the action of Christ Himself, when He knew He was twenty-four hours from His death, instead of having Hid disciples serve Him, He got up and washed their feet in an act of service. Are we expecting others to serve us because of our rank or position? Instead we should be serving others just like Christ's example before His death.

Notes:_____

_____

_____

_____

_____

_____

_____

_____

_____

_____

_____

January 26

Striking a Nerve

Striking a Nerve. Every view strikes a nerve nowadays. Whether you talk sports, religion or politics, you are bound to offend someone with what you believe and the stance you take on a topic. Politics seems to strike a nerve more than anything else these days. Views have become completely polarized. There is no longer any middle ground; you are either for or against whoever is in office. But what does the Bible tell us about how we are to treat those in charge?

Back in the book of Exodus when Moses was going through all the Laws that God had given him to instruct the Israelites, He gave them this little line: "You shall not revile God, nor curse a ruler of your people." - Exodus 22:28. Now I know that this was given to the nation of Israel and not to Christians but there are Old Testament truths that still hold true no matter what.

If you don't think that the Old Testament laws apply to you, here you go: "Remind them to be submissive to rulers and authorities, to be obedient, to be ready for every good work" - Titus 3:1. The New Testament gives us the same advice. We, as Christians, are to be obedient to those in office. We are to be honorable people and we are to honor the office no matter who holds it.

We do not have to agree with all things that the person in office does but we are instructed to be obedient (unless it goes against God's Word). We don't always agree with our spouse, but we honor our spouse because we love them, and God instructs us to do so. We don't always agree with our bosses, but we honor that they have authority over us, and we obey them. So why don't we do that with our elected officials? Why do we find it so easy to throw hate and anger at them for everything they do?

We ruin our witness to the world that doesn't believe in God when we take part in the same things that the world does. If we don't look any different than the world then why should they want to be Christians? We will never fully agree with any person that is in office, but we can always honor the position like God wants us to and be a great witness for Christ.

Notes:_____
_____
_____
_____
_____
_____
_____
_____
_____

God of Molech

God of Molech. There is nothing new under the sun! We treat things going on today as if it's the worst it has ever been in the history of mankind. I agree that the things we do as a society today are getting worse and worse by the hour it seems, but it's nothing new.

Let's take the wickedness of killing our children for example. We find these things going on all through the Bible. Do you remember when Israel was in captivity in Egypt? They were getting too numerous and caused a potential threat to the power of the pharaoh. He ordered all the male Jewish babies, that were born in Egypt, to be thrown into the Nile River and drowned. Luckily Moses was saved and rescued Israel from captivity.

It didn't get any better in the days of Jesus. Remember when He was born King Herod ordered all the male children around Bethlehem to be killed because Jesus posed a threat to his throne? Luckily Jesus and His family received word from an angel and were able to escape to Egypt (ironic) and survive. Jesus went on to die on the cross at Calvary to save the world from their sins.

In 2 Kings, chapter 23, we find the sacrifices of children to the Ammonite god Molech. Molech is mentioned in a handful of places in the Old Testament and once in Acts in the New Testament. The Israelites fell into the trap of sacrificing their own children to this pagan god as well, trying to be like the people around them. The section in 2 Kings said that people were sacrificing their sons and daughters to Molech by burning them alive. They felt that the sacrifice of their children would be more acceptable that the sacrifice animals to God of Israel.

The Bible speaks quite often of the blessing that children are: "Like arrows in the hand of a warrior are the children of one's youth.
Blessed is the man who fills his quiver with them!" - Psalm 127:4-5. Jesus ordered His disciples not to keep the children from Him. We are instructed to come to faith in Christ as a child. We should be protecting the lives of our children as God wants us too, not sacrificing them to the modern-day god of Molech.

Notes:_____
_____
_____
_____
_____
_____
_____
_____
_____

All In

"All in!!!" Remember back about seven or eight years ago and Texas Hold'em was all the rage? It seemed to be on ESPN almost every night. People were playing it on computers and signing up trying to get into tournaments. The best part was when they were down to the final table and someone would push all their chips to the center of the table and declare they were "all in". It meant they were risking everything on winning that hand.

Can you say that you are "all in" on this Christian life or are you just in it for the chance to go to heaven? There is a Biblical difference between salvation and Lordship. Most Christians have no problem accepting Christ for their salvation but very few sacrifice their life over to the Lordship of Jesus Christ. Very few say, "God, I am all in! Do with my life as you please". That's Lordship.

Remember when Thomas met Jesus for the first time after the Resurrection? He was having a hard time believing that Jesus had risen from the dead, but when he saw Jesus for the first time and Jesus instructed Him to put his fingers in the holes in His wrists and to put his hand in His side. Thomas's reaction was to cry out, "My Lord and my God". He was saying that Jesus Christ was God and he was giving over Lordship of his life to Him.

There are really two types of Christians in the world: the saved and the available. The saved thank God for saving them from the debt of their sins, but the available thank God for their salvation and then say use me as You will. That's what being an "all in" Christian means; being available for whatever it is God wants from you. It's not easy. It means giving up control of your own life and giving it all to God.

The Apostle Paul gives us an outline of what an "all in" Christian looks like in Romans 12:1-2. He tells us that we are to present ourselves a "living sacrifice" to God. We'll investigate what that means tomorrow as we go through those two verses this week.

Notes:_____
_____
_____
_____
_____
_____
_____
_____
_____
_____
_____
_____
_____

January 29

A Living Sacrifice

A Living Sacrifice. What is it that God wants from us as Christians? Romans 12:1 answers that question clearly. The Apostle Paul commands us to present our bodies (ourselves) as a living sacrifice. But why? Because of the mercy that God has shown us in sacrificing His own Son and removing our sins.

He asks for total commitment, not a half-hearted try. Webster's dictionary defines total commitment as "the alignment of one's motives, resources, priorities and goals to fulfill a specific mission, accomplish a specific task or follow a specific purpose."

Total commitment to something is usually viewed in a negative light centering around what you lose, the rules you need to follow or the fun you miss out on. Total commitment isn't done on a whim; it's done with wisdom, logic and shrewd evaluation.

We live as though a total commitment to God would be a crushing blow to our personal dreams and future happiness when in reality, He has so much more for us than we can ever dream of. Paul asked the Romans in chapter 8 verse 32 - "He who did not spare His own Son but gave Him up for us, how will He not also with Him graciously give us all things?"

Verse 1 of chapter 12 of Romans gives us a command, a motivation and a reason. The command is to offer your body. The motivation is the mercy of God. And the reason is that it's the worship God desires. We are to present our physical bodies as an act of true, inner, Spirit-directed service to God.

Notes:_____

_____
_____
_____
_____
_____
_____
_____
_____
_____
_____
_____
_____
_____
_____
_____
_____
_____
_____
_____

Why?

Why? I think the favorite word of a soon-to-be three-year-old is "why?" It doesn't matter what the answer may be to the question he asks; it's going to get the response of "why?" It's enough to about drive you crazy. I think that's why God makes little kids so cute; it helps keep them alive!

So, we found out "what" God wants from us as Christians in the first verse of Romans chapter 12: total, all-in surrender. Verse two gives us the "how" and the "why". We saw yesterday that we, as Christians, are commanded to surrender our bodies as a living sacrifice to God as our act of worship because of what He has done for us through Jesus Christ.

That's great, but "how" do we go about doing that so that we can worship God with our sacrifice? Paul says we surrender our bodies to God by no longer conforming to this world. The word "conform" means to be poured into a mold of something and take on its outward appearance. We must stop acting like the rest of the world and start acting like Jesus. Whatever we put into our hearts and minds will be what we live out in our lives. If we put in the things of this world, we live out the things of this world. If we put in God's Word, we live out God's Word.

We also have to be "transformed" in the things we put in our minds. This transformation happens from the inside out. A metamorphosis must take place. That word "transformed" is the same word used to describe the change that happened to Christ on the Mount of Transfiguration.

Now that we know "what" God wants us to do and "how" He wants us to do it, the second part of verse two tells us the "why": so we can "discern the good, acceptable and perfect will of God".

Imagine what the Christian life would be like if we break free from the performance-oriented life based upon "doing" things. We are saved by grace, but then we change it to works after salvation. What if we just kept living this Christian life under God's grace?

Notes:_____

_____
_____
_____
_____
_____
_____
_____

Money Where Your Mouth Is

Put your money where your mouth is! We always want proof, don't we? The Apostle
Thomas wanted proof that Jesus had risen from the dead as the other apostles had told
him. We wanted to see it with his own eyes. He wanted to touch and handle Him. There is
nothing wrong with wanting proof of some things. The world wants proof that we are what
we say we are. They want us to put our money where our mouth is.

We have been looking at Romans 12 and the first two verses showed us "what" God
wanted from Christians (total submission), "how" to do it (transformation by the renewing
of our minds), and "why" we should do it (receive perfect will of God). Verses nine through
thirteen gives us the marks of an "all in" Christian.

The Apostle Paul gives us the following list of what our lives should look like if we have
totally surrendered to Christ:
• we will be authentic. Authenticity happens when the real you, meets real needs, for the
right reasons, in the right way.

- we show a sincere love.
- abhor what is evil.
- hold fast to what is true.
- be devoted to one another.
- honor one another.
- not be slothful in zeal (laziness).
- fervent in spirit.
- serving the Lord.
- rejoicing in hope.
- patient in troubles.
- constant in prayer.
- contribute to the needs of others.
- be hospitable

Now there is no way we can be perfect in all of these things. We are all at different places
along our journey for each one of these and we will never perfect any of them. But our goal
should be to keep striving after the mark of being like Jesus in each of these and the result
will be that people will know that we are followers of Christ. Even the Apostle Paul said,
"Not that I have already obtained this or am already perfect, but I press on to make it my
own, because Christ Jesus has made me his own". - Philippians 3:12

Notes:_____
_____
_____
_____
_____
_____
_____
_____
_____
_____
_____

February 1

Lost

Lost. Have you ever been lost while you were out driving in an area you weren't to certain about? As men, we don't like to admit that, but our spouses would usually be pretty quick to let everyone know of our misadventures. That's ok because being lost happens to the best of people. It's much harder to do nowadays with the invention of all sorts of navigational technology like Google Maps and Waze.

I remember when I first got my license back in the late 80's and there was no such thing as navigational devices through technology, I don't even think there were cell phones yet that were not in a bag! We navigated locally by landmarks to get someplace we weren't sure of. We would work from known places of interest and then navigate by odd looking houses or funny shaped trees to decide if we were going left or right. If that didn't work, we had those large maps that once you unfolded you could never fold back to its original position. If you were a frequent traveler, you may have purchased one of those large books with all the maps of each state in it.

Sometimes during our Christian lives, we can get into situations where we feel "lost" and don't quite know where we are or where we might be heading, not knowing where God wants us to go. I'm not talking about salvation lost but lost in a sense as to where does God want us to go, or what is God's will for our lives. He gives us a map and he gives us a GPS.

God's Word, the Bible, is our map to what He wants for our lives. In it He gives clear instructions of how He wants us to live, how we are to act, and wat His general will is for the lives of all Christians (see yesterday's post). The more time we spend in God's Word, the clearer it becomes to us as to how we are to live. The Holy Spirit is our internal GPS system that guides us to what God's will is for us personally. He speaks to us through His Spirit about personal things like relationships and occupations. He uses it to guide us towards His particular will for our individual lives.

Do you feel "lost" at times? Are you using the directional tools that God has provided you: His Word and the Holy Spirit? These are the map and GPS systems for our spiritual lives. If not, start today by getting into God's Word and praying that He speaks to you and guides you by His Spirit.

Notes:_____

_____

_____

_____

_____

_____

_____

_____

_____

February 2

Groundhog Day

Happy Groundhog Day! Well it was just reported that spring is on its way because Punxsutawney Phil did not see his shadow this morning. It always made me wonder because the first day of spring is a set day on the calendar and it is coming no matter what he says. I know, he predicts the weather until spring!

This day always reminds me of the movie Groundhog Day with Bill Murray. It's such a funny movie. I'm sure most of you have seen it but if you haven't here's what it's about. A weatherman travels to cover the event and ends up waking up every day on Groundhog's Day to relive that day repeatedly. Each day he tries to improve on the day before.

He spends each day trying to better himself in order to win over the female reporter that is with him because he falls in love with her. Finally, at the end....... well, I won't ruin it for you if you haven't seen the movie. If you have seen it, you know how it ends anyway.

Life doesn't work out that way for us. We don't get to live the same day over and over until we get it right or get what we want. We only get one chance at this thing called life. It will come to an end for each of us one day and then the Bible says it is followed by the judgement.

The Book of Proverbs gives us a lot of wisdom about how we are to live this life. Here are just a few:

"Hear, my son, and accept my words, that the years of your life may be many." - Proverbs 4:10

"For whoever finds me finds life and obtains favor from the LORD," - Proverbs 8:35

"Whoever pursues righteousness and kindness will find life, righteousness, and honor." - Proverbs 21:21

Jesus also speaks a lot about life in the four Gospels. He speaks of how we must decide to follow Him in this life because it will be too late after we die. Have you made that decision? We don't get a "do-over" in this life like Bill Murray did in the movie Groundhog Day.

Notes:_____
_____
_____
_____
_____
_____
_____

Sticks and Stones

Sticks and stones. You know how the rest of it goes, "they may break our bones, but words will never hurt us!" I remember that was our parent's advice they gave us when bullies use to pick on us. They lied! Words do hurt and most of the time they hurt worse than physical scars. Things that we say out of anger or in a joking way, have long lasting affects on those that the comments were made to. It usually takes a lot longer, if ever, for those emotional wounds to heal than it does for physical wounds. Our words are powerful tools for either good or bad.

Proverbs 18:21 says that "death and life are in the power of the tongue". What a true statement that is. The words that come out of our mouth have such power on the people that we are speaking them to. They have the power to build up or they have the power to destroy. The Bible instructs us, as Christians, to use our words to build others up, "Let no corrupting talk come out of your mouths, but only such as is good for building up, as fits the occasion, that it may give grace to those who hear." – Ephesians 4:29

How do we speak to those around us: our spouses, our kids, our friends and our co-workers? Do we think about what we say and how it is going to affect them before we let the words come out of our mouths? Are we always sarcastic in our responses and is the other person taking it as sarcasm or are we killing them with our words?

Or words are the most powerful things we have. We speak about 5000 of them a day. Are they being used to edify others? James wrote "but no human being can tame the tongue. It is a restless evil, full of deadly poison. With it we bless our Lord and Father, and with it we curse people who are made in the likeness of God. From the same mouth come blessing and cursing. My brothers, these things ought not to be so." - James 3:8-10.

Notes:_____
_____
_____
_____
_____
_____
_____
_____
_____
_____
_____
_____
_____

February 4

God is Good

God is good. All the time. We had a great message yesterday at Church about the importance of prayer in the church. We went through multiple sections of scripture showing different ways that prayer was important and the different aspects of prayer by members of the church.

But one section of the scripture that we looked at yesterday really stuck out in my mind and I felt the Holy Spirit really speak to me when I read it. It wasn't even the main point of the sermon but as we read through it I knew it was God's message to me for today.

Each time we sit in church or in a Sunday school class, God has a different message for each person that is present. He speaks to us through His Word to meet our needs for the things that we are going through in our lives. We never know what we may be teaching or what we may even be preaching that is going to meet someone right where they are.

Our job is to go into God's house ready to hear from Him each time we are there. It may be from a teacher, it may be from the preacher, or it just may be through a simple conversation with someone else between services. Whatever the situation, or the messenger, God is good all the time and He is always ready to meet our needs in His time.

So, what was the scripture that hit me today? A simple message of the Gospel found in just a few verses in 1 Timothy chapter 2: "This is good, and it is pleasing in the sight of God our Savior, who desires all people to be saved and to come to the knowledge of the truth. For there is one God, and there is one mediator between God and men, the man Christ Jesus,
who gave himself as a ransom for all, which is the testimony given at the proper time."

Notes:_____
_____
_____
_____
_____
_____
_____
_____
_____
_____
_____
_____
_____
_____
_____
_____
_____

February 5

An Anchor for the Soul

Who's your anchor? As Christians, our eternal, heavenly anchor is our Lord and Savior Jesus Christ. We have a hope in Him that is a sure and steadfast anchor of the soul as the writer of Hebrews tells us. But who do we have as our earthly, spiritual anchors? Notice that I said anchors and not just a single anchor.

It is important that we have earthly mentors in our lives that guide us spiritually and act as anchors to keep us safe in times of storms. Most of the time our anchors are our spouses, or our parents, or maybe even our grandparents or pastors. But there will come a time in our lives that one of them will no longer be there to guide us through life. That is why it is important to have more than one and it's even similarly important that they are from different generations.

One example in the Bible showing this need is the relationship between Abram and Lot. Abram acted as Lot's father figure and was the one that Lot spent almost all of his early life with. Abram was Lot's only anchor. But when things got too big for them to stay together, Lot left and went to the big cities of Sodom and Gomorrah. He lost his anchor in Abram and started hanging around the wrong crowd that offered him no spiritual guidance. Lot didn't finish as well as he had started because he lost his anchor in Abram.

Another example is the story of the child king of Judah named Joash in 2 Kings. He was hidden away in the temple for six years and grew up only knowing the high priest Jehoiada. Jehoiada was Joash's only anchor. When Joash began to reign at the age of seven, he followed the spiritual advice of Jehoiada and thrived as the king of Judah. But when Jehoiada died at age 130, Joash surrounded himself with the wrong people and had lost his anchor. Just like Lot, Joash started strong but did not finish well.

Who are your anchors? What would happen if you lost one of them? Would you have other anchors to keep you close to the Savior when the storms of life come your way? Make it a point to have multiple anchors in your life over multiple generations.

Notes:_____
_____
_____
_____
_____
_____
_____
_____
_____
_____
_____
_____
_____
_____

February 6

Addicted

I'm an addict! There, I said it. I'm addicted to my smart phone. I'm sure I'm probably not the only one out there that has this same problem. We have become a society of instant gratification and constant entertainment and I am one of those that have this addiction. My wife lovingly pointed it out to me just the other night.

I come home and instead of having a conversation with her, I'm on my phone. Instead of playing with the kids for the short time that I get to see them during the day, I'm on my phone. Yes, it's been a long day and I just want to "veg" for a while, but that is no excuse for the amount of time I spend on this stupid little contraption. I think I take for granted that the kids will be little forever and I can make up that time at a later date. That way of thinking is so far from the truth I don't know why I convince myself of it. And it's not only my kids, spending time with my wife is even more important because a time will come where the kids will be gone and it will just be the two of us again. Our relationship needs to remain strong so that we don't drift apart these years that the children are in our care.

It is so easy to get trapped into scrolling and scrolling through social media like Facebook not realizing how long you have been looking at it. Or maybe it's a certain game on your phone that keeps you sucked in for long periods of time. It's addicting and it's a problem. It's a problem for me and I'm sure it's a problem for many others. It takes self-discipline to be able to put the phone away and concentrate on the things that really matter in life: people!

The Apostle Paul told the believers at Colossae to "make good use of the time". There are better ways we can make good use of the time than being on our phones. Our marriages depend on it. Our children depend on it. It's time to work more on my relationships and spend less time on the smart phone.

Notes:_____

_____
_____
_____
_____
_____
_____
_____
_____
_____
_____
_____
_____
_____
_____

The Wall and the Book

A Wall and a Book. First, let me tell you about the wall. I was driving to work yesterday morning and I flipped over to the classic country channel and heard a song by the Statler Brothers called "More Than a Name on a Wall". It was the first time I had ever heard it but it immediately meant a great deal to me.

The song is about a mother visiting the Vietnam Memorial Wall in Washington, DC with a pencil and a piece of paper to make a marking of her son's name from the wall. She talks about how much more he was than just another name on a wall. She talked about how special he was to her and how much she missed him.

It meant something to me because I lost my father to the effects of Agent Orange from his time fighting in the Vietnam War. Although his name will never be on the wall in Washington because he didn't die in the war, about ten years ago we did go to Washington for a ceremony for those that loss their lives because of the war later in life. It was a very touching event.

Most of us will go through life and never get our names enshrined on any type of wall or monument, and most of us are too old to win any trophies, even if they are just participation ones. But there is one place that we can still make sure our name appears and it's the most important place of all: The Lamb's Book of Life.

Now let me tell you about the Book. This book holds the names of all those that have put their faith and trust in Jesus Christ as their Savior. Once your name is written in this book, you will spend eternity in the presence of the Father and the Son. If you are not found in the Lamb's Book of Life, you will be cast into hell to spend eternity in anguish and torment.

I don't need any more trophies at my age, my best trophy is that my name is forever written in the most important place of all; the Lamb's Book of Life. Is your name there? If it is, I look forward to spending eternity with you. If it's not, now is the time, today is the day of salvation. I would love to show you how to make sure your name is there.

Notes:_____

_____
_____
_____
_____
_____
_____
_____
_____
_____
_____

February 8

Bench Warmers

Bench warmers. I recently started a new job after being with the same company for almost twelve years. I am a project manager by trade for a manufacturing company with a global presence. I switched companies but both my old company and my new company are in very similar industries with many of the same customers. I'm not one to switch jobs very often, so this was a big step for me leaving one company that I was comfortable in to having to start brand new in another company. When you switch jobs, many times you go from being highly involved in everything that is going on, to being the new person with very little to do until you get up to speed.

I'm working through this situation right now and it's making me feel like a bench warmer on a sports team. Everyone else is so busy doing their jobs and going from place to place and meeting to meeting, and I'm just sitting there watching all of the events take place. Its like being on a basketball team and everyone else gets to play while you have to sit on the bench and just watch. It makes it so much harder when you have been so used to being one of the players out on the court for the past twelve years at your other company.

As Christians, when God saves us, He doesn't save us just to sit and watch other Christians live the so-called "Christian life". He doesn't save us to watch others grow and witness for Him. He doesn't save us to be bench warmers in this life. He wants us to et in the game and take parts and be active contributors in spreading His Gospel and showing His love for the lost. In reality, we spend too much of our Christian lives as bench warmers. We go to church and just sit in the pews and don't take part in meeting the needs of our church. We don't take part in singing in the choir, we don't teach that Sunday school class that needs a teacher, we don't volunteer to work in the nursery so the moms can have an hour break from their kids each week, and on and on. We are more comfortable watching from the bench.

"For we are His workmanship, created in Christ Jesus for good works, which God prepared beforehand, that we should walk in them." Ephesians 2:10. We aren't saved because of our works, but when we get saved, we show the results of our salvation by doing work for God. God has blessed you with talents through the Holy Spirit to do things in His local church that others have not been gifted with. If you are not doing them, the church body is incomplete.

Notes:_____
_____
_____
_____
_____
_____
_____

February 9

Trust in Me

"Trust in me". That's from one of my favorite Disney movies, The Jungle Book. I loved the original animated movie and I love the new version that came out a couple years ago with the real-life Mowgli. I even bought the soundtrack because the songs are awesome. The new version was on last night, so of course I watched it because the kids were in the room. They didn't watch any of it but I watched the whole thing for them.

I never realized how much the snake, Kaa, was so much like Satan. It was the voice of a woman in the new movie but was a man in the original. Her voice was so calm and so relaxing it almost lulled you into a trance. Satan works the same way, slowly lulling you to relax your guard and do something against God's Word.

Kaa uses that famous line, "you can trust me", while all the while knowing that her plan was to slowly strangle Mowgli to death. Satan tries to do the same thing to us, slowly luring us into sin. First, it's just something small and then the sins continue to progress into something worse and worse. The whole time lying to us that we can "trust him".

It's nothing new, it all started in the Garden of Eden when he lied to Eve over something that seemed so insignificant. "Did God really say......?" That's his way into our hearts, asking us if what we believe is what God said. He tried it on Christ too, but all three times Jesus answered him with the exact words of God! We should know God's Word so well that when the temptation comes, we can say, "thus says the Word of God".

Notes:_____
_____
_____
_____
_____
_____
_____
_____
_____
_____
_____
_____
_____
_____
_____
_____
_____
_____
_____
_____

Big Sin Verses Little Sin

Big Sin Verses Little Sin. Is there a difference between big sins in our lives and little sins in our lives? Maybe there is when we look at one another and judge the severity of sin, but God sees all sin as just that: sin. We like to judge sin like a skyline view of a city. Each building is a different sin and we judge it based on the height of it. God looks at sin like a bird's eye view of a city. He looks down on the buildings and the height of each one can't be differentiated. They all look the same to Him just like sin does.

One of the kings of Israel, Jehu, looked at sin from a skyline perspective and it cost him dearly. Jehu was one of only four kings that was anointed to be king (Saul, David and Solomon were the others). With his anointing came specific instructions: eliminate the descendants of Ahab and Jezebel and wipe out the pagan religions in Israel.

Jehu had no problems with the first instruction, he eliminated the house of Ahab and Jezebel and even took it too far by eliminating the servants of their household as well. But that wasn't the issue. When he came to the second instruction of eliminating the idol worship in Israel, he only chooses the big sin. He wiped out the Baal worship but allowed the worship of other false religions to continue.

He chose the big sin to eliminate but left the little sin to continue in his nation. Because of this mistake, God limited the length of time his family would rule on the throne of Israel to just four generations.

Do we do the same things in our lives? Do we eliminate the big sins in our lives but let the little ones continue to live in our hearts? Does that little sin keep us from the full blessing of God? God sees no difference between big sins and little sins, to Him they are just sin. Let's be vigilant to work on keeping all sins out of our lives by confessing them daily. 9 If we confess our sins, he is faithful and just to forgive us our sins and to cleanse us from all unrighteousness. "If we say we have not sinned, we make him a liar, and his word is not in us."

- 1 John 1:9-10

Notes:_____
_____
_____
_____
_____
_____
_____
_____
_____
_____
_____

God's Will - Part 1

God's will. What is it and how do we find it? I mentioned in a video a couple of weeks ago that there are really two aspects to God's will. First, there is a corporate aspect that God has a will for all Christians to follow. Second, God has a specific will for our lives as individuals. I can't help you with the second one (that's between you and God), but I can help you with the first one.

God lays out specific actions for the lives of His children that he wants us to perform. We find at least seven of these in the New Testament. Over the course of this week we will investigate what God's will for our lives as Christians should be based upon His Word and not our own opinions.

The first will God has for our lives can be found in 1 Thessalonians 4:3-7. "For this is the will of God, your sanctification: that you abstain from sexual immorality; that each one of you know how to control his own body in holiness and honor, not in the passion of lust like the Gentiles who do not know God; that no one transgress and wrong his brother in this matter, because the Lord is an avenger in all these things, as we told you beforehand and solemnly warned you. For God has not called us for impurity, but in holiness."

Isn't it awesome that the beginning of verse three actually tells us that what is following is the actual will of God! How can we get that wrong? Sadly, we do get it wrong because our will of selfishness fights against the pure and perfect will of God. However, we are instructed to live holy lives, controlling our own bodies from committing sexual immorality and not acting like the unsaved world acts.

Why should we take this seriously? Because God has called us to holiness and not to lives of impurity. That is the first will God has for your life: Be holy because God is holy. How can we preach of a holy God if we are not trying to live holy lives?

Notes:_____

_____
_____
_____
_____
_____
_____
_____
_____
_____
_____
_____
_____
_____

God's Will - Part 2

So, we know that the first thing that God wills for our lives is to be holy. We saw that in 1 Thessalonians yesterday. Today we'll look at the second will God has for us as Christians. It's not as obvious as yesterdays was, but we will see it pretty clearly once we dive into it.

The second thing that God wills for our lives as Christians is to witness in our world. We find it in 2 Peter 3:9 - "The Lord is not slow to fulfill his promise as some count slowness, but is patient toward you, not wishing that any should perish, but that all should reach repentance." Now just looking at that from the outside, one would question how that is God's will for the Christian life.

You would ask, "if He wishes that no one should perish and all would repent and come to the saving knowledge of Jesus Christ, doesn't that happens before we are Christians?" You are correct! But God wants us to be a witness in our world so that we can share the Gospel and others can come to that same saving knowledge. That is God's will for our lives: that we would share the Good News with others so that they too may be saved.

The Apostle Paul said it best, "How then will they call on him in whom they have not believed? And how are they to believe in him of whom they have never heard? And how are they to hear without someone preaching? And how are they to preach unless they are sent? As it is written, "How beautiful are the feet of those who preach the good news!" - Romans 10:14-15.

Has anyone ever told you that you have beautiful feet? You do if you preach the Good News of Jesus Christ! That is God's will for you; to witness to your world about what Jesus Christ has done for you.

Notes:_____

_____

_____

_____

_____

_____

_____

_____

_____

_____

_____

_____

_____

_____

God's Will - Part 3

Holiness. Witnessing. Those were the first two topics we looked at that are the will of God for the Christian life. We have five more to go. Today we go back to Paul's first letter to the Thessalonians for the third way in which we fulfill the will of God. This one is just one sentence out of a whole paragraph that could be argued as God's will for our lives.

If you get a chance today, read 1 Thessalonians 5:12-22 in it's entirety to get the whole context of what Paul is saying to the believers in Thessalonica. But for this post we are going to look at just one sentence, three short verses, to see God's will for our lives. "Rejoice always, pray without ceasing, give thanks in all circumstances; for this is the will of God in Christ Jesus for you." - 1 Thessalonians 5:16-18

We get three commands in one and once again Paul makes it a point to specifically tell us that these things are the will of God. First, we are to rejoice always! That's hard to do, if we want to be honest about it. It's hard to rejoice in a broken relationship, it's hard to rejoice in the illness of a loved one and it's hard to rejoice in the death of those we love. But we are expected to rejoice because this world is not our home. This life is the worst it will ever be for a Christian. For the non-Christian, this is the best life will ever be. So rejoice!

Second, we are to pray without ceasing. That phrase "without ceasing" means that we do it in all circumstances. When we wake up, when we drive to work, while we are eating, when we face issues, and before we go to bed. Our prayer life is our direct connection to the will of God. I wish my prayer life was better than it is (just being honest).

Finally, we are commanded to give thanks in all circumstances. We have so much to be thankful for, I couldn't even begin to list all the things in this little post. Our family started something new this year; at the end of each week we write on a piece of paper the things we were thankful for this past week and put it in a jar. Our plan is to go back through them at the end of the year and remember all the things God blessed us with in 2019.

Rejoice always!
Pray without ceasing!
Give thanks in all circumstances!
This is the will of God!

Notes:_____
_____
_____
_____
_____
_____

February 14

God's Will - Part 4

The post a couple of days ago on the will of God about witnessing in our world used the phrase from scripture, "beautiful are the feet". Today's post will focus on the toes, stepping on them. It is not the aim of this topic to single out any particular political party as being right or wrong, it solely about following God's will based upon His Word.

We go back to Peter's first epistle, chapter 2, verses 13-15: "Be subject for the Lord's sake to every human institution, whether it be to the emperor as supreme, or to governors as sent by him to punish those who do evil and to praise those who do good. For this is the will of God, that by doing good you should put to silence the ignorance of foolish people."

The assumption people make is that we are to submit to and obey everything that the government does, but that is not what this is saying. Its context is that, as Christians, we should always look to do good and follow the laws that are in place. The government's purpose is to reward the good and punish the evil (seems to be opposite of that today). We should always strive to follow the laws because by doing so we are doing God's will.

But what if the laws of the land go against God's Word? What do we do then as Christians? We should always follow God's Word and obey Him over the law. When the council of the chief priests summoned Peter and the other apostles before them to command them to stop preaching the resurrection of Jesus Christ, Peter answered them by saying, "we must obey God rather than men". He gave us the answer to what we are to do when having to decide between the Laws of God and the laws of men.

In the end, we should do the best we can to be good citizens by obeying and submitting to all the laws of the land that do not go against the Word of God. In this way, we are fulfilling to will of God in our lives. As the Apostle Paul said in Romans 13:1-7, "Let every person be subject to the governing authorities. For there is no authority except from God, and those that exist have been instituted by God."

God's will is for us to be holy, to witness in our world, to rejoice always, pray continuously, be thankful in all circumstances and now submit to authorities. This is God's will for you and me.

Notes:_____
_____
_____
_____
_____
_____

God's Will – Part 5

Hi-ho, hi-ho it's off to work we go. All of us, at one time or another, have had a job and have went to work to make a living, to pay the bills and enjoy vacations. Work is a part of our lives, some of us have started work at a very young age, mowing lawns or shoveling snow to make some spending money as a kids. Or maybe we helped clean the house or worked on the farm to make an allowance to buy things we wanted.

"Bondservants, obey your earthly masters with fear and trembling, with sincere heart, as you would Christ, not by the way of eye-service, as people-pleasers. But as bondservants of Christ, doing the will of God from the heart, rendering service with a good will as to the Lord and not to man, knowing that whatever good anyone does, this he will receive back from the Lord, whether he is a bondservant or is free." - Ephesians 6:5-7.

The Apostle Paul is referring to employees as bondservants and employers as masters. He calls us, as Christian employees, to submit to the authority of our employers and honor them. But Paul warns us a couple of ways that we are not to act towards our bosses, we are not to do things as eye-service, or lip-service, and not to do thing as people-pleasers; we are to honor and submit to our employers as if we were working for the Lord. Paul meant we aren't to be employees that "butter-up" our bosses in hopes of getting some sort of promotion for being the person that is always looking to please or always agreeing with everything the boss says.

Instead, we are to work for our employers as if Jesus Christ was our boss, doing things in a way that is honorable and obedient. This does not mean that we are to do things that go against what the Bible says is morally correct. We are not to do things that are illegal just because our employers told us to do it.

So what do we do if our bosses act like jerks or are in a position where they may be less intelligent than the rest of the employees and only got the position because they were people-pleasers? DO we rebel against their authority? No, we are to show the love of Christ in the workplace, knowing that we reflect our Savior. I know it's easy to join in with the crowd and complain, but we are to resist that temptation and honor our employers.

Notes:_____
_____
_____
_____
_____
_____
_____
_____
_____
_____
_____

February 16

God's Will - Part 6

Do you like to read? My beautiful bride loves to read and always has a book that she is working through, usually with a couple of more waiting in the wings. She is a regular at the public library checking out and renewing books. We are going to focus on that word "renewing" for this post.

So far, we have looked at five things that the Bible instructs us to do because they are the will of God for the Christian's life. We are instructed to be holy, to be witnesses in our world, to rejoice always, pray without ceasing, and give thanks in all circumstances, to submit to authorities and yesterday the video message was about honoring our employers. All of these are generalities for every Christian to follow. But what about God's will for our lives as individuals, how do we find that?

The final two posts, today's and tomorrow's, will be ways in which we can seek God's will for our lives that is specific just to us. We find the first way in Romans 12:2 - "Do not be conformed to this world, but be transformed by the renewal of your mind, that by testing you may discern what is the will of God, what is good and acceptable and perfect." If we want to find the will of God for our lives, we have to be different, we can't be like the rest of the world.

We will never find God's will for our lives if we spend the majority of our time doing the exact same things that the world does. We will never find His will in the examples shown on tv sitcoms, in how the world tells us we should live in commercials, or the lies that the more we have the better life will be. We won't find God's will at work, on the golf course, or in the mall; not that any of these are bad things in and of themselves.

We will only find God's specific will for our lives by renewing our minds, by changing the way we think. We will find it by putting in the effort to study God's Word and living out the general wills that we have already looked at so far. When we renew our minds and stop following this world, God will reveal to us what He has for us to do. But we have to be willing to change and willing to put in the work to seek His will.

We cannot think we will find God's will just by going to church for an hour each week and then living like the rest of the world the other six days and twenty-three hours the rest of the week. We have to diligently seek after God, and He will show us His will for our lives.

Notes:_____
_____
_____
_____
_____

February 17

God's Will - Part 7

"He who hesitates has lost!" My dad used to always say that to me when I was playing sports. What he meant was "do something" and not to just wait. That thought goes right along with our seventh and final message about God's Will for the Christian life.

The first five posts were about what the Bible says about general things that are God's Will for every Christian's life. Yesterday we started looking at one of two ways we can find the specific Will of God for our individual lives. Yesterday, the post told us we are to renew our minds and stop acting like the world. We need to be in God's Word so that He can speak to us about what He wants us to do.

Today's point is that as we wait and investigate God's Word, we need to do something. Our Scripture comes from Ephesians 5:15-17 - "Look carefully then how you walk, not as unwise but as wise, making the best use of the time, because the days are evil. Therefore, do not be foolish, but understand what the will of the Lord is." Making the best use of the time so we can find God's Will.

It reminded me of Tim Tebow's story. Growing up he went on family mission trips to Central American countries and worked with kids. He was doing something and making good use of his time as he waited for God to show him His specific will for his life. On his mission trips he was especially drawn to the children with special needs and this became his specific will for his life.

Every year, on the Friday night before Valentine's Day, he holds a global prom night called Night to Shine for kids around the world so that they have a special night just for them where they are celebrated and made to feel like royalty. The event was held in 655 churches in all 50 states and in 24 countries. To see videos of these children as they walk down the red carpet and people are cheering for them just brings tears to your eyes. Tim found God's Will for his life because he didn't wait, he made good use of the time in this evil world.

As you wait to find God's Will for your life, "do something", and in that time of action, God will show you what He is to have you to do. I hope you have enjoyed this little series on God's Will.

Notes:_____

_____

_____

_____

_____

_____

Giving When You Can't Be Repaid

I saw this story on Facebook and it's just too good not to share. I don't know what this guy's religious beliefs are, but he was such a shining example of being God's hands and feet. What he did was put the words of the story in Luke 14 into action and I'm not even sure he knew it.

This is what Luke 14:13-14 - "But when you give a feast, invite the poor, the crippled, the lame, the blind, and you will be blessed, because they cannot repay you. For you will be repaid at the resurrection of the just."

So here is the story I'm referring to. On Super Bowl Sunday of this year, a man in New York City reserved a room at a rooftop bar in downtown Manhattan. He went and bought seven or eight New England Patriots t-shirts and walked around the streets of the city inviting homeless men to a party.

He asked them if they were cold and if they were hungry and then invited them to join him in watching the Super Bowl at the place, he reserved a room. Of course, the homeless men were a bit suspicious of the invitation, especially with the cameras rolling. But they soon accepted the invite and made their way to the party.

For about four hours, these homeless men were able to get out from the cold, gain a new t-shirt and fill their bellies with great food. All of this at no cost to them (they had no way of paying anyway). They were in that bar with so many people that had never been in their situation, yet no one seemed to even notice they were there.

I was just so impressed by the way the guy went out of his way to give to these men a short period of time that they could never ever repay him for. The end of the video showed these homeless men in tears for what that guy had done for them out of sheer grace. They did nothing to deserve being invited and had no way to pay for the things they were given. Much like God's grace toward us through Jesus Christ.

This man was an example of Luke's story above, but he was also an example of Christ (even if he didn't know it). How are we being an example of Christ in showing grace to those that can do nothing for us in return?

Notes:_____
_____
_____
_____
_____
_____

Broken

Broken. Things in this world get broken all the time, especially when you live with a three-year-old. Most of the time things are broken by mistake, sometimes they are not. But it's not just kids who break things, adults do it too. My nephew broke his ankle playing basketball about a month ago and it wasn't on purpose. My truck is broken right now because it's just old and things like that happen.

People get broken too: physically, emotionally and spiritually. Sometimes our brokenness is because of the decisions we made and the actions we've taken. Sometimes it's God breaking us because our hearts have become filled with too much pride and we need to be humbled. Brokenness isn't always a bad thing. We may need to be broken to be built back up again better than before or we may need to be broken so the light of God can shine through our cracks.

The idea of being broken reminds me of the song from Matthew West called "Broken Things". Here's one of my favorite parts of the song:

"The pages of history they tell me it's true
That it's never the perfect; it's always the ones with the scars that You use.
It's the rebels and the prodigals; it's the humble and the weak
All the misfit heroes You chose
Tell me there's hope for sinners like me."

The Bible also talks about the broken and the humble. "He heals the brokenhearted and binds up their wounds." - Psalm 147:3. "For the LORD takes pleasure in his people; he adorns the humble with salvation." - Psalm 149:4. "Whoever exalts himself will be humbled, and whoever humbles himself will be exalted." - Matthew 23:12.

Are you broken spiritually right now? Is it of your own doing or has God broken you so His light can shine through the broken pieces? Either way, let this be a time of praises to God because He is getting ready to heal your brokenness and use your experience in a mighty way!

Notes:_____
_____
_____
_____
_____
_____
_____
_____
_____
_____

February 20

Overwhelmed

Overwhelmed! We've all been there at some point in our lives. The word means something different to each of us and we all have a different tolerance level before we feel overwhelmed. It's a word I've heard multiple times in the last few days and I felt like it was something God wanted me to share.

It started on Monday when my good friend and former college teammate, Peter Pessetto, discussed being overwhelmed on his Facebook Live chat that day. He was coming at being overwhelmed from a business standpoint and how he coaches his clients through the feeling. From his standpoint he instructs others to use that feeling of being overwhelmed as a chance to keep pushing through it and not letting off the gas, so to speak. Peter said it could be a time of growth and reflection on priorities if those in that position lean into the feeling and keep working to get through. I agreed with where he was coming from in regard to his topic.

I started thinking about the feeling of being overwhelmed from a spiritual standpoint and if the same instructions would work. Many times, when we, as Christians, get to a point of feeling overwhelmed, the first thing we do is to try to fix it ourselves. We look for ways to solve whatever is causing the feeling of being overwhelmed. We depend on self instead of depending on God. It is normally because of decisions we have made that we are in the position of feeling overwhelmed to begin with.

Jesus said to His followers, "Come to me, all who labor and are heavy laden, and I will give you rest. Take my yoke upon you, and learn from me, for I am gentle and lowly in heart, and you will find rest for your souls. For my yoke is easy, and my burden is light." - Matthew 11:28-30. As Christians, we need to step back and take our foot of the gas and go to God with the burdens that overwhelm us and let Him carry those burdens. Just like He traded places with us on the Cross, He is willing to trade yokes with us as well.

Are you overwhelmed today? Does life feel like it's too much for you to handle? We serve a God who is waiting to take your burdens from you and give you His rest instead, all we must do is ask. If He was willing to die for you, He's more than willing to take your burdens too.

Notes:_____

_____

_____

_____

_____

_____

_____

_____

_____

February 21

Fear

Fear......it is a liar (according to singer Zach Williams). Fear......you don't own me (according to singer Francesca Battistelli). There a lot of things to be afraid of if you watch the news anymore. We are all afraid of something. Some people have extreme phobias that keep them almost frozen in their tracks. How do we get past our fears?

The Bible gives us many Scriptural truths about fear. But, as Christians, how do we take those truths and apply them to our lives? It's easy to read them in our Bibles and say, "that is so true" and then never take what we read and put it into action. It takes real faith to transfer our fears to God and let Him control what happens.

I have always thought that both fear and worry were wasted emotions. There is nothing we can do about the things we worry about or the things we fear might happen, it's usually not in our control anyway. Most of the things we fear and worry about never work out as bad as we fear or even come to fruition.

The Bible uses the phrase "fear not" 365 times; one use for every day of the year. What if each day we woke up with the mindset that on that particular day, we are not going to fear anything because God told us specifically for that day not to fear?

Here are some good verses about not fearing anything and trusting in God: "The LORD is on my side; I will not fear. What can man do to me?" - Psalm 118:6. "Fear not, therefore; you are of more value than many sparrows." -Matthew 10:31. ""Fear not, little flock, for it is your Father's good pleasure to give you the kingdom." - Luke 12:32.

I know it's hard not to fear things in life: getting sick, losing loved ones, having something happen to our children; but our faith in God must be greater than our fear of life. Hand your fears over to God and let Him work things out, He wants what's best for you. Strengthen your faith in God by overcoming your fears, because in the end, fear is a liar and fear does not own you.

Notes:_____
_____
_____
_____
_____
_____
_____
_____
_____
_____
_____

Hope – the Answer to Trials

Hope. The last few days in our daily devotions, we have looked at different types of emotions that we all face, believers and non-believers, things like being broken, overwhelmed and fearful. These are not emotions that Christians are somehow immune to because we have accepted Christ as our personal Savior. These are emotions that everyone is prone to and emotions that many of us face for long periods of time. They can sometimes take the joy out of living and make us question why we are here and why God is allowing this to happen.

So what makes us as Christians different from the non-believers? The answer to that question is the word "hope". As believers, we now have this hope in things that are greater than this life here on earth. We have a hope in God, a hope in Jesus Christ and a hope in the promises of God and His truths found in the Bible.

This "hope" that we talk of is not a "hope-so" type of hope, like we hope it's not going to rain tomorrow, it's a "know-so hope" because it is built upon the promises of God. "For all the promises of God find their "Yes" in Him. That is why it is through Him that we utter our Amen to God for His glory." – 2 Corinthians 1:20

We have the promise that Christ is going to return and call all believers to Himself to spend the rest of eternity in His presence, praising and worshipping Him. "And if I go and prepare a place for you, I will come again and will take you to myself, that where I am you may be also." – John 14: 3. We know that the promises of God are reliable because they have been proven true over and over again. If He has been truthful in all past promises, why would we not have hope that His future promises are true as well?

"Waiting for our blessed hope, the glorious appearing of our great God and Savior Jesus Christ" – Titus 2:13. Is your hope found in that wonderful promise of Scripture? Or is your hope found in the things of this world? This world will let you down because of broken promises, but the promises of God are faithful and true.

Notes:_____

_____
_____
_____
_____
_____
_____
_____
_____
_____
_____
_____
_____

February 23

Dry Seasons

Dry. It's not really a word that can be used for our neck of the woods right now. I've never seen it rain so much in North Carolina for the twenty-three years I've been down here. It seems like it rains five or six days out of the week, every week! And it's been like this for about six months or so now. When will it be dry again?

I don't know when it will be dry again but when it does dry out, we'll probably complain that we need rain, that's just how we are, complainers. We go through the same things in our spiritual lives as well. We have seasons of great blessings and then we have seasons of feeling like those blessings have dried up. Those dry seasons are hard.

When we go through those dry seasons in our spiritual lives, it's easy sometimes to question where God is and why He is letting us go through this. We wonder if we have done something wrong or if He is mad at us or even if He's abandoned us. He hasn't left us or abandoned us, He's just silent for some reason. His Word says that He will never leave us or forsake us and we have to trust in what He's doing during that time.

I think of King David and so many of the Psalms that he wrote during his life when he felt that God had left him. That time period when he was anointed king even though Saul was still on the throne and was trying to take David's life. David spent most of that time in hiding or on the run and he questioned where God was and why He was letting this happen.

I think of the story of Job. I think of Habakkuk and his question to God: "O LORD, how long shall I cry for help, and you will not hear? Or cry to you "Violence!" and you will not save?" There are so many Biblical examples of people feeling like God was distant and not listening to them. You shouldn't feel like you are the only on that has gone through this.

Keep calling out to God during your dry season. Keep praying that He will open your eyes to why you may be going through this. Keep the faith that He will never leave you or forsake you. The blessings of rain are coming, and your dry season will soon be over.

Notes:_____
_____
_____
_____
_____
_____
_____
_____
_____
_____

The Sun and the Son

The sun. I know it's out there even if it hasn't been seen in a while. It was out for about an hour or so last week and the forecast says it should be out tomorrow and the next day possibly. Even though it hasn't physically been seen, I know it's there.

Just like I don't physically feel the earth rotate every day and I don't physically feel it revolve around the sun every year, I know it does. I know the sun is there because it's lighter during the day than it is at night and it gets warmer too. I don't have to physically see it to know it's true.

The Son. I know He's there even if I have never physically seen Him. He was here for about thirty-three years about two thousand years ago and the Bible says He's coming back soon. Even though He hasn't physically been seen by me, I know He's there.

That's what we call faith. Just like we have faith that the sun is going to rise each morning and we are going to make one trip around the sun each year even though we don't see it or feel it, we know that Jesus Christ lived and still lives today even though we don't see Him.

It reminded me of the words of Jesus to Thomas after the Resurrection: "Eight days later, his disciples were inside again, and Thomas was with them. Although the doors were locked, Jesus came and stood among them and said, 'Peace be with you.' Then he said to Thomas, 'Put your finger here, and see my hands; and put out your hand and place it in my side. Do not disbelieve but believe.' Thomas answered him, 'My Lord and my God!' Jesus said to him, 'Have you believed because you have seen me? Blessed are those who have not seen and yet have believed.'"- John 20:26-29

The writer of Hebrews says it best: "Now faith is the assurance of things hoped for, the conviction of things not seen." - Hebrews 11:1. The whole of chapter 11 in Hebrews tells us of the faith that the heroes of the Bible had in God. Do you have faith that the Bible is true? Do you have faith that Jesus Christ is who the Bible says He is? And do you have faith that He is coming back again to receive His Church and then the judgement?

Notes:_____
_____
_____
_____
_____
_____
_____
_____
_____
_____
_____

February 25

Clingers

Clingers. Did you ever have children that are or were "clingers"? Maybe they clung to your leg when you were out in public and someone tried to talk to them, but they were so shy they just grabbed ahold of one of your legs and hid their face. My little guy doesn't cling onto my leg because he's shy, he clings on to my leg because he thinks it's funny when I walk around, and he holds on for dear life.

There are adults that are clingers too. They are extremely needy and though they may not physically cling to you (that would be embarrassing for both parties), they do cling to you emotionally. They seem to be in constant need of someone in their lives emotionally. They tend to drain the person that they cling to.

God does not have this problem, in fact, He prefers that we seek Him to cling to and not the things of this world. At the end of Joshua's life, he instructed Israel to continue to cling to God: "but you shall cling to the LORD your God just as you have done to this day." - Joshua 23:8.

The psalmist also spoke of clinging to the Lord: "My soul clings to you; your right hand upholds me." - Psalm 63:8. "I cling to your testimonies, O LORD; let me not be put to shame!" - Psalm 119:31.

What are you clinging to - other people and the things of this world, or are you clinging to God and His promises? He desperately wants you to cling to Him. The things of this world, people included, will pass away, but the promises of God never will. Choose to cling to Him and you will never be disappointed.

Notes:_____
_____
_____
_____
_____
_____
_____
_____
_____
_____
_____
_____
_____
_____
_____
_____

February 26

Security

Security. We all want security in our homes, for our families, in our relationships and in our jobs. We work hard to make sure that our things are secure. We lock our doors when we leave the house and some even go as far as having security systems with cameras and all to make sure we are safe. It's natural to want to feel secure in our homes and that the things we worked hard to accumulate are well protected.

But what about our eternal security? What do we have to do to protect that? Nothing! Once we have put our faith and trust in the atoning work of Jesus Christ on the Cross of Calvary, we are eternally secure. The Apostle John wrote in his first epistle: "I write these things to you who believe in the name of the Son of God, that you may know that you have eternal life." - 1 John 5:13. Read 1 John when you get a chance.

Three amazing things happen when we accept Christ as our Savior. First, we are sealed by the Holy Spirit: "In him you also, when you heard the word of truth, the gospel of your salvation, and believed in him, were sealed with the promised Holy Spirit, who is the guarantee of our inheritance until we acquire possession of it, to the praise of his glory." - Ephesians 1:13-14

Second, we are placed in the hand of Christ: "My sheep hear my voice, and I know them, and they follow me. I give them eternal life, and they will never perish, and no one will snatch them out of my hand." - John 10:27-28.

Finally, we are also in the hand of the Father: "My Father, who has given them to me, is greater than all, and no one is able to snatch them out of the Father's hand." - John 10:29.

Our eternal security is sealed by the Holy Spirit, is in the hand of Jesus Christ and is in the hand of God. All three persons of the Trinity have a part in securing our eternity. If we could do nothing to earn our salvation, we can do nothing to lose it. We would have to be more powerful than all three persons of God. We're not that powerful.

Notes:_____
_____
_____
_____
_____
_____
_____
_____
_____
_____
_____

February 27

Free

Free! I love free stuff and I bet you do too. When you go someplace expecting to pay for whatever service it may be and it ends up being free for some reason, that's awesome! Free Wi-Fi, free food, free parking, whatever it might be, it always seems better when it's free.

Many of the politicians lining up for the next election are offering all kinds of free stuff too: free healthcare, free college education and a whole slew of other free things. Only catch is that someone must pay for it: the taxpayers. All those things that are advertised as free really aren't when you pull back all the layers of the onion.

The greatest free gift is the gift offered by Jesus Christ. The free gift of salvation. There is nothing you must do to get it, there are no works great enough to earn it. It's free! "For the wages of sin is death, but the free gift of God is eternal life in Christ Jesus our Lord." - Romans 6:23. The free gift of eternal life offered up through the death, burial and resurrection of Jesus Christ.

That free gift of salvation also cost something too. It cost Jesus Christ, the Son of God, His life. It was a cost He was willing to pay because of His great love for us. "But God shows his love for us in that while we were still sinners, Christ died for us." - Romans 5:8. It's free for us but cost Christ His life. It's the greatest free gift in the history of the world.

Have you received this free gift? "Because, if you confess with your mouth that Jesus is Lord and believe in your heart that God raised him from the dead, you will be saved." - Romans 10:9. The free gift is there and available to you, all you have to do is accept it by faith. Believe in your heart and confess with your mouth.

Notes:_____
_____
_____
_____
_____
_____
_____
_____
_____
_____
_____
_____
_____
_____
_____
_____

February 28

Garbage

Garbage. It's everywhere. We create so much garbage in the course of our day, over the course of a year and over the course of our lifetime. As I drive an hour to and from work each day, I see the amounts of garbage that are along the roads. I wonder how people could be so careless that they just throw it out the window. I wonder how much blows from the speed of the cars and where it originated? How much blows out of the back of garbage trucks that originally picked it up?

Garbage isn't only trash that we throw away. There a lot of definitions for garbage. Noise can be garbage. Speech can be garbage. Time can be garbage. What we accomplish can be garbage. It reminds me of what the Apostle Paul said, "But whatever gain I had, I counted as loss for the sake of Christ. Indeed, I count everything as loss because of the surpassing worth of knowing Christ Jesus my Lord. For his sake I have suffered the loss of all things and count them as rubbish, in order that I may gain Christ"- Philippians 3:7-8.

All that Paul had accomplished in his life, he counted as garbage in comparison to knowing Christ and Him crucified. What about the things we accomplish in life, do we count on them or count them as garbage in comparison to knowing in Christ? Are we defined by our status, our belongings, our degrees or our fame? Or do we see those things as ways to glorify Christ?

Let us not get caught up in what the world defines as being accomplished and instead look at those things as garbage in comparison to the eternal blessing of knowing Christ. For the things of this world that are not done to the glory and honor of Jesus Christ will be burned up like hay, wood and stubble. Only those things that were done for the glory of God will survive the fire like precious jewels. It is better for us to do things for God's glory than our own.

Notes:_____
_____
_____
_____
_____
_____
_____
_____
_____
_____
_____
_____
_____
_____

March 1

The Dog Track Rabbit

The dog track. It always makes me think of the 80's sitcom "The Golden Girls". Sophia always spent some of her free time going to the dog track to wager some money. Sometimes she would come back successfully and sometimes she would not. In the south Florida area of Miami, dog tracks are a big thing.

I don't know if I would find it interesting to go to a track to watch muzzled dogs run around a track chasing a fake rabbit that they will never be fast enough to catch, but I've never been to one. I do love watching the Triple Crown horse races every year, but I don't know if they are comparable. Why go to a track to watch something chase after a fake prize with all their heart and soul never having the chance to catch it when you can watch humans do it every day.

We are programmed by the world to chase after fake rabbits in hopes that someday we will finally be satisfied by catching it, even though we will never do it. Every time we feel like we are going to catch the rabbit, it gets a little further away than before. We do the same thing in this life we live: if we just had a nicer car, a bigger house, a better paying job, and on and on and on. We never catch the rabbit because we want something more.

The Bible says we are to be content in all things. "Not that I am speaking of being in need, for I have learned in whatever situation I am to be content. I know how to be brought low, and I know how to abound. In any and every circumstance, I have learned the secret of facing plenty and hunger, abundance and need. I can do all things through him who strengthens me." - Philippians 4:11-13.

That's the real context of the popular verse Philippians 4:13. Paul was saying he could do all things (those listed in verse 12) because Christ gave him the strength to be content in what he had. Paul was no longer chasing rabbits like he was before his conversion on the road to Damascus.

Are you content in what God has given you? Are you truly finding strength in Christ to do all things in the situations He has put you in? Or are you chasing rabbits around the course hoping to find satisfaction in things you'll never find as satisfying? Find satisfaction in Jesus Christ and not the things of this world.

Notes:_____
_____
_____
_____
_____
_____
_____
_____

Zip the Lip

"If you don't have something nice to say, then don't say anything at all!" How many heard that growing up as children? Yet when we become adults, we seem to forget those sage words of advice. Whether it's gossip, backbiting, or just flat out being ugly, we should all go back to that wonderful saying we were told as children, especially if we call ourselves Christians.

We can't turn on the evening news any longer without most of the stories being "hearsay" or "a person speaking in anonymity". Lies, hurtful, and jumping to conclusions without having all the facts seems to be all the news channels work off of nowadays. Sitcoms aren't any better. Awards shows aren't even worth turning on. All of them seem to thrive on tearing others down that don't agree with their way of thinking.

As Christians we have the obligation to have our words to be powerful and uplifting and not use them to hurt others. The Apostle Paul told Titus "to speak evil of no one, to avoid quarreling, to be gentle, and to show perfect courtesy toward all people."- Titus 3:2. We should all go back to that great saying above.

Our words are to be positive and used to build up, or edify, other. "Let no corrupting talk come out of your mouths, but only such as is good for building up, as fits the occasion, that it may give grace to those who hear." - Ephesians 4:29. This includes what we post on social media! I don't know how many times I have cringed at some of the things I used to post that was hurtful or unnecessary. I have tried to make it a point not to do that any longer.

If I don't have anything good to post, I don't post anything at all. I don't share it or comment on it (no matter how much it may make my blood boil or how wrong it may be). Our words should be positive and uplifting.

Notes:_____
_____
_____
_____
_____
_____
_____
_____
_____
_____
_____
_____

March 3

Grateful

Grateful. Today I had the awesome opportunity to fill in for my preacher at our church. I am grateful that he trusts me enough to take on such an important responsibility and I don't take it lightly. So, because of my gratefulness, I preached on the topic of being grateful. I spoke about the story found in Luke 17 about the one grateful leper.

There were ten of them suffering from the same disease that was really a death sentence for those who had it. These ten men cried out to Christ as he passed through the area of Samaria asking the Master to have mercy on them. As Jesus usually did, He showed them mercy and sent them to see the priest so that the priest could declare them clean even though they were yet to be healed.

Following His direction, the lepers went off in the direction of the priest and along the way they were healed. I would assume all ten of them were grateful that the disease was gone, but only one turned that feeling of gratefulness into worship. The one turns back and falls at the feet of Jesus worshipping Him for the mercy He had shown.

Do we do that enough? Do we actually stop and think of the death sentence that awaited us until Jesus had mercy on us? That the Good News of the saving power of Jesus Christ was even presented to us? Do we turn that grateful feeling into a time of worship at the feet of the Savior?

Or do we continue on like the other nine lepers who were healed did? Do we take our salvation for granted like it was something that we deserved or was owed to us? God forbid we ever get to that point! We should have grateful hearts daily and return to the feet of Jesus to worship Him daily. His mercy and grace is deserving of our gratefulness and worship.

Notes:_____
_____
_____
_____
_____
_____
_____
_____
_____
_____
_____
_____

March 4

Inheritance

Inheritance. We have all wished, at one point or another, that we would get that letter in the mail, or that phone call, that some extremely rich relative that we never knew we had passed away and left us an inheritance of millions of dollars and we were set for life. It's the thing movies are made about but never really come true. There's no rich uncle, no millions of dollars and no inheritance. Just dreams.

We may have an inheritance of some sort left to us by our parents but probably not worth millions. We may even be working towards leaving an inheritance for our children when we are gone. But if we know Christ, our inheritance is already set and just waiting for us in the future.

That's what's unique about inheritances, someone usually has to die for it to take place, unless you are as bold as the prodigal son and demand it while your parents are still alive. In the case of Christians, someone did die for our inheritance to be put in place: Jesus Christ. We have not received the full reward of our inheritance yet, but we have received the guarantee of the Holy Spirit. The Holy Spirit is God's down payment of our future inheritance.

The Apostle Peter put it this way - "Blessed be the God and Father of our Lord Jesus Christ! According to his great mercy, he has caused us to be born again to a living hope through the resurrection of Jesus Christ from the dead, to an inheritance that is imperishable, undefiled, and unfading, kept in heaven for you" - 1 Peter 1:3-4.

The Apostle Paul said this about our guarantee - "And it is God who establishes us with you in Christ, and has anointed us, and who has also put his seal on us and given us his Spirit in our hearts as a guarantee." - 2 Corinthians 1:21-22.

Our inheritance is waiting for us in the future. It is imperishable. It is undefiled. And it is unfading. Awaiting us in heaven. Right now, we have the gift of the Holy Spirit as a guarantee of that future inheritance.

Notes:_____
_____
_____
_____
_____
_____
_____
_____
_____
_____
_____
_____

Courage

Courage. It was what the Cowardly Lion from the Wizard of Oz longed for. Although he pretended to be fierce, in reality, he was nothing more than a coward. All roar and no bite. Like one of those little tiny dogs that barks and barks and barks and as soon as you take one step towards them they run off with their tails between their legs.

That word "courage" always reminds me of the book of Joshua in the Bible. It was a time of transition for the nation of Israel. They were getting a new leader as the torch was being passed from Moses to Joshua. They were getting a new land, the Promised Land, as their forty years of wandering was coming to an end. It was a scary time for them individually and as a nation.

I couldn't imagine the fear that Joshua must have had in his heart as he takes over for one of the most beloved leaders in Israel's history. Everyone he knew and loved, besides Caleb, had died over the past forty years because of their disbelief and rebellion. Joshua is now taking over with the knowledge that across the Jordan River awaited multiple battles with strong enemies to claim the land God has promised them. He needed courage.

God encourages him with these words: "No man shall be able to stand before you all the days of your life. Just as I was with Moses, so I will be with you. I will not leave you or forsake you. Be strong and courageous, for you shall cause this people to inherit the land that I swore to their fathers to give them. Only be strong and very courageous, being careful to do according to all the law that Moses my servant commanded you. Do not turn from it to the right hand or to the left, that you may have good success wherever you go." - Joshua 1:5-7.

And, "Have I not commanded you? Be strong and courageous. Do not be frightened, and do not be dismayed, for the LORD your God is with you wherever you go." - Joshua 1:9.

God has not given us a Spirit of fear, but has instead instructed us to have courage, not in our own strength, but in who He is. He will never leave us, and He will never forsake us. He loves us way too much. Whatever you may be going through, go through it with courage that God is with you. He knows the battles that are ahead, and He is going into them with you.

Notes:_____
_____
_____
_____
_____
_____
_____
_____

Smarts

Smarts. All the scarecrow from the Wizard of Oz wanted was a brain. He just wanted to be smart. He wanted to make informed decisions. It wasn't too much to ask for. I'm sure there have been many times when people have looked at me and the decisions I have made in my life and said, "man, if that guy only had a brain!" I've felt like the scarecrow at times in my life.

I've heard the argument many times that Christians believe in the "fairytale" of Jesus Christ. That we use our belief in Him as a crutch to get through the difficulties of life. That we have some sort of "blind faith" in a make-believe religious person. I thought that way myself when I "didn't have a brain". But belief in Jesus Christ is not a blind faith, actually it should be the exact opposite. It should be a "know so" faith.

I got on a plane last week and went to Cincinnati. I have no degree in aerospace engineering or anything like that, but I got on the plane with the faith that it was going to get off the ground, fly to Cincinnati and land safely when we got there. It wasn't "blind faith" that I got on the airplane. I didn't believe in a fairytale pilot. It was based upon experience and knowledge. I know thousands of planes a day, for months and years leave airports every day and land safely at their destination. I don't know everything about how that works but I trust those that do and design and fly the airplanes.

It's the same thing with our faith in Christ. We don't know all the answers to all the things about God and Jesus Christ, but as we gain knowledge and we see Him working in the lives of others, we begin to grow our faith. The Bible instructs us to use the minds that God has given us to search the Scriptures, to seek after truth and to know more about Him. There is nothing "blind" about it. God gave us a brain so that we can know him with all our hearts, all of our souls and all of our MINDS!

Don't ever let someone treat your faith in Christ as a mindless fairytale. Let them know that you studied the Word, you've experienced His truth in your life, and you know He is who He says He is. You are no scarecrow!

Notes:_____
_____
_____
_____
_____
_____
_____
_____
_____
_____

March 7

Heart

Heart. That was the request of the Tin Man to the Great and Powerful Oz. All he wanted was a heart to fill that empty barrel chest of his. It wasn't too much to ask for, was it? He just wanted a heart so that he could feel love and care for others but be careful what you wish for!

The Bible makes it clear that man's heart is wicked and evil right from the very beginning. We saw it in Noah's day: "The LORD saw that the wickedness of man was great in the earth, and that every intention of the thoughts of his HEART was only evil continually." - Genesis 6:5. And it was no different during the days of Jeremiah: "The HEART is deceitful above all things, and desperately sick; who can understand it?" - Jeremiah 17:9.

But when we come to Christ in a humble manner and confess our need for a Savior and repent of our sins, He gives us a new heart and we can echo the words of David: "Create in me a clean HEART, O God, and renew a right spirit within me." - Psalm 51:10. The heart can be both wicked and it can be a joy to God. It starts out completely wicked until we give our hearts to God.

As I watched the Tin Man get his heart, I imagine it to be like the new heart that God gives us when we accept the free gift of eternal life through His Son. He takes from us the old wicked heart and places within us a new heart, full of love for Him and other people. Have you had a heart transplant? Or are you still holding on to that old wicked heart from your birth? God wants to give you a new heart, a heart that longs for Him.

Notes:_____
_____
_____
_____
_____
_____
_____
_____
_____
_____
_____
_____
_____
_____
_____
_____
_____
_____

March 8

Home

Home. Dorothy just wanted to go back home. She just wanted to get back to Kansas. She wanted to get back so bad that she followed the yellow brick road all the way to Oz in hopes that the Great and Powerful Wizard could grant her that wish. With the help of the Cowardly Lion, the Scarecrow and the Tin Man, she made it to Oz and ultimately made it home. It's a great feeling to make it home.

Every year, my family and I travel north to visit my family for Thanksgiving. It's always great to see them and spend time with them since it only happens once a year, but there is nothing like the feeling you get when you make it home.

As Christians, we long for going home. Not this place called earth and not this short period of time we call life, we long for our eternal home with Christ. This life we now live here on earth is just a vapor of time in comparison to spending eternity with God. That hope that we have allows us to endure the trials and tribulations of this world because we know it is just temporary.

"So we are always of good courage. We know that while we are at home in the body we are away from the Lord, for we walk by faith, not by sight. Yes, we are of good courage, and we would rather be away from the body and at home with the Lord. So, whether we are at home or away, we make it our aim to please Him" - 2 Corinthians 5:6-9. This world is not our home, we are just passing through on our way to glory.

"But as it is, they desire a better country, that is, a heavenly one. Therefore, God is not ashamed to be called their God, for He has prepared for them a city." - Hebrews 11:16. Do you desire a better home? Are you not ashamed to call God your God? He has prepared a place for those that are His children, a place we can call "home".

Notes:_____
_____
_____
_____
_____
_____
_____
_____
_____
_____
_____
_____
_____
_____

March 9

We're Not Worthy

"We're not worthy! We're not worthy!" That famous line was made popular by Wayne and Garth on Saturday Night Live and then in their own movie "Wayne's World". They would fall down at the feet of some movie star or rock star and bow up and down yelling "we're not worthy". They did it because they were in awe that they were in the presence of a star.

As Christians, we will one day do the same thing, but not at the feet of a star. Instead we will fall at the feet of the Son, in awe, with a feeling of not being worthy of being in His presence. It happened to so many people in the Bible when they realized who He was, even the Apostle Peter: "But when Simon Peter saw it, he fell down at Jesus' knees, saying, 'Depart from me, for I am a sinful man, O Lord.'" - Luke 5:8.

There are times in all of our lives as Christians that we do not feel worthy of being called Christians. But our worth is not found in the things we do, it is found in who we are in Christ. God looks at us and sees His Son and His righteousness and not our own (because we have none). I feel that way sometimes when I get to teach and preach God's Word. I think to myself, "I am not worthy to be doing this". But it's not about me, it's about Him.

"'Worthy are you, our Lord and God, to receive glory and honor and power, for you created all things, and by your will they existed and were created.'" - Revelation 4:11. He is worthy of our praise because He died in our place for our sins. Remember that you are worthy to God, so much so, that He sent His own Son to bear the punishment of your sins on the Cross of Calvary.

Notes:_____
_____
_____
_____
_____
_____
_____
_____
_____
_____
_____
_____
_____
_____
_____
_____
_____

Coexist

Coexist. I see these bumper stickers all the time on the back of cars as I drive throughout the country. It's the lie of Satan and people are falling for it left and right. There will never be coexistence because there never has been coexistence. Even the first two brothers in the Bible, Cain and Abel, couldn't coexistence and had to be separated. The world views represented in the bumper sticker can never coexist with one another, and especially not Christianity.

The first symbol, "C", is the crescent moon and star of the religion of Islam. Even though Muslims claim to share the same God with Christians, their writings and beliefs prove that to be incorrect. The second symbol is the iconic "peace" sign. It is actually and anti-Christian symbol using an upside-down cross. The third symbol represent both male and female signs and represents the feminist movement, transgenderism and homosexuality spoken against in the Bible.

The fourth symbol is the Star of David and represents Judaism. Even though it is closely related to Christianity and where Christianity started, it denies Christ as the Messiah. The fifth symbol is the "i" dotted with a witchcraft pentagram (no explanation needs here). The sixth symbol is the yin and the yang of Far Eastern religions of Buddhism and Hinduism which believes in nature as god.

The final symbol of the bumper sticker is the Cross of Christianity. It's very fitting because when you finally come to the Cross of Christ, no other religion will ever follow after it. Many times people have to go through trying so many other things like those symbolized in the bumper sticker before they come to the Truth.

"For many deceivers have gone out into the world, those who do not confess the coming of Jesus Christ in the flesh. Such a one is the deceiver and the antichrist. - 2 John 1:7.

"And there is salvation in no one else, for there is no other name under heaven given among men by which we must be saved." - Acts 4:12.

Don't let the world force you into believing this lie of Satan. There is no coexistence. There is only one Truth. It didn't come from Muhammad, Buddha or Allah. It comes from God, Jesus Christ and their Word; the Bible.

Notes:_____
_____
_____
_____
_____

March 11

Imprint

Imprint. Those of you that live up north are still leaving imprints of your boots in the snow or maybe you can still make snow angels. Down here in the south the imprints being made are in the mud because of the amount of rain we have gotten so far this year. And some of you have made a trip to the beach already this year and have left some imprints in the sand as you walked along barefoot.

An imprint is the exact replica of what has been pushed into whatever the medium is that was used: snow, mud or sand. We make imprints of the hands and feet of our little children to remember one day how little they once were while they eat us out of house and home. Our fingerprint is an imprint that is unique to only us and cannot be replicated by another.

The writer of the book of Hebrews tells us that Jesus Christ was the exact imprint of the nature of God the Father. "He is the radiance of the glory of God and the exact imprint of his nature, and he upholds the universe by the word of his power." - Hebrews 1:3a. Jesus Christ was not a reflection of the Father but an imprint. The two terms, reflection and imprint, mean two different things.

A reflection gives off the glory of something else. The moon offers no light of its own but reflects the light of the sun. An imprint is the exact replica of what has been impressed into it. The glory of Jesus Christ was the same exact glory of God the Father. Jesus was not reflecting the light of the Father; He was also that same light. The Father and the Son have the same radiance of glory.

Jesus told His followers that if they have seen Him, they have also seen the Father. Jesus had the imprint of the exact nature of God, not the exact physical appearance because God is Spirit. We are to be a reflection of the glory of God, but we'll discuss that tomorrow.

Notes:_____
_____
_____
_____
_____
_____
_____
_____
_____
_____
_____

March 12

Reflection

Reflection. I have to admit that the reflection in the mirror in the morning isn't all that pretty. If I'm truly honest, it isn't that pretty when I fix myself up either. Our reflection tells us a lot about ourselves. When we look in the mirror, we often see all the blemishes and faults looking back at us instead of the things God sees in us.

Yesterday we looked at Jesus Christ as the exact imprint of the Father. We saw that he was not a reflection of God's glory but was the same glory that the Father was, that's what made Him an imprint. As Christians, we are commanded to reflect the glory of God by how we live out our lives. We are to reflect the light of Jesus Christ.

Jesus gave us the instruction to be a light so that people see us and glorify the Father: "Nor do people light a lamp and put it under a basket, but on a stand, and it gives light to all in the house. In the same way, let your light shine before others, so that they may see your good works and give glory to your Father who is in heaven." - Matthew 5:15-16.

Do the people we come across day in and day out whether at work or just when we are out and about see God in our lives? Do they see the reflection of His light? When we look in the mirror, do we see only our flaws, or do we see the glory of God reflecting from within us? God wants us to draw others to Him because we let our lights shine.

Notes:_____

Thorns

Thorns. It's that time of year again when those thorn bushes along the edge of my property start growing back. We had them bush hogged this winter, so I need to make sure I keep up with them this year and not let them get out of hand again. There is nothing worse than mowing along the line of thorn bushes and getting pricked by every one of those bushes. The littlest one seem to hurt the most when they get ahold of your skin.

We have thorns in our lives too. Things that seem to feel like a hindrance to living the full Christian life possible. Things in our lives that seem to hold us back. Maybe it's mistakes we made when we were younger that we wish we could go back and do over again differently. Maybe they are physical handicaps or shortcomings that we feel are keeping us back. Whatever they might be, they are not a hindrance to the power of God.

The Apostle Paul has his own thorn: "So to keep me from becoming conceited because of the surpassing greatness of the revelations, a thorn was given me in the flesh, a messenger of Satan to harass me, to keep me from becoming conceited." - 2 Corinthians 12:7. We are never told what this "thorn" was, but there have been multiple ideas of what it might have been.

Whatever the thorn was, Paul pleaded for God to remove it: "Three times I pleaded with the Lord about this, that it should leave me." - 2 Corinthians 12:8. But God did not remove it and instead used it as a way to make Paul lean on the strength of God: "But he said to me, 'My grace is sufficient for you, for my power is made perfect in weakness.' Therefore, I will boast all the more gladly of my weaknesses, so that the power of Christ may rest upon me." - 2 Corinthians 12:9.

What is your thorn? Have you prayed to God to remove it? Has He not answered your prayer? He may want you to depend on His strength and not your own. He may want to use that thorn as part of your testimony. Whatever it may be, thank God for it and asked Him for strength to use it to glorify Him.

Notes:_____
_____
_____
_____
_____
_____
_____
_____
_____
_____
_____

March 14

Well Done

Well done! Everyone loves to get that praise when we have worked extremely hard on something and when it's finished, it worked out exactly how we wanted it to, and people notice and praise us for it. Kids especially love to be praised for the little things they accomplish on their own. It gives us that warm and accomplished feeling inside that we did it.

I heard those words this morning from my boss praising one of my coworkers on an awesome job they did in finding a solution to a difficult problem. You could just see the pride in that person's face for being recognized for that accomplishment. When things like that happen and you are publicly praised for what you did, it makes you strive to do more because you feel appreciated.

It reminded me of the story found in Luke: "When he returned, having received the kingdom, he ordered these servants to whom he had given the money to be called to him, that he might know what they had gained by doing business. The first came before him, saying, 'Lord, your mina has made ten minas more.' And he said to him, 'Well done, good servant! Because you have been faithful in a very little, you shall have authority over ten cities.' And the second came, saying, 'Lord, your mina has made five minas.' And he said to him, 'And you are to be over five cities'" - Luke 19:15-19.

The Lord has given each of us specific gifts and talents that He wants us to use for His glory. If we use those gifts and talents, one day we will hear the Lord say to us, "Well done my good and faithful servant!" If we don't use them, we will feel the shame of letting down our Savior. We won't lose our salvation, but we will not get to hear those wonderful words.

Are you using your gifts and talents to glorify God? If you are, keep up the good work. If you aren't, there still time to get to work!

Notes:_____
_____
_____
_____
_____
_____
_____
_____
_____
_____
_____

Horrific Tragedy

Tragedy. The events of the tragedy that occurred in Christchurch, New Zealand can be described only as horrific. With almost fifty people killed and dozens more injured, it makes it hard to understand the evil that is going on in the world. The shooting of individuals, no matter their faith, at two separate mosques is just an extreme example f hate in this world. Four people that were labeled as "right wing" radicals carried out a well-planned attack on a group of people during their time of worship.

Our hearts become so callous and numb to events like mass shootings that are reported in the news because we have become accustomed to events like that as they are becoming more frequent. It hurts my heart that news of things like this and the loss of lives has become sort of "ho-hum" in my life.

The irony of the situation is that the shooting took place in a town in New Zealand called Christchurch. Although none of us are probably ever going to be resident of Christchurch, New Zealand, as believers, we are residents of the Church of Christ. The universal church, made up of all believers worldwide, goes beyond the four walls of the physical structure called the "church". We are a body of believers that are not limited to a specific location. I am sure that even though this tragedy occurred in two mosques, there are Christians in that town as well that possibly lost friends and neighbors.

What is the Biblical response of Christians to the loss of lives at a location of a mosque by people who believe things hat are at odds to what we believe? Our response should be sorrow because even though they do not believe like we do, our God loves them just as much as He loved us before we knew Him. We should be in prayer for the community that God's love shows up in a mighty way and changes hearts from being at odds with Him to searching for Him.

The Bible commands us to do three specific things in our lives as Christians. First, we are called not to judge others, "Judge not, that you be not judged." - Matthew 7:1. Second, we are not to hate, "But I say to you who hear, 'Love your enemies, do good to those who curse you, pray for those who abuse you." - Luke 6:27. Finally, we are commanded to love our neighbor. Our neighbor is anyone who we come across. We will never judge someone into the kingdom of God. We will never hate anyone into the kingdom of God. We can only show the love of Christ to make people want to be part of the kingdom.

Notes:_____
_____
_____
_____
_____
_____
_____

Be Different

Be different! We celebrate differences between people. The color of our skin, our nationalities, our sexes, and our handicaps. Everyone is different in some way from everybody else and that's okay. It would be a very boring world if we were all the same. But God didn't create robots to just follow programmed orders, He created individuals that have a free will to think and do as they see fit.

But when we become Christians, God has a new set of standards that He sets for us based upon His Word and we are no longer to live like the rest of the world. The world will never lead people to salvation, it will lead them to the falsehood that living good will be good enough. That is the lie of Satan because he is the current prince of this world. But the King of kings wants us to live differently.

Paul told the Ephesians the following: "Now this I say and testify in the Lord, that you must no longer walk as the Gentiles do, in the futility of their minds. They are darkened in their understanding, alienated from the life of God because of the ignorance that is in them, due to their hardness of heart. They have become callous and have given themselves up to sensuality, greedy to practice every kind of impurity. But that is not the way you learned Christ!" - Ephesians 4:17-20.

We are to be different than the unbelievers because they don't know any better and we do. Their heart has been hardened and calloused by this world. Our eyes have been opened to the truth and we should live like we now know it.

Paul continued: "assuming that you have heard about him and were taught in him, as the truth is in Jesus, to put off your old self, which belongs to your former manner of life and is corrupt through deceitful desires, and to be renewed in the spirit of your minds, and to put on the new self, created after the likeness of God in true righteousness and holiness." - Ephesians 4:21-24.

Live differently. Be different. Not because of pride but out of humility of knowing the truth.

Notes:_____

_____

_____

_____

_____

_____

_____

_____

_____

_____

God Only Knows

God only knows. I have heard it said that character is who you are in the dark, who you are when nobody is around. Those moments when we are all by ourselves and nobody would know what decisions we made, right or wrong. We would get away with it and nobody would ever know. But God knows.

I put that in a negative connotation that the decision we make are always going to be bad ones when nobody is around to see them. I'm sure there are many times we make the right decision even when there is no one around to see them because we are people of good character. The Bible tells us to do our good deeds in a manner that one hand doesn't know what the other one is doing (Matthew 6:3).

All of us go through things that the rest of the world has no idea that we are going through, not even those closest to us. Things that go on in our thoughts and internal conversations that we keep inside and don't share with anyone else. God knows every one of those conversations. He is part of that thought process because He is always listening even when we don't speak. God always knows.

He cares about everything we are going through. Every struggle that we face externally and every struggle that we face internally. God knows everything about us. All the things that we hide from the world by the masks we wear when we are in public, God knows. All the times we may cry all alone when no one is around, He knows about those moments. He is right there by your side.

The Bible puts our worth to God this way: "Are not five sparrows sold for two pennies? And not one of them is forgotten before God. Why, even the hairs of your head are all numbered. Fear not; you are of more value than many sparrows." - Luke 12:6-7. We are not forgotten by God and we have great worth to Him.

Maybe you are going through something and no one else even knows about it because you have kept it inside. Maybe you are facing some internal struggle about a major decision and feel like you are all alone in this. God knows all about it and you are not alone. He cares for you and is waiting on you to come to Him with your fears. God only knows.

Notes:_____
_____
_____
_____
_____
_____
_____
_____
_____
_____

Mulligan

Mulligan. That unofficial "do over" you get when you are playing golf with a bunch of your buddies. You know, when you hit the ball five feet off the tee on the first hole or you hit it directly in the pond and you have to grab another ball out of the bag and hit it again. You only get a certain number of mulligans until your friends just won't let you pull that anymore.

Ever had a mulligan in life? One of those times you did something you could never imagine yourself doing and you wish you could just go back in time and take a "do over"? I've had my share of mulligans in life both before I became a Christian and even after I became one. I've wished many times I could go back in time and change some of the things I did, but we can't. There are no real mulligans in life. We have to face our mistakes and move forward.

It reminds me of the story of the Apostle Peter. After boldly stating he would never forsake the Lord by denying he knew Him, a few hours later he did just that, just as Christ told him he would. And in the moment Christ needed His followers to be by His side, Peter was hiding in the shadows watching all the events of the evening unfold. I'm sure at that very moment Peter wished he could take a mulligan.

Days later he had the opportunity to face Christ once again after the Resurrection and make things right. Even though he couldn't go back to that fateful night, he could go forward from where he was. Christ asked him three times if he loved Him and all three times Peter responded that he did. The mulligan that Peter could not take on his own was granted to him by Christ. Christ gave him the mulligan he so deeply desired.

The same thing happens to us in our lives, Christ offers us the mulligan we wish we could use. By His death on the Cross, our sins are forgiven and are removed from God's memory as far as the east is from the west. What I have been calling a mulligan, the Bible calls grace. The free gift that we do not deserve to receive. Grace, grace, God's grace. Grace that is greater than all our sins.

Notes:_____

_____
_____
_____
_____
_____
_____
_____
_____
_____
_____

Who?

Who? Not the band from back in the day. Not the World Health Organization. It's a question that we often ask throughout the day. Who is it? Who did it? Who was it? And I could go on and on with who questions. But the question "who" was asked by Jesus two times with two very different answers. One of those answers is the most important answer you can ever give.

Who? That was the question that Jesus asked his disciples. First, He asked them who other people said He was. "Now when Jesus came into the district of Caesarea Philippi, he asked his disciples, 'Who do people say that the Son of Man is?'" - Matthew 16:13. We hear all sorts of answers when we ask the world who Jesus was. Some say He was a great teacher, some say that He was a good moral example and some say He was just a fictional character that was made up by man to fill a religious void.

But that was not how the disciples answered the question by the response of what the people of their day thought. "And they said, 'Some say John the Baptist, others say Elijah, and others Jeremiah or one of the prophets.'" - Matthew 16:14. Their answer was that the people thought Jesus was one of the very important historical figures of Jewish history. Even though they were all incorrect.

Then the most important question ever followed right after their answers, "He said to them, 'But who do you say that I am?'" - Matthew 16:15. He asked this question of those who knew Him best. Those that had spent both night and day with Him. It's the question that will be asked of those that stand before God. "Who do you say Jesus Christ is?" What will your answer be? That He was just a good teacher, a good man or a fictional character?

Simon Peter jumped right in with the correct answer because he knew who Jesus was. "Simon Peter replied, 'You are the Christ, the Son of the living God.'" - Matthew 16:16. Jesus was, and is, the Christ, the Messiah, the Son of God. That is the answer to the most important "who" question in life. The answer you give will change your eternity. There is only one right answer to the question of who Jesus is: the Christ, the Son of the living God!

Notes:_____
_____
_____
_____
_____
_____
_____
_____
_____
_____

Prison

Prison. At this exact moment in time while you are reading this post, whenever that is, God is in prison. Does that shock you? If God is omnipresent, which He is, He is in all places at all times which means that right now He is behind bars. Ever think of it that way? In the worst of places that we can think of, God is there.

Do you believe that there are Christians today that are in prison? There are! Here in the United States and elsewhere around the world. In some countries Christians are put in prison because of their faith. They have not broken any laws other than following Christ and now their lives consist of confinement. There are men and women in the United States that may not have went into prison as a Christian but found Christ while they were incarcerated and will come out as a Christian.

Is there any Biblical evidence that God is in prison? I think if we asked Paul and Silas, they would certainly say God was in that prison in Philippi on that night they were there. The story is found in Acts 16. Paul and Silas removed an evil spirit from a slave girl that was making her owner quite a living by fortune telling in the city. Because they did this, they were arrested, beaten and thrown in prison. "And when they had inflicted many blows upon them, they threw them into prison, ordering the jailer to keep them safely. Having received this order, he put them into the inner prison and fastened their feet in the stocks." - Acts 16:23-24.

That evening God showed up! While being in chains, Paul and Silas started praying and singing hymns of praise to God and when the time was right God caused an earthquake to bust open the prison door and remove the shackles. "About midnight Paul and Silas were praying and singing hymns to God, and the prisoners were listening to them, and suddenly there was a great earthquake, so that the foundations of the prison were shaken. And immediately all the doors were opened, and everyone's bonds were unfastened." - Acts 16:25-26. God showed up to prove to the people of Philippi that He was real, and that Paul and Silas were His messengers. It turned the life of the Philippian jailer and his family upside down.

There isn't anywhere that we can go that God is not with us. No matter your situation, God sees you and when you praise Him even in that situation, He will show up! Ask Paul and Silas.

Notes:_____
_____
_____
_____
_____

Unanswered Prayers

Unanswered prayers. A phrase that Garth Brooks made famous by a song by the same name. I bet some of you are even singing the lyrics to that song now as you continue reading. What are we to do as Christians when we feel that God is not answering our prayers? Maybe we feel that our prayers are just hitting the ceiling and not making their way up to the throne of God. Rest assured that God hears your prayers.

I have always heard that there are three answers that God gives to all prayer requests: yes, no and not yet. There are prayers that we pray that are completely in tune with the will of God and the timing is right and because so, He says "yes" to our prayer request. Then there are prayers that we pray that God directly tells us "no" because they are either outside the will of God or we are asking for the wrong reasons. The final answer that God gives to our prayers is "not yet". There may be prayers that we pray that are in the will of God but are not in the timing of God or right for us at that particular point in time. So, He asks us to wait. These seem to be the prayers that we feel are "unanswered".

In the story of Hannah in 1 Samuel chapter 1, she was barren and prayed desperately to have a son, even promising to give him back to the Lord if He answered her prayer. It had seemed to her that the Lord's answer was "no" but she kept at her request. When the priest Eli saw her praying, he thought that she was drunk because her mouth was moving but no words were being spoken. Once he found out that she was just pleading with God that He would answer her request, Eli told her to return home, her request would be granted. Not long after, Hannah conceived and brought forth the prophet Samuel. It was never a "no" from God, just a "not yet". It was in God's will for Samuel to be born but the timing had to be right.

Maybe there is something in your life that God just doesn't seem to be answering and you feel like giving up, don't do it if you haven't received a definite "no" from God. You may just be going through the "not yet" stage. Keep asking and keep praying. "And I tell you, ask, and it will be given to you; seek, and you will find; knock, and it will be opened to you. For everyone who asks receives, and the one who seeks finds, and to the one who knocks it will be opened." - Luke 11:9-10.

Notes:_____

_____
_____
_____
_____
_____
_____
_____

Unpardonable Sin

The unpardonable sin: what is it and who commits it? Have you ever watched the news and have seen the horrific crimes that people are committing today and thought to yourself, "God can never forgive someone like that!" Or maybe someone has done something so terrible to you that you have said you would never forgive that person. Maybe you have done something in your own life that you are sure God could never forgive you of that sin. Forgiveness is hard from a human perspective, but thankfully God doesn't forgive like we do.

We tend to get this view of life that there is some sort of imaginary line that once we cross it with a certain sin, we can never be forgiven and brought into a relationship with God. We minimize the power of God by thinking our power to sin is somehow greater than His power to forgive. But that is such an un-Biblical thought process and such a limit on the God of the Bible. God is not only able to forgive us of all our sins, but He is willing to forgive us. "If we confess our sins, He is faithful and just to forgive us our sins and cleanse us from all unrighteousness." – 1 John 1:9.

So, is there a sin God can't forgive; the unpardonable sin? There is no sin got cannot forgive, but there is a sin God will not forgive and that is what is termed the unpardonable sin. The context is Matthew 12:31-32 says, "Therefore I tell you, every sin and blasphemy will be forgiven people, but the blasphemy against the Spirit will not be forgiven. And whoever speaks a word against the Son of Man will be forgiven, but whoever speaks against the Holy Spirit will not be forgiven, either I this age or in the age to come."

The work of the Holy Spirit is to convict those that do not believe in Christ of three things:: that they are sinners, that Christ died for their sins and that Jesus Christ is the only way to salvation. When unbelievers are convicted of those three things but reject Christ and die in their sins, that is the unpardonable sin. It is unpardonable because there is no second chance when they die to get it right. They cannot stand before God after death and say, "I want to try again, I know the answer, I just didn't accept it when I was alive." Men and women don't get a second chance to accept Christ after they die.

Have you accepted Christ as your Savior? Have you been convicted of your sin, been told that Christ dies as a payment for those sins and that He is the only way to God? If so, and you reject that and die, you will not get a second chance.

Notes:_____

_____

_____

_____

_____

_____

_____

It Should've Been Me

It should've been me! Have you ever used that line when you didn't get something you deserved? Maybe it was that promotion at work that someone else got, who doesn't work nearly as hard as you do, but seems to be best buddies with the boss. Maybe it was that girl or that guy that you thought you'd spend the rest of your life with, but they chose someone else instead of you. We've probably all had situations in our past that we look back on and say, "it should've been me".

My moment was just after college when I had a baseball tryout with a minor league team near my home in New York. There were three of us trying out that day and I felt I performed better than the other two guys in almost all the drills they put us through. But in the end, they kept the other two guys and sent me home with my tail between my legs. I left that day with the strong feeling that it should've been me and not them. But God had different plans for my life than baseball. A few months later I got the call to move to North Carolina and the rest is history.

There may even be some of you that had a horrible event happen in your life that may have taken the life of another person but by God's grace you survived. Maybe it was an accident or maybe something else happened, but you look back at that event and say "it should've been me"! That is a really hard thing for some people to get over when they survive something that someone else doesn't, and they question God as to why He let them survive. If that happened to you, God allowed you to live because it wasn't your time and He has something still left for you to do.

The only thing in life that we can really say that "it should've been me" is the punishment for our sins. It should've been me hanging on the cross for my own sins and not my Savior. It should've been me wearing that crown of thorns for the things I did. It should've been me beaten and spit upon for the life that I lived and not Jesus Christ. But He loved me so much that He was willing to take my place, to take my punishment and to pay my penalty. He died on that Cross of Calvary so that I could be forgiven of my sins. He died for me!

He died for you too! Have you accepted His free gift of salvation? Have you accepted that it should've been you on that cross instead of Him? Put your faith and trust in Him and He will save you from the punishment of your sins. All He wants is for you to believe that He is who the Bible says He is.

Notes:_____
_____
_____
_____
_____

The big "G"

Big "G" or little "g"? Which do you worship? Who has the biggest part of your life, the God of the universe or the gods of this world? It's a tough question and if we are really honest about it, the little "g" gods have way too much of our lives. The little "g" gods are all those things that we put a greater priority on than big "G" God. When we do that, the Bible calls that idolatry. We are all guilty to some extent.

The idea of the big "G" and little "g" came from reading the story of Paul in Athens in Acts 17. As he makes his way up to Mars Hill to give his Gospel message to the intelligent men of Athens, he passes through all these altars to the gods of Greece. Noticing there was one altar to the "unknown god", Paul uses this as his point of entry into their world.

He talks about how religious they must be to have so many gods. He points out that this "unknown god" that they have made an altar to is the Lord God. Paul shares the Gospel message with them through the resurrection of Jesus Christ and that all men will stand before their "unknown god" and be judged. Some of the men mocked him, others wanted to hear more and some even believed and joined Paul by accepting Christ.

People in this world today are searching, even if they won't admit it. They are looking for truth, they are looking for peace and they are looking for a way. We have the answer! We know the One who is the way, who is the truth, and who is the life - Jesus Christ.

Which one is more important to us, the little "g" gods that take us away from our worship of God, or the big "G" God that we will one day stand and give an account of our lives to?

Notes:_____
_____
_____
_____
_____
_____
_____
_____
_____
_____
_____
_____
_____
_____
_____
_____
_____
_____

March 25

My Father's Business

Sanford and Son. I used to love that show back in the 70's. Yes, I'm old enough to remember watching that show. Old man Fred Sanford ran a junkyard and his son, Lamont, worked along with him. As Fred tried to wheel and deal on all those money-making scams that never seemed to work out in his favor, Lamont was running the business the way it should have been. Lamont was about his father's business.

In our sermon at church yesterday, Pastor Phillip spoke about Jesus being about His Father's business. The story is found in Luke chapter 2. Joseph and Mary went to Jerusalem for the Feast of the Passover and when the Feast was over, headed back home to Nazareth. After a full day's journey, they realized their twelve-year-old son, Jesus, was not with them. They had to go back to Jerusalem to find him. In today's society they would be reported to child welfare services for losing their child!

But when they get to Jerusalem, they find Him, three days later, teaching in the Temple. He is sitting among the teachers of the Temple listening and asking questions. Not only that, He was answering their questions as well to their amazement. Imagine the awe of these learned men as they sat and listened to the knowledge of this twelve-year-old and His insight to the Word of God. But He was the Word of God in the flesh! They just didn't know it yet.

When His parents find Him, they ask Him what He is doing and if He understood how much that He has scared them by not being with them. Jesus gave no apology for what He had done, He just responded to them, "Why were you looking for me? Don't you know that I have to be about my Father's business?" However, He submitted Himself to the authority of His parents and returned with them to Nazareth.

Let me ask you, are you about your Father's business? Are you about sharing the saving message of the Gospel of Jesus Christ? Are you about winning souls to God for all of eternity? That is the business of the Father and that is what He has entrusted you to while you are still here on earth. I want to be found being about my Father's business when He returns for me, how about you?

Notes:_____
_____
_____
_____
_____
_____
_____
_____

March 26

Pain

Pain. As I sit here writing today's post, I have some serious pain in my chest and left arm. I used to think it was a heart attack and went to the doctor to make sure it wasn't. After about doing that five or six times, I realized it wasn't my heart. I found that I have a gluten intolerance and one of my side effects of eating gluten is fibromyalgia. I get serious pains in my chest and arm every time I eat something by mistake that I shouldn't have eaten. It goes away over time but it's not fun to go through.

As I go through this pain, I feel bad that I even complain about it, thinking of the pain my Savior went through for me. To be put through a fake trial before the Jewish religious leaders, blindfolded and smacked, have the beard ripped out of His face and spit upon, what do I have to complain about?

After the fake trial, He is taken out into the courtyard, stripped down, and beaten with a cat-of-nine-tails. That's a whip with shards of bone woven into the end of the straps of the whip. As He's beaten, the skin of His back is ripped off to the point where His bone is showing through and He is bleeding profusely.

When the whipping is over, He is forced to carry His Cross from the courtyard, where He was beaten, to the Place of the Skull, Golgotha. As He carried His Cross through the streets of Jerusalem and out the gate of the city, the crowds are screaming at Him along His path.

When He gets to the place of His death, He is laid upon the Cross with spikes driven through His wrists and ankles to hold Him up on the Cross until He dies. The crown of thorns still cutting into His skull since the beating He took in the courtyard. There on the Cross, He hangs until He gives up His own life in place of mine. And I have the nerve to complain about this current and temporary pain. God forgive me!

Notes:_____
_____
_____
_____
_____
_____
_____
_____
_____
_____
_____
_____
_____

March 27

Boring

Booooooooring! Ever had one of those teachers in school or maybe a lecturer at a work conference that was so monotone and boring that you had to fight to stay awake? Makes you wonder why they even do what they do for a living if they can't be somewhat excited about their job. How can you not show enthusiasm for something that you spend most of your waking day doing? Really makes you look at them and wonder why they even do it.

I bet non-Christians look at us sometimes and see how unenthusiastic we take being a Christian and wonder why they would even want to be like us. There are some Christians that make you wonder why they have no joy in their lives and how they could be so bored with life. If anyone should be excited about life, it should be us!!! We have been given a new life in Christ and we should be shouting about it from the rooftops. People should look at us and say, "wow! I want what he/she is having!"

But too often we portray this mundane and monotone lifestyle that doesn't attract anyone to want to have what we have. I'm not saying we should be out partying it up, but we should be living life with some excitement. Our sins have been paid for! We once were dead but now we are alive! Isn't that what the father of the prodigal son said? People should look at us and know who we are: Christians!

"But God, being rich in mercy, because of the great love with which he loved us, even when we were dead in our trespasses, made us ALIVE together with Christ-by grace you have been saved" - Ephesians 2:4-5. He made us alive to show that Christ too is alive. We don't serve a dead Savior; we serve a Savior who is ALIVE! We should also be alive in how we live our lives. Don't be a boring Christian, show the people around you that you are alive because your Savior is alive!

Notes:_____
_____
_____
_____
_____
_____
_____
_____
_____
_____
_____
_____
_____
_____
_____

Old Friends

Old friends. It's always great to catch up with old friends when we get the chance. I got the chance earlier this week when I got to go to lunch with a former colleague. I get that chance when I travel back to my hometown once a year. It's always great when we can just sit down and reminisce about the days we used to spend together.

I also think about those that are no longer with us. Either because of old age or sickness, they have passed away and we can no longer spend time with them. I think about my dad often this time of year because it's opening day of baseball season. He loved baseball and he loved his Orioles. I miss talking baseball with him.

But the Bible talks about a time when we will once again get to be with those we loved and that have passed on. Those that have passed away and accepted Christ as their Savior will be awaiting us that have done the same. We will have the rest of eternity to spend with our old friends but even better we will have all eternity to spend worshiping our Savior.

"But we do not want you to be uninformed, brothers, about those who are asleep, that you may not grieve as others do who have no hope. For since we believe that Jesus died and rose again, even so, through Jesus, God will bring with him those who have fallen asleep. For this we declare to you by a word from the Lord, that we who are alive, who are left until the coming of the Lord, will not precede those who have fallen asleep. For the Lord himself will descend from heaven with a cry of command, with the voice of an archangel, and with the sound of the trumpet of God. And the dead in Christ will rise first. Then we who are alive, who are left, will be caught up together with them in the clouds to meet the Lord in the air, and so we will always be with the Lord." - 1 Thessalonians 4:13-17

I look forward to seeing my Christian friends and family that are now in the presence of Christ.

Notes:_____
_____
_____
_____
_____
_____
_____
_____
_____
_____
_____
_____

Faithful. Just. All.

Faithful. Just. All. What do we do as Christians wen we feel that there is something in our past that God cannot forgive us for or something that we have done that we feel God could never use us again to glorify Him? It is usually an argument used by non-believers as a way out of accepting Christ. They like to say, "If you know what I have done in my past, you would understand that there is no way that God could forgive me." But nothing could be further from the truth. God already knows what you have done and it doesn't matter if I know what that was or not.

If God cannot forgive you of your sins then God is not God. If God won't forgive you of your sins then there was no reason for Jesus to go to Calvary and die on the Cross in your place. But what about things in the past that still are hard to let go for the Christian? Things that we may have done before we accepted Christ or things that we have done after we became Christians, how do we let go of our past?

"If we confess our sins, he is faithful and just to forgive us our sins and to cleanse us from all unrighteousness." – 1 John 1:9. There are three key words found in that one sentence of Scripture: faithful, just and all. First, God is faithful. God is the same God today as He was yesterday and will be tomorrow. He doesn't pick and choose what sins He will and will not forgive. Second, God is just. Justice has already been served for the cost of our sins through the death, burial and resurrection of Jesus Christ. Finally, Jesus paid for all sins. There is not a sin, as a Christian, that God cannot and will not forgive. He will forgive us for *all* of our sins and cleanse us from *all* unrighteousness.

God has forgiven the sins of our past, He is forgiving the sins of our present and He will forgive the sins of our future if we confess them. Do not let Satan lie to you and make you believe there is a sin God cannot forgive, he wants you to stay in your sin and be out of fellowship with God so that you cannot be used by Him. Keep your sins confessed, stay in fellowship with God and watch Him use you.

Notes:_____

_____
_____
_____
_____
_____
_____
_____
_____
_____
_____
_____

March 30

Spring

Spring. Green. Allergies. It that time of the year and the weather has been beautiful the last couple of days. Everything is green. The trees are budding, and the Bradford Pear trees are all white and pink and in bloom. The sound of lawnmowers have been rumbling the past couple of weekends and so it begins. Everything that was once dead has sprung back to life and the rebirth has begun.

It is so fitting that this is the time of year that we celebrate Easter and the resurrection of our Savior. What the world thought was dead and over, arose again in final victory. We celebrate the Risen Savior. Just like spring and the rebirth of all the flowers and trees, so too was the rebirth of Jesus Christ.

Just like he had told His disciples, He arose from the grave and appeared to them and hundreds more. The grave couldn't hold Him. The power of Satan had been broken. Every Sunday when we go to church, we are celebrating the resurrection of our Savior on the first day of the week.

"But the angel said to the women, 'Do not be afraid, for I know that you seek Jesus that was crucified. He is not here, for He is not here, for He has risen, as He said. Come, see the place where He lay.'" – Matthew 28:5-6.

Even though spring brings about things that we may dislike, such as allergies and mowing, the events of spring remind us of the resurrection of our Savior. Enjoy the rebirth of the creation of God and remember our Savior.

Notes:_____
_____
_____
_____
_____
_____
_____
_____
_____
_____
_____
_____
_____
_____
_____
_____
_____
_____
_____

March 31

Farming

Farming. Yesterday I talked about spring being sprung and the rebirth of all that has been dead all winter and how that reminds us of the resurrection of our Savior. This past week, as I've driven back and forth to work and especially in the area around my house, the sight of tractors on the road and in the fields have been unmistakable. They have been everywhere, and we even saw one working well after dark on Friday night. It's that time of year to get the fields ready to be sown.

It got me thinking back a few months ago when these same farmers were out in their fields reaping what had been sown the previous spring. As they work this spring turning over the soil and getting the ground ready for it's crop, it reminded me of the teaching of reaping and sowing in the Word of God.

"Do not be deceived: God is not mocked, for whatever one sows, that will he also reap. For the one who sows to his own flesh will from the flesh reap corruption, but the one who sows to the Spirit will from the Spirit reap eternal life." - Galatians 6:7-8. This is always the scripture that is usually used when the idea of reaping and sowing is talked about. It is usually in a negative light, which is a true teaching, but it is not the only idea spoken about in terms of reaping and sowing.

The idea of reaping and sowing is used by the Apostle Paul when he speaks about giving, "The point is this: whoever sows sparingly will also reap sparingly, and whoever sows bountifully will also reap bountifully. Each one must give as he has decided in his heart, not reluctantly or under compulsion, for God loves a cheerful giver." - 2 Corinthians 9:6-7.

Maybe you get discouraged because you don't seem to be winning lost souls to the Lord, but maybe God has you working for Him as the planter of the seed. Or maybe God has you working as the one who waters that seed that has already been planted by offering encouragement to those seeking Christ. Or maybe you are one of the ones God is using to experience someone accepting Christ. All of those roles are important to God's plan of saving lost souls. But in the end, it is the final work of the Holy Spirit of God that saves people, not us.

Keep sowing the seeds of Christ's love for lost sinners. Keep watering the seeds that have already been sown. And keep alert for the opportunity to watch as God does the reaping of the work, we have already put in. To God be the glory!

Notes:_____

_____

_____

_____

_____

April 1

Good Person

Good person. We all know people that we would consider "good people". You know them as "a good dude" or as "the sweetest lady". We look at their lives and maybe see no flaws. We know they aren't perfect, but the mistakes they make are so far and few that we overlook them in the face of the entire picture of their lives. We love having them as friends and we trust them in the advice that they give.

However, the "good person" is sometimes the hardest to reach with the Gospel and to show them their need for a Savior. They look at their lives and they say, "in comparison to everyone else, I'm a pretty good person." And that is what makes it so hard; they are a pretty good person, but that will not save them from the penalty of their sin. It's usually the person that has really messed up their lives that understands their need for a Savior. It reminded me of the story from Luke that I read yesterday.

"He also told this parable to some who trusted in themselves that they were righteous, and treated others with contempt: 'Two men went up into the temple to pray, one a Pharisee and the other a tax collector. The Pharisee, standing by himself, prayed thus: 'God, I thank you that I am not like other men, extortioners, unjust, adulterers, or even like this tax collector. I fast twice a week; I give tithes of all that I get.' But the tax collector, standing far off, would not even lift up his eyes to heaven, but beat his breast, saying, 'God, be merciful to me, a sinner!' I tell you; this man went down to his house justified, rather than the other. For everyone who exalts himself will be humbled, but the one who humbles himself will be exalted.'" - Luke 18:9-14.

Our works will never save us. Our being a "good person" will never save us. The only thing that can save us is the work of Jesus Christ on the Cross of Calvary: His death, burial and resurrection. When we put our faith in the fact that He was God and died for our sins, He will save us when we ask Him to. "He who calls upon the name of the Lord will be saved!" Have you put your trust in Him or are you trusting that you are "good" enough?

Notes:_____
_____
_____
_____
_____
_____
_____
_____
_____
_____
_____
_____

April 2

Airport People

People. Everywhere. I spent most of my waking hours yesterday in an airport terminal. As I sat in the white rocking chair in the Charlotte airport, I watched people for hours. Some were just taking their time walking from one terminal to another and some looked like they were trying out for the Olympic track and field team. As I watched people, because of the multiple delays of my flight, I got to thinking about a song on the radio by Brandon Heath called "Give Me Your Eyes".

There were big ones, and there were small ones. There were tall ones, and there were short ones. There were skinny ones, and there were not so skinny ones. There were old ones, and there were young ones. There were some that looked rich and some not-so-much. There were black ones, and there were white ones, and there were ones of every color in between. There were local ones, and there were out-of-town ones. But as I thought about it, they all had one thing in common.

The song goes:
"Looked down from a broken sky
Traced out by the city of lights
My world from a mile high
Best seat in the house tonight
Touch down on the cold black-top
Hold on for the sudden stop
Breathe in the familiar shock of confusion and chaos
All those people going somewhere, why have I never cared
Give me your eyes for just one second
Give me your eyes so I can see,
Everything that I keep missing,
Give your love for humanity.
Give me your arms for the broken-hearted
The ones that are far beyond my reach.
Give me Your heart for the ones forgotten.
Give me Your eyes so I can see."

That song took on a whole new meaning to me today as I sat and watched. There is no possible way I could share Christ with all of them, but I can share Christ with the ones that He puts in my path. I can plant a seed, or I can water a seed that has already been planted. Give me Your eyes Lord so I can see.

Notes:_____
_____
_____
_____

April 3

Fatherhood

Fatherhood. I don't know if there is a better word in the English language. I never knew how much being a father would change me. My first child made me a father and my second one made it even better. I was worried about something though when we found out we were having another child so many years after having the first one.

Would my love for my first little girl, Christina, be divided when our little guy, Timothy, came along. That was my biggest fear. For almost eight years all my love for my daughter was all her's and now I had a second one coming and I was afraid that my love for her would be taken, to some extent, and given to my son. But you know what, my love was not divided, it was multiplied.

The love I had for my daughter stayed exactly the same as it had before the birth of my son and he received his own amount of love that I didn't know I had inside me. I look at them now, three years later, and I can still say that both of them have 100% of my love. This multiplying of love made me think of God.

Every time someone becomes a new believer and accepts Christ as their Savior, God's love is multiplied. He doesn't love those that have been Christians for many years any less than He ever did just because someone else is now His child. His love multiplies, just like mine did for my own children.

Every day my children make be proud to be called their father. Yesterday Christina gave a big presentation at her homeschool group on the life of Ester. This is way out of her comfort zone and my wife said she knocked it out of the park. Timothy (because every Paul must have a Timothy) is learning his days of the week and months of the year and he impresses me every day in how much he is learning. Him and Jen pray together every night before bed, and it makes my heart bust with joy. I'm the most blessed father in earth (a little bias there!).

Notes:_____

_____
_____
_____
_____
_____
_____
_____
_____
_____
_____
_____

A Thousand Words

A picture can speak a thousand words sometimes. Like the picture that goes along with this post. We come to times in our lives that the road ahead is definitely washed away and God does not want us to go in that direction or maybe He wants us to wait there until the road is ready, but we come up with our own plans on how to keep going. We devise all sorts of ways to keep on the same path because it's easier than finding another way.

I don't know about you, but sometimes I don't like change and sometimes it doesn't bother me at all. We head off on our little plan of life thinking it's going to be a nice, smooth and relaxing journey and then all of a sudden, we come around the bend and the road is gone. It's a lot of effort to turn back in life and find a new route to take. It's difficult to sit and wait for that road to be opened back up as well.

So, what do we normally do? We come up with all sorts of ideas on how we can continue on the same path we were heading even though we have crystal clear evidence that we should not and there are dangerous risks involved if we do. It reminds me of many times in my life that I pushed on and it didn't work out to well.

We make plans on how our life is supposed to progress and we have dreams that we want to fulfill, but we have to be open to the plan of God for our lives. We need to see that the roadblocks that we come across and the roads that are washed away may be God telling us that this is not the direction He wants us to go. Maybe He wants us to turn back or maybe He wants us to wait. What He doesn't want is for us to make our own plans on how to get past the situation. He will let us, because He gave us free will, but we will suffer the consequences for not being obedient.

Notes:_____
_____
_____
_____
_____
_____
_____
_____
_____
_____
_____
_____
_____
_____

April 5

Exercise

Exercise. My wife had joined a local gym that had just opened up and was really enjoying working out and the great people that were there working out with her. She had asked me several times, over about three months, to try it out myself, but I was so out of shape that I did not want to start and suffer through those first couple of weeks of being sore. I also didn't want to embarrass myself in front of other people with how badly out of shape I was. But, after some time, I decide to go ahead and join the group and start working out. I was right – I was sore for weeks and I made a fool of myself to start with, but after a few weeks I started to see some differences.

Exercising really made a big difference. After about four months of going three days a week, I had lost over fifteen pounds and had to buy the next size down in pants and shirts. The daily pain in my knees had disappeared and I was feeling better in general. But I started a new job that doubled my distance from home and I wasn't able to get to the gym any longer. As you can imagine, everything I had improved has slowly gone back to almost where it was before I started.

There is nothing wrong with physical exercise, I enjoyed it when I was able to do it, but what about our spiritual fitness? Do we put as much time and energy into our spiritual well-being as we do into our physical well-being? This body is going to grow old and slowly deteriorate and one day die, but our souls are going to live forever either in a place called heaven or a place called hell. Doesn't our eternal welfare mean more than our temporal welfare?

When we stop reading God's Word, when we stop meeting in fellowship with other believers in the local church and when we stop praying and communicating with God, our spiritual fitness begins to decline. Unlike physical changes that we se when we stop working on our physical bodies, spiritual weakness is not always visible, but we feel it. We know in our own hearts that we are not where we once were with God. We feel like we are farther away than we once were, understanding that God hasn't moved, we have.

Do you need to get back into spiritual shape? Can you tell there is a difference in your life because you are not spending as much time as you once did? Today is the day to get back into spiritual shape. It may be hard but make it part of your daily routine once again, you won't regret it.

Notes:_____
_____
_____
_____
_____

April 6

Adoption

Adoption. I read a great story the other day that some of you may have seen as well. A nurse adopted a little girl from the hospital that no one had visited during her time there. The little girl was born very premature and addicted to drugs because of the drug use of her mother. The nurse would visit her every day at the end of her shift.

After nine months, the nurse was given foster care rights to the little girl and took her home. Two years later, the nurse was able to legally adopt her and become her legal parent. Amazingly enough, the woman was unable to naturally get pregnant herself and couldn't afford the treatments to do so. This got me thing about the word "adoption" and what it means to us as Christians.

The Apostle Paul loved the word "adoption" and used it when writing to the church in Rome, to the Ephesians and to the Galatians. When we become Christians, God adopts is into His family. We are given all the same rights that belong to His Son, Jesus Christ. We become joint heirs to all that is His. "The Spirit himself bears witness with our spirit that we are children of God, and if children, then heirs-heirs of God and fellow heirs with Christ, provided we suffer with him in order that we may also be glorified with him." - Romans 8:16-17.

We are adopted out of the family of Satan and into the family of God. "To redeem those who were under the law, so that we might receive adoption as sons. And because you are sons, God has sent the Spirit of his Son into our hearts, crying, 'Abba! Father!' So, you are no longer a slave, but a son, and if a son, then an heir through God." - Galatians 4:5-7.

Have you been adopted into the family of God? Just like that little girl that was adopted by the loving nurse, her life was changed forever. Your life and eternity can be changed forever by adoption into the family of God.

Notes:_____
_____
_____
_____
_____
_____
_____
_____
_____
_____
_____
_____
_____

April 7

I Deserve

I deserve it!!! You deserve better!!! I hear these words more and more often. Even the legendary Joe Namath is on a commercial to tell you that you deserve something better. When did we become a group of people that somehow "deserves" something? And when did we "deserve" better? When we compare what we have now to the generations before us, how do we even dare to demand such a thing?

The Bible is clear that when we do not belong to Christ, we are deserving of the punishment for our own sins. We are deserving of the condemnation of God. We deserve to be the one that hangs on the Cross for our sins. That is truly what we deserve! But God offers us a way to escape the punishment that we deserve. His name is Jesus Christ.

Mercy is God withholding from us what we deserve to get, punishment. Grace is God giving us what we don't deserve, salvation. We deserve punishment but instead receive grace, all because of God's perfect plan of salvation through Jesus Christ.

So the next time you say that you deserve something (a raise, break today, or something else), stop and think about what you really deserve. Then thank God that He withheld from you what you really deserved because of what Jesus Christ did. Have you thanked Him today?

Notes:_____
_____
_____
_____
_____
_____
_____
_____
_____
_____
_____
_____
_____
_____
_____
_____
_____
_____
_____
_____
_____
_____
_____

April 8

Jigsaw Puzzles

Jigsaw puzzles. I love putting together jigsaw puzzles. My love for them comes from my grandmother. She used to have them when I was a kid and I remember going to her house and spending hours sitting at the card table next to the window putting puzzles together with her. She used to be very meticulous in how she laid out all the pieces. I do the same thing now.

Where I work always has a jigsaw puzzle laid out for anyone to work on as just a break from work. I work on them now and again and it brings back such wonderful memories. The last puzzle that was out for us to put together was made more difficult because one of the guys decided we would put it together without the use of the box as our guide. It was much more challenging, but a fun way to put together a puzzle once in a while.

Life is like that too. We don't get to see the box of the finished picture as we go through this puzzle of a life. We only see brief pieces that somehow fit together to form the entire picture. Sometimes that one piece is missing that keeps us from understanding what that little moment in time was all about. Each event, each moment and each season in our lives brings the puzzle into focus a little clearer.

God sees our whole lives from beginning to end because He is not bound by time. We see what we have already been through and what we are going through in the present, but we have no understanding of what lies ahead in our future. We live by faith that the God of the universe holds our lives in His hands.

"Beloved, we are God's children now, and what we will be has not yet appeared; but we know that when he appears we shall be like him, because we shall see him as he is." - 1 John 3:2. We don't know the whole story of our lives. We do know that when He returns and we see Jesus, we will be like Him and all things in our lives will be made clear.

Notes:_____
_____
_____
_____
_____
_____
_____
_____
_____
_____
_____

April 9

Redemption

Redemption. There is something about redeeming yourself after something goes wrong that is extremely satisfying. Watching the game last night exemplified the thought of redemption. The team that won the championship last night was the same team that suffered a tremendous and humiliating loss last year that had never happened before. They were the punchline to many jokes for the past year and last night they were able to redeem themselves.

Thinking about the idea of redemption got me to wondering how many people think that they have the power and the ability to redeem themselves spiritually. The answer is that no one has the power or the ability to redeem themselves. Redemption has to come from another source. A source that is like us but different from us.

Jesus was born in the likeness of men so that He could redeem man. Up until His coming, sins were covered by the blood of goats and lambs. That was only a temporary fix until the true Redeemer came in the form of Christ. His sacrifice on the Cross with His blood didn't just cover the sins of man, it removed the punishment for the sins of man. There is a big difference from having them covered (still there) to having them removed.

"He (Jesus Christ) entered once for all into the holy places, not by means of the blood of goats and calves but by means of his own blood, thus securing an eternal redemption. For if the blood of goats and bulls, and the sprinkling of defiled persons with the ashes of a heifer, sanctify for the purification of the flesh, how much more will the blood of Christ, who through the eternal Spirit offered himself without blemish to God, purify our conscience from dead works to serve the living God."- Hebrews 9:12-14.

Redemption is a word that is thrown around lightly in today's day and age, but spiritually speaking, it should be a word that has profound meaning to the believer. It's a word that means we have been taken out of the humiliation we were once sentenced to face, and instead, placed in heavenly places with our Savior. Have you been redeemed by the blood of the Lamb?

Notes:_____
_____
_____
_____
_____
_____
_____
_____
_____

April 10

Vanity Plates

Vanity plates. I always get a kick out of trying to figure out why some people have the vanity plates that they have. Sometimes it's very obvious and sometimes not so much. I drive an hour to work each day and come across so many cars that my chances of seeing vanity plates are probably higher than yours. I saw one yesterday that said "BIGKNTRY" and was attached to a Dodge 2500 Ram pickup truck. As I drove past, the teenager wasn't as big as I thought he was going to be. I wonder how many guys were called "Big Country" among their friends in rural America?

I still can't figure out the appeal of owning vanity plates. I guess it may help you make sure you get in the right car if you drive a car similar to everyone else. It's not like you can see the plates while you're driving! People also judge you right away based upon what your plates may say. I guess it's all just vanity.

Solomon had a lot to say about vanity in Ecclesiastes, "I have seen everything that is done under the sun, and behold, all is vanity and a striving after wind." - Ecclesiastes 1:14. "Then I considered all that my hands had done and the toil I had expended in doing it, and behold, all was vanity and a striving after wind, and there was nothing to be gained under the sun." - Ecclesiastes 2:11.

We all have some level of vanity in our lives and I think it differs at different ages. When we are younger, we worry about the clothes we wear and the cars we drive. As we get older, we start to make sure we have the right house and our cars might still be important. But as we come to the later years in life, like Solomon, we look back and agree that it was all just vanity and chasing of the wind.

If you have vanity plates please don't take offense, I have nothing against them, they're just not for me. But we all have some level of vanity in our lives, take a second and reflect if there is anything in your life that seems like you are just chasing the wind.

Notes:_____
_____
_____
_____
_____
_____
_____
_____
_____
_____
_____
_____

April 11

Birthdays

Birthday. Well, today officially marks another trip around the sun. My dad used to always say we only had one birthday and all the rest were just the anniversaries of our births. He was right in a way. When I think about birthdays, I think about the fact that I had nothing to do with it. I didn't decide who my parents were going to be, or at what point in history I was going to be born, or in which country and I didn't decide on my race or gender. All of those things were decided by God.

Even though I didn't get to have a say in my physical birth, I do have a say in my spiritual birth. It easy to see that we have all had a physical birth, you wouldn't be reading this if you didn't, but a spiritual birth is not as easily recognizable. The idea of a spiritual birth can be very confusing, so much so, that even the most educated have a hard time understanding it.

In the Gospel of John, chapter 3, we have the story of the exchange between Jesus and Nicodemus, a ruler of the Jews. He knew that Jesus was from God and Jesus agreed with this statement. Jesus then told Nicodemus that in order to see the kingdom of God, a person must be born again. This statement completely confused Nicodemus. He asked how someone that is old, like himself, be born again. Was he supposed to climb back in his mother's womb once more?

Jesus' answer was that a person has to be born of both water (physical) and of the Spirit (spiritual) to enter into the kingdom of God. According to Christ, we need to experience two "birth" in order to get into heaven. The first birth, physical, we have no control over, but the second birth, spiritual, we have the option to choose to put our faith in the saving work of Jesus Christ or not to.

Just as the Bible speaks of two births, it also speaks of two deaths. The first is a physical death that everyone that had a physical birth will experience. The second death is a spiritual one. Those who face a second death are those who have not accepted Jesus Christ as their Savior. Those who have, will not experience a second death. So, if your only born once (physical) you will die twice (physical/spiritual). If you were born twice (physical/spiritual) you will only die once (physical).

As I celebrate my physical birth today, I am more thankful for my spiritual birth, knowing I will only die once. Have you experienced two births or are you headed towards two deaths? I hope you choose two births; you will never regret it.

Notes:_____
_____
_____

A Day of Silence

A Day of Silence. The day in between Good Friday and Resurrection Sunday. It seemed like all hope was lost with the crucifixion of Christ and nothing good was going to come for His followers now that their leader was gone. That day of silence was a national day of rest for the Jewish culture, it was the Sabbath. A day God created for His people to rest and reflect on Him. It was a day in Jewish culture where they couldn't really do anything related to work. The women followers of Jesus were preparing the oils and spices to anoint the body of the Messiah the following day at first light.

Can you imagine was the closest followers of Christ had been thinking that day? There was no busy work they could attend to in order to take their minds off of the events that just took place less than twenty-four hours earlier. They had given up everything to follow Him over the last three years. They had left family, friends and their livelihood to follow Him, and now they must have felt like it was all for nothing.

Even though Christ had tried multiple times to prepare them for these things that had just taken place, they had not listened to His warnings or they didn't believe that it was going to turn out this way. "For just as Jonah was three days and three nights in the belly of the great fish, so will the Son of Man be three days and three nights in the heart of the earth." – Matthew 12:40.

"You know that after two days the Passover is coming, and the Son of Man will be delivered up to be crucified." – Matthew 26:2.

But even though the disciples thought all hope was gone, God was still working. Jesus had told the thief on the cross next to Him, "today, you will be with me in Paradise." So, we know that after the death of Christ, He went to a place called Paradise to witness to those Old Testament saints that put their faith in the Word of God.

When we feel all hope is gone in our lives, understand that God is still working. Even though it may seem like a period of silence in your life and God doesn't seem near, understand that Sunday is coming! We all have a day when that silence will be broken and God will show up in a miraculous way.

Notes:_____
_____
_____
_____
_____
_____
_____
_____
_____
_____

April 13

Forgive Them

Forgive them. One of the hardest things to do is to forgive someone who has done something bad to you. We tell ourselves that we will never be able to forgive that person for the harm they have done to us. We usually harbor that unforgiving spirit for the rest of our lives if the act was bad enough. Not being able to forgive does more damage to us than it usually does to the other person.

Over the next seven days, we are going to look at the last seven sayings of Christ before dying on the Cross of Calvary. This will lead us up to Good Friday and His death. These next posts come from a book by Stu Epperson called "The Last Words of Christ".

As Jesus was nailed to the Cross and the Cross was dropped into the hole in the ground with a painful jolt, the first thing on the mind of the Savior was forgiveness. He goes to the Father in prayer, not for Himself, but for others; for you and me. I can't imagine the pain that He was in as He hung there, but what is even more unimaginable is that He would ask for forgiveness for those that had put Him there.

He wasn't just asking God to forgive the people immediately responsible for doing this, He was asking for forgiveness for the sins of every man and woman that He was representing by dying on that Cross. He was paying for the sins of the entire human population, from Adam through those that have not even been born yet as of today. He was our substitute.

The first saying of Christ while He was dying on the Cross was a saying that was wrapped up in a prayer, "And Jesus said, 'Father, forgive them, for they know not what they do.'" - Luke 23:34. If He could forgive us while dying in our place for sins He did not commit, shouldn't we also have a forgiving spirit and forgive others that have sinned against us. We are never more like our Savior than when we forgive others.

Notes:_____
_____
_____
_____
_____
_____
_____
_____
_____
_____
_____
_____
_____

April 14

Pardon

Pardon. We hear that word a lot at the end of a president's term in office. They will use their power to pardon certain individuals that may have been targeted for political reason or possibly have been innocent all along. Most of the time the pardon is given because of some relationship the person has with the president. Pardon removes all guilt of the person being pardoned. Christ does the same for us.

The second phrase that Christ spoke while on the Cross dealt with pardon. The first one that He spoke was a prayer to His Father asking for forgiveness of all of us. Today's phrase deals with the pardon of one particular person; the thief on the other cross. Jesus wasn't crucified alone, there was a criminal crucified one either side of Him. While He was crucified for the sins of others, the two criminals were being crucified for their own crimes.

As one criminal mocked Christ and taunted Him that if He was God, to get off the Cross Himself and get him down too. The other criminal showed awe and reverence for who He knew was the Messiah. He asked Jesus to remember him when He got to paradise. With that, Jesus spoke His second saying from the Cross, "And he said to him, 'Truly, I say to you, today you will be with me in paradise.'" ~ Luke 23:43.

Jesus pardoned the sins of the criminal that truly sought His forgiveness. The criminal never got his life together before that day, never went to church, wasn't a good person, didn't give to charities, and never got baptized. He just confessed his need for a Savior and Christ saved him that day, within hours of his death.

Jesus wants to pardon you too. You don't need to get your life together first, He'll meet you right where you are. Then, just like the thief was promised, one day you will be with Him in paradise. Let today be your day. Ask Him to save you from the punishment of your sins. He's already paid it all.

Notes:_____
_____
_____
_____
_____
_____
_____
_____
_____
_____
_____
_____
_____

April 15

Others-Centered

Others-centered. In a world that tells us to "have it our way" and sings about "I did it my way", there are those that put others before themselves. Mothers usually spend most of their lives putting the needs of their family before their own needs. But that is not how the world would have us think, they would want us to make sure our needs are met and that we are satisfied. That brings us to the third phrase of Christ while He was hanging on the Cross to die.

"When Jesus saw his mother and the disciple whom he loved standing nearby, he said to his mother, 'Woman, behold, your son!' Then he said to the disciple, 'Behold, your mother!' And from that hour the disciple took her to his own home." - John 19:26-27. As He hung in agony from the torture of being beaten and flogged and nailed to a cross, he was concerned about the wellbeing of His own mother.

It seems as though Joseph, Jesus' earthly father, may have already died and Jesus, being his mother's firstborn, had taken over the role of providing for his widowed mother. With His impending death, He makes sure that the well-being of His mother will be settled. He appoints John, the only disciple that was at the Cross, to be a son to His mother and take care of her. He turns to His mother and lets her know that John was now her son.

I cannot imagine being in that position and not being concerned for my own well-being, but Jesus shows us what it means to be others centered. He shows what the heart of being "like" Him is all about. He put His own needs aside and made sure that the future needs of His mother were secured.

It should make us look at our own lives to see if we are more self-centered than we are others centered. It's a hard road to walk, but that is the road Christ asked us to walk. We are to lay down our lives and pick up His Cross and follow Him.

Notes:_____

_____

_____

_____

_____

_____

_____

_____

_____

_____

_____

_____

April 16

Forsaken

Forsaken. How many have had someone in your lives forsake you for maybe something you did or maybe even because you became a Christian. We really don't know what it means to be forsaken like some others might know it. I think of those in the Middle East that choose to leave Islam and become Christians, that's what it means to be forsaken. Family, friends, even people they don't really know forsake them because of their new relationship with Christ.

Christ definitely felt forsaken in an earthly sense when almost all of His disciples left Him when He was arrested in the Garden of Gethsemane. But I don't think being forsaken by them hurt as much as it did to be forsaken by His Father. That brings us to the fourth saying of Christ on the Cross.

"And at the ninth hour Jesus cried with a loud voice, 'Eloi, Eloi, lema sabachthani?' which means, 'My God, my God, why have you forsaken me?'" - Mark 15:34. As Jesus nears the point of death, God the Father turns His back on His own Son. At that point, God had laid the sins of the entire world on the body of Jesus. And because God is Holy, He could not look upon His Son in sin. He had to turn from Him and forsake Him for that time.

Since before the foundation of the world, the Father and the Son has always been in perfect fellowship with one another, and now for the first time that fellowship is broken. Jesus is now feeling something He has never felt before and it makes Him cry out in agony.

Because of our sin nature, we often break fellowship with our Heavenly Father. But we have the promise that He will never leave us nor forsake us. Isn't that a great promise to rely on?

Notes:_____

_____

_____

_____

_____

_____

_____

_____

_____

_____

_____

_____

_____

_____

Thirst

Thirst. That time of the year is coming up when the temperature down south is about to get HOT. When we have to spend time outside in the heat, it is easy to get thirsty. We lose a lot of fluid from sweating and we have the need to drink water to keep ourselves hydrated. This brings us to the fifth saying of Christ on the Cross. "After this, Jesus, knowing that all was now finished, said (to fulfill the Scripture), 'I thirst.'" - John 19:28.

This is the only time out of the seven sayings from the Cross that Christ references His own physical pain and suffering. Out of all the pain that He has endured so far, it seems kind of odd that He would worry about being thirsty. But He said what He did to fulfill what the Scriptures said about the Messiah (Psalm 69:21).

He became thirsty so that we would never have to thirst again. This is what He told the woman at the well: "Jesus said to her, 'Everyone who drinks of this water will be thirsty again, but whoever drinks of the water that I will give him will never be thirsty again. The water that I will give him will become in him a spring of water welling up to eternal life.'" - John 4:13-14.

He is the Living Water so that when we accept Him as our Savior, we will never have to utter the words "I thirst". He becomes in us a spring of water that satisfies our every need. Are you thirsty? Do you have the Living Water? He wants to quench that thirst you have in your life for truth. Come to the well of Living Water and drink.

Notes:_____

_____
_____
_____
_____
_____
_____
_____
_____
_____
_____
_____
_____
_____
_____
_____
_____

April 18

Finished

Finished. It is the best feeling when we have a task in front of us, that may seem daunting at the start, that finally comes to and end and we can say "it is finished!" Maybe it's a home project, or something out in the garden, or a project for work or school; it doesn't matter because we get the same feeling when it's done. It is satisfying to know that whatever it was we started out to complete has been finished.

That brings us to the sixth of Christ's seven saying on the Cross. After He prayed to the Father to forgive mankind for what they were doing, and after He pardoned the thief on the cross next to Him, and after He makes sure His mother is cared for, and after He asks His Father why He was being forsaken, and after He tells the onlookers that He's thirsty, He says, "When Jesus had received the sour wine, he said, 'It is finished,' and he bowed his head and gave up his spirit." - John 19:30.

What was it that He finished? He finished what He was sent to do. He finished what the Father required of Him. He died a sacrificial death on the Cross of Calvary to pay for the sins of the world, sins He did not commit. That's what was finished. He finished what He was born to do!

The finished work of Christ on the Cross was only the beginning of what was left. He had told the Pharisees that if they tore down the Temple (meaning Him) that He would raise it up again in three days. They ridiculed Him for His arrogance that He could rebuild the Temple that took decades to build. But they missed what He was saying.

As we celebrate Good Friday tomorrow, it reminds me of a cartoon I once saw. One character asked, "if this is the day Christ died, what makes it so good?" The other character answered, "it's good because it should have been us!" Christ's death means nothing if the Resurrection doesn't happen three days later. He would be just like all of the other heads of world religions: still dead! But Christ is alive! And He is seated at the right hand of the Father right now making intercession for you and me.

We serve a risen Savior, one that came to this earth for the sole purpose to die for our sins. And just like He said, "it is finished". But Sunday is coming, and the tomb is still empty! Praise God, what a Savior!

Notes:_____
_____
_____
_____
_____
_____

April 19

Our Own Terms

Our own terms. We like to do things on our own terms when we want to do them. The last thing we want is for someone else to dictate our lives. Whether it's parents, teachers, bosses, spouses or the government, we do not like to be told what to do. We have a natural instinct to buck authorities. I have had my share of bucking authority from a very young age and it's still difficult to control sometimes.

The authorities thought that they were in control of the death of Jesus Christ, but they were not. It had nothing to do with the authority of the Pharisees or the authority of Pilate, it was completely in the control of God. This brings us to our seventh and final saying of Christ from the Cross.

"Then Jesus, calling out with a loud voice, said, 'Father, into your hands I commit my spirit!' And having said this he breathed his last." - Luke 23:46. Christ was in complete control of His own death. I believe if He wanted to stay there any longer, He could have, but the time had come, and He was "finished" with what He came to do. He decided when it was time to die and He decided to commit His Spirit back to the Father!

Jesus had told His followers that He was the one that would decide to lay down His own life and that He was the one able to take it up again. "'For this reason, the Father loves me, because I lay down my life that I may take it up again. No one takes it from me, but I lay it down of my own accord. I have authority to lay it down, and I have authority to take it up again. This charge I have received from my Father.'" - John 10:17-18.

As Jesus was dying on the Cross, He told the world that "it is finished", and once it was finished, He told the Father that He was coming home! The seven sayings started with Jesus praying to the Father that He would forgive "them" and now it ends with Jesus addressing the Father once more to tell Him that He is giving His Spirit back to the Father. What a wonderful picture of love.

The definition of love can be summed up in this, ""For God so loved the world, that he gave his only Son, that whoever believes in him should not perish but have eternal life." - John 3:16. God loves you. He loves you so much He sent His one and only Son to die in your place! Have you accepted Him as you Savior?

Notes:_____
_____
_____
_____
_____
_____

All that Glitters is not Gold

All that glitters is not gold. Traveling for work is not all that people believe it is. It isn't about going to different cities and getting to sight see and visit places all over the country that other people never get to visit. Traveling for work is about busy airports with rude people in a hurry to get from once place to another that are only concerned about their needs. It's about renting cars and trying to find your way around cities you have never been to before in order to find your hotel. Traveling is about staying in different hotels all the time and not being able to sleep because the bed is different and you are in a different time zones messing with your internal clock. It's about being there for work purposes and not vacationing and doing whatever you want. Trust me, all that glitters is not gold.

Being away for the fourth week in the last six weeks gets old. I miss my wife and I miss my kids. I miss my kid's activities; I miss eating dinner with my family and I miss the daily nighttime routine of them going to bed. But, being on the road means that I am providing for my family in a way that allows us to live in a way different than others live.

Do we look at other people's lives and envy what we think their life is like? Do we look at other people's social media accounts and think that they are living some sort of lifestyle that we have always wanted to live ourselves. Let me give you some advice, what you see and think people's lives are like are probably way different than the lives they live behind closed doors. People like to show you the best of times but keep the worst of times hidden from public view.

As Christians, let's not envy the lives of other's and what God may be doing with them that we feel He should be doing through us. God had a different plan and will for each one of our lives. Some of His followers may be ones that are out front in the public eye while others He may be using behind the scenes. Whichever it is, one is not better than the other if we are doing what God's will for our life is. "For as in one body we have many members, and the members do not all have the same function, so we, though many, are one body in Christ, and individually members of one another." – Romans 12:4-5.

Notes:_____
_____
_____
_____
_____
_____
_____
_____
_____
_____
_____
_____

April 21

Borrowed

Borrowed. We all have times in our lives that we need to borrow something, whether it's a car, tools or money, we have needs that we can't meet on our own. I always remember my father's advice on borrowing something: always give back what you borrowed in better condition than when you received it. That sage advice has always stuck with me when I ask someone if I can borrow something they have.

Jesus Christ borrowed something after His life had come to an end as well: a tomb. "Now there was a man named Joseph, from the Jewish town of Arimathea. He was a member of the council, a good and righteous man, who had not consented to their decision and action; and he was looking for the kingdom of God. This man went to Pilate and asked for the body of Jesus. Then he took it down and wrapped it in a linen shroud and laid him in a tomb cut in stone, where no one had ever yet been laid." - Luke 23:50-53.

There was no need for Jesus to have ownership of the tomb, He wasn't staying long. He only needed it for three days. "For just as Jonah was three days and three nights in the belly of the great fish, so will the Son of Man be three days and three nights in the heart of the earth." - Matthew 12:40. He knew the outcome of His crucifixion long before He ever went to the Cross.

"And he began to teach them that the Son of Man must suffer many things and be rejected by the elders and the chief priests and the scribes and be killed, and after three days rise again." - Mark 8:31. In order to fulfill the will of God, Christ died on Good Friday and was placed in the borrowed tomb. But that wasn't the end of the story, Sunday was coming.

We celebrate today, Easter Sunday, in remembrance that we serve a Risen Savior. Our God is not dead, He is alive and still in control today. The Bible says that He is currently sitting at the right hand of the Father making intercession for us. All other leaders of the world's religions are still dead and, in the tomb, but our Savior only needed a borrowed tomb for just three days.

"When I saw him, I fell at his feet as though dead. But he laid his right hand on me, saying, 'Fear not, I am the first and the last, and the living one. I died, and behold I am alive forevermore, and I have the keys of Death and Hades.'" - Revelation 1:17-18. He is alive! He is alive indeed!

Notes:_____

_____

_____

Ashamed

Ashamed. I've done many things in my life that I look back on now that I'm ashamed of. Some of you who know me may understand what I'm talking about and those of you who don't, you'll just have to trust me. Maybe you may have a past that you're ashamed of too. It's okay, our past is our past and does not reflect our future. If we have accepted Christ, our past sins are separated from us as far as the east is from the west.

There is one thing that I will never be ashamed of and that is accepting Jesus Christ as my Savior. I'm not ashamed of my belief in God or in the truth of His Word. I am not ashamed of how my life has changed since He found me. I have nothing to be ashamed of in any of those things I just listed because I know that my future is in His hands.

The Apostle Paul said the same thing, "For I am not ashamed of the gospel, for it is the power of God for salvation to everyone who believes, to the Jew first and also to the Greek." - Romans 1:16. The Good News of Jesus' sacrificial death at Calvary is nothing to be ashamed of. His death is what brings salvation to those who believe.

Paul told Timothy not to be ashamed of the Gospel either, "Therefore do not be ashamed of the testimony about our Lord, nor of me his prisoner, but share in suffering for the gospel by the power of God, who saved us and called us to a holy calling, not because of our works but because of his own purpose and grace, which he gave us in Christ Jesus before the ages began" - 2 Timothy 1:8-9.

And Paul's final plea to Timothy should be how we feel as well, "But I am not ashamed, for I know whom I have believed, and I am convinced that he is able to guard until that day what has been entrusted to me." - 2 Timothy 1:12.

Maybe you have done something in your life that you are ashamed of, trust that Christ has forgiven you of your past sins and cleansed you from all unrighteousness. Never be ashamed of the Gospel of Jesus Christ; wear it as a badge of honor.

Notes:_____
_____
_____
_____
_____
_____
_____
_____
_____
_____
_____

April 23

Scars

Scars. We all have them. I have sports related scars, surgery related scars, construction related scars and scars from just being stupid. I have emotional scars as well that people can't see, but they are there, whether visible or not. All of our scars have stories that go right along with them as well as lessons learned from those same scars. I bet you have your own scars, visible and invisible, that have some pretty interesting stories that go with them.

Scars are nothing to be ashamed of, they mean that at one time we were in a bad situations and they also mean that we survived those very same situations. Scars mean we've been hurt, and scars mean we've been healed. Scars mean that we have gone through battles and came out victorious on the other side. We have no reason to hide our scars because they show the world that we have overcome the worst that has been thrown our way.

Jesus was unashamed of His scars. After His Resurrection, He appeared to the eleven disciples multiple times but one of them still had his doubts until he saw Him for himself. Thomas has been given the nickname "Doubting Thomas" because of his need to see Jesus after the Resurrection with his own eyes. When Jesus appeared to Thomas and the others in the upper room, He proudly showed off His scars.

"Now Thomas, one of the twelve, called the Twin, was not with them when Jesus came. So, the other disciples told him, 'We have seen the Lord.' But he said to them, 'Unless I see in his hands the mark of the nails and place my finger into the mark of the nails, and place my hand into his side, I will never believe.'" ~ John 20:24-25.

"Then he said to Thomas, 'Put your finger here, and see my hands; and put out your hand and place it in my side. Do not disbelieve but believe.' Thomas answered him, 'My Lord and my God!' Jesus said to him, 'Have you believed because you have seen me? Blessed are those who have not seen and yet have believed.'" ~ John 20:27-29.

Our scars are something to be proud of. Our scars make us who we are. Jesus bears the scars of the Cross to remind us of what He did for us and He does so unashamedly. We should not be ashamed of our scars or of our love for our Savior. By His wounds we are healed.

Notes:_____
_____
_____
_____
_____
_____
_____

April 24

Relationships

Relationships. Some relationships we decide to get into and some relationships we have no choice in the matter. I chose to be in a relationship with my wife, but my children have no choice but to be in a relationship with me. I had no choice in having a relationship with my parents and sister. My children have no option but to be in a relationship with each other, they're brother and sister and they always will be.

I will always be my children's father and there is nothing they can do to change that. I will always be my parent's son and there is nothing I can do to change that. My blood and my DNA will always be connected with my parents and now my children. It is undeniable that they are mine and I am theirs.

The same thing happens when we become Christians, we become a child of God and have a new relationship with Him. When we choose to accept Christ as our Savior, we become joint heirs with Christ to all that belongs to the Father. "The Spirit himself bears witness with our spirit that we are children of God, and if children, then heirs-heirs of God and fellow heirs with Christ, provided we suffer with him in order that we may also be glorified with him." - Romans 8:16-17.

Nothing can separate us any longer with that relationship we have with the Father through Christ. "Who shall separate us from the love of Christ? Shall tribulation, or distress, or persecution, or famine, or nakedness, or danger, or sword?" - Romans 8:35. "No, in all these things we are more than conquerors through him who loved us. For I am sure that neither death nor life, nor angels nor rulers, nor things present nor things to come, nor powers, nor height nor depth, nor anything else in all creation, will be able to separate us from the love of God in Christ Jesus our Lord." - Romans 8:37-39.

Or relationship to God is secure, but our fellowship with Him can be broken by our actions. We will talk more about fellowship in tomorrow's post.

Notes:_____
_____
_____
_____
_____
_____
_____
_____
_____
_____
_____

April 25

Fellowship

Fellowship. It's being in harmony with one another. It's walking hand-in-hand in agreement with someone. Fellowship is based upon being in accord with the other person that we are in a relationship with. Yesterday I wrote about our relationship as unchanging based upon our actions. Our fellowship does change based upon our actions. My children can do nothing about our relationship, but their actions can have a serious impact on our fellowship.

The same is true when we become Christians. As I said yesterday, once we accept Christ as our Savior, our relationship with God cannot be changed, we are now His children. However, when we sin against God, our fellowship with Him is impacted. We are no longer in accord with His will. We haven't lost our relationship, but we have hurt our fellowship.

In the Apostle John's first epistle, he put it this way, "If we say we have fellowship with him while we walk in darkness, we lie and do not practice the truth." - 1 John 1:6. If we harbor sin in our lives we are no longer walking hand-in-hand with God. We are out of fellowship with the Father.

"But if we walk in the light, as he is in the light, we have fellowship with one another, and the blood of Jesus his Son cleanses us from all sin." - 1 John 1:7. If we keep our sins confessed and we are walking according to His will, then we are in fellowship with God.

But what if you are out of fellowship with God right now, how do you get back into fellowship? John gives us the answer in this same section of scripture, "If we confess our sins, he is faithful and just to forgive us our sins and to cleanse us from all unrighteousness." - 1 John 1:9. Confession of sin puts us back into fellowship with the Father.

My children will never lose their relationship to me because they have no choice, I am their father. However, they do have a choice of remaining in fellowship with me based upon their actions. The same thing applies to us as Christians, we will always have a relationship with God but we may not always be in fellowship.

Notes:_____
_____
_____
_____
_____
_____
_____
_____
_____

April 26

Group Think

Group think. When you spend a lot of time in meetings at work, you get to see how group dynamics work based upon the attendees of the meeting. Over the last few weeks I have had the opportunity to travel with a different group of co-workers each time. It's interesting to see how a person's title or rank at work affects the decision-making of the rest of the team. Just because someone in a meeting has a particular title, it doesn't always mean that their idea or line of thinking is always the best way. Now, many times it is because they are speaking from past experiences and have a lot of knowledge to draw from. But, just agreeing because of who they are and not proposing an alternate view can be dangerous.

When the nation of Israel had made their escape for Egypt through the Red Sea, God had planned for them to enter into the land He had promised them from the days of Abraham. Moses sent twelve spies into the land, one from each tribe of Israel, to determine if the land was going to be able to be taken. After forty days of viewing the land and the people already living in it, they reported back to Moses and the rest of Israel. Ten of those twelve spies said that they could not take the land because there were giants living there and they couldn't defeat them.

But two, Caleb and Joshua, spoke up that they could take the land that God had promised their fathers because He would fight for them. "And he said to all of the congregation of the people of Israel, 'The land, which we passed through to spy it out, is an exceedingly good land. If the Lord delights in us, He will bring us into this land and give it to us, a land that flows with milk and honey. Only do not rebel against the Lord. And do not fear the people of the land, for they are bread for us. Their protection is removed from them, and the Lord is with us; do not fear them'". – Numbers 14:7-9.

But the people of Israel did not listen to the two, instead, they listened to the ten who gave a bad report and the group thought won out. Because of their decision to listen to the negative group, they spent the next forty years wandering in the desert until they all died out except for Caleb and Joshua.

Are you listening to the negative advice of the group instead of what God has called you to do? If God has spoken to you to do something for Him, no matter what the group thinks, you follow the will of God.

Notes:_____
_____
_____
_____
_____
_____
_____
_____

April 27

Construction

Construction. All I wanted to do was get home after being gone for three days. After flight delays and having to wait to get a gate at the airport so we could get off the plane, I was finally in the car and on my way home. It started off just fine until I came to about 30 miles of nighttime construction. We came to a standstill as we went down to just one lane. An hour drive turned into over an hour and a half and it was after midnight when I walked through the door and I was finally home.

If we think about it, we want our Christian life to be just like my expectation after I got off the plane: just a straight smooth shot home without any bumps in the road. Unfortunately, life isn't like that at all. There are bumps, slowdowns, detours and pit stops. Each one of those delays come at just the right time and for specific reasons. God uses them to redirect us, to slow us down or to keep us safe.

James said it this way, "Count it all joy, my brothers, when you meet trials of various kinds, for you know that the testing of your faith produces steadfastness. And let steadfastness have its full effect, that you may be perfect and complete, lacking in nothing." - James 1:2-4.

Paul said something similar to the Romans, "Not only that, but we rejoice in our sufferings, knowing that suffering produces endurance, and endurance produces character, and character produces hope, and hope does not put us to shame, because God's love has been poured into our hearts through the Holy Spirit who has been given to us." - Romans 5:3-5.

When we come to bumps, delays and detours, we can have faith that they are for our good and not for our destruction. We can use these situations to grow in our faith in God by knowing that He is fully aware of our path and the best route for us to get there safely and according to His will.

So, as I sat in line last night waiting to get through the construction zones, I turned up the radio and sang along (I am not a very good singer but by myself I sound just like one of the band) praising God for the fact that He had gotten me back home safely even though it may not have been in my timing.

Notes:_____
_____
_____
_____
_____
_____
_____

April 28

Synagogue

Synagogue. Yesterday there was another terrible attack on a religious center. A month ago, there was one at a Muslim mosque in New Zealand, on Easter Sunday there was one at a Christian Church in Sri Lanka and yesterday there was an attach at a Jewish synagogue in San Diego. All crimes against people of faith by someone out of hatred.

As Christians, we are commanded to love our neighbors no matter what their beliefs may be. By showing them love, we extend the love of Christ to them. We may not believe in their belief system, but that does not mean we are to hate them or do anything malicious to them. God loves them too and Christ died in their place as well. We all were once enemies of God.

God still has a plan for His people the Jews. Right now, we are in what is called the "church age" but God will come back to focusing on the Jews once again after the Rapture. Our focus should be praying for those that are still lost and without Christ; Muslims, Jews, atheists and every other group of people.

The Apostle Paul, who was once a Jew himself of the highest degree, always started with his Jewish heritage when he came to a new city. "And immediately he proclaimed Jesus in the synagogues, saying, "'He is the Son of God.'" And all who heard him were amazed and said, "Is not this the man who made havoc in Jerusalem of those who called upon this name? And has he not come here for this purpose, to bring them bound before the chief priests?'"- Acts 9:20-21.

"When they arrived at Salamis, they proclaimed the word of God in the synagogues of the Jews. And they had John to assist them." - Acts 13:5.

"But they went on from Perga and came to Antioch in Pisidia. And on the Sabbath day they went into the synagogue and sat down." - Acts 13:14.

Paul has a deep desire for his people to turn to God like he did. We should have that same desire for the lost to turn to Christ like we have. Pray for those that are terrorized by hatred. Pray that God will turn their hearts towards Him and save them.

Notes:_____
_____
_____
_____
_____
_____
_____

April 29

Darkness

Darkness. I used to drive most of my journey into work in darkness, but now that the time has changed the breaking of dawn has started when I am leaving for work. I have to say that I enjoy driving in the light better than I do driving in the dark. It make it so much easier to see up ahead on the road.

I had some interesting conversations with unbelievers through social media this past weekend. They were questioning the legitimacy of Christianity and things I had posted. I wouldn't say it was an argument, but it definitely was a chance to expose some of their misconceptions. Both conversations ended because darkness was exposed by light.

I find it funny how quickly someone will leave a conversation when their path leads them down a dead end. They quickly end the conversation, and in one instance, ended the Facebook relationship all together. Unfriend, as it may be. But that's okay, a seed was planted that may get watered later. We can "win" every battle. All we can do is let the Word of God speak for itself.

"And this is the judgment: the light has come into the world, and people loved the darkness rather than the light because their works were evil. For everyone who does wicked things hates the light and does not come to the light, lest his works should be exposed. But whoever does what is true comes to the light, so that it may be clearly seen that his works have been carried out in God." - John 3:19-21.

"For God, who said, 'Let light shine out of darkness,' has shone in our hearts to give the light of the knowledge of the glory of God in the face of Jesus Christ."- 2 Corinthians 4:6. Let your light shine so that darkness can be exposed.

Notes:_____

_____
_____
_____
_____
_____
_____
_____
_____
_____
_____
_____
_____
_____
_____

Heaven

Heaven. Are you going? Many people think so but that is opposite of what the Bible teaches. If you ask people where they are going to go when they die, most people will automatically say they have been good enough to get into heaven. I see many people talk about loved ones that have died that they are now in heaven even though they have never made a profession of faith in Christ. Why do people believe that their default destination will be heaven when they die? Is it because they don't want to face the fact that they might be going to hell? Who wants to think that?

The fact that most people choose heaven is because they feel they have been a "good enough" person in comparison to others they may know. We like to rank our behavior to those around us and decide that we are better than them, so we must be some of the ones going to heaven. We have been programmed to believe that "bad" people go to hell and "good" people go to heaven. The Bible teaches that those that accept Christ as their Lord and Savior go to heaven and those that reject Him go to hell.

"Enter by the narrow gate. For the gate is wide and the way is easy that leads to destruction, and those who enter by it are many. For the gate is narrow and the way is hard that leads to life, and those who find it are few." Matthew 7:13-14. Those verses should prove that the numbers of those that will end up in hell is much greater than the numbers of those that end up in heaven.

I have heard it referenced in terms of popular songs that have been written over the years; "Stairway to Heaven" and "Highway to Hell". Even though neither of the songs are written with a Christian theme, the titles of the two songs are biblically accurate if we put it in comparison to Matthew 7:13-14. A stairway is much narrower than a highway.

We do not get to heaven by our good works or because we are so-called "good" people (whatever that means). We get to heaven by putting our faith in the death, burial and resurrection of Jesus Christ. We acknowledge that we are sinners in need of a Savior and we realize that Jesus Christ is that Savior. Have you put your faith in Him?

Notes:_____

_____

_____

_____

_____

_____

_____

_____

_____

_____

May 1

Static

Static. There is nothing worse than when you are traveling long distances and you start to move out of range of the radio station that you are listening to. It happens very slowly, where you start to get a slight static interruption in the music, and it cuts in and out. But as you keep getting further and further away, the static increases to the point that you can no longer hear that sweet sounding music that you were just listening to and it's off to seeking a new station within range.

Sin causes static in our fellowship with God. It also happens slowly, when we allow a sin to fester and not confess it. Soon as more unconfessed sins are added to our lives the static between us and God gets greater. We can no longer hear Him and our prayers to Him are blocked. As we get further from God the static grows increasingly larger and instead of turning back into range with God, we usually search for another station. It could be relationships, activities or substances to fill in the vacuum left from being out of fellowship with God.

In my live video post with Nathan yesterday, the echo from feed was almost unbearable. All I could here in my earphones was my own voice echoing back to me. That made it extremely hard to speak as I felt I was speaking over myself. It effected my message and interrupted the flow of the conversation. It was nothing either one of us planned, it just seemed to be a technical issue. That static caused a break in our effectiveness and fellowship.

Our need is to eliminate static (sin) in our lives by keeping in range (fellowship) with the signal (God). We do that by keeping our sins confesses and staying in fellowship. "If we confess our sins, he is faithful and just to forgive us our sins and to cleanse us from all unrighteousness." - 1 John 1:9. Keeping a clean sheet with God eliminates the static in our conversations between Him and ourselves. It also keeps our relationship with one another in better fellowship. If you feel God is distant in your life, find the static that is causing that interruption in fellowship.

Notes:_____

_____

_____

_____

_____

_____

_____

_____

_____

_____

May 2

I Don't Know

I don't know. It's okay for that to be the answer sometimes when we are asked questions that we don't know the answer to, especially as Christians. I don't know why the horrible things that happened on the campus of UNCC took place. I don't know why evil things happen in this world. I don't know why some people were allowed to survive and some were not. It's okay to not have all the answers! Sometimes trying to explain what your opinion is only makes it worse.

Evil does exist in this world and it will continue to do so. Times like these make people question why God allows evil to exist. They ask that if He really exists, why doesn't He just stop all evil things from happening. It's not a question that has an easy answer, but it does have an answer. Evil exists because of our rebellious nature and evil hearts.

God create the angels and humans with a free will, a will to choose how we act and what we decide to do. God did not create robots that were automatically programmed to do exactly how they are instructed. Instead, He made the angels and mankind with the opportunity to choose to love and follow Him. Our free will allows us the opportunity to rebel or to submit. Evil exists because of man's nature to want to rebel.

Even some of the angels, who have always been in the presence of God since they were created, chose to rebel against God and were cast out of heaven. If they were in the presence of God and still chose to rebel, how much more likely is man to rebel who have not been in His presence? "The heart is deceitful above all things, and desperately sick; who can understand it? "- Jeremiah 17:9.

I don't know why God allows certain things to happen in this world that we deem as evil. To deem something as "evil" means we must understand that there is a standard in which we judge evilness. God's Word is that standard. What I do know is this; even though evil things happen, God is still good! People want to blame God for the evil deeds of man. When I do things that are deemed evil, it's not the fault of God, it's because of the wickedness that resides within me. God is good, all the time.

Notes:_____

_____
_____
_____
_____
_____
_____
_____
_____

Lips

Lips. When I was an art student back in my high school and early college years, I used to love drawing portraits of people. I would draw people out of magazines or from pictures. It is very difficult to make a drawing look exactly like the person's picture, very few people can do it. Certain features can make or break your drawing: the eyes, the nose and the lips. If you don't get any of those just right, your drawing will be a disaster.

Our lips say a lot about us. We have all different shapes and sizes of lips based upon our genes. Our lips say a lot about us in who we are, and what we believe as well, based upon what comes out of them. Our lips are the gateway to our hearts.

As Christians, we like to say that we have given our hearts to Jesus, but what about other body parts, like our lips; have we given them to Jesus as well? Would Jesus be proud of what we allow to come out of our lips in ordinary conversations or behind closed doors? Would he be proud of the songs we sing when we are in the car alone and the lyrics may be questionable? Jesus doesn't just want our hearts; He wants all of us.

"Keep your tongue from evil and your lips from speaking deceit." - Psalm 34:13.

"O Lord, open my lips, and my mouth will declare your praise." - Psalm 51:15.

"Because your steadfast love is better than life, my lips will praise you." - Psalm 63:3.

"My lips will shout for joy, when I sing praises to you; my soul also, which you have redeemed." - Psalm 71:23.

Our lips are an important mirror to our hearts. Lips that praise the Lord reflect a heart that does so as well. If the Lord is the Lord of our hearts, then He should also be the Lord of our lips.

Notes:_____

_____
_____
_____
_____
_____
_____
_____
_____
_____
_____
_____

May 4

Hot!

It was hot! When an air conditioner goes out, people get in a bad new when the temperature is too hot. I flew into the Charlotte airport yesterday and the concourse I arrived in was experiencing an outage in their air conditioning. It wasn't just one section of the concourse; it was the entire concourse. It wouldn't have been that bad if I had to just pass through the concourse on my way to my connecting flight, but my next flight happened to be going out of that same concourse, so I just had to sit there and deal with it.

People were not happy! Passengers were arguing with one another, the ticket agent was arguing with the passengers, the ceiling tiles were tore out as the maintenance people were trying to fix the problem and airport personnel were handing out free bottles of water to try to help people stay cool. It wasn't really working. Luckily my connecting flight boarded only ten minutes after I landed, so I didn't have to deal with it very long.

Hell is going to be hot! Hotter than the concourse with the broken down air conditioning unit in the Charlotte airport. Hell is not going to be fixed at some point in time and everyone will then be comfortable. Hell is going to stay hot for all of eternity with no escape. Hell is a place where thirst will not be quench; no one will be coming around with ice cold bottles of water. Hell is going to be a place of constant torment, utter darkness, screaming and wailing and the gnashing of teeth according to God's Word.

If people at the airport acted so unruly just because the air conditioner was out for a short period of time, how are they going to act for all eternity when there will be no relief? All the people in that concourse left at some point in time and found relief on the airplane or at their own home, the people in hell will never have the opportunity to escape.

Oh, the assurance I have that I will never have to experience what it is going to be like in hell. It's not because I'm too good of a person to go to hell, it's because I have put my faith and trust in Jesus Christ and what He did at Calvary. I have accepted Christ as my personal Savior and because of that I will spend eternity where He is. Have you made your eternal decision on heaven or hell? Don't wait, today is the day of salvation.

Notes:_____
_____
_____
_____
_____
_____
_____
_____
_____
_____

May 5

Lucky

Lucky. That word always reminds me of the 80s/90s country song by Mary Chapin Carpenter, "I Feel Lucky". I tell my wife all the time how lucky I am to have her, and her response is "it's not luck, it's a blessing!" From a Christian point of view, she's right, there is no such thing as luck. God is sovereign over all things and nothing happens according to luck. Things happen because He blesses us with those things.

We may barely miss being in a car accident and we are quick to say, "I was lucky I avoided that", when in actuality, it was the blessings of God that we avoided it. Even those that are not Christians are afforded the blessings of God over luck. The Bible says, "For he makes his sun rise on the evil and on the good and sends rain on the just and on the unjust." - Matthew 5:45.

The blessings of God have nothing to do with four leaf clovers, rabbit's feet, horseshoes or pennies; it is purely the love of God that He has for His creation. "Are not two sparrows sold for a penny? And not one of them will fall to the ground apart from your Father. But even the hairs of your head are all numbered.
Fear not, therefore; you are of more value than many sparrows." - Matthew 10:29-31.

As Christians, do not rely on "luck", but count all things as blessings from God. "Blessed are the people to whom such blessings fall! Blessed are the people whose God is the LORD!" - Psalm 144:15. Even though Mary Chapin Carpenter may have sung about felling lucky, it all comes down to the blessings of God. Have you realized how blessed by God you really are? Blessed that you don't have to pay the penalty of your own sins! That's not lucky my friends, that's being blessed!

Notes:_____
_____
_____
_____
_____
_____
_____
_____
_____
_____
_____
_____
_____
_____
_____
_____
_____
_____
_____

May 6

Graduation

Graduation. It's coming up on that time of year once again. Little ones will be graduating from kindergarten, teenagers will be graduating from high school and people of all ages will be graduating from college. It's one of the great achievements in life. We've reached a certain level of knowledge that the school tells us we are free to go on to the next stage of life whether we are really ready or not.

I've been through three graduations myself with my high school graduation being the most eventful. We were outside and they got about halfway through the 200 students and a storm cloud came rolling through and they stopped it at about the letter "G". They had us all stand up at once and they announced us as graduates. Two seconds later everyone was sprinting for the gymnasium because the bottom fell out. College and graduate school were much more uneventful.

Graduation is a big life changing moment. We go from the routine of going to class, eating in the cafeteria, hanging out with friends and staying up all night studying for exams to all of a sudden, we are kicked into the real world where nothing seems to be in any type of order. The same thing happens when we become Christians.

When we give our life to Christ, the routine of what we used to do all of a sudden is replaced with this whole new life. The things we once did now seem foreign to us. This new thing we call the Christian life seems just as foreign. We become "new creatures" like the Bible says, "Therefore, if anyone is in Christ, he is a new creation. The old has passed away; behold, the new has come." - 2 Corinthians 5:17.

Once the initial shock wears off and we start a new routine of a job or career, we start finding that what we learned from school was just the tip of the iceberg. What we expected doesn't always meet reality. The same thing happen with the Christian life. We have this expectation that life is going to be all rainbows and butterflies but it's not. The Christian life is hard, "Count it all joy, my brothers, when you meet trials of various kinds, for you know that the testing of your faith produces steadfastness. And let steadfastness have its full effect, that you may be perfect and complete, lacking in nothing." - James 1:2-4.

Congratulations to all the new graduates and congratulations to those that may be new in Christ. Your best life lies ahead.

Notes:_____
_____
_____
_____
_____

No Man is an Island

No man is an island. That's the start of a famous poem by English poet and priest, John Donne. As he laid dying in his bed and hearing the church bells toll for funeral after funeral, knowing his own death was soon to come, he wrote these famous words, "No man is an island, entire to himself." It was recently turned into a Christian song by Tenth Avenue North.

We are created by God for relationships, first and foremost with Him, and then with others. We were not created to be solitary beings. We are not islands unto ourselves. So many letters in the New Testament, especially those written by the Apostle Paul, uses the phrase "one another" when exhorting its readers. Paul used this phrase multiple times in his letters to the Romans and to the Corinthians.

Paul, through the prompting of the Holy Spirit, directs believers to love one another, pray for one another, live in harmony with one another, encourage one another, and welcome one another. There are many more that could be listed that I'll let you look up on your own. Are we doing these things or are we escaping to our own little world thinking we will be okay without interaction with anyone else?

Do we think that we can still grow in Christ and not attend church? The writer of Hebrews says, "And let us consider how to stir up one another to love and good works, not neglecting to meet together, as is the habit of some, but encouraging one another, and all the more as you see the Day drawing near." - Hebrews 10:24-25. We are instructed not to neglect meeting together. It is important to gather with like-minded individuals to worship together in Spirit and in Truth.

Even Jesus said, "For where two or three are gathered in my name, there am I among them." - Matthew 18:20. If you don't have a church family, find one! Make sure they are preaching the Gospel of Jesus Christ and not just fanciful sayings.

Notes:_____
_____
_____
_____
_____
_____
_____
_____
_____
_____
_____
_____

May 8

Retirement

Retirement. Not long ago, when I was in my new home-away-from-home, the airport, I was following an older couple and their friend down the jetway to get on the plane and I was listening to their conversation with another older lady. The retired group of three were telling the other woman about their upcoming adventure of hiking 300 miles through Portugal and Spain. As you can imagine, this story caught my attention and the amazement of the older lady whom they were telling the trip details to.

This got me thinking about growing older and a future retirement on my part. I'm still quite a few years away from retiring, especially with young children, but hopefully someday I can retire and have more time to do things like taking adventures with my wife. But what about our Christian lives? Do we ever retire from doing the work of God? The answer to that is "no"!

Our work for the Kingdom of God never comes to an end. Jesus never gave any of His followers a retirement party for their long years of service. All of the Apostles went to the grave, mostly against their will, proclaiming the Gospel of Jesus Christ. Christians never retire, we just leave this world and enter into the glory of the Lord.

I look forward to retiring from the secular world but recognize the fact that retirement from a relationship with Jesus Christ will never end. I will never retire from my relationship with my beautiful wife, so why would I assume I would retire from my beautiful relationship with my Savior? You may never get a paycheck from being a Christian, but the benefits are for eternity. "So even to old age and gray hairs, O God, do not forsake me, until I proclaim your might to another generation, your power to all those to come." - Psalm 71:18.

Notes:_____

_____
_____
_____
_____
_____
_____
_____
_____
_____
_____
_____
_____
_____
_____
_____
_____

More

More. Our sin nature seems to always crave more. More money, more status, more love, more stuff! We seem to be satisfied with not being satisfied. I was scanning through the channels last night and came across the show Deal or No Deal with Howie Mandel. As I watched the show, the gentleman playing made it to the last five cases with some big money still on the board. He was offered six figures to bow out but his need for more pushed him to turn it down and keep pressing his luck. It turned out that he made the wrong choice and ended with the $10 case, all because he wanted more.

"For all that is in the world-the desires of the flesh and the desires of the eyes and pride of life-is not from the Father but is from the world." - 1 John 2:16. Part of the issue is our lust for the flesh and the eyes and the other part of the problem is the world tells us we need more.

That verse shows us that the problem lies within our sinful nature. Things we see are things we end up lusting after. That new car that drives by catches our eye and all of a sudden, we talk ourselves into how old our current car is and the need we have to want more. Our flesh wants to be satisfied and our eyes tempt our flesh to fulfill those desires to have more

"Keep your life free from love of money, and be content with what you have, for he has said, 'I will never leave you nor forsake you.'" - Hebrews 13:5. We defeat the desire to have more with having contentment with what God has blesses us with. There is no sin in having things, that's not what I'm saying, the sin is in the desire to want more. If God blesses us with material things then so be it, but we should have grateful hearts and be content in our lives.

The gentleman on Deal or No Deal kept pushing for more because he wasn't content with the six figures that they offered him. He kept saying how much that money could help him financially, but the list of the flesh, the list of the eyes, and the pride of life kept him from stopping. The world (the audience) kept pushing him to go for more and the world was wrong. He left with so little money he couldn't even fill up his gas tank.

Take inventory of your life and thank God for all you have and be content in your life. "Not that I am speaking of being in need, for I have learned in whatever situation I am to be content. I know how to be brought low, and I know how to abound. In any and every circumstance, I have learned the secret of facing plenty and hunger, abundance and need." - Philippians 4:11-12.

Notes:_____
_____
_____
_____
_____

Forgetful

I was out and about today riding around with my little guy doing some errands after spending the morning working in the yard. We went to the hardware store to get some things that I need to finish off what I was working on. After picking up what we needed and checking out, we got all the way home just to realize that we, or I, had forgotten one thing: the most important thing that we went for in the first place. So, we had to load back up in the truck and head back to the hardware store for that one item.

I thought to myself, the older that I get, the more things I seem to forget. It gets hard some times just to remember the simple things. Even before I left the house, I reminded myself that I needed two of one item and one of the other, but it turned out I only got one of each, so I had to go back for the second one.

That got me thinking about God and the that He never forgets and that He always forgets. That's kind of confusing right? Let's start with the fact that God never forgets. When God makes a promise, He will always fulfill those promises. Throughout the Bible, God has made promises with individuals and covenants with nations and He has always followed through on what He has promised. He promised Abraham that He would make a great nation out of him even though Abraham and Sarah were well up there in age. God fulfilled His promised and gave them Isaac. From Isaac came Jacob, who was renamed Israel, and he had twelve sons that became the tribes of Israel.

Not only does God never forget, God also always forgets. When we give our lives to Christ and accept Him as our personal Savior, God forgets every sin that we have ever committed and will commit. God is always forgetful when it comes to the sins of His children. Now He may hand out earthly punishment for our sins, but He will never hold them against us when it comes to eternity.

We are always on the mid of God, He never forgets about us. He will never say to Himself, "I have forgotten all about so-and-so, I need to check on them and see if they are okay and what they are doing." We are constantly on the mind of God. He always knows what we are doing, He always knows what we need and He always cares for us.

Notes:_____
_____
_____
_____
_____
_____
_____
_____
_____
_____

Blame

Blame. "You ruined it!" Have you ever said those words to someone? Has someone ever said those words to you? Maybe a parent, or a teacher, a coach, or a boss. Maybe you even said that to your own children or maybe even your spouse. We think things are ruined because they are not going according to our plans. We feel things are ruined because of the amount of time that we have put into something that now seems to be turned upside down.

I think about all the times in the Bible that God could have looked down on His creation and could have said, "You ruined it!" He could have easily said those words to Adam and Eve, He could have said it to the nation of Israel and He definitely could have said it to those that persecuted and killed Jesus Christ. But in all those ways that mankind could have ruined the plans of God, He never once said that.

We can't ruin the plans of God. We will never read or hear the words, "you ruined it", from the lips of God. He knows all things, and nothing catches Him by surprise. He knew that Adam and Eve would fall, He knew the nation of Israel would be unfaithful and He knew that Christ can to die for the sins of the world. He knows all things and is not restricted by our concept of time.

He knows all about us too. He knows that we struggle and make mistakes. He knows that the plans we have for ourselves may be ruined. "For I know the plans I have for you, declares the LORD, plans for welfare and not for evil, to give you a future and a hope. Then you will call upon me and come and pray to me, and I will hear you. You will seek me and find me, when you seek me with all your heart.
I will be found by you, declares the LORD, and I will restore your fortunes and gather you from all the nations and all the places where I have driven you, declares the LORD, and I will bring you back to the place from which I sent you into exile." - Jeremiah 29:11-14.

Notes:_____

_____
_____
_____
_____
_____
_____
_____
_____
_____
_____
_____
_____

May 12

Mother's Day

Mother's Day. It only comes around once a year on the calendar, but in reality, it's something that is celebrated every day. None of us would be here without our mothers. None of us probably would have survived this long without them either. Mothers have a great responsibility in the lives of their children, Christian mothers have an even greater one. The Bible gives us some great examples of Godly mothers (and grandmothers) that can be used in guiding the raising of our children.

Mothers and grandmothers can do four things that can have a Godly influence on their children and grandchildren. First, they can show the watching eyes of children that they take God's Word seriously by reading, studying and meditating on it. "All Scripture is breathed out by God and profitable for teaching, for reproof, for correction, and for training in righteousness, that the man (and woman) of God may be complete, equipped for every good work. - 2 Timothy 3:16-17.

Second, mothers and grandmothers can have an active prayer life, both in private and with their children. "But you, beloved, building yourselves up in your most holy faith and praying in the Holy Spirit, keep yourselves in the love of God, waiting for the mercy of our Lord Jesus Christ that leads to eternal life. And have mercy on those who doubt; save others by snatching them out of the fire; to others show mercy with fear, hating even the garment stained by the flesh." - Jude 1:20-23.

Third, to be a great example to their children, mothers should be an active participant in the church. If children see that church is important to their mothers, they are more apt to continue when they grow older. "Do not be slothful in zeal, be fervent in spirit, serve the Lord." - Romans 12:11.

Finally, mothers should train up their children in the way they should go and then be willing to let them go when God's call on their children's lives takes place. "Paul wanted Timothy to accompany him, and he took him and circumcised him because of the Jews who were in those places, for they all knew that his father was a Greek. As they went on their way through the cities, they delivered to them for observance the decisions that had been reached by the apostles and elders who were in Jerusalem. So, the churches were strengthened in the faith, and they increased in numbers daily." - Acts 16:3-5. When Timothy's time had come to go with Paul, his mother had trained him and then let him go.

Notes:_____
_____
_____
_____
_____

Squad

Squad. You know, that small group of close friends that has been given the term "my squad". I heard recently that the older we get the less friends we make. Studies show that as we age, we make less friends and it may be at least five years since you made a new friend. We all have acquaintances, people we work with, people we say hi to at church and even thousands of them on social media, but our "squad" usually consists of less than five people.

By "squad", I mean those few people that if something went wrong in your life, they would be the ones you reach out to for support, not including your family. The small group that you feel free to stop by their house uninvited or that they stop by yours. The friends you don't mind spending hours of just one-on-one time with, that's your "squad". It's okay if you are thinking to yourself right now who your "squad" is and it's okay if the number is greater or less than five.

Jesus had his own "squad" so to speak. He had the multitudes that followed him from town to town looking for miracles, but they would be more like His Facebook followers nowadays, not really part of the "squad". Then He had His twelve disciples that He was much closer to than the multitudes, but even they wouldn't be termed as His "squad".

Jesus had a very small group that He opened Himself up to more than any others in the group of twelve. His "squad" consisted of three: Peter, James and John. Those three men were the ones that Jesus usually separated from the crowd to give them insight to the deep things of God. And out of the three, John says he was the one that Jesus loved.

It's okay to have acquaintances, and it's ok to have friends, but it's important that we have a "squad", a group that we share life with, the good and the bad. We need that small group of people that we can lean on in times of trouble and that we can truly show our hearts to without fear of being judged. Do you have a "squad" or are you part of a "squad"? It's important spiritually to have one, Jesus did.

Notes:_____
_____
_____
_____
_____
_____
_____
_____
_____
_____

Desire

Desire. We all have that fire inside of us that desires to excel at something. That little flame deep down inside to chase after the thing that makes our hearts happy. I watch the posts that people share on Facebook every day and you can see by the subject what that person's desire is. For some it's animals like dogs and horses, for some it's sports and politics, and for others their desire is to know God and make Him known.

That desire is the flame that is inside of us that needs to be fanned into a greater fire. The Apostle Paul told Timothy the same thing, "For this reason I remind you to fan into flame the gift of God, which is in you through the laying on of my hands, for God gave us a spirit not of fear but of power and love and self-control." - 2 Timothy 1:6-7. Paul encouraged Timothy to fan that spark that was in him into a flame. That spark was Timothy's sincere faith that Paul wanted to grow into a flame.

Many times in our lives we have the ability to fan the flame of others by encouraging them in the things they do. Paul was definitely encouraging Timothy, but the wording encourages Timothy to fan his own flame and not to look to someone else to do it for him. We are instructed to take what is a spark inside us for some "cause" and fan that spark into a flame by encouraging ourselves.

"Delight yourself in the LORD, and he will give you the desires of your heart." - Psalm 37:4. What are the desires of your heart? What is that spark within you that makes you get up each morning? What are you doing to fan that spark into a flame? Seek after the Lord and He will give you the desires of your heart according to His will.

Notes:_____
_____
_____
_____
_____
_____
_____
_____
_____
_____
_____
_____
_____
_____
_____
_____
_____
_____

May 15

Adjustments

Adjustments. I have to say that I have never once been to a chiropractor. I know some people that swear by them, but I have never really had any back problems that made me go. I have this strange feeling that if you go once, you're stuck having to go the rest of your life. I would love to hear your comments about going to a chiropractor.

I have heard that when you do go to the chiropractor, that it can be very painful until they are done adjusting you. They will push and pull on all the spots that are hurting to work out the soreness and make you feel like you are back to feeling like your normal self. Again, I have never been to the chiropractor so I'm just repeating what I have heard.

God does the same things to us sometimes that a chiropractor does in adjusting our backs. God will take the sore spots in our lives and push and pull at them and it will hurt at the beginning. He shines a light into our lives exposing the dark spots He wants to work on and it's painful. He will push and prod at those "knots" in our lives until He works them out and gets us back into His will. It will be uncomfortable at the beginning but when He is done, our lives seem to be back in correct working order.

The idea of God being like a chiropractor reminds me of the verses in Jeremiah, "'Arise, and go down to the potter's house, and there I will let you hear my words.' So, I went down to the potter's house, and there he was working at his wheel. And the vessel he was making of clay was spoiled in the potter's hand, and he reworked it into another vessel, as it seemed good to the potter to do." - Jeremiah 18:2-4.

If something seems amiss in our lives to God, He will use his caring hands to remold us into something more beautiful. Just like the chiropractor use their hands to massage out the bad areas of our bodies, so too does the Master Potter use His hands to work out the areas in our lives He wants to fix. We need to be willing to allow God to work on those sore spots so that He can restore us back to where He wants us.

Notes:_____
_____
_____
_____
_____
_____
_____
_____
_____
_____
_____

Perfect Timing

Perfect timing. Ever have one of those moments when you thought all hope was lost and there was no way out of your current situation? And then all of a sudden, the improbable happens, something you thought could never take place to get you out of a situation. That's God showing up right on time.

I heard a story on the radio the other day about God showing up with perfect timing that I want to share. A military husband and wife, with a newborn baby, had just moved to a new city. Most of their important stuff was in a storage unit they had rented. The husband, on deployment in another state, called his wife to tell her that he was notified by the police that their storage unit had been broken into.

Of course, his wife was very upset and started praying on her way over to meet the police at the storage unit. When she got in the car and turned on the radio, a line from Mercy Me's song came on saying, "Your day's about to get better!" She laughed and told God that it was pretty ironic that that line was on and that there was no way that her day was about to get any better. In fact, she thought her day was about to get terribly worse.

However, when she arrived at the storage unit, the police notified her that someone had cut the padlock on the unit but the way the lock was cut, they couldn't remove it from the hole it was locked through. So even though the lock was destroyed, they were unable to open the door meaning everything was still secure in the unit. Her day had gotten better, and God was just letting her know through the song on her way over. He had perfect timing.

The Bible tells us that the birth of Jesus was based upon perfect timing, "But when the fullness of time had come, God sent forth his Son, born of woman, born under the law, to redeem those who were under the law, so that we might receive adoption as sons." - Galatians 4:4-5.

The Bible also tells us that our salvation came at the perfect time as well, "but God shows his love for us in that while we were still sinners, Christ died for us." - Romans 5:8. God's timing is perfect. As the Karen Peck and New River song goes, "even when He is four days late, He's still right on time!"

Whatever it is you may be going through right now, stay faithful, God is working in His time and His timing is always right on time. A perfect God always has perfect timing.

Notes:_____
_____
_____
_____
_____

Plans Change

Plans change. The best laid plans don't always work out the way we want them to. We depend on technology and sometimes technology lets us down. My plan was to stay at home today and work from the comfort of home and get a lot of things done. I had any things that need to get done today, but it doesn't look like its going to happen. When I went to log into the system at work, it wouldn't let me log in. After about a dozen tries, I decided to call someone at the office and see what was up. Came to find out that our entire system is down and nobody can gain access whether they are in the office or working remotely.

So, my best laid plans didn't work out. Ever have that happen to you? Something you had been planning on for days, or months, or maybe even years, didn't work out for some unforeseen reason? It happens to everyone because our plans are not always God's plans. Now, I'm not saying that what happened today with work was in the plans of God, we live in a fallen world and things happen, but what I am saying is sometimes our plans are not what God wants for us.

"For I know the plans I have for you, declares the Lord, plans for welfare and not for evil, to give you a future and a hope." – Jeremiah 29:11. The apostle Paul had plans to bring the Gospel message of Jesus Christ to Asia and that was where he started his journey towards. But, in a dream at night, he had a vision of a man calling out to him from Macedonia, and at that moment Paul's plans where changed by God. He scrapped his plans for Asia and headed towards Macedonia. God had plans for Paul that he did not have for himself.

Paul was in the complete will of God and completely open to the call of God. He could have been stubborn and told God that was not what he wanted to do, tat his plan was to go to Asia and that the people of Macedonia would just have to wait. But Paul didn't do that; instead he obeyed the voice of God and dropped his plans to follow God's will

When God calls us to do something that is different then what we have planned, do we dig in our heels and tell God that we are going to do what we want? Or are we like Paul and change our plans for the better and perfect plans of God? God wants us to be obedient to Him because He knows so much better than we do. God's plans are perfect!

Notes:_____
_____
_____
_____
_____
_____
_____

Battles

Battles. We all face them. Whether they are battles within us, with family or coworkers, or even with culture. Some we win and some we lose. We need to be careful what battles we fight as Christians because some aren't worth losing a chance to witness of our Lord over.

The Bible describes many battles between groups of people and between individuals. There are all the battles listed in the Bible when Israel was taking the promised land. There were battles when Israel was being taken into captivity because of their idolatry. We see battles between David and King Saul. Battles are a part of history and they will still be a part of the future.

The Book of Revelation tells of a final battle between Satan and Christ called the Battle of Armageddon. Satan will attempt one last overthrow of Christ but will lose and be thrown into the lake of fire to suffer for eternity.

Maybe you are facing some of your own battles and you don't know where to turn for help. You can pray like David did, "Contend, O LORD, with those who contend with me; fight against those who fight against me!" - Psalm 35:1. The battle belongs to the Lord, let Him fight for you, for His strength is greater than our own.

Notes:_____

_____
_____
_____
_____
_____
_____
_____
_____
_____
_____
_____
_____
_____
_____
_____
_____
_____
_____
_____
_____
_____
_____
_____

Full Moon

Full moon. Last night showed us the glory of God with an amazing full moon shining bright in the sky. I love when we have a full moon because it just lights up everything. It's almost bright enough to be outside doing yard work. As we drove home last night, it was like the moon was guiding our way.

What's amazing is that the moon produces no light of its own, it just reflects the light of the sun. What a Biblical principle that is. God and Christ are the source of the light, we are to be the reflection of their light. We produce no light of our own, we are nothing but sinners saved by the grace of God.

"In him was life, and the life was the light of men. The light shines in the darkness, and the darkness has not overcome it." - John 1:4-5. Jesus Christ came to this world to be the light of the world. He came to reflect the light of His Father even though the same light was within Him.

The purpose of His coming to earth was "to give light to those who sit in darkness and in the shadow of death, to guide our feet into the way of peace." - Luke 1:79. As the moon reflects the light of the sun, so should we reflect the light of the Son!

Our job is to now reflect the light of Jesus Christ in how we live our lives, "for at one time you were darkness, but now you are light in the Lord. Walk as children of light (for the fruit of light is found in all that is good and right and true) and try to discern what is pleasing to the Lord." - Ephesians 5:8-10.

Notes:_____

_____
_____
_____
_____
_____
_____
_____
_____
_____
_____
_____
_____
_____
_____
_____
_____
_____

Mailman

Mailman. I grew up the son of a mailman. We moved back to New York from North Carolina when I was in the third grade because my dad got a job with the post office back home. My dad loved being a mailman. He loved meeting and talking to all the people on his route. He would carry dog treats with him for all the dogs along the way. He loved to just deliver the mail to people.

Christ asks us to do the same thing. He asks us to deliver the Good News of the Gospel. He asks us to love being the "mailman". He asks us to love on, and talk to, the people along our route called life. He asks us to be His hands and feet.

What he doesn't require us to do is make sure that the mail is received. We are not responsible for whether or not the receiver accepts the message, just like my father was not responsible for whether or not they paid their bills. He just asks us to deliver the message. After that, we have to let the Holy Spirit work from there. We cannot "save" anyone, we can only make Him known.

How much of our own mail do we throw away when we get it because we feels it's just junk mail. We will come across people that we share the message of Christ with, that will feel it's just junk, however, we are to still deliver the message. We never know if the Holy Spirit has been working beforehand when we share the News. It may just be that they have thrown the message away dozens of times before because they thought it was "junk", but something happened in their lives and they are ready to receive the Gospel.

Continue to be God's mailman. Continue to share the Good News of Jesus Christ. You never know when the Holy Spirit has already prepared the path for you to share the Gospel. "And he said to them, 'Go into all the world and proclaim the gospel to the whole creation. Whoever believes and is baptized will be saved, but whoever does not believe will be condemned.'" - Mark 16:15-16.

Notes:_____
_____
_____
_____
_____
_____
_____
_____
_____
_____
_____

Amazed

Amazed! I've used that word a time or two to describe events that have happened in my life. I've been amazed that my gorgeous wife chose to spend the rest of her life with someone like me. I've been amazed that God has blessed me with two beautiful and healthy children. I'm still amazed that God would choose to save a rotten sinner like me and chose to use me to share His Good News. But God works in amazing and mysterious ways.

That word, "amazed" shows up many times in the four Gospels and it Is always in reference to someone's reaction to what Jesus had said or done. The crowds were amazed at His miracles, the religious people were amazed at His knowledge and teaching, and it was even said that Pilate was amazed with Christ when he questioned Him.

It's not hard to believe that people were amazed with Jesus Christ when they encountered Him. However, there is one place in the Gospels where the tables were turned and Jesus was the one that was amazed. "And He could do no mighty work there, except that He laid His hands on a few sick people and healed them. And He was amazed because of their unbelief." - Mark 6:5-6a.

He was in His own hometown of Nazareth and the people would not believe in Him. Because of their unbelief, He could not do any mighty works there. These were people that knew Him, had heard of His miracles and still would not believe. If those who physically had the opportunity to see and hear him would not believe, why are we amazed that this generation will not believe?

Just like I wrote about yesterday, we are to continue to share the message of Jesus Christ, but we should not be amazed when that message is rejected. Our Lord and Savior was rejected in His own hometown and it left Him amazed.

Notes:_____

_____
_____
_____
_____
_____
_____
_____
_____
_____
_____
_____
_____

May 22

Wardrobe

Wardrobe. I have to admit that my wardrobe isn't much to write about. It consists mostly of khakis, jeans and polo shirts. That's about all I wear to work. I do have one suit for those "special" occasions. I just don't feel the urge to spend money on clothes. If I get anything new it's usually because my bride bought it for me.

But there is coming a day when I will get a whole new wardrobe and it will go with anything. "The one who conquers will be clothed thus in white garments, and I will never blot his name out of the book of life. I will confess his name before my Father and before his angels." - Revelation 3:5.

"After this I looked, and behold, a great multitude that no one could number, from every nation, from all tribes and peoples and languages, standing before the throne and before the Lamb, clothed in white robes, with palm branches in their hands" - Revelation 7:9.

"And the armies of heaven, arrayed in fine linen, white and pure, were following him on white horses." - Revelation 19:14. We will all be clothed in white for all eternity because our sins have been removed as far as the east is from the west. Our white clothes will never have a spot or stain because Jesus took them from us on the Cross.

"Come now, let us reason together, says the LORD: though your sins are like scarlet, they shall be as white as snow; though they are red like crimson, they shall become like wool." - Isaiah 1:18.

Notes:_____
_____
_____
_____
_____
_____
_____
_____
_____
_____
_____
_____
_____
_____
_____
_____
_____
_____

May 23

Camels

Camels. One of my favorite all time commercials is the camel walking through the office asking everyone what day it was. Everyone tried to ignore him until he finally got someone to admit that it was Hump Day! I used to have a guy I worked with named Mike and I would ask him every Wednesday what day it was and he would make me happy by telling me it was Hump Day. Little things make me happy.

One of the most confusing sections of Scripture involves the mention of a camel. "Again, I tell you, it is easier for a camel to go through the eye of a needle than for a rich person to enter the kingdom of God." - Matthew 19:24. Putting it context, a rich young man had approached Jesus about what good deed he need to do to have eternal life. When He overconfidently confirmed he had done all things Jesus required of him, Jesus told him to sell all his stuff and give it to the poor and follow Him. He couldn't do it.

That leads to Jesus telling the crowd that it was easier for a camel to go through the eye of a needle than a rich man to get into heaven. There is some debate about this saying. In the 15th century a story originated that the "eye of the needle" was a small entrance in the wall around Jerusalem that was used after the gates have been shut for the night. However, no opening has ever really been found to confirm this. Second, it is said that the word "camel" was misspelled during translation and the word should read "rope". They are very similar in the original Hebrew. Either way, a rope nor a camel can fit through the eye of a needle.

Either debate really doesn't matter to the context of the story. The point is this, whether "rope" or "camel," Jesus' point still stands; no matter whom you are and what you've accomplished, it is impossible to enter the Kingdom of God on your own "good works". Which is exactly why Jesus had to take on human flesh and come to earth. It goes against our desire to be self-sufficient, the Gospel tells us that apart from being in Christ Jesus, we are deserving of the eternal judgment that God is going to hand out to the unrighteous on the last day.

It does not mean that rich people can't get into heaven and that they need to sell all their stuff if they want a chance to make it. Remember, Jesus was talking to an unbeliever and not a Christian. In Jesus' day, being rich was believed to be an outward sign of God's blessing on someone. Jesus was trying to prove to the young man that material possessions don't always mean that you are blessed by God. Having accepted His Son means you are blessed by God.

Notes:_____
_____
_____
_____
_____

Salesman

Salesman. Within the first seventy-two hours of being in our brand new house, three security system salesmen rang our doorbell to try and sell us new home security systems. The first one showed up while we were unpacking the moving truck, he came walking right down the driveway with his company literature. Another one rang the doorbell the following day and one more two days later. They must be in cahoots with either the real estate agents or the moving companies.

There's nothing like moving into a new home and being pestered by salesmen trying to sell you something else after you just spent loads of money on a new house. I understand that they have to make a living and the best time to sell a security system is when someone first moves in, but they could at least give us a week or two! I'm not a big fan of salesmen in the first place, whether it's selling cars, furniture or Girl Scout Cookies (just kidding on the cookies). I always feel like I'm getting only one side of the story: the positive.

When we witness to others about Christ, do you think we come across as salesmen? Are people turned off from Christianity because we can be too pushy or we "sell" them on only the positive things about a relationship with Christ? Do we make it seem like all the troubles of the world will go away when they become Christians? Nobody is going to "buy" that, they understand that life is still hard as a Christian. "I have said these things to you, that in me you may have peace. In the world you will have tribulation. But take heart; I have overcome the world." - John 16:33.

Don't "sell" Jesus, witness to people about how accepting Jesus as your Savior changed your life. Tell them who you were before Christ and who you are now with Him. Tell them that life isn't always easy, even after becoming a Christian, but that you now have someone to turn to in times of trouble that understands. "For because he himself has suffered when tempted, he is able to help those who are being tempted." - Hebrews 2:18. Tell them that your relationship with Christ is about eternal blessings and not earthly blessings. People are much more open about hearing your experiences than they are being "sold" something. No one can ever argue with what Christ has done for you.

Notes:_____
_____
_____
_____
_____

May 25

Music and Dance

Music and dance. Two things my daughter loves is dancing and playing the piano. We got to watch her perform last night at her piano recital and tonight we get to watch her at her dance recital. I couldn't be happier that she follows her heart and does what she loves to do even though most of her friends play sports.

Her love of dancing and music reminds me of David in the Bible. He was musically inclined and even soothed the soul of King Saul by playing for him on his harp. "And David and all the house of Israel were celebrating before the LORD, with songs and lyres and harps and tambourines and castanets and cymbals." – 2 Samuel 6:5. Almost all of the psalms are written by David and most believe they were sung to music. "I will give to the LORD the thanks due to his righteousness, and I will sing praise to the name of the LORD, the Most High." – Psalm 7:17.

David loves to dance as well. "And David danced before the LORD with all his might." – 2 Samuel 6:14. Whenever I think of David dancing I think of the scene from Footloose when they stood before the town council trying to get them to approve letting them have a dance in their town. They used Biblical Scriptures to show that singing and dancing were ways of showing praises unto the Lord.

I pray that Christina continues to pursue both her music and her dancing and that she uses both of them to glorify and praise the Lord as she grows closer to Him. "Then shall the young women rejoice in the dance, and the young men and the old shall be merry. I will turn their mourning into joy; I will comfort them and give them gladness for sorrow." – Jeremiah 31:13.

Notes:_____

_____
_____
_____
_____
_____
_____
_____
_____
_____
_____
_____
_____
_____
_____
_____

Crying

Crying. It was a late-night last night and our little guy fell asleep at the dance recital. When he woke up as we were leaving, he got to crying and every little thing stoked the tears. We finally got in the car and started driving home and he fell back asleep. Every parent that I passed carrying a sleeping little one seemed to understand the problem.

We cry when we are hurt. We cry when we are sad. And we cry when we are happy. It's part of the emotional package that God gave us. For some of us, our days of crying will cease to exist. "He will wipe away every tear from their eyes, and death shall be no more, neither shall there be mourning, nor crying, nor pain anymore, for the former things have passed away." - Revelation 21:4.

But for others, crying will be a part of the emotions they will experience for all of eternity. "I tell you, many will come from east and west and recline at table with Abraham, Isaac, and Jacob in the kingdom of heaven, while the sons of the kingdom will be thrown into the outer darkness. In that place there will be weeping and gnashing of teeth." - Matthew 8:11-12.

The Bible tells of two places that man will spend eternity: heaven or hell. In one place there will be no more tears as God will wipe away every one of them. The second place will be a place of weeping and utter darkness. We all have a decision to make in regard to where we spend our eternity. Accepting Christ will lead to eternal life. Rejecting Christ will lead to eternal suffering. Your choice.

Notes:_____

_____
_____
_____
_____
_____
_____
_____
_____
_____
_____
_____
_____
_____
_____
_____
_____
_____
_____
_____

May 27

Memorial Day

Memorial Day. A day set aside for those that fought for our freedom and lost their lives in doing so. It's a day to remember our past and the freedoms we have because of those that paid the ultimate price. Not all that went to battle came home, and some who went to battle came home and died because of what they were exposed to. My dad passed away almost 35 years after he came home from Vietnam because of his exposure to Agent Orange.

We set up a day to remember them and we probably all have different ways of doing that. It reminds me of the story in Joshua. As they crossed the Jordan River into the Promised Land, they were getting ready to go into battle with the people already living there. Joshua sent twelve men, one from each tribe of Israel, back into the river to grab a large stone and bring it out. Once they were in the Promised Land, they built a memorial so that future generations would remember what God had done in allowing Israel to cross over on dry ground.

"And Joshua said to them, 'Pass on before the ark of the LORD your God into the midst of the Jordan, and take up each of you a stone upon his shoulder, according to the number of the tribes of the people of Israel, that this may be a sign among you. When your children ask in time to come, 'What do those stones mean to you?' then you shall tell them that the waters of the Jordan were cut off before the ark of the covenant of the LORD. When it passed over the Jordan, the waters of the Jordan were cut off. So, these stones shall be to the people of Israel a memorial forever.'"- Joshua 4:5-7.

As we celebrate this day, let it be in remembrance of those that sacrificed all for those they never knew. "Greater love has no one than this, that someone lay down his life for his friends." - John 15:13.

Notes:_____
_____
_____
_____
_____
_____
_____
_____
_____
_____
_____
_____
_____
_____

May 28

Stories

Stories. We all have them. Some stories make us feel good and some stories not so much. We tell our stories and we listen to others tell their stories. Some people have a story for every situation in life and some people seem to love to tell them. Some people keep their stories to themselves and that's okay too.

Sitting in airports and on airplanes, you get to hear a lot of people tell stories. Most of the time they aren't even talking to you, you just get to overhear the conversations of others. Sometimes they are on the phone and you only get to hear one side of the story. Other times you hear the stories being shared between two people that just met and they are telling about themselves or what they do.

I always wonder how much of the story is exaggerated to make it either more interesting or make the story teller come across in a better light. Very rarely will anyone ever tell a story to a stranger to make themselves look bad. That got me thinking about the stories in the Bible.

Many people believe the stories in the Old Testament are just fairy tales or fables. But the Bible makes sure that it shows all the people at their best and their worst. No one is spared from having their total lives on display: the good, the bad and the ugly. When stories are told in that way, it brings a higher level of truth to the story because we aren't just given the "good" stuff.

We are told the sinful sides of Noah, Abraham, Moses, David and a list of others. That allows us to believe that the stories are true and accurate; not fairy tales or fables. "Knowing this first of all, that no prophecy of Scripture comes from someone's own interpretation. For no prophecy was ever produced by the will of man, but men spoke from God as they were carried along by the Holy Spirit." - 2 Peter 1:20-21.

"All Scripture is breathed out by God and profitable for teaching, for reproof, for correction, and for training in righteousness, that the man of God may be complete, equipped for every good work." - 2 Timothy 3:16-17. While the stories of man may be inflated with lies and exaggeration, the Word of God is truth.

Notes:_____
_____
_____
_____
_____
_____
_____

Error

Error. A few days ago, a baseball legend passed away. Bill Buckner, a lifetime .289 hitter, a NL batting champion and an all-star, passed away in Idaho at 69. He was a great ball player that played for 22 years with five different teams, but he will always be remembered for one fateful night in New York during the 1986 World Series.

In game six of the World Series against the New York Mets, Bill let a ground ball go through his legs in the tenth inning allowing the game winning run to score to force a game seven. The Mets would eventually win the World Series and the curse of the Red Sox continued. Every great play and every great season Bill Buckner had, took a back seat to that one error at first base.

Things like that happen in our lives too, except we don't call them errors, we call them sins. Many times, our sins become what defines us to others. They look at us and see our past sins over everything else we may have done in our lives. We could have been an all-star in everything we had done, but one error is all anyone remembers. When Bill died the other day, all they kept playing when the talked about his death was that fateful error.

We can't let that continue to define us, Bill didn't. He spoke about it when asked, but he didn't let it haunt him from continuing on with his life. It reminds me of the story of Peter when he denied Christ three times. He could have let that define him, but Christ made sure that He forgave him so he could continue on to do great things like his sermon on the day of Pentecost (Acts 2).

Don't let your past sins define your future. Don't let other's remembrance of your past sins define you either. God has forgiven you and is ready to use you to glorify His name.

Notes:_____
_____
_____
_____
_____
_____
_____
_____
_____
_____
_____
_____
_____
_____
_____
_____
_____

May 30

Lion

Lion. Whenever I come across the movie "The Lion, the Witch and the Wardrobe" on television, I always stop and watch it no matter what part of the movie it is at. There is just something about that movie that draws me to watch it any time it is on. I love the book as well, and my wife and daughter are reading the entire Chronicles of Narnia series together.

I recently watched a movie about C.S. Lewis, where they spoke about why he chose to portray Aslan as a Lion in his story. He said that most people view God as this heavenly grandfather in the sky that just gives into all of our wildest desires just to make sure we are happy. He said that he wanted to portray Aslan as both an approachable character, but also as a fierce character. He chose a Lion to portray the character Aslan in is Chronicles of Narnia stories.

The world wants to look at God as just this deity of love, that all He wants is everybody to be happy and that He will not pass any judgement on anyone, instead He will just welcome them with open arms and a big hug. He will do that if we repent and turn our lives over to Him and accept His Son as our Savior. But if man does not do that, the Bible says that God will judge man for his sins and punish him for eternity for not accepting the free gift of eternal life.

Jesus came to this world the first time representing a lamb. "The next day he saw Jesus coming toward him, and said, 'Behold, the Lamb of God, who takes away the sin of the world!'" - John 1:29. His first trip was to offer Himself as a sacrificial lamb for the sins of the world. His second trip He will return as the Lion from the tribe of Judah to judge the sins of the world. "And one of the elders said to me, 'Weep no more; behold, the Lion of the tribe of Judah, the Root of David, has conquered, so that he can open the scroll and its seven seals.'" - Revelation 5:5.

The Lamb of God has come and gone, doing His sacrificial work. The Lion of the tribe of Judah is set to return to judge and conquer. Have you accepted the work of the Lamb or are you planning on facing the judgement of the Lion? You still have time to choose.

Notes:_____
_____
_____
_____
_____
_____
_____
_____

Drafted

Drafted. It's that time of year again when many young athletes get the opportunity to make their career in a professional sport. Around this time of year, the athletes that play football, basketball and baseball await a phone call that a professional sports team had selected them in their yearly draft. Some of these young men that are in their late teens and early twenties, will go from never having a full-time job to now being a professional athlete making millions of dollars if they are the best of the best. They will go from being reliant on their parents to meet their basic needs to now having more money than they will ever know what to do with. That has to be a hard transition for some of them.

With this new job, many changes will take place in the lives of these young athletes outside of just the money. They will possibly have to move to a different part of the country. They will have newfound fame that they never experienced before. They will be living on their own and having to manage on their own. All of these changes at one time can make it very difficult to be successful.

We face some of the same things when we decide to accept Christ as our Savior. Not in the sense that we get "drafted" by God, but we do change realms of what we once were to what we now are. We go from being enemies of God before we were Christians to now being the children of God after our conversion. We have a newfound lifestyle in Christ that we didn't have before. We have an access to God we never had before and we have a new requirement to how we are to live our lives.

There should be a change in us that comes from being a new child of God. The things we do should be different. The words that come out of our mouths should be different than they used to be. And the place we go should be different than what we used to go to. "Therefore, if anyone is in Christ, he is a new creation. The old has passed away; behold, the new has come." 2 Corinthians 5:17. When this change happens from the old person, we were to the new person that we are, it can be very difficult. The things we have always done now conflicts with the things that we are commanded to do.

Are you a new Christian and struggling with this new person that you are and the battle between the person you used to be? I understand, and I think all Christians do, but keep fighting the good fight, it will get easier.

Notes:_____
_____
_____
_____
_____
_____
_____
_____

Asleep

Asleep. Are we asleep at the most important times of our lives, when Christ needs us to be His witnesses? As I traveled recently, I sat next to a lady that was from India and she had a little two year old boy with her. She sat with that wiggly little guy for the entire two and a half hour flight with him on her lap. They were on the inside seat next to the window and he sat in that confined area as patiently as a two year old could. As the flight came to an end and we hit the runway and started taxiing to the terminal, that little guy fell asleep. He stayed awake the entire flight and as soon as we got to our destination, he fell asleep.

I'm sure the rest of her family was waiting for them in the terminal and anxious to see her and the little guy. And I'm am sure she had talked up the trip and the excitement that he must have had to see his family when he arrived. And then when he gets to his final destination and is only minutes away from what he has been waiting for, for who knows how long, he falls asleep.

It reminded me of the apostles in the Garden of Gethsemane just before the arrest of Jesus. He had asked his three closest disciples to stay with Him and pray. When He went out to check on them, they were fast asleep! The most important moment in their time with Christ so far, and they couldn't stay awake. He had told them this time was coming and they didn't believe Him, and when He needs them most to be in prayer, they fail Him.

When Christ calls on us to do something for the kingdom of God, will we be alert and ready, or will He find us asleep at the most important time? I have to ask myself all the time, am I asleep or awake? Am I watching the people in this world for opportunities to share the love of Christ and introduce them to the Good News of Jesus Christ? God wants us not to wander through this world as if we are asleep, He wants us to be alert and always watching for opportunities to witness to others for Him.

Notes:_____

_____
_____
_____
_____
_____
_____
_____
_____
_____
_____
_____
_____
_____
_____

June 2

Prayer

Prayer. The spiritual leaders of our country have asked the nation to make today a National Day of Prayer for our political leaders and our president in particular. We live in dangerous times both within our country and from our enemies abroad. Satan has blinded the eyes of so many and has gain the hearts and minds of many that are in powerful positions. The Bible is clear that he is the prince of the power of the air at this current time. "For we do not wrestle against flesh and blood, but against the rulers, against the authorities, against the cosmic powers over this present darkness, against the spiritual forces of evil in the heavenly places." - Ephesians 6:12. The prayers of God's people are extremely important and powerful.

"Let every person be subject to the governing authorities. For there is no authority except from God, and those that exist have been instituted by God. Therefore, whoever resists the authorities resists what God has appointed, and those who resist will incur judgment. For rulers are not a terror to good conduct, but to bad. Would you have no fear of the one who is in authority? Then do what is good, and you will receive his approval, for he is God's servant for your good. But if you do wrong, be afraid, for he does not bear the sword in vain. For he is the servant of God, an avenger who carries out God's wrath on the wrongdoer."- Romans 13:1-4.

Notice that Paul's command to believers was not reliant on any of the leaders being from our favored political party. We should pray for our leaders first and foremost to have a relationship with Jesus Christ and second that they would make decisions based upon the Word of God. "Remind them to be submissive to rulers and authorities, to be obedient, to be ready for every good work, to speak evil of no one, to avoid quarreling, to be gentle, and to show perfect courtesy toward all people." - Titus 3:1-2.

Pray for our country and our leaders today and every day that we may live in peace.

Notes:_____
_____
_____
_____
_____
_____
_____
_____
_____
_____
_____

Planner

Planner. Are you a planner or do you just go with the flow? Do you make to-do lists and stick to them no matter what and if it gets messed up it just ruins your day? Are you married to your opposite? Do you make plans and your spouse goes with the flow, or the other way around? I spend all week at work making timelines and trying to keep the team in line with following them, so when I get home I would rather just go with the flow.

There is absolutely nothing wrong with making plans: short term or long term. I think it is good to make plans about what we want to accomplish for the week and even plans for what we want to accomplish for the next several years. However, we need to make sure that our plans aren't so rigid that God can't use us in ways that He wants to because our plans get in the way. We have to be ready to allow God to direct our paths. "In all your ways acknowledge him, and he will make straight your paths." - Proverbs 3:6.

Our plans are fine as long as they match up for God's will for our lives. If we become too attached to our plans, God may have to break us from them in order to use us, just like the potter does the clay. Our only concrete plan should be to use our lives to bring glory and honor to God and to share His message of salvation through His Son Jesus Christ.

Notes:_____

_____
_____
_____
_____
_____
_____
_____
_____
_____
_____
_____
_____
_____
_____
_____
_____
_____
_____
_____
_____
_____

Weeds

Weeds. I think I do a better job at growing weeds in my yard than I do growing grass. I can grow grass like a champion in my gravel driveway, but not in the yard. I spray for weeds constantly and my wife pulls weeds like it's going out of style. Why is it so easy for weeds to grow and so hard for grass to grow? Is it the soil? Is it too rocky or is there too much clay? I don't know the answer but it does remind me of one of the parables of Christ.

"And he told them many things in parables, saying: 'A sower went out to sow. And as he sowed, some seeds fell along the path, and the birds came and devoured them. Other seeds fell on rocky ground, where they did not have much soil, and immediately they sprang up, since they had no depth of soil, but when the sun rose, they were scorched. And since they had no root, they withered away. Other seeds fell among thorns, and the thorns grew up and choked them. Other seeds fell on good soil and produced grain, some a hundredfold, some sixty, some thirty. He who has ears, let him hear.'" - Matthew 13:3-9.

When we share the Gospel of Jesus Christ, we do not know much about the ground we are planting the seed in. Some of those we share with may not be interested at all because maybe things are going too well in their lives and they don't feel they need a Savior. Some may be so distracted by the things of the world that they listen but soon go back to the pleasures of the world.

But sometimes, that soil has been worked by someone else who has the shared the Gospel before us and it softened their hearts. And when you share the Good News with them, the time is right for that seed to take root. We never know the soil that has been prepared before we arrive. Our job is to continue to plant seeds and sometimes it's our job to just till the soil. Maybe our job is to just pull and kill the weeds that may choke out future seeds.

Whatever it is the Lord would have us to do, we are to continue to leave seeds along our journey called life. Sometimes we till, sometimes we weed and sometimes we plant. Either way, keep doing what Christ commanded us to do, "Go therefore and make disciples of all nations, baptizing them in the name of the Father and of the Son and of the Holy Spirit, teaching them to observe all that I have commanded you. And behold, I am with you always, to the end of the age." - Matthew 28:19-20.

Notes:_____
_____
_____
_____
_____
_____
_____

Reputation

Reputation. Someone's reputation is a valuable thing. It is also a very delicate possession. It takes years to develop your reputation and seconds to kill it. Your reputation also varies from person to person based on events that happen between the two of you. You may have a stellar reputation with one person only to find that your reputation with someone else is the exact opposite.

As Christians, our reputation is extremely important. We are sometimes the reason why unbelievers feel they don't need Christ. If we call ourselves Christians but live our lives the same way the world lives, then why would they need a Savior? We are the reason that people don't come church because they feel the church is filled with "hypocrites". Sometimes we are! We say one thing and do the opposite. That is not drawing unbelievers to Christ.

Believe me, I'm talking to myself here too. This all goes through my heart before it ever reaches your eyes. I have to ask myself often if my reputation matches up with what my mouth claims to be. To be honest, it hasn't always been so. I've done many things to ruin my reputation as a Christian. It's a daily struggle to make sure I am walking with Christ. I'm sure you feel the same way as well. Our reputation is important. How people see us is important too, not for our egos, but for our witness of Christ.

We can't be like the church in Sardis though, "You have the reputation of being alive, but you are dead. - Revelation 3:1. What we can't do is be fake. We must be real and we must be genuine or people will see right through us. That's where they feel we are "hypocrites" which means to wear a mask.

Notes:_____

_____
_____
_____
_____
_____
_____
_____
_____
_____
_____
_____
_____
_____
_____
_____
_____
_____
_____

Both Ends of the Spectrum

What a difference a week makes. Just last week, I had reached out to the people who follow the page with a very important prayer request for one of my friends. His son had been involved in a freak accident while on vacation outside of the United States. I reached out to all the prayer warriors to pray for this very concerning situation and everyone made intercession to God on his behalf and the best possible outcome occurred from the accident. All glory, honor and praise go to God for the answered prayers.

Now, a week later and my feelings are on the opposite end of the spectrum. I got news today that a long time childhood friend of mine had passed away after a long battle with cancer. One thing both of these incidents reminded me of is that life is fragile, no matter what age we are: children, middle-aged, or elderly.

I know that death will come upon all of us at some point unless the Lord returns soon and calls His church home. I understand that people we know and love can face death at any time during their lives and we don't have any say about it. God is in control of when we are born and when we die, who are parents are and in what country we are born in. God is completely sovereign over His entire creation.

Death still hurts us that are left behind to deal with it. Even though I hadn't seen my friend in decades, I still hurt knowing that he left behind a wife and children, both his parents, and three sisters who have children he was an uncle to. He was the same age that I am and it really made me take a look at my own life and the people I have in it. Do they know how much I love them and how important they are to me?

I don't know what relationship he had with God, whether he had accepted Christ as his Savior or not. That, too, made me think; am I doing all that I can to make sure my friends and family know Christ so that when the day comes of their passing, I can have the assurance of knowing where they are? Our most important job here as Christians is that we witness to others, especially our friends and family, so that their eternity is secured.

Notes:_____
_____
_____
_____
_____
_____
_____
_____
_____
_____
_____
_____
_____
_____

June 7

Disappointment

Disappointment. We all go through it at different stages in life. When we are young, we may be disappointed that we didn't get a lollipop when we asked for it. As teenagers we may be disappointed when someone turns us down when we ask for a date. When we are older, we may be disappointed when we don't get the job or promotion we want or expected. Disappointment happens in many ways and it happens to all of us.

So how do we move on from disappointment? We have to remember that our plans for our lives are not always God's plans for us. The things we desire in our hearts for how our lives should go may not be the best overall direction God has for us. "For my thoughts are not your thoughts, neither are your ways my ways, declares the LORD." - Isaiah 55:8. There is nothing wrong with having dreams and goals. However, we need to be ready for them to take a back seat to what God has planned for us.

I know some people in my life that are disappointed with how things have gone recently and that's okay. We need to keep moving forward knowing that God knows best, and even if we are disappointed now, God loves us and will never do us wrong. If you are disappointed today because something you planned didn't go how you expected it, take heart, God may just have something better for you up ahead.

Notes:_____

_____
_____
_____
_____
_____
_____
_____
_____
_____
_____
_____
_____
_____
_____
_____
_____
_____
_____
_____
_____

Pride

Pride. We have become a society that celebrates sin by calling it "pride". We have a whole month celebrating this original sin of pride. It was pride that Satan used to lure Adam and Eve to sin against God by promising them they would become like Him. Why do we have pride in sin and celebrate some sins and not all sins? What makes some socially acceptable and others not? What makes some sins illegal and some, something to have "pride" in?

The Bible is pretty clear on what God thinks about pride, and being proud: "I will punish the world for its evil, and the wicked for their iniquity; I will put an end to the pomp of the arrogant, and lay low the pompous pride of the ruthless." - Isaiah 13:11. The root of all sins usually starts with pride. "For all that is in the world-the desires of the flesh and the desires of the eyes and pride of life-is not from the Father but is from the world." - 1 John 2:16.

If you did a search of your Bible about the words "pride" and "proud" you will find that almost all of the references are shown as being a negative thing. The only thing that we should really have pride in is what Jesus Christ did for us because we had nothing to do with it. Most lists of things that God hates has the word pride or proud in it. "The fear of the LORD is hatred of evil. Pride and arrogance and the way of evil and perverted speech I hate." - Proverbs 8:13. "Pride goes before destruction, and a haughty spirit before a fall." - Proverbs 16:18.

There is a coming day in which those that are proud will be brought low. "And the haughtiness of man shall be humbled, and the lofty pride of men shall be brought low, and the LORD alone will be exalted in that day." - Isaiah 2:17. It is better that we humble ourselves now then being humbled against our will later. We can bow the knee now and recognize God for who He is, or we can bow it later and confess what we denied for all of our lives. "Therefore, God has highly exalted him and bestowed on him the name that is above every name, so that at the name of Jesus every knee should bow, in heaven and on earth and under the earth, and every tongue confess that Jesus Christ is Lord, to the glory of God the Father." - Philippians 2:9-11.

Notes:_____

_____

_____

_____

_____

_____

_____

_____

_____

_____

_____

Power

Power. It's a pain when it goes out. Due to getting so much rain so fast last night, our power went out at the house just before we went to bed. It was only out for less than ten seconds, but it was just annoying enough to have to reset all the clocks. As soon as it goes out, everyone seems to panic for a split second. We worry about it getting hot in the house because the air conditioning is off and we worry about the food in the refrigerator going bad.

What about when we lose our connection with God? When our so-called "power" is out with Him? We lose connection with the power of God when we have sin in our lives. Sin causes us to lose fellowship with our source of power. "If we say we have fellowship with Him while we walk in darkness, we lie and do not practice the truth." - 1 John 1:6. Sin keeps the Holy Spirit from working in our lives to be in the will of God.

To keep the power on in our lives we need to make sure our account is right with God and that we keep our sins confessed. "But if we walk in the light, as He is in the light, we have fellowship with one another, and the blood of Jesus his Son cleanses us from all sin." - 1 John 1:7. Our lives work better when we keep our sins confessed and allow the Holy Spirit to work. "If we confess our sins, he is faithful and just to forgive us our sins and to cleanse us from all unrighteousness." - 1 John 1:9.

Does the power of God seem to be missing in your life? Maybe sin is keeping you from possessing the full power of God. Confess your sins to Him and let Him cleanse you from all unrighteousness and see the power come back on in your life.

Notes:_____
_____
_____
_____
_____
_____
_____
_____
_____
_____
_____
_____
_____
_____
_____
_____

Bus

Bus. My senior year of high school, a group of us took a yellow school bus to our senior prom. We got all dressed up and rode as a group to the prom instead of all of us riding separately. The lady who drove us to all of our high school sporting events drove us to the prom, picked us up and drove us to the after-prom party and then came back and picked us up the next morning. We used to call her "Fred" and she got all dressed up as well and even decorated the bus for the occasion. What a fun time we all had together that night.

When I tell that story to people now, they sort of cock their heads and look at me strange. But we knew who was on our bus and that we were ultimately safe during all of our travels. My good college buddy, Peter Pessetto, always tells his clients to check who they have on their bus. Some people don't need to be on our buses with us because they drag us down and we need to make sure we only have those on our bus who build us up. The same thing goes in the Christian life. We have to make sure we don't let Satan on our buses.

Not only do we need to check who we have in our lives but we also need to check what things we let into our lives that can give Satan a foothold. "Be angry and do not sin; do not let the sun go down on your anger and give no opportunity to the devil." - Ephesians 4:26-27. It's not just the people on our bus that can lead us into temptation to sin, but there are also things we let into our own lives that tempts us to sin. We can't let those things have a seat on our bus either.

"Do not be unequally yoked with unbelievers. For what partnership has righteousness with lawlessness? Or what fellowship has light with darkness? What accord has Christ with Belial? Or what portion does a believer share with an unbeliever?" - 2 Corinthians 6:14-15. "Therefore go out from their midst, and be separate from them, says the Lord, and touch no unclean thing; then I will welcome you, and I will be a father to you, and you shall be sons and daughters to me, says the Lord Almighty." - 2 Corinthians 6:17-18.

It's good for each of us to take a look at who, and what, we have allowed on our buses. Sometimes we need to remove people from our bus because they are not equally yoked with us. We also need to remove actions in our lives from our bus that do not glorify God. Have you looked recently to see what you have on your bus? It may be a good time for a roll call.

Notes:_____
_____
_____
_____
_____
_____

Edification

Edification. About a dozen years ago or so, my wife and I went to the NC State Fairgrounds for a concert of one of my favorite Christian bands, Third Day. A group opened for them that I didn't know much about, called Building 429. They were very good and we both became fans of their music. What I always find interesting is how Christian bands come up with their band names. Some of them are very evident, Third Day, Casting Crowns, etc.

Building 429 had a very interesting story of how they came up with their name. They took their name from the scripture found in Paul's letter to the Ephesians. "Let no corrupting talk come out of your mouths, but only such as is good for building up, as fits the occasion, that it may give grace to those who hear." - Ephesians 4:29. So, the "429" comes from chapter 4 and verse 29 in Ephesians. And the word "Building" comes from the word used right in the verse.

As a Christian, we should not allow any corrupt talk to come out of our mouths. Whether we are talking with unbelievers, and most importantly, if we are talking to believers. Every word should be used to edify, or build up, one another. There is enough negativity in today's world that, as Christians, we should not be adding to it. As our mothers always told us, "if we don't have anything good to say, don't say anything at all!"

We never know what problems and issues other people are going through and we should be the type of people that change someone's day for the better instead of adding any additional grief. We need to be careful with our words. We live in a culture where sarcasm and quick wit seem to rule our conversations. I admit, I can be a sarcastic person most of the time and need to do a better job at biting my tongue.

If you get the chance today, or the rest of this week, use it as an opportunity to build someone up instead of tearing them down. Remember Building 429 and let no corrupt words come out of your mouth. Some people may be surprised at the change in your conversation.

Notes:_____
_____
_____
_____
_____
_____
_____
_____

Lawn Mowers

Lawn mowers. Lawn equipment and I don't play well together. It seems that both lawn mowers and weed eaters like to mess with me no matter how well I try to maintain them. Well, the lawn mower monster showed up again yesterday and bit me. There is nothing worse than being in the middle of mowing and have the lawn mower break down and you have to leave the rest of the yard looking like a jungle. I have about a quarter of a well-groomed lawn.

I was riding the mower yesterday and all of a sudden it started running a bit rough and then it just cut off completely like it had run out of gas. I knew I had a full tank when I started so that couldn't be what the issue was. When I lifted up the hood of the mower, a small fuse connected to the carburetor was smoking. I knew that couldn't be good. I went to the hardware store to see what their thoughts were on what had happened. They sold me a small part and said that should fix it. Well, not being mechanical at all, I did more damage to it than I had started with.

I got upset with the fact that I didn't get the yard done. Then a got more upset that the lawn mower was broken and then it just rolled into being disappointed in general. I came in the house and my wife knew it was bothering me even though there really wasn't much I could do about it at that point. I felt bad that I had let my situation dictate my attitude for the rest of the evening.

I have so much to be thankful for: no one was hurt, the lawn mower can be fixed and I have awesome friends that have offered to let me borrow their mowers so I can finish my yard. The Bible says, "Finally, brothers, whatever is true, whatever is honorable, whatever is just, whatever is pure, whatever is lovely, whatever is commendable, if there is any excellence, if there is anything worthy of praise, think about these things." - Philippians 4:8.

So through all of this I will think of the good things that God has blessed me with and I will praise Him for it.

Notes:_____
_____
_____
_____
_____
_____
_____
_____
_____
_____
_____

Scared

Scared. Have you ever been scared to death? Have you ever scared someone else to death? I have to admit; I like scaring people. I get a kick out of scaring people and I know for a fact some of you do too, but I won't mention any names. I remember scaring one of my friends from high school pretty good.

There was this man who built an elaborate labyrinth out of the middle of the woods as a tribute to his son who had died in a car crash when he was a teenager. Why he decided to build a labyrinth, no one knows. What we did know was that it was a painstaking task because it was a brick and mortar labyrinth and not just made of bushes. There were statues and everything inside the labyrinth. The entrance slowly came up out of the ground until it was well above ten feet tall at the center.

Well, as the story goes, we were in the local grocery store and we heard one of our friends planning a trip up to the labyrinth that night with a group of girls in the next aisle over. So, we decided to beat them up there and hide within the labyrinth until they got there. We made it there and parked somewhere different so our car didn't give us away. After about a mile trip into the woods to find it, we were ready for our visitors.

As you can imagine, when we jumped out from inside the labyrinth, our unsuspecting visitors were scared out of their minds. A lot of screaming and running ensued and people were a little upset with us. But everyone got over it and we still laugh about it.

It's scary to come across things we don't expect along our path. We probably spend way too much time being scared about things that we create in our own minds that never materialize. The Bible speaks pretty often about the idea of fear, in fact it tells us 365 times to "fear not". "You came near when I called on you; you said, 'Do not fear!'" - Lamentations 3:57.

"There is no fear in love, but perfect love casts out fear. For fear has to do with punishment, and whoever fears has not been perfected in love." - 1 John 4:18.

Notes:_____
_____
_____
_____
_____
_____
_____
_____
_____

June 14

Who Do You Think You Are?

Who do you think you are? Have you ever asked your kids that question when they talk back to you when you tell them to do something? Have you ever gotten that response from your parents when you were a little kid and thought you knew more than they did? Have you ever had Satan whisper that in your ear when you are witnessing to someone about Christ or telling them your story about how you accepted Christ as your Savior? The devil likes to put doubt in our minds that we are worthy to share Christ with others based upon our background.

Satan likes to remind us of our past, of the things we have done that he thinks somehow disqualifies us from sharing the Gospel. If that is true, none of us would be worthy of sharing the Gospel because we all have a past, some more colorful than others. SO how do we respond when that doubt creeps up in our minds and our heart that we somehow are unworthy to share Christ?

The answer to that question is: I am a child of the King, that's who I am! I am a different person today than who I used to be. I am not perfect and never will be, if I am waiting for that to happen before I share Christ, I will never be good enough to do it. See, I'm just a nobody, trying to tell everybody about a Somebody who saved my soul. That's it! God has used "nobodies" throughout the Bible to share His message, to do great things for Him and to be a part of the plan He has for man.

We are saved by grace, given the power of the Holy Spirit and commanded to proclaim the Gospel everywhere we go and there is nothing Satan can do about that but make us doubt ourselves. Don't let him deceive you into thinking that you are not good enough; you are! Yu are a child of the King!

Notes:_____
_____
_____
_____
_____
_____
_____
_____
_____
_____
_____
_____
_____
_____
_____
_____

Mr. Grinch

"You're a mean one, Mr. Grinch!" Doesn't seem like the right time of year to be talking about the Grinch, does it? The kids watched the new Grinch movie yesterday on Netflix and Timothy spent the rest of the day singing those words. I ended up watching it with them too as I worked from home.

As I watched the end of the movie when the Grinch's heart grew three sizes that day and he decided to bring back all the Christmas stuff that he had stolen from Whoville, I realized just how much of a Christian theme the end of the story had.

The people of Whoville did not arrest him, they didn't chastise him for what he did and they didn't kick him out of town telling him
never to return. They showed him grace. That's forgave him. They invited him in to join in the celebration with them. They allowed him to have a place of honor in the festivities.

That's what God does for us. When we spend most of our lives robbing and stealing from the love of God, He still shows us grace. When we see the error of our ways and our hearts grows three sizes and we decided to return to Him, He shows grace. He doesn't condemn us; He doesn't turn from us and He doesn't send us away telling us never to come back. Like the prodigal son, He puts us in a place of honor and celebrates our return to Him.

Do we treat people that come back to us with a changed heart with that same grace? Do we look to really find what the root of the issue was? The Grinch wasn't really mad at Christmas, he was lonely and looking for friends and a family. What are those that hurt us really looking for? Love? Friendship? Family? Let us show grace to those who repent and seek our forgiveness. "Bearing with one another and, if one has a complaint against another, forgiving each other; as the Lord has forgiven you, so you also must forgive." - Colossians 3:13.

Notes:_____
_____
_____
_____
_____
_____
_____
_____
_____
_____
_____
_____

June 16

Father's Day

Father's Day. This is always one of the hardest days of the year for those of us that have lost our fathers. For those of you that still have your fathers, be thankful for the time you still have with them and that you have the ability to celebrate with them today. This day always reminds me of my father and the things that he had taught me throughout his life.

My dad taught me the meaning of work and providing for your family. He taught me that, as a dad, we have to do whatever we have to in making sure that our family is provided for. In all the things that my dad provided for us, the most important thing he provided was his time. He was always present for everything we did as kids. He was at all of the sporting events, even coaching most of the time, and all of our school events. It never stopped, even with all my traveling for college sports.

My father was loyal to my mother and loyal to his friends. My dad taught me to help those that are in need and whenever you borrow something, you give it back better than you got it. This post would be too long if I listed everything my father taught me. I'm thankful and blessed to have had him as my dad.

I'm a father now, have been for almost 11 years, and I know that at times I fail, but I do my best to do the things that my father taught me with my own children. I have a lot of improvements to make, but I'm trying. If I can become half the day that my father was, I'd be happy.

We have a Heavenly Father that is the greatest example of what true Fatherhood looks like. He is always accessible, He is always providing for us, and He always has our best interests at heart. Do you know Him as your Heavenly Father too? There is never a better Father than God.

Notes:_____

_____

_____

_____

_____

_____

_____

_____

_____

_____

_____

_____

_____

_____

_____

Reunion

Reunion. I had the privilege to head down to South Carolina this past weekend to spend time with my wife's family on her father's side. I got to meet her aunts and uncles as well as most of her cousins and their children. She hadn't seen some of them in over fifteen years, so it was a great reunion with a lot of hugging, laughing and eating. It was great for me to get to know that side of her family.

It got me thinking about reunions and stories the Bible tells about seeing family that you haven't seen in many years. It brought me to the story of Joseph and his brothers. After being sold into slavery by his brothers, Joseph made his way up the chain of command in every situation that he was in. It culminated in being the second highest in command in the empire of Egypt.

When his brothers arrived in Egypt because of a drought, Joseph was finally reunited with the very members of his family that tried to do away with him. For most of us, that would have been the time of retaliation, but not for Joseph. These were his brothers, and whatever they had done to him was in the past and he was overjoyed to see them after many years.

It also brought to mind the story of Jacob and Esau and the opportunity they had to reunite after a major falling out over a birthright. The point is, no matter what trials and tribulations we go through as families, when we have the opportunity to reunite and see each other once again, our family bond is stronger than anything else we go through.

There will be a final reunion that Christians should be looking forward to; the reunion of believers to Christ and to other believers. That glorious day is coming, hopefully soon, when we will be able to spend eternity in the presence of our Lord and Savior. We will once again see family that also put their trust and faith in Christ. Oh, glorious day!

"Then we who are alive, who are left, will be caught up together with them in the clouds to meet the Lord in the air, and so we will always be with the Lord. Therefore encourage one another with these words." - 1 Thessalonians 4:17-18.

Notes:_____
_____
_____
_____
_____
_____
_____
_____

Bullying

Bullying. We can probably all say that we have been bullied at one time or another in our lives, either when we were young or possibly even as adults. Some of us may even be bold enough to admit we have been the bullies at some point in our lives too. A vast majority of us, if we are honest, could say that we have been on both sides of the bullying issue. We have most likely bullied others that have been smaller or weaker than us and we have probably been bullied by people older and stronger than us.

The idea of bullying made me think if there were any examples in the Bible of well-known bullies. I thought of two, one Old Testament and one New Testament, but there are probably many more. Just happened that my two bullies share the same name: Saul! King Saul bullied David to the point that he chased him around the nation of Israel trying to kill him because he knew he had been anointed to be the next king. Saul, later known as Paul, was a bully to all the Christians in and around Jerusalem. He was such a bully, that he even chased them down and put them in jail for their beliefs. Stephen was stoned, with Saul's approval, because of his belief that Christ was the Son of God.

No one has ever been bullied into believing in Christ as their Savior. People make that decision because they are loved into it. We show the love of Christ to them in all that we do and they see how we live our lives and that should draw them into wanting what we have. If you can bully them into Christianity, then someone can bully them out of it.

"In the same way, let your light shine before others, so that they may see your good works and give glory to your Father who is in heaven." - Matthew 5:16. Let the light of Christ draw men/women to Him, not bullying. "Above all, keep loving one another earnestly, since love covers a multitude of sins."- 1 Peter 4:8.

Notes:_____
_____
_____
_____
_____
_____
_____
_____
_____
_____
_____
_____
_____

The Greatest of All Time

G.O.A.T. The Greatest of All Time. We hear that little phrase more and more when we talk of sports and music. Who is the greatest of all time in a certain field and why do we believe so? It makes sports radio and casual talk with friends more interesting. There can never be a consensus because most often we are comparing people who never competed against each other during the same time period.

Is it Michael Jordan or Lebron James? Is it Babe Ruth or Barry Bonds? Is it Gordie Howe or Wayne Gretzky? Is it Bart Starr or Tom Brady? There is no right or wrong answer that you can defend with absolute facts and statistics. What we do know is that they were all great in their time against their opponents according to the rules of their era. That's it, no further discussion needed on who the Greatest of All Time is.

In reality, it doesn't matter. In eternity, no one will be discussing who the greatest was in any particular field at any particular time because we will be standing at the feet of the One that has been and always will be the Greatest: God the Father and Jesus Christ the Son. There is no argument over this fact!

"For I will proclaim the name of the LORD; ascribe greatness to our God!" - Deuteronomy 32:3.

"Great is the LORD, and greatly to be praised, and his greatness is unsearchable." - Psalm 145:3.

The is only One who deserves the title "Greatest of All Time" and that is the God of the Bible. He is the only One worthy of our praise. He is the only One worthy of the glory of being great.

Notes:_____
_____
_____
_____
_____
_____
_____
_____
_____
_____
_____
_____
_____

Award or Reward

Award or Reward? I really never thought about the difference between the two words until I heard someone talking about it on the radio. I have always known that we will be receiving rewards in heaven so I wanted to see why God's Word said about awards. Nothing. It's not even in the Bible one time. So that got me looking into the difference between an award and a reward.

What I found was that an award was usually given for some sort of achievement, for example, winning a spelling bee, competing on a sports team or finishing a project at work. There is usually nothing of value given for the award, it is only seen as intrinsic value. An award is usually given by one person to another person in front of a large group of people as a means of recognition for one's achievements. All based upon human ability.

A reward on the other hand is different. It is usually received for some sort of work being accomplished that is measurable and above the norm, like returning a lost wallet or pocketbook. There is usually something of value given as the reward whether it is monetary or a prize. The reward is usually given to one person but not always in a public setting as a means of recognition.

In Heaven, we are told that we earn rewards for our service as Christians here on earth. The reward that is most often discussed in the New Testament are crowns. Believers will receive the reward of Crowns for what they have accomplished here on earth that is measurable and above the norm. Not everyone will receive the rewards. We don't know if we will receive the rewards in front of all of the Heavenly host or just one-on-one in front of God. We do know that rewards, and not awards, will be given in Heaven.

"Watch yourselves, so that you may not lose what we have worked for, but may win a full reward." - 2 John 1:8.

"The nations raged, but your wrath came, and the time for the dead to be judged, and for rewarding your servants, the prophets and saints, and those who fear your name, both small and great, and for destroying the destroyers of the earth." - Revelation 11:18.

Notes:_____
_____
_____
_____
_____
_____
_____
_____

It's OK to be Not OK

It's okay to be not okay. I was having a conversation with a fellow coworker the other day about Christians in general and the conversation turned to how Christians always act like everything in their life is perfect and they have no problems. This person went on to say that he would have an easier time believing in Christianity if Christians weren't so fake. That really made me think about how I go about my own life; do I make it look like I live a perfect life and look down on people who have problems? Trust me, I have my own problems.

Why do we tend to keep our struggles hidden from the world so that they think that we have no problems? Not only to we portray that façade to nonbelievers, but we do the same thing with believers. Are we afraid that if we admit to struggles in our lives that we will somehow be less of a Christian? When we go to church and ask people how they are, they immediately respond, "great", and all the while they are struggling with their spouse, their kids, their jobs, or paying bills. But we like to come across to others that our lives are fine.

You know what, it's okay to be not okay! If we would be transparent with others about things we are struggling with, we become real people. People will know that they are not the only ones going through the issues we are going through. Our brothers and sisters in Christ can now pray for us if they know that we need help. People who have been through the same things we are facing can now offer advice on how they made it through.

"Blessed be the God and Father of our Lord Jesus Christ, the Father of mercies and God of all comfort, who comforts us in all our affliction, so that we may be able to comfort those who are in affliction, with the comfort with which we ourselves are comforted by God."
– 2 Corinthians 1:3-4.

Be honest, we struggle, even as Christians, with this thing called life. Things happen, we make mistakes, things don't go our way, others hurt us and we make bad decisions. It's called life and it's a struggle for everyone. But we are called to support one another in prayer and in physical needs. We belong to the same family, the family of God, and we should see one another as people who can help, not as people we need to impress. Let's be real with nonbelievers and believers alike and watch our lives flourish by being transparent.

Notes:_____
_____
_____
_____
_____
_____
_____
_____

Tug-of-War

Tug-of-war. It's one of those great games that you can still play at any age. I've seen pictures lately of kids playing it at their end of the school year field days and I've seen pictures of adults playing it during Memorial Day picnics. Bragging rights are at stake as soon as you pick up that one end of the rope and start pulling. But what about that inner tug-of-war that we battle with ourselves everyday whether to do what we should or to do what we want?

That inner battle is real in the Christian life! I face it every day. I know what I should be doing in a spiritual sense, but my flesh wants to do the exact opposite and satisfy itself. The Apostle Paul calls it the battle between our spiritual life and our earthly, or carnal, life. He even struggled with the same things we do.

"For we know that the law is spiritual, but I am of the flesh, sold under sin. For I do not understand my own actions. For I do not do what I want, but I do the very thing I hate. Now if I do what I do not want, I agree with the law, that it is good. So now it is no longer I who do it, but sin that dwells within me. For I know that nothing good dwells in me, that is, in my flesh. For I have the desire to do what is right, but not the ability to carry it out. For I do not do the good I want, but the evil I do not want is what I keep on doing. Now if I do what I do not want, it is no longer I who do it, but sin that dwells within me." - Romans 7:14-20.

I see this tug-of-war in my own life in my marriage and my family. I come home from work in the evening and my flesh just wants to sit down and relax and sit in my recliner. My wife and kids haven't seen me all day and they want my attention too. I know in my heart that I need to help out when I get home, whether it's helping clean up after supper, playing outside with the kids or getting them ready for bed, but my selfishness wants to just sit and relax. It's a battle, and I know what to do, but the flesh just doesn't want to do it. Can I get an "amen"?

Don't feel like your failing because of this inner tug-of-war that we all go through. Keep pushing on and feeding the spiritual side and we will find ourselves winning more battles than losing. The battle never ends, it's waiting for us every morning when we wake up.

Notes:_____
_____
_____
_____
_____
_____
_____
_____
_____
_____

June 23

Lost and Found

Lost and found. That random collection of odds and ends that seem to never have a match and never find and owner, only to be discarded in the end. Jewelry, hats, gloves, umbrellas, keys, sunglasses, and on and on. There are lost and found locations at schools, work, churches and even at malls. It's the place where the collection seems to be always growing and no one ever claims a thing. Are we embarrassed to look in the box and say, "hey, I think that's mine"?

Whenever I see a lost and found box, it always makes me think of the story of the prodigal son. You probably know that story very well yourself; a young man demands his inheritance from his living father and goes off to another town and blows it all on a wicked lifestyle. When he's broke and living in a pig pen, he decides to go back and ask forgiveness from his father and be hired as a servant.

He gets home and his awaiting father runs to meet him and throws his arms around his filthy neck and celebrates his return. He calls for his servants to bring the boy a new pair of shoes, his finest robe, his signet ring and to kill the fatted calf because they were having a celebration. This welcome completely surprises the young man. And then the father says the words that always makes me think of the lost and found box, "'For this my son was dead, and is alive again; he was lost, and is found.' And they began to celebrate." - Luke 15:24.

If we are Christians, that's our story and that's how our Heavenly Father sees us. We once were dead in our trespasses and sins and we decide to turn back home. God anxiously awaited our return and when we were still making our way towards Him, He ran to meet us to celebrate our coming to Him. We went from a state of being "lost" to now being "found".

Have you ever been found, or are you still in the lost box? Have you ever been claimed by God as being His son or daughter because you claimed the death, burial and resurrection of Jesus Christ as your own? God doesn't want you to be lost, He wants you to be found. Those items that never get claimed in the lost and found box always end up being discarded. Don't let that be your eternal fate.

Notes:_____

_____

_____

_____

_____

_____

_____

_____

Rude

Rude. Some people are just so rude it's hard to imagine what goes through their heads when they act that way. Do they feel like they are the most important people on the face of the earth that certain courtesy rules don't apply to them? This is especially true when flying. I was on a flight this morning and a "gentleman" (I'll use that word loosely) felt that having his music blaring through his earphones wasn't disturbing to all the people sitting within three rows of him.

I mean it's not just in airplanes either, in restaurants, shopping areas and anywhere else you have to come across people in a public place, people are rude! I always wonder if they do it on purpose because they just don't care or if they are hoping someone my complain so they can go ballistic. I certainly hope they aren't Christians that act this way.

So, how are we supposed to act when we are in public place and call ourselves Christians? The Bible makes it perfectly clear what our actions and attitude should be. "Have nothing to do with foolish, ignorant controversies; you know that they breed quarrels. And the Lord's servant must not be quarrelsome but kind to everyone" - 2 Timothy 2:23-24a.

"Put on then, as God's chosen ones, holy and beloved, compassionate hearts, kindness, humility, meekness, and patience, bearing with one another and, if one has a complaint against another, forgiving each other; as the Lord has forgiven you, so you also must forgive. And above all these put-on love, which binds everything together in perfect harmony.
And let the peace of Christ rule in your hearts, to which indeed you were called in one body. And be thankful." - Colossians 3:12-15.

Don't be rude when you are in public places, it doesn't show well for calling yourself a Christian.

Notes:_____
_____
_____
_____
_____
_____
_____
_____
_____
_____
_____
_____

Turbulence

Turbulence. As you can probably tell, I did some traveling yesterday. About halfway through the flight from Charlotte to Milwaukee, we hit some major turbulence. It must have been some air pockets from a storm below us because we dropped about three times in a matter of fifteen seconds. Big drops too, like cups coming off the tray drops! Everyone gets a little nervous when something like that happens and they start grabbing onto arm rests and the back of the seats in front of them.

I was watching a movie on my iPad, so I didn't pay much attention to it. I've been on enough flights the past three months that it doesn't really phase me anymore. Flying into El Paso gets you used to turbulence because of the desert heat below the plane. I'm not saying I like it; I just know to expect it on most flights so I don't concern myself with it when it happens.

Life provides us with turbulence at times as well. Things seem to be going so smooth and then all of a sudden, boom! Turbulence! Things get bumpy for a while or we have sudden drops in life when we thought it was going so smoothly. If we go into life with the expectation that turbulence is going to come, we can handle it better than if we think life will always be a smooth ride. It's not that we have to like it, we just need to expect it so we aren't thrown for a loop.

Jesus told His disciples, "I have said these things to you, that in me you may have peace. In the world you will have tribulation. But take heart; I have overcome the world." - John 16:33. He told them, and us, that this world is going to give you some turbulence, but that we should have peace because He has overcome this world. Jesus' three-plus years of ministry was filled with turbulence, but He knew it was coming so He did not concern Himself with it. He knew why He had come into the world: to save the world from their sins. Everything else was just a part of the process; turbulence and all.

Are you going through turbulent times in your life right now? Take heart and have peace, there is a time when it will be over. Take with you the peace of Christ and hold on to Him.

Notes:_____
_____
_____
_____
_____
_____
_____
_____
_____
_____

Marriage

Marriage. Today marks fifteen years since I was blessed to marry my best friend and my better half. Honestly, she's probably the better three-quarters of our marriage. She is such a Godly woman and great example for our kids. She shows our daughter how a Godly wife and mother should act and she shows our son a wonderful example of the type of woman he should look for in a future bride. I am blessed to have such a wife.

Marriage isn't always easy, but besides my salvation, it's the best things that has ever happened to me. It has changed me for the better (I hope she thinks so too). Marriage takes a lot of work to be successful from both of us and many times I fail to hold up my end of the covenant. The patience of my wife has grown stronger over the past fifteen years due to my testing it so many times.

"The heart of her husband trusts in her, and he will have no lack of gain. She does him good, and not harm, all the days of her life." - Proverbs 31:11-12.

"She opens her mouth with wisdom, and the teaching of kindness is on her tongue. She looks well to the ways of her household and does not eat the bread of idleness." - Proverbs 31:26-27.

"Her children rise up and call her blessed; her husband also, and he praises her: Many women have done excellently, but you surpass them all." - Proverbs 31:28-29.

Thank you for loving me all these years. I couldn't, and don't, want to do this life without you. Love you more than anything.

Notes:_____
_____
_____
_____
_____
_____
_____
_____
_____
_____
_____
_____
_____
_____
_____
_____
_____

Room Service

Room service. I'm not one to really take advantage of room service when I travel because I'm more inclined to just go and get something to eat and not want to bother someone to have to wait on me in my room. However, on my recent stay, there weren't any restaurants around the hotel and the hotel restaurant was under construction. Even though it was under construction, they did offer room service.

So, for I think for the first time, I took advantage of room service for my evening meals. I called down my order and within twenty minutes or so I had my food right in my room. It was pretty cool to just be sitting there and have someone bring you your food. It was a great service and one I could take advantage of going forward, but I probably won't.

It got me thinking about serving and being served. It's nice to be waited on sometimes and have certain services provided to you when it is outside the norm. It is also important that we act as servants too and provide to others what they possibly cannot provide for themselves. Our nature tends to lean toward wanting to be served and against wanting to serve others.

Even Christ touched on this subject when speaking to His own disciples, "It shall not be so among you. But whoever would be great among you must be your servant, and whoever would be first among you must be your slave, even as the Son of Man came not to be served but to serve, and to give his life as a ransom for many." - Matthew 20:26-28.

So, as my time traveling ends and I enjoyed the room service on this trip, I find myself wanting to serve more than be served. It's a battle of my spirit to move away from the tendency to want to be served towards the will to want to serve others. I'm sure I'm not the only one battling these feelings.

Notes:_____
_____
_____
_____
_____
_____
_____
_____
_____
_____
_____
_____
_____
_____
_____
_____

Limited Time Offer

Limited time offer. As I was sitting in the airport yesterday waiting for the last leg of my journey, the flight a couple of gates over was overbooked. The lady working the desk kept making offers for travel vouchers to anyone who would wait for the next flight to the same location. She started out at $250 for anyone who would give up their seat on the flight and the offers kept going up from there every 15 minutes or so. I think that the last offer I heard was at $750 to anyone willing to give up their seat.

As with most things, it was a limited time offer because that flight was going to have to push back from the gate at the scheduled time. The opportunity was going to pass and when it came right down to it, if no one took the offer, people were going to be removed from the flight and have nothing to show for it. I don't know if anyone was kicked off the flight or the limited time offer was accepted by someone or not. I do know the flight left and there were no shouting matches at the gate when it left.

Eternal life in the presence of God has a limited time offer as well. We are given this life to make the choice to either accept Christ as our Savior or to reject the free gift of salvation. No one gets a second chance after they die, the decision has been made and no one can pray you into heaven after you're dead. The Bible says, "For he says, 'In a favorable time I listened to you, and in a day of salvation I have helped you.' Behold, now is the favorable time; behold, now is the day of salvation." - 2 Corinthians 6:2.

"Besides this you know the time, that the hour has come for you to wake from sleep. For salvation is nearer to us now than when we first believed." - Romans 13:11.

"For God has not destined us for wrath, but to obtain salvation through our Lord Jesus Christ, who died for us so that whether we are awake or asleep we might live with him." - 1 Thessalonians 5:9-10.

This life has a limited time offer in place for securing our eternal destination. We choose to spend it in heaven or in hell by what we do with the free gift of salvation through the death, burial and resurrection of Jesus Christ.

Notes:_____
_____
_____
_____
_____
_____
_____
_____
_____

Black and White

Black and white. For the most part, we like things in the world to be black or white, right or wrong. It helps us to better understand our world, but when the lines between black and white begin to blur, that's usually when the trouble starts. Grey areas tend to be the areas where division starts and wars begin.

God and His Word are definitely black and white. What He says is truth Is truth, and what He says is sin is sin. We get into trouble when we start to question His truth by making comments like "that was only during Bible times and doesn't apply today". It is also a mistake to try to take God's Word and interpret it to make it fit into the lifestyle we want it to fit in. I see it quite often in the news that people want to say if Jesus was here today He would support this or that.

Jesus definitely loves people wherever they are at in life but He definitely doesn't love the sin they are living in. The woman at the well, the woman caught in adultery, and the Pharisees in the Temple. He loved them all but told them to repent from their sin. Things were black and white with Christ and there was no grey. "This is the message we have heard from him and proclaim to you, that God is light, and in him is no darkness at all." - 1 John 1:5.

Satan is the master of blurring the lines between black and white. It started in the Garden of Eden with Adam and Eve. "Now the serpent was more crafty than any other beast of the field that the LORD God had made. He said to the woman, "Did God actually say, 'You shall not eat of any tree in the garden'?" - Genesis 3:1. See how he took what God used as a black and white statement and turned it into a great area by using their doubt in what God actually said? He made them use their own judgement of the Word of God to cause them to sin.

Don't fall for the grey of this world that wants to blur the lines of God's black and white Word. What God says in His Holy Word is the Truth and not up to our interpretation. Live by His Word and don't fall victim to the lies of the devil's grey areas.

Notes:_____

_____

_____

_____

_____

_____

_____

_____

_____

Debate

Debate. That's what they call it, but it has become less debate and more like mudslinging, back-biting and quarreling. It's not a one party issue either, if it was the opposite party, the same thing would have occurred. It's hard to believe they are so-called "all on the same team" as you watch them. The debates have been on this week and even though I didn't watch any of it, I did read about them after the fact. This is what our political system has come down to: one-line zingers that gets you the most press the day after.

The sad fact is, is that most of our churches have become the same way. We have divided up into denominations, or factions, declaring our way of thinking and translation of the Bible is better than another's in hopes of bringing in more congregants. We quarrel over minute facts that are meaningless to the overall plan of salvation. The Apostle Paul dealt with these same things in the Corinthian church, so it's not just a modern day issue. "What I mean is that each one of you says, "I follow Paul," or "I follow Apollos," or "I follow Cephas," or "I follow Christ." Is Christ divided? Was Paul crucified for you? Or were you baptized in the name of Paul?"- 1 Corinthians 1:12-13.

The Bible is clear in how we are to live our lives as Christians, especially with one another, "Remind them of these things, and charge them before God not to quarrel about words, which does no good, but only ruins the hearers." - 2 Timothy 2:14. If we are set apart by Christ, shouldn't we act like we are different from the world? Now, I'm not saying that if someone if doctrinally wrong, that we approve of their teaching, but if they believe and teach the Gospel of Christ, we should not be tearing them down. We are one with Christ and belong to Him.

This world already does whatever it can to discount the teachings of the Bible and if we discount one another, we are only playing into their hands. It was so good to see recently, that our little county in North Carolina, came together to improve the lives of people in our community. Churches from every denomination working together to make our county and better place. No arguments, no quarrels, and no back-biting, just brotherly love with one goal in mind: to show the love of Christ to our community. Well done to the 1200+ people who represented Christ during Impact Yadkin!

Notes:_____
_____
_____
_____
_____
_____
_____

July 1

Terms and Conditions

Terms and conditions. I am going to go out on a limb here and say that I am probably not the only one who has accepted terms and conditions without ever ready through what they are. Can I get an "amen"? Who has time to read through all of that legalese to just get to the end and not understand what you just read anyway? You need a lawyer to read through all of that to make sense of it, and who really has the time and money for that? So, instead, we just click on the "accept" button and continue on with life.

The Bible has terms and conditions too. Some of them take no effort of our own, God takes care of all of it for us. Others have certainly conditions we must meet for God to fulfill His end of the agreement. We had an awesome sermon at church yesterday by Pastor Phillip about one of the most important terms and conditions found in God's Word. Now before you jump all over me, I understand that this was originally given to the nation of Israel, but I'm sure it still holds true today to those of us that call ourselves Christians.

"If my people who are called by my name humble themselves, and pray and seek my face and turn from their wicked ways, then I will hear from heaven and will forgive their sin and heal their land. - 2 Chronicles 7:14. The two words "if" and "then" are the terms and conditions of the agreement. If we do what God has laid out for us to do, then He will follow through with what He has agreed to.

God asks us, as individuals and as a country, to do four very specific things: humble ourselves, pray, seek Him and turn, or repent, from our wicked ways. I think they need to be done in the very order as well. We live in a society nowadays that thinks to be humble is to be week. We instructed to take the tiger by the tail and go after the things we want, even if it's against God's will. The final task in the lost is to repent, to turn in the complete opposite direction from where we are currently heading.

If we do those four things, God says that He will in turn do three things for us: hear, forgive and heal. He will not hear us until we have completed the four requirements listed above. Once He knows that we are sincere and completely turned from our sinful ways, then, and only then, will he hear us, forgive us, and heal both us individually and as a country.

Our country is headed in the wrong direction and it's partly to blame for the lack of backbone found in Christianity today. Will you do your part?

Notes:_____
_____
_____
_____
_____

The Walking Dead

The Walking Dead. Anyone reading this fans of the show? I've never seen a single episode even though it ran for nine seasons. I've also never seen a single episode of Game of Thrones either. I have lived vicariously through the information of others for both of those shows, so I do have a general understanding of what both shows were about. I'm not a big fan of either of those genres, so it doesn't attract me to watch, even though millions of people love them.

I have always heard that art imitates life and would have to say that this show imitates what spiritual life in this current world looks like. As the tide sways from this country being considered a Christian nation to it now becoming more secular, the number of Christians is growing smaller as the number of non-Christians is growing larger. In a nutshell, the spiritually dead is outnumbering those that are alive spiritually.

Before we became Christians, we too, were once spiritually dead, "And you were dead in the trespasses and sins in which you once walked, following the course of this world, following the prince of the power of the air, the spirit that is now at work in the sons of disobedience- among whom we all once lived in the passions of our flesh, carrying out the desires of the body and the mind, and were by nature children of wrath, like the rest of mankind." - Ephesians 2:1-3. We were counted among the Walking Dead.

If you have accepted Christ as your Savior, you are no longer dead, but alive in Christ. "But God, being rich in mercy, because of the great love with which he loved us, even when we were dead in our trespasses, made us alive together with Christ-by grace you have been saved- and raised us up with him and seated us with him in the heavenly places in Christ Jesus, so that in the coming ages he might show the immeasurable riches of his grace in kindness toward us in Christ Jesus." - Ephesians 2:4-7.

Has there been a specific moment in time when God "butted" into your life? A time that you can put your finger on and say, you went from being spiritually dead to alive in Christ? If not, let today be the day that you leave the Walking Dead and move into life with Christ.

Notes:_____
_____
_____
_____
_____
_____
_____
_____

July 3

Truth

Truth. There are a lot of things in our government going on about what the truth is about different topics. It seems that both sides of the "truth" from each party is very different from one another. Each side is calling into question the other side's version of their "truth". Fact is that the truth doesn't belong to either party, it stands on its own ground without input from either side. Our feelings, experiences and personal convictions tend to bend the truth when we share our version of it.

The four Gospels seem to have different versions of the "truth" about what happened during the ministry of Jesus Christ. Skeptics like to use this argument as a way to discount the validity of the four Gospel writers. However, this is an false argument because the four writers, led by the Holy Spirit, were writing to different audiences. The focus of their audience prompted them to focus differently on the same events. So, what seems to be different versions of the same events, is in actuality the same truth only recorded for a different audience.

Just like in a car accident, which involves both those in the accident, as well as, those who were witnesses, they may have different versions of the same events. Those that were involved in the accident, and possibly the cause of it, will have one version, while the other party involved may have another version. Those that witnessed the accident from afar will have a completely different view than those involved. All of them have a version of the truth and are just reporting it from their standpoint.

The Gospels are the Truth of God brought to man by individual writers trying to reach specific groups of people: some Jews and some Gentiles. All four of them were presenting Christ in a different light. Even though the versions may have some points that may seem to contradict each other, they all still provide the Truth of God.

"So Jesus said to the Jews who had believed him, "If you abide in my word, you are truly my disciples, and you will know the truth, and the truth will set you free." - John 8:31-32.

"But the hour is coming, and is now here, when the true worshipers will worship the Father in spirit and truth, for the Father is seeking such people to worship him." - John 4:23.

Seek the truth in all things but know the Truth has already been given to us in the Word of God.

Notes:_____
_____
_____
_____
_____

July 4

Freedom

Freedom. Independence Day has always been my favorite holiday. The parades, the cookouts, fireworks and it always involved playing baseball. It's just an all-American holiday. I have such fond memories of this day being a day of fun and family. The whole nation, town by little town, came together to celebrate our independence from Britain all the way back in 1776.

I used to love teaching this subject to my students. The Revolutionary War, the Declaration of Independence, the Constitution and Bill of Rights. It was such an unprecedented time not only in America, but in the history of the world. A new nation set upon Christian principles and governed by the people.

Even though this was a major event in the history of the world in which America declared it's freedom from Britain, it wasn't the most important event in world history in regards to freedom. The thirty-three years that Jesus Christ spent on earth and His death, burial and resurrection was the greatest event in the history of mankind. It is the only event that brings true freedom to us as individuals.

"Now the Lord is the Spirit, and where the Spirit of the Lord is, there is freedom." - 2 Corinthians 3:17.

"For freedom Christ has set us free; stand firm therefore, and do not submit again to a yoke of slavery." - Galatians 5:1.

"Live as people who are free, not using your freedom as a cover-up for evil, but living as servants of God." - 1 Peter 2:16.

Enjoy living in the greatest country in the world today and celebrating our Independence Day.

Notes:_____
_____
_____
_____
_____
_____
_____
_____
_____
_____
_____
_____

July 5

Ungrateful

Ungrateful. I've noticed lately that there are many people that are ungrateful for the many things that this country has provided to them. Most of the people that are coming across as being ungrateful seem to be the same people that have gained the most by living in this great country. I'm not blind to the fact that there are issues within our country and things that can be improved, but I also realize we live in a country made up of people from many different backgrounds and philosophies and there will never be a time when everyone feels that things are perfect because we live in a fallen world.

As Christians, we should be grateful for the things in our lives no matter what situation we may be in. God has provided us with so much, most of all, the gift of His Son and the forgiveness of our sins. We can't get caught up in the things of this world and comparing what we have and don't have with others around us. All of these material things are going to go away or become the possession of someone else at some point. Our treasures are laid up for us in heaven.

It's easy to get caught up in the complaining and ungratefulness of others, but we need to remind ourselves, probably daily, of what we are grateful for: our health, our loved ones, a roof over our heads, food on our tables, etc. God has so richly blesses us with eternal things that the earthly things in this life should be viewed as minuscule.

"Therefore let us be grateful for receiving a kingdom that cannot be shaken, and thus let us offer to God acceptable worship, with reverence and awe, for our God is a consuming fire." - Hebrews 12:28-29. Have you thanked God with a grateful heart today for His blessings on you?

Notes:_____

_____
_____
_____
_____
_____
_____
_____
_____
_____
_____
_____
_____
_____
_____
_____
_____

July 6

Earthquakes

Earthquakes. It's been a very hectic two days for Southern California in terms of earthquakes. They had a 6.4 on Thursday and then a 7.1 yesterday. The first one didn't cause much damage but the second one did. I've never experienced an earthquake before but people I know have said it's a frightening experience. Earthquakes are nothing new and will continue on until the Lord returns.

The Bible talks quite a bit about earthquakes. The prophets all mention earthquakes as signs of things to come. Elijah went through an earthquake along with wind and fire, "And he said, "Go out and stand on the mount before the LORD." And behold, the LORD passed by, and a great and strong wind tore the mountains and broke in pieces the rocks before the LORD, but the LORD was not in the wind. And after the wind an earthquake, but the LORD was not in the earthquake." - 1 Kings 19:11. Isaiah, Ezekiel and Amos all talk about earthquakes. Jesus Christ talked about earthquakes in three of the four Gospels when He is describing the events of the end times, or the Tribulation period.

I think of Paul and Silas in the Philippian jail as they sang praises to the Lord and a great earthquake came and released their chains and burst open the jailhouse door, "and suddenly there was a great earthquake, so that the foundations of the prison were shaken. And immediately all the doors were opened, and everyone's bonds were unfastened." - Acts 16:26

Or the earthquake that happened at the death of Christ, "When the centurion and those who were with him, keeping watch over Jesus, saw the earthquake and what took place, they were filled with awe and said, "Truly this was the Son of God!" - Matthew 27:54. And the earthquake that was felt when the stone was rolled away at His Resurrection, "And behold, there was a great earthquake, for an angel of the Lord descended from heaven and came and rolled back the stone and sat on it." - Matthew 28:2.

Earthquakes are nothing new, they been around since at least the days of Elijah and they will continue on during the Tribulations. We must not misunderstand Jesus' warning about the last days as things that are happening now. His warning was for the time period after the Rapture of the Church and the events going on today are not part of His warning. But are you ready for His return?

Notes:_____
_____
_____
_____
_____

July 7

Bad Days

Bad days. We all have them, whether we are young or old, bad days just come along. Our little guy had one of those days yesterday. Nothing seemed to go right for him and everything turned into a crying session. It's one thing to have a bad day when you're an adult and can understand what is happening, and then it's another thing when you're three and can't express what you're feeling. It's hard to be patient during those times with little ones and try to get them to understand why they can't do certain things they feel they have the right to do.

I think God goes through the same thing with us as His children. We go through bad days and we don't understand why we can't do what we feel we have the right to do. We get frustrated, we get mad, we may even cry as we search for answers. With our limited knowledge of what lies ahead of us, we want to forge our own path ahead no matter what, and sometimes God tells us "no". We are like our three year old, who doesn't understand what we know and the dangers we may be keeping him from by telling him "no". He is living only in the current moment and doesn't understand fully what we do based upon our experiences and our own past failures.

God has no past failures, but He does have eternal experience that we do not; it's called sovereignty. "For my thoughts are not your thoughts, neither are your ways my ways, declares the LORD. For as the heavens are higher than the earth, so are my ways higher than your ways and my thoughts than your thoughts." - Isaiah 55:8-9.

So, as we experience bad days like my little guy did yesterday because of his lack of understanding, let us remind ourselves that God's ways are higher than our ways and His thoughts are higher than our thoughts. Let us go to Him in obedient prayer and not as little children throwing a fit because we did not get our way. He may just let us have our way to show us our limited understanding.

Notes:_____
_____
_____
_____
_____
_____
_____
_____
_____
_____
_____
_____

July 8

Flight Cancelled

Flight cancelled. I was all set to fly out last night to El Paso, when about 45 minutes before I had to leave my house, I got a notification that the first leg of my flight had been delayed by over two hours. Not an issue if my connection was only 40 minutes in Dallas. Due to my first flight arriving after my second flight was scheduled to take off, I had to cancel my travel plans for yesterday.

There is nothing more frustrating that having plans changed at the last minute, especially if it involves flights, hotels and rental cars. Meetings will be missed but I was able to reschedule a flight for today and as you read this I'll be on my way to Texas. The positive thing about the delay was that I got to spend more time with my family last night.

My wife and I spoke about my plans changing as we were getting ready for bed. She mentioned that God was probably just protecting me from something during my journey last night. Whether it was during my drive to the airport or while on the plane, God had a purpose for my cancellation last night. When we look at disruptions to our plans in that frame of reference, we can be thankful instead of disgruntled.

"The heart of man plans his way, but the LORD establishes his steps." - Proverbs 16:9.

Notes:_____

_____

_____

_____

_____

_____

_____

_____

_____

_____

_____

_____

_____

_____

_____

_____

_____

_____

_____

_____

_____

_____

_____

_____

July 9

Simple

Simple. I don't know about you, but I like things when they are simple. Like instructions on putting something together or directions on how to get somewhere. I like books that are simple to read and don't take a lot of brain power to understand. Don't get me wrong, sometimes I like things that are challenging too, but there are times when simple is just better. The Bible can be both simple and difficult at the same time.

The Gospel message is simple to understand we are sinners that need a Savior in the person of Jesus Christ. There are parts of the Bible, like the book of Daniel and the book of Revelation, that can be very difficult to understand because of all the symbolism. Imagine living in the times of the Old Testament and having to live under the Law. There were thousands of things that you could and could not do. Who could remember them all? The point was you couldn't, that's why we need a Savior.

The New Testament makes it pretty simple for the Christian to abide by. Jesus narrows it down to just two rules: "'Teacher, which is the great commandment in the Law?' And he said to him, 'You shall love the Lord your God with all your heart and with all your soul and with all your mind. This is the great and first commandment. And a second is like it: You shall love your neighbor as yourself. On these two commandments depend all the Law and the Prophets.'" - Matthew 22:36-40.

That's how simple it is to be a Christian: love God and love your neighbor! That's it! It doesn't tell us to choose who to love out of all the people, it doesn't tell us to love people that think and believe like we do, and it doesn't tell us to love people that look like us; it tells us to love our neighbor. When we love others like Christ loves us, we are never more like Him then at that moment. Jesus loved all of the people that society thought were unlovable: the tax collectors, the adulterous, the sick and the lame. He loved them because He knew His Father loved them.

Have you loved your neighbor today? The neighbor that doesn't believe the same things you do. The neighbor that doesn't look like you do. The neighbor that doesn't go to the same "church" you do? God loves them, so should you.

Notes:_____
_____
_____
_____
_____
_____
_____
_____

July 10

Awe and Wonder

Awe and wonder. As I sat in the airport this morning, there were two young children, probably around 7 and 9, waiting to board as well. As I listened to them speak, they mentioned that this was only their second time flying, the first being their journey to El Paso. I listened as they spoke of everything that was happening in the terminal in such awe and wonder. I listened to them explain everything that was happening outside the windows to the plane we were getting ready to board.

As I listened, I thought about how many times in the past few months I've sat in a terminal somewhere in this great country with just boredom of all that was going on. Each terminal only slightly different than another. But these children saw such excitement in this new experience they were having and I enjoyed their joy as I watched. Their mother, like me, wasn't too impressed by the whole event, but those kids were making memories they will never forget of their first round trip flight.

It got me thinking of the early days of becoming a Christian. The awe and wonder of this new life, this new feeling and my new outlook on life. I was excited for what lay ahead. I couldn't contain the joy I had in my heart for what had happened to me. I was like these kids in the airport terminal this morning. Everything was exciting as I saw life with new eyes.

But now, I sometimes feel, as a Christian, like I do as I sit in the terminal on another trip. Like it's just routine and I feel bored with the whole journey. I realize this morning that the awe and wonder that once filled my heart for this newfound life has turned into routine. Oh, how I long to go back to that feeling I first had. "But I have this against you, that you have abandoned the love you had at first. Remember therefore from where you have fallen; repent and do the works you did at first. If not, I will come to you and remove your lampstand from its place, unless you repent." - Revelation 2:4-5.

Create in me Lord a new heart! One that longs for the first love I once had for you. Forgive me for letting this life you have given me become routine.

Notes:_____
_____
_____
_____
_____
_____
_____
_____
_____
_____
_____

False Witness

False witness. There's something extremely hurtful when someone says something about you that is the exact opposite of the truth, especially if it's done out of jealousy or even a lack of knowledge. My sister had this happen to her this week as some people published some harsh criticism of her husband and herself. It was the complete opposite of what really happened and she had to defend herself against the false witness. Most people already knew the truth but it's the ones that don't and cause the lies to get bigger that you have to set right.

The Bible speaks quite a bit about bearing false witness against our neighbors and against one another. It starts all the way back in the Ten Commandments: "You shall not bear false witness against your neighbor." - Exodus 20:16. The same idea is found in Psalms and Proverbs that God forbids us from telling lies about someone. Some of those lies come from a lack of information and some of it comes from just being downright rude.

If we feel like people are bearing false witness against us, we stand in good company. At the trial of Jesus Christ, false witness were brought in to tell lies about the Savior. "Now the chief priests and the whole council were seeking false testimony against Jesus that they might put him to death, but they found none, though many false witnesses came forward. At last two came forward and said, "This man said, 'I am able to destroy the temple of God, and to rebuild it in three days.'" - Matthew 26:59-61.

The Apostle Stephen faced the same issue in his day as he spread the Good News of the Gospel. "And they stirred up the people and the elders and the scribes, and they came upon him and seized him and brought him before the council, and they set up false witnesses who said, "This man never ceases to speak words against this holy place and the law, for we have heard him say that this Jesus of Nazareth will destroy this place and will change the customs that Moses delivered to us." - Acts 6:12-14.

I hurt for my sister having to go through this but it's something we all face at different levels throughout our lives. It's the sin of man that God warned us about from the initiation of the Law. Do not bear false witness against your neighbor.

Notes:_____

_____

_____

_____

_____

_____

_____

_____

July 12

Revival?

Revival? For years, major stars from the movie industry, the music industry and the athletic industry have been outspoken about their anti-Christian views. We have heard from actors and actresses, musicians and athletes that push views that go against God's Word, but there seems to be a new wave of these people coming to Christ. Only they know if their conversion is real or not, and so does God, but our job should not be to cast doubt on their newfound salvation. We should support them in prayer.

Recent big name converts like Justin Bieber, Kanye West and Lamar Odom possibly show an opportunity for revival in this country. People like these three men are put high on pedestals and young people are highly influenced by the things they do and say. The conversion of these men, and others, can have a profound impact for Christ. It is still the truth of God's Word and the convicting work of the Holy Spirit that draws people to God, but the publicity that these men are getting could spur an interest in seeking God.

"And in the last days it shall be, God declares, that I will pour out my Spirit on all flesh, and your sons and your daughters shall prophesy, and your young men shall see visions, and your old men shall dream dreams; even on my male servants and female servants in those days I will pour out my Spirit, and they shall prophesy."- Acts 2:17-18.

Are we seeing the last great revival of our time where many hearts will turn back to God before Christ returns to bring His Bride home? I pray that we are for two reasons. First, it means that many will be saved before it is eternally too late. And second, it means we are that much closer to the return of our Savior and the rapture of the church.

Pray for revival to break out, not only in our country, but across the world, as the universal church continues to grow. "For the Lord himself will descend from heaven with a cry of command, with the voice of an archangel, and with the sound of the trumpet of God. And the dead in Christ will rise first. Then we who are alive, who are left, will be caught up together with them in the clouds to meet the Lord in the air, and so we will always be with the Lord.
Therefore encourage one another with these words." - 1 Thessalonians 4:16-18.

Notes:_____
_____
_____
_____
_____
_____
_____
_____
_____

True Love

True love. As I get to celebrate my beautiful bride's birthday today, the words "true love" kept popping up in different forms as I thought about what to write. She hates the movie "Princess Bride" and I love to watch it just to make her complain about it. The movie is about "true love" between Westley and Princess Buttercup. The movie "Shrek" was on this morning, again talking about the idea of "true love". It made me think of my own "true love", Jennifer.

Many times the idea of true love seems like a fairytale as we all go through times in our lives where we have struggles and it seems far from being "true love". But "true love" pushes through all of those struggles and difficult times. That's what makes it "true love"! It is love that doesn't let any situation stop the love you have for one another. No matter what one person may do, true love keeps on keeping on. It's a love that lays down its own life for the wellbeing of the other person.

"Greater love has no one than this, that someone lay down his life for his friends." - John 15:13. True love was shown that day at Calvary, when Jesus Christ laid down His life for all of us. He who had no sins took on our sins to give us eternal life. There has never been a greater true love than that.

Just like my true love for my bride, Jesus has shown His true love for us by His death, burial and resurrection to give us life. Have you accepted His true love?

Notes:_____

_____
_____
_____
_____
_____
_____
_____
_____
_____
_____
_____
_____
_____
_____
_____
_____
_____
_____
_____

July 14

Vacation Bible School

Vacation Bible School. That week during the summer when churches have VBS for all the children in the church and the surrounding community. There are themed Bible lessons, arts and crafts, singing, games and snacks. It is usually a big event at each church that takes weeks of preparation and draws dozens of children anxious to learn about God. I never got to experience VBS growing up but our kids have had the opportunity every year and I appreciate the opportunity that they have.

Our children being able to learn about the truth of God's Word is of the utmost importance, especially in today's society that is becoming more and more anti-truth and anti-God. A moral foundation being established with children at a young age, that continues throughout their upbringing, is so important. Our church does a wonderful job with educating the youth.

"Hear, O Israel: The LORD our God, the LORD is one. You shall love the LORD your God with all your heart and with all your soul and with all your might. And these words that I command you today shall be on your heart. You shall teach them diligently to your children and shall talk of them when you sit in your house, and when you walk by the way, and when you lie down, and when you rise." - Deuteronomy 6:4-7.

"Train up a child in the way he should go; even when he is old, he will not depart from it." - Proverbs 22:6. Our duty as parents is to teach our children the Truth of God's Word so that they are exposed to the commandments, love and grace of God. It is said that children's minds are shaped at a very young age. As parents, we are responsible for the shaping of those young minds. If we don't do it, the world will.

"And calling to him a child, he put him in the midst of them and said, "Truly, I say to you, unless you turn and become like children, you will never enter the kingdom of heaven. Whoever humbles himself like this child is the greatest in the kingdom of heaven. Whoever receives one such child in my name receives me, but whoever causes one of these little ones who believe in me to sin, it would be better for him to have a great millstone fastened around his neck and to be drowned in the depth of the sea." - Matthew 18:2-6. Jesus showed us the importance of our children. Are you training up your children to love the Lord?

Notes:_____

_____

_____

_____

_____

_____

_____

July 15

Ownership

Ownership. We generally like to own things and not have to rent stuff from people where we really get no return on our investment. Whether it's renting a house or leasing a vehicle, it is always better, financially, to own whatever it is you possess. There's also no better felling than making that last payment on a house or car and the title becomes your possession as proof of ownership. At that point, we can say it is ours and not the possession of the bank.

I'm a big fan of Dave Ramsey and his Total Money Makeover plan of getting out of debt. My wife and I did that plan to reduced much of our debt and we are closing in on paying off almost everything else. It is satisfying to see the value of our debt reduce month after month and the thought of the freed up money that will result when we are completely debt free. At that point, our "stuff" will actually be our stuff. We will finally have ownership of our things.

Outside of having ownership of physical things, it's important that we take ownership of spiritual things as well. Our salvation is based upon our ownership of what we have decided about Christ personally. Our salvation is not based upon our parent's relationship with Christ or our spouse's relationship with Christ. We have to have ownership of our own salvation. We also need to make sure that our children don't grow up believing that their eternity is secure because of the decisions we made about Christ. Every single person is responsible for their own relationship with Christ. Ownership is non-transferable!

Sometimes it's good to step back for a second and reflect where our personal relationship with God is through His Son. Have we personally taken ownership of our own salvation by making the decision to accept Christ as our Savior, or are we just renting and leasing our salvation through someone else's relationship? Take some time today to reflect on your own relationship to Christ and make sure you own it.

Notes:_____

_____
_____
_____
_____
_____
_____
_____
_____
_____
_____
_____
_____
_____
_____

Tolerance

Tolerance. A word that has seemed to take over society the last couple of years. It's always in the news and used as argument if someone disagrees with your own opinion. It has been in some stories lately regarding the women's World Cup soccer team. I looked up the definition of tolerance and it revolves around the acceptance of someone's opinion or actions, and not of the person themselves.

I think that is where the misconception arises. We can be tolerant of people but intolerant or their opinions or actions. We can disagree with what they do and still love them as a person. However, those that tend to disagree with the actions of others are usually quickly labeled as either a racist, a bigot or some other word that ends with the suffix "phobic". It sometimes comes across that those screaming for tolerance the most can be the most intolerant of others disagreeing with their opinions.

What does Jesus teach us about tolerance? First off, he always loved and respected the person. Second, He never tolerated anything that went against the Word of God. A great example is the woman caught in adultery that was getting ready to be stoned for her sin. As Jesus requested her accusers to look at their own lives and only those found to be without sin were allowed to cast stones at her, he spoke to her separately. "But when they heard it, they went away one by one, beginning with the older ones, and Jesus was left alone with the woman standing before him. Jesus stood up and said to her, "Woman, where are they? Has no one condemned you?" She said, "No one, Lord." And Jesus said, "Neither do I condemn you; go, and from now on sin no more." - John 8:9-11.

He has tolerance for our nature to sin as humans, but He never tolerates us to continue in that sin. "Go, and from now on sin no more!" As Christians we are to tolerate the fact that people are sinners by nature, because we are too! However, as Christians, we are never to tolerate the sin and approve or accept it if it goes against God's Word. We can be loving and intolerant at the same time, just like Jesus was.

Christians get a bad stereotype of being intolerant because we adhere to the truth of God's Word. I think we can do a better job of doing both, loving the sinner but hating the sin. If we do it in the reverse order, people begin to draw conclusions that we are hateful, intolerant bigots because that is how we come across without loving them first. It's easier for those we disagree with to accept our opinion of sin if they know that we love them first, for the sinner that they are, even though we may hate the sin they commit.

Notes:_____
_____
_____

July 17

Children

Children. The Bible tells us that children are a blessing to their parents. I have to fully agree with that statement. As our family gets to celebrate the eleventh birthday of our oldest child, it gives us the opportunity to really look back at how much God has blessed us as a family and our daughter in general.

It's so wonderful to watch our children grow and their personalities really develop from year to year. We look at our daughter and see so much of ourselves in her actions and demeanor. She really is a collection of both my wife and I, but she leans heavily to the traits of my wife. As she grows, so does our relationship with her. Our conversations are deeper, our expectations of her grow, and our excitement for her future increases.

All of these things are blessings from God that He chose us to be her parents. We have a great responsibility in making sure that she grows in her relationship with Jesus Christ more than any other aspect of her life. If we can continue to point her towards God and His will for her life, all other things will fall into place according to His plan.

"You shall therefore lay up these words of mine in your heart and in your soul, and you shall bind them as a sign on your hand, and they shall be as frontlets between your eyes. You shall teach them to your children, talking of them when you are sitting in your house, and when you are walking by the way, and when you lie down, and when you rise. You shall write them on the doorposts of your house and on your gates, that your days and the days of your children may be multiplied in the land that the LORD swore to your fathers to give them, as long as the heavens are above the earth." - Deuteronomy 11:18-21.

Notes:_____
_____
_____
_____
_____
_____
_____
_____
_____
_____
_____
_____
_____
_____
_____
_____

Detours

Detours. Yesterday, my wife and kids had to go out to run some errands; doctor's office, bank, grocery store, you know, just normal stuff. Well, on their way they noticed that the traffic was stopped in the opposite direction and decided to take an alternate route on the way back home to avoid the delay.

When the errands were complete, they headed off on their detour to avoid the traffic issues they saw on their way out. Traveling the back roads, they came across some construction in the small town they were traveling through that had the road down to one lane. The original traffic jam that they saw obviously increased the traffic on the back roads as others searched for a quicker path as well.

As they waited because of the construction, a train passed through the middle of town at super slow speed and eventually came to a complete stop across the intersection. They ended up waiting over thirty minutes to get through all the additional congestion caused by the train in addition to the construction. Needless to say, my wife was a bit perturbed when they got home.

But that's life right? Even our most prepared plans get detoured by things outside of our control. Sometimes what we see as inconveniences, are God's way of protecting us or slowing us down. He may be keeping us from dangers we do not see and at times He may be putting us in the path of someone that needs us at that moment in time.

It reminds me of the story of Paul on his missionary journey when God did not permit him to go into Asia and instead directed him through a dream to go to Macedonia. "And when they had come up to Mysia, they attempted to go into Bithynia, but the Spirit of Jesus did not allow them. So, passing by Mysia, they went down to Troas. And a vision appeared to Paul in the night: a man of Macedonia was standing there, urging him and saying, 'Come over to Macedonia and help us.' And when Paul had seen the vision, immediately we sought to go on into Macedonia, concluding that God had called us to preach the gospel to them." - Acts 16:7-10.

Even though detours may be a nuisance at the time, God is in control of each and every situation. We need to learn to ask ourselves, "what does God want me to do as I face this detour in life?" Allow Him to work through us in our moments of waiting.

Notes:_____
_____
_____
_____
_____

Masterpiece

Masterpiece. Have you ever wished you were cleaning out your house and found something that looked like trash only to find out it was worth millions? That happened to a ninety year old French woman a few weeks ago. Getting ready to move, the old Renaissance painting of Jesus Hanging in her hallway was heading to the dump if it wasn't appraised within the week before the move. The appraiser thought it was worth some money, but when it sold for $26.8 million, it was a much greater treasure than he even imagined.

Imagine having that treasure sitting in your house for decades, thinking it was nothing more than a flea market find, only to find out at the end of your life it was worth millions? It made me wonder what her life would have been like if she knew about that painting fifty years ago. Would she have sold it and spent the rest of her years living in the lap of luxury on the French Riviera? Or would she have used the money to help those in need or started a shelter for abandoned children? We'll never know!

It reminded me of the story of the man who found a treasure and sold everything he had to get it. "The kingdom of heaven is like treasure hidden in a field, which a man found and covered up. Then in his joy he goes and sells all that he has and buys that field." - Matthew 13:44.

Or what about the merchant that found the pearl. "Again, the kingdom of heaven is like a merchant in search of fine pearls, who, on finding one pearl of great value, went and sold all that he had and bought it." - Matthew 13:45-46.

When we finally realize the treasure that is available to us when we put our faith in Christ, are we willing to give everything else away to possess what He makes available to us? When we accept Him as our Savior, we become His masterpiece. Isn't that a wonderful trade-off?

Notes:_____

_____
_____
_____
_____
_____
_____
_____
_____
_____
_____

July 20

Brain Freeze

Brain Freeze. Oh, the pain is real. To close out our week of Vacation Bible School last night, the church had an ice cream social when it was all over. Homemade ice creams of every flavor were available for tasting. Styrofoam cups were filled with either one favorite flavor or a combination of every flavor available. There aren't many things that I love more than ice cream, especially chocolate.

As I ate my cup of ice cream in our fellowship building, I looked around the room at about one hundred other adults and children enjoying their ice cream as well. Every few minutes you would see someone stop eating really quick and get that look of absolute pain on their faces as they reached for their forehead. One by one, the brain freeze monster attacked innocent people just trying to enjoy their frozen refreshments. It got me twice. There is really nothing you can do about it but wait and let it pass on its own.

As I mentioned yesterday, I lost a childhood friend to cancer this week and the pain is real. I hurt not for him, as his pain is now gone, but for his family. His parents and sisters, his wife and children, and his friends that were left behind. The pain of losing someone hits hard when we are not expecting it. It sometimes becomes overwhelming and we feel that we can't make it through. There seems to be no immediate relief from the pain of our lose. But like the brain freeze we receive from ice cream, over time the pain slowly begins to ease.

The pain of brain freeze from eating ice cream will eventually go away, but the pain of losing someone never really does. I've lost all of my grandparents and my father, and the pain of losing them has never really fully gone away. The memories of all the good times have become a way of getting through their not being here, but they are still missed.

My heart goes out today for the family that are burying loved ones and saying their final goodbyes. I pray for the pain and hurt that you are feeling. The memories of the good times will soon push out the feelings of emptiness and hurt.

Notes:_____
_____
_____
_____
_____
_____
_____
_____
_____
_____
_____
_____

Alarm Clock

Alarm clock. The best thing about Saturday mornings is that no alarm clocks go off on that particular day in our house. Monday through Friday it goes off to jolt me out of my peaceful sleep to head off to work. Sunday it goes off so that we can all get up on time and head out to church to worship God. But Saturday, no alarm clock needed (most of the time).

Due to being woken up routinely during the week, my internal alarm clock usually wakes me up about the same time on Saturday mornings anyway. Some Saturdays I can roll back over and get some extra sleep, but most of the time my body says it's time to get up and use the restroom. The body gets so used to a routine that it will keep it no matter if there is an external alarm or not.

God has given us an internal alarm clock, not to physically wake us up, but to spiritually wake us up. The Holy Spirit is our internal alert system to keep us in tune with the expectations of God. It alerts us to things that aren't right externally and things that aren't right internally. It's that uneasy feeling you get in situations that you know aren't where God wants you to be. The Holy Spirit works the same way internally when we are thinking of sinning against God's Word.

"But the Helper, the Holy Spirit, whom the Father will send in my name, he will teach you all things and bring to your remembrance all that I have said to you." - John 14:26. The Holy Spirit is not only our alarm clock but is also our teacher. As we read God's Word, the Holy Spirit helps us to learn the truth and apply it to our lives.

This internal alarm clock called the Holy Spirit is only possessed by those that have accepted Jesus Christ as their own personal Savior, He is not present in unbelievers. Do you possess the power of the Holy Spirit? Have you been saved by the redeeming work of Jesus Christ? Only then will you know the indwelling power of the Holy Spirit.

Notes:_____
_____
_____
_____
_____
_____
_____
_____
_____
_____
_____
_____

Peace

Peace. It was the big time slogan of the 60's. Songs were written about it with titles like "Give Peace a Chance" and others. We use it as a catchphrase when we are saying goodbye to our friends. The logo has been used for decades to sell merchandise. But will there ever really be peace in the world with some many cultural, political and religious differences? How will peace ever be achieved when so many people have so many opposing views on almost every subject that faces mankind?

As humans we search for peace, both for ourselves and for everyone. We look to all sorts of external things in search for some semblance of peace: money, fame, possession, sex, drugs and the list can go on and on. We look for external peace by passing more laws only to upset those that don't agree with the law. We look to be "tolerant" of everyone's view only to argue that those that disagree are being intolerant. Peace seems so far away from being achieved internally and externally.

The is only One that gives us the peace internally that we so desire in our lives and His name is Jesus Christ. "Peace I leave with you; my peace I give to you. Not as the world gives do I give to you. Let not your hearts be troubled, neither let them be afraid." ~ John 14:27. True peace, eternal peace, only comes from the One who has the authority to give it. "I have said these things to you, that in me you may have peace. In the world you will have tribulation. But take heart; I have overcome the world." ~ John 16:33.

World peace will never come until after Jesus Christ comes back and sets up His kingdom here on earth for one thousand years. Even during those one thousand years, with Christ available for everyone to see, people and nations will rebel until there is one final battle. Once that battle ends, then peace will finally rule the land (Revelation 20). Peace will come through the completed work of our Lord and Savior Jesus Christ.

Are you searching for inner peace? Are you longing for the day where there is peace on earth? Both of those are only found in Jesus Christ when we put our faith in His finished work on the Cross of Calvary.

Notes:_____
_____
_____
_____
_____
_____
_____
_____
_____

July 23

Foothold

Foothold. Last year I was able to attend a project management seminar in which Manley Feinberg was the keynote speaker. He is a world famous mountain climber that has scaled almost all of the world's tallest and most dangerous peaks. He was such an interesting speaker in terms of setting goals and how that relates to mountain climbing. But he said the most important aspect of climbing was the foothold.

He talked about the fact that climbing the steep faces of mountains is not about upper body strength, although it is helpful, it's about pushing upward with your legs. In order to be able to push, a climber has to be able to have their feet on strong footholds to get the leverage they need. The foothold is the key to successfully making your way up the mountain.

The same is true in the Christian life, where we place our feet and the footholds, we establish are the key to successfully progressing through this mountain called life. Christ is the solid rock in which our footholds should be placed upon. "Everyone then who hears these words of mine and does them will be like a wise man who built his house on the rock. And the rain fell, and the floods came, and the winds blew and beat on that house, but it did not fall, because it had been founded on the rock. And everyone who hears these words of mine and does not do them will be like a foolish man who built his house on the sand. And the rain fell, and the floods came, and the winds blew and beat against that house, and it fell, and great was the fall of it." - Matthew 7:24-27.

If we are not careful, negative thoughts and actions can also get footholds in our lives that gives access to Satan to use against us in our walk with God. "Be angry and do not sin; do not let the sun go down on your anger and give no foothold to the devil." - Ephesians 4:26-27. We can allow footholds, both positive and negative, to appear in our lives. It is our job to make sure that our footholds are placed in the strength of God. Do not give opportunity to the devil to use footholds in your life to sin. We must guard where we place our feet. "My steps have held fast to your paths; my feet have not slipped." - Psalm 17:5.

Notes:_____

_____
_____
_____
_____
_____
_____
_____
_____
_____
_____

July 24

Fans

Fans. Last night I got to take some time and go to a Major League Baseball game between the Milwaukee Brewers and the Cincinnati Reds. It's been years since I've been to a professional game and it was all that I remembered it to be. The sounds, the smells and the fans. There were fans of all shapes and sizes there last night. There were fans young and old and almost every single one of them was wearing a jersey of their favorite team and player.

We walked through the souvenir shop looking at all the clothing and trinkets, I have to say, there was nothing cheap in that store. Yet all these fans were sporting these expensive jerseys for the game. Kids had them on along with their gloves in their hand hoping to catch a foul ball, homerun or have the ball thrown to them from their favorite player.

These fans were fanatics about their home team and its players and it got me thinking; are we as fanatic about our Savior as these people are about these baseball players? I mean, what if we got up every day with the same fervor for Jesus Christ as all these people did for this one game played by ordinary men? What if we went to church as excited about worshiping God as these young kids did about worshiping these ball players?

"Whoever loves father or mother more than me is not worthy of me, and whoever loves son or daughter more than me is not worthy of me. And whoever does not take his cross and follow me is not worthy of me. Whoever finds his life will lose it, and whoever loses his life for my sake will find it." - Matthew 10:37-39.

What would our Christian life look like if we sold out to being true disciples of Christ? What would our Christian life look like if we followed Christ like we may follow things of this world? I believe our lives would be turned upside down, just like the original disciples of Christ and His Church.

Notes:_____
_____
_____
_____
_____
_____
_____
_____
_____
_____
_____
_____
_____

Greek to Me

It's all Greek to me. Spending so much time in airport terminals lately exposes me to so many different people from so many different cultures and backgrounds, especially in the major airports. I get to hear people speaking all sorts of languages as I walk and sit in the terminal. Sometimes I can recognize what language it might be even though I don't know the language.

I was sitting near a father and son today and they appeared to be from an Asian country but I'm not sure which one. I sat and listened to them behind me as they talked in their native tongue, not knowing what language it was or what they were saying. Whatever they were saying, I could tell that the middle-aged son was trying to explain something to his older father as they waited for the plane to board. The language may have been foreign to me but the tone of the conversation was not.

It got me thinking about heaven and the verses John wrote in the book of Revelation, "After this I looked, and behold, a great multitude that no one could number, from every nation, from all tribes and peoples and languages, standing before the throne and before the Lamb, clothed in white robes, with palm branches in their hands, and crying out with a loud voice, "Salvation belongs to our God who sits on the throne, and to the Lamb!" - Revelation 7:9-10. That verse always makes me think, if the great multitude made up of so many different people, were speaking so many different languages, did John understand every language now that he was in Heaven, or did all the people speak the same language?

After the Flood, God instructed Noah and his sons to spread out and repopulate the earth, but they disobeyed God and all settled in one place. God had to scatter all the people and confound their language to get them to spread out. I believe when we are all gathered back to God on that great day in Heaven, God will give us back one unified language that we all will speak. That is why John could understand that all the people he saw in Heaven cried out, "Salvation belongs to our God who sits on the throne, and to the Lamb!"

So, as I sit here today in wonder at what those around me are saying in their own native tongue, I believe the day is coming soon that I will no longer wonder because I will understand everything because we will all be in the presence of a mighty God who makes everything known to us who put our faith and trust in His Son, Jesus Christ. Praise God!

Notes:_____
_____
_____
_____
_____

July 26

Ultimate Sacrifice

Ultimate Sacrifice. I read a story today about a father that made the ultimate sacrifice to save the lives of his three daughters. A Tennessee family was vacationing in Florida when the man's youngest daughter got caught in a riptide out in the ocean. The man's two older daughters went out to help their younger sister and they too got caught in the riptide. The father and another man paddled out on boards to rescue the girls and he lost consciousness on the way back to shore and later died.

I have always wondered what adrenaline must kick in as a parent when our children are in serious danger, life threatening danger. This man's quick actions to save his children ultimately cost him his own. He sacrificed his life in exchange for the possibility of saving the lives of his daughters. His wife and his daughters now have to go on with their lives without him, but the assurance they have of his love for them has been proven.

I believe almost every parent would lay down their own lives to save the lives of their children, of course there are some that would not. But what about laying down our lives for just a friend, or maybe even a stranger, would we do that? Some would without thinking twice. The very words of the Apostle Paul touch on this very topic, "For one will scarcely die for a righteous person-though perhaps for a good person one would dare even to die- but God shows his love for us in that while we were still sinners, Christ died for us." - Romans 5:7-8.

Jesus made mention of it as well, "Greater love has no one than this, that someone lay down his life for his friends." - John 15:13. Jesus Christ laid down His perfect, sinless life in our place so that we may take on His righteousness when we accept Him as our Savior. There is no greater love that that; to lay down your life for those that are your "enemies" to give them the opportunity to become your "friends".

"For this reason the Father loves me, because I lay down my life that I may take it up again. No one takes it from me, but I lay it down of my own accord. I have authority to lay it down, and I have authority to take it up again. This charge I have received from my Father." - John 10:17-18.

Notes:_____
_____
_____
_____
_____
_____
_____
_____

Poison Ivy

Poison Ivy. I have been working in the yard all morning and afternoon today trying to make the yard look pretty. It's been one of the cooler days the past couple of weeks allowing me to be out during the middle of the day. One of the last things I did was cut down some wild weeds growing at the edge of our property to try and reclaim some of our yard.

Among the regular looking weeds were patches of poison ivy mixed in and if I wasn't careful, I would have been right up in it. Special thanks to my beautiful bride for pointing out where it was so I could avoid getting too close to it. I wasn't so lucky about a month ago as I was pulling some weeds around the bushes and happened to get a whole handful of poison ivy. I had it on the back of my hands and up my wrists for about a week.

Just like poison ivy, sin can hide itself among the normal mundane things we do every day until it sneaks up on us and catches us unaware. We may not even know until it's too late and we are covered in the aftereffects of touching it. Wouldn't it be great if sin came with a flashing neon sign telling us right where it is; pointing out to us to be careful and take caution in that particular area because sin awaits us?

My wife was kind enough to point out the areas for me to be careful because poison ivy was lurching. Too bad we couldn't have someone go before us each day pointing out areas where sin is waiting to catch us unaware. We do, it's called the Holy Spirit. We also have God's Word instructing us in areas of our lives that we are to be mindful and aware of letting sin in.

"Be sober-minded; be watchful. Your adversary the devil prowls around like a roaring lion, seeking someone to devour. Resist him, firm in your faith, knowing that the same kinds of suffering are being experienced by your brotherhood throughout the world." - 1 Peter 5:8-9.

Do not let sin spread like poison ivy. "If we confess our sins, he is faithful and just to forgive us our sins and to cleanse us from all unrighteousness." - 1 John 1:9.

Notes:_____
_____
_____
_____
_____
_____
_____
_____
_____

Buffet

Buffet. There are few things in life better than an all-you-can-eat buffet. After church this morning, we took the family to a pizza buffet by our house because our daughter loves spaghetti and our son loves pizza. What better treat than being able to pick what style you want and how much of it you are willing to endure. It allows the possibility of a great feast for those that are hungry enough. Our crew probably didn't get our money's worth at the buffet, but that's okay, they enjoyed the treat.

The past few months I have been teaching on what Heaven will be like when we get there and last week we focused on if we will eat and drink in Heaven and what the Bible tells us about it. The Scriptures are pretty clear that eating and drinking will not be in the spiritual sense, but we will actually physically eat and drink for all of eternity. "On this mountain the LORD of hosts will make for all peoples a feast of rich food, a feast of well-aged wine, of rich food full of marrow, of aged wine well refined." - Isaiah 25:6.

Not only was the idea of a future feast an Old Testament promise, Christ also spoke of it to His followers, "I tell you, many will come from east and west and recline at the table with Abraham, Isaac, and Jacob in the kingdom of heaven." - Matthew 8:11. "You are those who have stayed with me in my trials, and I assign to you, as my Father assigned to me, a kingdom, that you may eat and drink at my table in my kingdom and sit on thrones judging the twelve tribes of Israel." - Luke 22:28-30. If Christ promises that His followers will eat and drink at His table in the future Kingdom, why would we believe that eating and drinking will only be in a spiritual sense?

I look forward to eternity, when we can eat and drink of the feast God has prepared for us. Food like we have never tasted before, unaffected by the curse currently on the earth. We can eat and drink and be filled with the bounty of God. I look forward to sitting at the table with you who are believers in Christ.

Notes:_____
_____
_____
_____
_____
_____
_____
_____
_____
_____
_____
_____

Hello, My Name Is

Hello, my name is....... I just started a new job at the beginning of the year and have now been there almost seven months. One of the hardest parts of starting a new job, or moving to a new place, is learning the names of so many people that you have never met before. They have the easy part of just learning one new name, yours, while you have to learn hundreds. It takes months' worth of time to remember names and even so, I find myself still not remembering everyone's.

One thing that we will never have to worry about is God knowing our name. When we get to stand in His presence, we will not be asked to remind Him of what our name is. For one, He's omniscient and knows all things, but more than that, He knows us. Each and every one of us He knows by name. He's known us since the foundation of the world. "Before I formed you in the womb, I knew you, and before you were born, I consecrated you...." - Jeremiah 1:5. "Even as he chose us in him before the foundation of the world, that we should be holy and blameless before him." - Ephesians 1:4.

God knows us so well, even better than we know ourselves, that there will be no need to tell Him, "hello, my name is....". When we see Him, He will call us by name because He knows every hair on our heads. "But even the hairs of your head are all numbered." - Matthew 10:30. Doesn't that give you an overwhelmingly comforting feeling that you are not unknown? In this big world we live in with billions of people, God knows you so intimately that He not only knows your name but knows the exact number of hairs on your head. That's a loving and personal God.

Notes:_____
_____
_____
_____
_____
_____
_____
_____
_____
_____
_____
_____
_____
_____
_____
_____

July 30

Not Quite

Not quite. We have probably all had times in our lives when we were "not quite". Maybe we were not quite the right person for the job. Or we were not quite the marrying type. We could have been not quite smart enough, tall enough, good looking enough, athletic enough and on and on. In measuring up to someone else's standards, we might always fall into the group of "not quite". It's okay to be not quite for someone else, what we have to be worried about is being "not quite" right with God.

I hear it in so many conversations with people who may believe in God but don't think they have to believe in what Just Christ did. They live their lives on a works-based mentality. They believe if they can just be good enough, if they can just go to church often enough or if they give just enough to charity, that they will somehow be accepted by God. However, on judgement day, when God judges them on their works, they will not quite be good enough, because acceptance by God isn't about what we do, but what Jesus did.

The Bible is clear on man's standing with a Holy God:

"For all have sinned and fall short of the glory of God" - Romans 3:23.

"For the wages of sin is death, but the free gift of God is eternal life in Christ Jesus our Lord." - Romans 6:23.

Eternal life in Christ Jesus is clearly listed as a free gift of God, not the works of man!

"For by grace you have been saved through faith. And this is not your own doing; it is the gift of God, not a result of works, so that no one may boast. - Ephesians 2:8-9.

The only way to be a "not quite" is to put your faith in the free gift of eternal salvation, the death, burial and resurrection of Jesus Christ. The last thing anyone ever wants to hear from the mouth of a Holy God are these words: "And then will I declare to them, 'I never knew you; depart from me, you workers of lawlessness.'" - Matthew 7:23. ""Then he will say to those on his left, 'Depart from me, you cursed, into the eternal fire prepared for the devil and his angels." - Matthew 25:41.

Put your faith in Jesus Christ before it is eternally too late. If you want to know how, please feel free to reach out to me.

Notes:_____
_____
_____
_____
_____

July 31

Harvest

Harvest. As I drive around the great state of North Carolina, I have noticed that the harvest season has begun on some of the crops along the sides of the road. I have noticed that the lower leaves of the tobacco plants have started the process of being primed. It's so interesting to watch over the next couple weeks as the tobacco fields become less and less populated with tobacco leaves and the field starts showing through. It won't be much longer and the corn will start going through the same process.

As fall arrives, the activity of the local farmers starts to get increasingly more frantic. The end of the season is coming and the crops have to be harvested so that they do not die and become useless and money is not lost. Farmers spend their hard earned money each year to plant seeds in hopes that their investment in the seeds will provide profit in the crops.

This time of the year always brings to mind the words of Jesus to His disciples, "Do you not say, 'There are yet four months, then comes the harvest'? Look, I tell you, lift up your eyes, and see that the fields are white for harvest. Already the one who reaps is receiving wages and gathering fruit for eternal life, so that sower and reaper may rejoice together. For here the saying holds true, 'One sows and another reaps.' I sent you to reap that for which you did not labor. Others have labored, and you have entered into their labor." - John 4:35-38.

"Then he said to his disciples, 'The harvest is plentiful, but the laborers are few; therefore, pray earnestly to the Lord of the harvest to send out laborers into his harvest.'"- Matthew 9:37-38. Are you taking part in the Lord's harvest? Are you planting seeds, watering those that have already been planted, or are you taking part in the reaping? This world is in desperate times and the great and terrible Day of the Lord is closer every day. Let us do our part in taking part in the harvest.

Notes:_____
_____
_____
_____
_____
_____
_____
_____
_____
_____
_____
_____
_____
_____
_____

August 1

Sharing

Sharing. It's hard to share our possessions with others, especially as young children and it doesn't seem to get any easier as we grow older. Having a three year old just confirms what I already thought I knew: people don't like to share. Why is it that we feel that the objects God blesses us with, somehow are ultimately ours and not still His? God is the ultimate example of what it means to share. Sharing is different from giving.

We are much more apt to "give" somebody something that belongs to us than we are to "share" in our belongings? Why is that? I think it comes down to having an obligation to still be connected in some way to what we share. When we give something to someone else for them to take ownership of, we rid ourselves of any obligation to what is done with that object. We know that whatever it is we gave away is no longer ours and will probably never return back to us. We can cut our connection to that object and move on.

But when we share, we are keeping our connection, and we are also opening ourselves up to a relationship with someone else over our object. We still have ownership but someone else now has part in our object. A connection has been made between the two people that are now sharing in ownership of the object. There is an obligation by both parties for the well-being of that object.

As Christians, we don't "give" the Gospel away. We don't tell people of Christ and then walk away with no connection, like we've done our part and now it's over and on them. We share the Gospel of Jesus Christ because we retain ownership, but we are inviting others in to share in our relationship with God through Jesus Christ. We now have an obligation with those that we share the Good News to make sure we continue to foster this new relationship and water the seed that we have planted.

Just as Paul told Timothy, "They are to do good, to be rich in good works, to be generous and ready to share, thus storing up treasure for themselves as a good foundation for the future, so that they may take hold of that which is truly life. - 1 Timothy 6:18-19. Share the Gospel and be obligated to see your sharing through to the salvation of lost souls.

Notes:_____
_____
_____
_____
_____
_____
_____
_____
_____

August 2

Dead End

Dead End. I remember growing up in a little neighborhood where all the kids spent all day outside playing with the other kids in the neighborhood. It was a mix of boys and girls of different ages and abilities and the older ones looked after the welfare of the younger ones. We played in people's yards and we played things like kickball and whiffle ball in the streets. We always had to stop and clear the road when any cars came through, but most of the drivers understood we were playing and were very patient.

If we didn't want to be bothered with stopping as much, we would all make our way down to one of the dead end streets in our neighborhood and play there. With no through traffic, our games were interrupted less often. The dead end streets always seemed to be the best places to play. I remember one of the streets had a vacant wooded lot and we went in and build a small BMX track to ride our bikes in. Dead end streets were a valuable life experience growing up.

Now that I look at life with a whole new set of eyes as a Christian, I can see that the dead end streets that this world promises lead to nothing but eternal destruction. You can watch television commercials and think your whole life could be fixed if I just had this product or that job, but in reality, the only way your life can be fixed is through Jesus Christ. It reminds me of what the Apostle Paul said about one of his former colleagues for Christ, "For Demas, in love with this present world, has deserted me and gone to Thessalonica." - 2 Timothy 4:10.

Demas fellow in love with this current world and not only deserted Paul, but it seems he deserted his relationship with Jesus Christ, if there truly ever was one. A prominent US pastor and author recently renounced his relationship with Christ for the love of this world sending shockwaves through the Christian community. Begs the question, did he know Christ or just know about Him. There are many people in this world that think they are Christians because they know about Jesus, but in reality are not Christians because they don't know Him.

"Do not be conformed to this world, but be transformed by the renewal of your mind, that by testing you may discern what is the will of God, what is good and acceptable and perfect." - Romans 12:2.

Notes:_____
_____
_____
_____
_____

Shoes

Shoes. We went shopping this morning for new shoes for my little guy. We signed him up to play soccer for the first time this fall so we had to make sure he had all the right gear before his first practice this Thursday. We had to get a pair of shin guards and socks and most importantly new soccer boots. There aren't a whole lot of places that make soccer shoes for a three year old, but we finally found him a pair and to say he's excited is an understatement.

As I was putting his shoes on in the sports store, the Bible verses from Ephesians all of a sudden popped into my head, "Therefore take up the whole armor of God, that you may be able to withstand in the evil day, and having done all, to stand firm. Stand therefore, having fastened on the belt of truth, and having put on the breastplate of righteousness, and, as shoes for your feet, having put on the readiness given by the gospel of peace. In all circumstances take up the shield of faith, with which you can extinguish all the flaming darts of the evil one; and take the helmet of salvation, and the sword of the Spirit, which is the word of God" - Ephesians 6:13-17.

"As shoes for your feet, having put on the readiness given by the Gospel of peace"(v. 15). The Gospel of Jesus Christ give us peace, peace from the penalty of our own sins, peace with the Father and peace with others. This newfound peace that we receive from the Gospel makes us ready to withstand the wickedness of this world. It makes us ready to share the Good News of Jesus Christ.

My son is ready to start his soccer career this Thursday and it will be an exciting few days as we await the arrival of that first practice. He will be ready to go out there and at least run around and tire himself out for an hour or so. Are you ready? Not to run around a soccer field, but the share the peace of the Gospel of Jesus Christ? The world is looking for peace, and they aren't able to find it in any "thing" but only in the Savior. But the world need you to share that peace with them. That's our mission and that's Christ's command to us, "And he said to them, "Go into all the world and proclaim the gospel to the whole creation." - Mark 16:15.

Notes:_____
_____
_____
_____
_____
_____
_____
_____
_____

August 4

Listen

Listen. It's a hard thing to do sometimes, to actually listen to words that are being spoken to you. I was curious as to what was the difference between hearing and listening, so I googled it to find out and this is what I learned. Hearing is accidental, involuntary and effortless. On the other hand, listening is focused, voluntary and intentional. Hearing is the simple act of perceiving sound by ear but listening requires concentration so that your brain processes meaning from words and sentences.

How often do we just hear words as noises in the background, never really processing what is being said. I'm sure we are all guilty of just hearing what our spouses and children are saying and not intentionally focusing on listening to their words. I'm sure we are just as guilty as we sit and listen to the preacher on Sundays. Things may distract us and our minds may wander allowing us only to hear God's Word and not listen to what is being said.

"Come, O children, listen to me; I will teach you the fear of the LORD." - Psalm 34:11. Listen to me and I will teach you! Learning comes by listening and not just hearing. We hear so many sounds and words throughout the course of our day, but what do we really take time to intentionally listen to? "Blessed is the one who listens to me, watching daily at my gates, waiting beside my doors." - Proverbs 8:34.

I'm so glad that God doesn't just hear us but he listens to us, taking our pleas and prayers to heart intentionally. "For he says, 'In a favorable time I listened to you, and in a day of salvation I have helped you.' Behold, now is the favorable time; behold, now is the day of salvation." - 2 Corinthians 6:2. God is waiting to hear our cry for salvation. He is listening intently for unbelievers to cry out to Him for help. He is willing to save the lost.

As the world begs for peace, love and acceptance, do we hear them or are we listening to them? Are their pleas just background noise in our lives or are we concentrating on what they are saying and processing their need for a Savior? Be intentional. Be focused. And be voluntary in what the lost are saying to you. Introduce them to our Savior, Jesus Christ.

Notes:_____
_____
_____
_____
_____
_____
_____
_____
_____
_____
_____

August 5

Growth

Growth. Every time that someone I haven't seen in a while sees my kids, the first thing that usually comes out of their mouths is, "man, look how much they have grown!" The same response happens if I send someone pictures of the kids. I'm not sure if they expect them to stay the same size for years on end, or if that is just a common response when they've seen them for the first time in quite a while. Little ones grow so quickly from month to month, but they slow down some as they get older.

As adults, most of our growing is done outward, as we gain weight, our hair grows grey or maybe even goes away, our eyes grow dim and our memories grow distant. Age takes a toll on our growing. But what about growing spiritually? As we age, that is one thing in our lives that should continue to grow stronger and not grow weaker. "The righteous flourish like the palm tree and grow like a cedar in Lebanon." - Psalm 92:12. There is no reason, other than our own slack in doing so, for us to not continue to grow in our walk with Christ as we age.

"Rather, speaking the truth in love, we are to grow up in every way into him who is the head, into Christ, from whom the whole body, joined and held together by every joint with which it is equipped, when each part is working properly, makes the body grow so that it builds itself up in love." - Ephesians 4:15-16. Our Christian lives should continue to grow in Christlikeness. If we aren't growing, we're dying spiritually.

"Like newborn infants, long for the pure spiritual milk, that by it you may grow up into salvation-if indeed you have tasted that the Lord is good." - 1 Peter 2:2-3. As we grow, our desire for the deeper things of God should grow as well. We should be moving from the simple things of God (milk) and into the deeper things of God (meat).

"But grow in the grace and knowledge of our Lord and Savior Jesus Christ. To him be the glory both now and to the day of eternity. Amen." - 2 Peter 3:18.

Notes:_____
_____
_____
_____
_____
_____
_____
_____
_____
_____
_____
_____

August 6

Explosion

Explosion. During my layover between flights this morning, I stopped at one of the little places in the airport to grab some breakfast since I had started out so early this morning. I chose a thing of fresh fruit and a drink. They didn't have anything but water and soda to choose from, and I'm not a big soda drinker, but I grabbed a Dr. Pepper and went on my way to my gate. I put the bottle of soda in my back pocket as I walked from one end of the airport to the other.

When I got to my gate and sat down, I put the bottle of soda on the floor and ate my little package of fresh fruit. After about ten minutes, I reached down and got my soda and when I opened it up it exploded all over me. I figured that after ten minutes, any shaking that had occurred from being in my pocket while I walked had settled itself. But there I was, sitting at the gate with my lap soaked on my left side from my knee to my belt. Nothing like starting your long journey to the west coast with soda soaked jeans.

Things don't always go the way we plan them to go. When we hope for just smooth sailing, sometime there are unexpected events that change our day. I had a decision to make this morning as I sat with wet jeans: either be angry at what I had done or go on with the day knowing that at some point my pants would dry and everything would be back to normal (but a little sticky). I chose not to be mad at what happened, I just grabbed some additional napkins and dried my jeans the best I could.

Things happen unexpectedly in our lives and we always have two decisions to make: be better or be bitter. "Let all bitterness and wrath and anger and clamor and slander be put away from you, along with all malice." - Ephesians 4:31. As believers, we are to live our lives without bitterness, without wrath and without anger. All of these things cause us to allow sin to creep into our hearts. As Christians, what do we really have to be bitter or angry about? We've accepted the free gift of grace from God by accepting Christ's payment on the Cross for our sins. That alone should keep us from being bitter or angry.

Notes:_____
_____
_____
_____
_____
_____
_____
_____
_____
_____
_____
_____

Tired

Tired. Yesterday was a long day of traveling from one side of the country to the other. It started out very early on the east coast and ended late on the west coast. After about twenty hours of being awake, I was finally able to get to bed last night, but my body had me back up early again this morning because that internal clock didn't care that I had traveled three time zones yesterday. So, to say the least, I'm tired again this morning.

There were things I wanted to do here yesterday when I arrived, but plans changed and I just went with the flow. I figured that I would catch up on those tasks when I got back to the hotel last night, but I was exhausted when I got here and they didn't get done. So, as I woke up early this morning, I was able to catch myself up with the items I didn't get checked off my list yesterday. It made me think about getting things done in eternity.

I have been teaching about Heaven in our Sunday school class and one of the items that we had discussed last week was that whatever things we want to complete in Heaven that do not get done on that day, we will have lost no time to get it done. Eternity loses no time. When we go to bed one day, and wake up the next, no time has been lost. Whoever we didn't get to talk to on one particular day, can be spoken to the next day without feeling like we ran out of time. Nothing will corrode, no one will die and we won't feel like we missed something.

I look forward to an eternity where time and tasks are not a priority in life. The idea of not having to rush through things because time is running out will not exist. I look forward to not being tired because there is not enough time in the day to get everything done. Oh, what a glorious time that will be. "Come to me, all who labor and are heavy laden, and I will give you rest. Take my yoke upon you, and learn from me, for I am gentle and lowly in heart, and you will find rest for your souls. For my yoke is easy, and my burden is light." - Matthew 11:28-30.

Notes:_____

_____
_____
_____
_____
_____
_____
_____
_____
_____
_____
_____

August 8

Homeless

Homeless. One of the things that is very noticeable as we drove through the areas around Los Angeles the last few days, was the amount of people that are homeless. At almost every stop light and stop sign, there were homeless people on the corner with cardboard signs asking for help. It's disheartening to see so many people facing hard times like that. It tugs at your heart as a Christian, as you long to help everyone but knowing that you just don't have the resources to do so.

The guy I was riding with mentioned that he tries not to give homeless people any money because he is afraid that they will use it for drugs or alcohol. I agreed that most will probably do that, and some will actually use it for food or towards getting a room for a night so they can shower and sleep on a bed. I told him that my job was to help when I can in those situations, just like Jesus asked us too; "For I was hungry and you gave me food, I was thirsty and you gave me drink, I was a stranger and you welcomed me, I was naked and you clothed me, I was sick and you visited me, I was in prison and you came to me.'"- Matthew 25:35-36. What they do with the money or things I may give them is their responsibility and they will be held accountable for their choices, not me.

As a society, we normally look down on the homeless like they are diseased, when all of us are just a few bad choices of being in the same situation they are. They are human beings and God's creation, just like us, nothing more and definitely nothing less. Even the Apostle Paul had times of homelessness, "To the present hour we hunger and thirst, we are poorly dressed and buffeted and homeless, and we labor, working with our own hands. When reviled, we bless; when persecuted, we endure; when slandered, we entreat. We have become, and are still, like the scum of the world, the refuse of all things." - 1 Corinthians 4:11-13.

There is a coming day that all who put their faith and trust in Jesus Christ will never face homelessness. For He tells us, "In my Father's house are many rooms. If it were not so, would I have told you that I go to prepare a place for you? And if I go and prepare a place for you, I will come again and will take you to myself, that where I am you may be also." - John 14:2-3. Why a glorious promise. If you know Him, your reservation in His Heavenly home is awaiting you. Praise God!

Notes:_____
_____
_____
_____
_____
_____
_____

Debt Relief

Debt relief. As I was flipping through the channels on the television the other night, I saw the same add multiple time for a debt relief company. They promised that they could help people get out of their overwhelming debt for pennies on the dollar. The idea of this sort of hit me the wrong way. Where is the accountability to the person who spent money that they didn't have? Now, this company is going to swindle the companies that they owe money to out of what they deserve. That just hit me the wrong way.

But, that is the society and culture we live in today: buy the things your heart desires and worry about how to pay for it later. It made me think of my grandparent's generation that saved the money they needed until they had enough to buy what they wanted. Whatever it was they needed or wanted was going to have to wait until they had enough money to pay for it. They didn't go into debt for their wants and they never had the need for a debt relief company. I believe this industry has sprung up in our generation as we wanted more than our pocketbooks could pay for.

As Christians, we have a "debt relief company" that goes by the name of Jesus Christ. When He left the portals of Heaven to take on human flesh, He came with the total understanding that He was here to pay the debt of the world's sins for the glory of the Father. "For our sake he made him to be sin who knew no sin, so that in him we might become the righteousness of God." - 2 Corinthians 5:21. Christ relieved the debt we owed for our sins; Christ paid it all. Those that have not accepted Christ as their Savior, are still in debt for the things they've done in the flesh.

"Blessed are those whose lawless deeds are forgiven, and whose sins are covered; blessed is the man against whom the Lord will not count his sin." - Romans 4:7-8. Have you had your debt relieved? Have you accept Christ's death, burial and resurrection as payment for your sins? Today is the day to call upon the name of the Lord to save you from the punishment of your sins. He has already paid your debt in full; He's just waiting for you to accept Him.

Notes:_____
_____
_____
_____
_____
_____
_____
_____
_____
_____
_____

Hatred

Hatred. It's such a strong feeling. What could be so influential in our lives that we actually hate it? I can understand hating cancer or some other disease, but there shouldn't be any reason that we hate other people. People have strong ties to politics, religion, race and even sports teams; so much so, that they hate anyone that opposes their line of thinking. Hate has become so prevalent in our world today and just seems to grow exponentially every day. It's almost to the point that I can say that I hate hate.

What are we to do as Christians? We're normal people too, who have strong opinions and feelings towards certain things, especially when it comes to moral topics. Should we get to the point of hatred towards others that don't see the world through the same eyes as we do? I would say no, and we should come to expect that the number of people who see the world through Biblical eyes will continue to grow smaller and smaller until the return of Christ.

So, what shall we do when we come across those that hate us for what we believe in? Should we fight fire with fire so to speak? Of course not. The great civil rights leader from the 1960's, Medgar Evers, said, "when you hate, the only person that suffers is you because half the people you hate, don't know it, and the other half, don't care." Hate is like the picture of this snake below wrapped around a saw. He keeps tightening his coils thinking he is strangling the saw, when the whole time he is actually cutting himself to death.

"You have heard that it was said, 'You shall love your neighbor and hate your enemy.' But I say to you, Love your enemies and pray for those who persecute you, so that you may be sons of your Father who is in heaven. For he makes his sun rise on the evil and on the good and sends rain on the just and on the unjust." - Matthew 5:43-45. The only hatred that a Christian should have in his heart is the hatred for his own sin. We should hate sin in us as much as God hates sin in us.

"There are six things that the LORD hates, seven that are an abomination to him: haughty eyes, a lying tongue, and hands that shed innocent blood, a heart that devises wicked plans, feet that make haste to run to evil, a false witness who breathes out lies, and one who sows discord among brothers." - Proverbs 6:16-19. These are the things we should hate within ourselves. We shouldn't hate others because they sin differently than we do.

Notes:_____

_____

_____

_____

_____

_____

August 11

Stains

Stains. Little kids and stains go together like peanut butter and jelly. My little guy was all dressed up for church today and by the time we made it through lunch, his nice pink button down shirt was covered with macaroni and cheese stains all down the front. As a three year old, we have come to the reality that his clothes are going to get stained when he eats, it's just a part of life with children. All we can do is depend on the capability of the washing machine to get out the stains.

Children aren't the only ones to get stains on their clothes, adults can be just as bad. But what about the stains of sin in our lives? There is no moral washing machine that we can throw our sin stained lives into that can make us clean again and ready to go on to the next stain. How do we go about washing away our sins and being made new again? The old hymn is pretty clear the only way this can happen; "What can wash away my sin? Nothing but the blood of Jesus!"

We shouldn't get our theology from a hymn book, so what does the Word of God say about cleansing us from our sins? "Come now, let us reason together, says the LORD: though your sins are like scarlet, they shall be as white as snow; though they are red like crimson, they shall become like wool." - Isaiah 1:18. Even in the Old Testament, before the incarnation of Christ, the answer to the cleansing of sins was the promise of One to come.

"If we confess our sins, he is faithful and just to forgive us our sins and to cleanse us from all unrighteousness." - 1 John 1:9. The first step of being cleansed of our sins is acknowledging that we have them. Then we must confess our sins and repent from doing them again. If we do that, God is faithful and just to forgive us and cleanse us from all of our unrighteousness. Have you been cleansed or do the stains of your sins still remain? God is waiting to cleanse you; all you have to do is ask.

Notes:_____
_____
_____
_____
_____
_____
_____
_____
_____
_____
_____
_____
_____

August 12

Jury Duty

Jury Duty. My beautiful bride had her first day of jury duty today and it could last all week. That wonderful privilege of sitting in a courtroom all day hearing both sides of an argument in regards to either a criminal or civil case, in which you are responsible to weed out the lies and decide on the facts of the case. I have always found it interesting that both sides have very different "facts" of the case, yet both parties have sworn that they will "tell the truth, the whole truth and nothing but the truth". At the end of the trial, someone has been lying the entire time. One of my favorite black and white movies of all time is Twelve Angry Men.

As my wife has to sit there this week listening to the testimony of several witnesses and perhaps the defendant themselves, she will have to piece together the statements of all the individuals involved to try and figure out exactly what the truth is. There will be false statements that won't add up with the rest of the stories and those will have to be thrown out in making her decision. She will need to consider so many little details to come to her final decision whether someone is innocent or guilty.

When we stand in judgement before Christ, as either believers or unbelievers, there will be no jury listening to our testimony. There will be no opportunity for us to try to persuade others of our guilt or innocence. We will stand alone and give an account for our lives. "So, then each of us will give an account of himself to God." - Romans 14:12. We will not be able to hire a lawyer to plead our case, we will stand on our own accord to give an account only of ourselves.

"I tell you, on the day of judgment people will give account for every careless word they speak, for by your words you will be justified, and by your words you will be condemned." - Matthew 12:36-37. Believers will stand before Christ to give an account for what they did with their lives as Christians, not for whether they have accepted Christ or not. Unbelievers will stand before God and give an account for all of their works and will be asked what they have done with Christ. Unbelievers will find their works are not enough to allow them access into the presence of God's eternity and they will be cast out into Satan's pit for the rest of eternity.

Notes:_____
_____
_____
_____
_____
_____
_____
_____
_____

Home Makeover

Home makeover. We've spent the last 15+ years remodeling an old farmhouse that I bought before we were married. It's been a painstaking task as we've pretty much done one room at a time as we have had the money to do so. But it's also been great to see the changes and have the ability to somewhat make the changes to fit our needs. It has not always been fun living in the house while we have been making the renovations, but it's been nice seeing how the house has improved.

We have two upcoming renovations in our future lives. Our mortal bodies will be renovated into glorious immortal bodies and this old earth will be renovated into a New Earth. I am so looking forward to both renovations.

"For this perishable body must put on the imperishable, and this mortal body must put on immortality. When the perishable puts on the imperishable, and the mortal puts on immortality, then shall come to pass the saying that is written: "Death is swallowed up in victory." "O death, where is your victory? O death, where is your sting?" - 1 Corinthians 15:53-55. What a glorious day it shall be when this old sinful body will be changed into a sinless body to forever be with the Lord.

"Then I saw a new heaven and a new earth, for the first heaven and the first earth had passed away, and the sea was no more." - Revelation 21:1. "But according to his promise we are waiting for new heavens and a new earth in which righteousness dwells." - 2 Peter 3:13. This earth that we currently live on will be burned up with fire and restored to its original state as a New Earth with a beautiful city in it called the New Jerusalem where God will reside with man.

Are you looking forward to the renovations that are to come? First our bodies and then our home. There will be no time and energy that we will have to put into those renovation projects, they will all be completed by the Savior.

Notes:_____
_____
_____
_____
_____
_____
_____
_____
_____
_____
_____

August 14

Routine Maintenance

Routine maintenance. I had to bring my car to the shop today for some routine maintenance, like getting the oil changed and all of the fluids topped off. My car kept notifying me every time I started it up that it was time for some fixes. It's nice that the newer cars nowadays have programs to alert you to the needs of the car. On my older truck, I just have to pay attention to that little sticker and my odometer to make sure I get the oil changed on time.

Just like our vehicles, we need routine maintenance in our physical lives, and more importantly, in our spiritual lives. We need to check ourselves and make sure that we are in God's will for our lives and that we are doing those things that we control to make sure we are walking close to Him. Things like our daily devotional time, our prayer life and regularly meeting to worship with other believers at church.

Along with the newer cars on the road, we have a built in "system" that will alert us when things are out of kilter in our spiritual lives. The Holy Spirit works as that system to tells us that something is wrong. If we listen to the Spirit, we can confess our sins and get back in fellowship with God. "If we confess our sins, he is faithful and just to forgive us our sins and to cleanse us from all unrighteousness."- 1 John 1:9. However, if we fail to heed to the work of the Spirit, we will continue to drift further from the will of God and life will be tougher.

"These things I have spoken to you while I am still with you. But the Helper, the Holy Spirit, whom the Father will send in my name, he will teach you all things and bring to your remembrance all that I have said to you." - John 14:25-26. Let us allow the Holy Spirit to teach us all things, to direct us to things in our lives that need routine maintenance and let Him work in us to draw us closer to God. We have been given the Spirit of God for a reason, to direct us to His will.

Notes:_____
_____
_____
_____
_____
_____
_____
_____
_____
_____
_____
_____
_____

Water

Water. You really never know how important water is in your life until it's taken away from you. On Tuesday afternoon we found that we no longer had water in our house. So, after checking the breakers and a few other things, we narrowed it down to either the well went dry because of the lack of rain the last two months or the pump in the well went bad. We did have a brief storm last week that we feel lightening may have went in on it and started the process of it going bad.

Luckily, after calling about five different plumbers, we got one to come out after supper on Tuesday and pull the pump and replace it. As I sat out there at the pump, with my little guy asking the plumber a thousand questions, I started thinking about the story of the woman at the well that met Jesus because He knew He had a meeting with her.

"A woman from Samaria came to draw water. Jesus said to her, "Give me a drink." (For his disciples had gone away into the city to buy food.) The Samaritan woman said to him, "How is it that you, a Jew, ask for a drink from me, a woman of Samaria?" (For Jews have no dealings with Samaritans.) Jesus answered her, "If you knew the gift of God, and who it is that is saying to you, 'Give me a drink,' you would have asked him, and he would have given you living water." The woman said to him, "Sir, you have nothing to draw water with, and the well is deep. Where do you get that living water?" - John 4:7-11.

Living water! As we sat for a few hours at the house with no running water (but plenty of bottled water) we came to realize how blessed we are to live in a place where water is not a scarcity. There are place around the world that people have to trek miles to get water and that water isn't in any way clean enough to drink. But we also live in a country that has ample access to the Living Water, Jesus Christ, that those around the world do not have access to like we do. I pray that God's Word goes out to those who long for this Living Water just like the woman at the well.

"How then will they call on him in whom they have not believed? And how are they to believe in him of whom they have never heard? And how are they to hear without someone preaching? And how are they to preach unless they are sent? As it is written, "How beautiful are the feet of those who preach the good news!" - Romans 10:14-15.

Notes:_____
_____
_____
_____
_____
_____
_____
_____

August 16

Holy Water

Holy water. I heard a new song on the radio called "Holy Water" and it brought me back to my youth. Growing up and playing baseball with the same group of guys for most of my childhood, there was one mother that was a very devout Catholic. When we played on all-star teams, she would bring holy water to all the games and use it on our bats, our gloves and on people themselves. I wasn't a religious person at that time, so it didn't really do anything for me but get me wet. We were very successful as a team but I'm pretty sure it didn't have anything to do with the holy water.

Whether the other guys on the team believed that the holy water helped them play better or not, I couldn't tell you. But, knowing what I do now about the Bible, I'm know that the holy water had nothing to do with our success. The outcome of our baseball game was not a priority to God. He has no interest in who wins or loses ball games, He does have an interest in how we glorify Him.

I'm not convinced in the power of holy water, but I am convinced in the power of the Living Water! "Jesus answered her, "If you knew the gift of God, and who it is that is saying to you, 'Give me a drink,' you would have asked him, and he would have given you living water." The woman said to him, "Sir, you have nothing to draw water with, and the well is deep. Where do you get that living water?" - John 4:10-11.

"Jesus said to her, "Everyone who drinks of this water will be thirsty again, but whoever drinks of the water that I will give him will never be thirsty again. The water that I will give him will become in him a spring of water welling up to eternal life." The woman said to him, "Sir, give me this water, so that I will not be thirsty or have to come here to draw water." - John 4:13-15.

Have you drank from the Living Water? The water that will never make you thirst again. Jesus Christ is the Living Water that we need to be drinking of, not the rotten water of this world.

Notes:_____

_____
_____
_____
_____
_____
_____
_____
_____
_____
_____

Fun

Fun. I have completely enjoyed watching the first few days of the Little League World Series. The pure excitement and joy on the faces of these eleven and twelve year old's makes it so enjoyable to watch. The pride in the faces of their parents as they are being interviewed about their children cannot be hidden. I enjoy watching these kids play so much more than I do watching professionals play.

I love how they get so excited for each other and pick each other up when they make mistakes. It's not just their own teammates that they celebrate, if an opposing player hits a homerun, they all give him a high five as they circle the bases. There seems to be no animosity between the players or coaches on opposing teams. When someone happens to get hurt, you can see the concern the players on the opposing team has for that player's welfare.

We can all take a valuable lesson from these kids. They have a complete understanding that what they are doing is playing a game, and at the end of that game, it doesn't really matter who won or lost but if they played the best they could. What if we, as Christians, cared less about winning and losing this thing called life, and instead worried about "playing" it right?

What if we cheered on others like these kids do, whether they are on our team or not? What if we, like the players lifted each other up when we fail instead of talking about those that messed up? What if we beamed with pride for believers that accomplished something great instead of tearing them down and finding faults in what they did? How much more will our Christian life reflect the life of our Savior?

These kids playing the game of baseball have such a wonderful faith in humanity at such a young age. They don't care about differences they have with the other kids not on their team, they care about the similarities they share with them instead. "And calling to him a child, he put him in the midst of them and said, "Truly, I say to you, unless you turn and become like children, you will never enter the kingdom of heaven. Whoever humbles himself like this child is the greatest in the kingdom of heaven." - Matthew 18:2-4.

Sometimes children can teach us better than we can teach them. All we have to do is step back and look once in a while to see what innocence and faith come from those that have yet to be soured by the world.

Notes:_____
_____
_____
_____
_____

August 18

Followers

Followers. It amazes me how many people from around the world follow Between Two Trees that I started about ten months ago. It seems to have spread like wildfire over the last couple of weeks. It is humbling to know that people are reading about events that are happening in your own life and can relate to those moments no matter where they live. But this blog is definitely not about the number of followers, but more importantly, about who we are following Jesus Christ.

I've heard it said so many times, "don't be a follower, be a leader!" I have a problem with that statement on a couple of levels. First, in order to be an effective leader, we have had to be a follower at some point in time. Following brings experience. We learn from others what works well and what doesn't work at all. Second, if we all become leaders, who will we have following us? In reality, we are both followers and leaders at the same time. We follow those that are more experienced than we are and we lead those that are less experienced than we are.

Jesus told his disciples, "Follow me." The Apostle Paul told others to, "follow me as I follow Christ". We have to be very careful in who we follow to make sure that we are not led astray. We also have to make sure those that follow us are of the same accord so that they do not cause division.

Who are you following? Is it the wisdom of man or the wisdom of God?

Notes:_____
_____
_____
_____
_____
_____
_____
_____
_____
_____
_____
_____
_____
_____
_____
_____

Nobody

Nobody. The Christian group, Casting Crowns, has an awesome new song out on the radio and the chorus goes like this:

"I'm just a nobody,
Trying to tell everybody,
All about somebody,
Who saved my soul"

That is who we are as Christians; a bunch of nobodies trying to tell the world about Jesus. The story isn't about us, it's about Him. God can, and will, use each of us and our talents to glorify Him by telling others about the saving power of Jesus Christ.

The song lists some of the "nobodies" in the Bible that did great things for God. Abraham was an idol worshiper before God called him. David was just a shepherd boy before God made him king. The disciples were just fishermen and tax collectors before God had them change the world. And Saul was a persecutor before God used him to write most of the New Testament. Just a bunch of nobodies who God used because they surrendered their will to God's.

Maybe you feel like I do some days, insignificant and useless to God's kingdom, but that is the furthest thing from the truth. When we submit ourselves to being nobodies, God can then use us greatly to tell others about the greatest "Somebody" who ever lived. We have to get past the feeling of having to change the world all in one day and just let God use us as He wills for this very day, we are in.

As John the Baptist said, "He must increase, but I must decrease." - John 3:30. Are we doing things for our own glory, or are we looking to glorify God in all that we do? I believe that is a question we should be asking ourselves rather often just to make sure the things we do are being done with the right motives.

Notes:_____

_____
_____
_____
_____
_____
_____
_____
_____
_____
_____

Flat Tire

Flat tire. It's been one of those weeks that everything seems to go wrong and it culminated with a flat tire. The pump in our well died last week, I had a strange load noise my car was making and both of those issues got fixed. But when I got home last night from getting my car fixed, I noticed that one of the tires on my truck was almost completely flat. I only use the truck on weekends to go to the landfill and such, but still, just another issue to deal with after a week full of issues.

Sometimes life gets us down and feeling "deflated" (pun intended), and we feel like we can't get ahead and make our way past what's weighing us down. We can get in a funk and let each new issue pull us further and further into a feeling of hopelessness. We feel that maybe God is punishing us for some reason we do not yet know about. Or we start looking back at our recent actions to see if we can figure out what we've done wrong that God can be punishing us for.

Truth is, God's probably not punishing us for anything, we just live in a fallen world where bad things happen. Well pumps die, cars make noises and tires go flat, not because we did anything wrong, it just happens. But why do we automatically want to respond like we are being punished? Do we see God as this Heavenly Judge just waiting for us to mess up so He can punish us? That is not the God of the Bible. His grace is always abounding for His children. Now don't get me wrong, He will correct His children when they need it, but that's not His ultimate goal.

"And God is able to make all grace abound to you, so that having all sufficiency in all things at all times, you may abound in every good work." - 2 Corinthians 9:8. The grace of God allows us to be able to look at the hard times and battles in our lives and know that we are not being punished for things but that we live in a fallen world where bad things happen to everyone. "For he makes his sun rise on the evil and on the good and sends rain on the just and on the unjust." - Matthew 5:45.

When bad things come, and they will, sometimes many at one time, know that God loves you and He wants what's best for you. Let us not look at every obstacle as punishment from God. Let us look at it as a chance to run to Him and ask Him for grace to get through it.

Notes:_____
_____
_____
_____
_____
_____
_____

August 21

Superheroes

Superheroes. My son loves superheroes. He will pretend he's a different one about every hour. Between Spider-Man, the Hulk and any others he can think of, he has their powers to shoot webs or smash stuff. I've never really been into the whole superhero thing. I think the only superhero movie I have ever seen is the original Batman with Michael Keaton. There seems to be a new superhero movie that comes out every month and I just can't keep up.

What is it with our fascination with superheroes? Is it the unique powers that they possess or is it the fact that we all have a longing to be saved from evil villains? I think it's a bit of both. Who hasn't dreamt of having some unique superpower as a child? Being able to fly, leap tall buildings in a single bound or be bulletproof? It's what childhood memories are made of.

When it comes right down to it though, I think it is that desire to be saved from the evil in this world and have a feeling of safety in our lives. Superheroes deliver both of those in the movies but they don't exist in real life. But God's Word tells us of the greatest "superhero" to ever live. He had extraordinary powers but didn't flaunt them. He knew all things yet kept many of them to Himself. He could escape death but decided not to for our sake. His name is Jesus Christ, the Savior of the world.

"Have this mind among yourselves, which is yours in Christ Jesus, who, though he was in the form of God, did not count equality with God a thing to be grasped, but emptied himself, by taking the form of a servant, being born in the likeness of men. And being found in human form, he humbled himself by becoming obedient to the point of death, even death on a cross. Therefore, God has highly exalted him and bestowed on him the name that is above every name, so that at the name of Jesus every knee should bow, in heaven and on earth and under the earth, and every tongue confess that Jesus Christ is Lord, to the glory of God the Father." - Philippians 2:5-11.

The greatest superhero story ever told is found in the Word of God! He died so that you could be saved and spend eternity in safety like we long to have. Do you know Him? Have you heard of Him? He knows you and wants a relationship with you.

Notes:_____
_____
_____
_____
_____
_____
_____

August 22

Practice

Practice. We had night number three of soccer practice for the three and four year old soccer team. With that age group, it's hard to get them to do much during practice, but we practice anyway and have a lot of fun doing it. We practice getting better even though the steps are little and hard to see, we do it because over time those small steps from practice build upon one another into habits that show progress.

The same thing occurs in our Christian lives. We don't become perfect followers when we accept Christ as our Savior. We have to take small steps by allowing the Holy Spirit to show us where we need improvement and then we practice those things. Over time those small steps build into healthy habits that begin to show themselves to others. We call it "growing in Christ". "Rather, speaking the truth in love, we are to grow up in every way into him who is the head, into Christ, from whom the whole body, joined and held together by every joint with which it is equipped, when each part is working properly, makes the body grow so that it builds itself up in love." - Ephesians 4:15-16.

Many times we believe that we should automatically be good at all aspects of the Christian life when we give our lives to God, but that is not what happens. We are to continue to grow and practice for the rest of our lives. As we become better at some things, there are other areas of our lives that the Holy Spirit will direct us to work on. It's a continuous journey of practice for the rest of our lives.

"Do not neglect the gift you have, which was given you by prophecy when the council of elders laid their hands on you. Practice these things, immerse yourself in them, so that all may see your progress" - 1 Timothy 4:14-15. My son had a meltdown today at practice because he didn't think he was good. It was the third time he practiced soccer, of course he wasn't going to be good yet. We think the same way as Christians, but as Paul told Timothy, "practice these things". Even someone like Timothy needing to continue to practice.

Notes:_____

_____

_____

_____

_____

_____

_____

_____

_____

_____

_____

_____

August 23

Haircuts

Haircut. Me and my little guy went to get haircuts yesterday morning. It was just the two of us going to get all cleaned up and looking sharp. We ended up getting the same style haircut so we could both look "slick" as he put it. When we got done, the two of us complimented each other on how good we looked with our new haircuts. He's come a long way since the first time he sat for a haircut. Now, he just sits there and lets Miss April go to work.

Sometimes we go a long time between haircuts and there is quite a bit of work to be done to get us looking like we once did. Other times we go even though we might not need it because we have an important event coming up that we want to look our best for. Our spiritual lives can sometimes take on the same condition as our haircuts. There are times we may go long stretches without confessing our sins to God and our lives seem empty and out of sorts. And then there are other times when our prayer lives are kept up to date and we feel like we are walking very close with the Lord.

"If we confess our sins, he is faithful and just to forgive us our sins and to cleanse us from all unrighteousness." - 1 John 1:9. For many of us, our prayer lives may be the weakest aspect of our spiritual walk, I know it can be for me. I find it much easier to pray for others than it is to go in prayer and confess my own sins. However, it is important that we keep our sins confessed so that there is no break in fellowship with the Father.

"If we say we have fellowship with him while we walk in darkness, we lie and do not practice the truth. But if we walk in the light, as he is in the light, we have fellowship with one another, and the blood of Jesus his Son cleanses us from all sin." - 1 John 1:6-7.

Notes:_____
_____
_____
_____
_____
_____
_____
_____
_____
_____
_____
_____
_____
_____
_____

Knocking

Knocking. We had a startle at our house last night with an unexpected knock on the door after 9:00. We were sitting in the living room and the kids were getting ready for bed and all of a sudden someone knocked on the side door to the kitchen. My wife and I looked at each other, kind of confused because we don't get many people at our house at any time of the day. I got up and answered the door a little concerned as to who it might be. When I opened the door, there was no one around.

A little confused if we actually heard a knock, I sat back down in the living room when a knock came at the door again. This time I turned on all the outside lights to see if I could see anything before opening the door. There was still nobody out there when I opened the door. Now I knew someone was messing around, but the way the world is today I wasn't sure what their intentions were. So, I got a baseball bat and a flashlight and out the door I went into the night. After a short search, I saw some neighborhood boys running through the woods. Just kids playing pranks. It brought back some of my own childhood memories.

As I thought about the events of last night, the idea of knocking has stuck with me and the words of Christ in the Book of Revelation, "Behold, I stand at the door and knock. If anyone hears my voice and opens the door, I will come into him and eat with him, and he with me." - Revelation 3:20. In the context of the book, He is writing to a church that has become lukewarm and He wants back in. But the same is true for our hearts. When the Holy Spirit speaks to us that we need to accept forgiveness for our sins, Christ is knocking on our hearts wanting us to accept Him in. Only He can forgive us of our sins. Only He can give us peace with the Father.

Is Christ knocking at the door of your heart wanting you to accept Him? "For he says, "In a favorable time I listened to you, and in a day of salvation I have helped you." Behold, now is the favorable time; behold, now is the day of salvation." - 2 Corinthians 6:2. Today is the day of salvation. Have you accepted Him?

Notes:_____
_____
_____
_____
_____
_____
_____
_____
_____
_____
_____
_____

August 25

Not Done with You Yet

Not done with you yet. Have you ever felt like your past has disqualified you from doing work for God? I have, and it's a total lie from the devil. If you are still alive, God has work yet for you to do for His Kingdom. It took a while for me to understand that, but now that I have, I no longer believe the lie that my past holds me back from my present and my future.

There are so many Biblical examples of people that had made mistakes at some point in their lives and God still used them for mighty things to His glory. Abraham was an idol worshiper. Moses was a murderer. Rahab was a prostitute. And I can go on and on all the way through the Bible. The point is that even though we all have a past, some worse than others, God's not done with you yet if you woke up this morning.

"For I know the plans I have for you, declares the LORD, plans for welfare and not for evil, to give you a future and a hope." - Jeremiah 29:11. God loves us even though we have a past. He has plans for us. Plans to give us a future and a hope that can only be found in our Lord and Savior, Jesus Christ. If you feel like you're insignificant, don't believe it. Each one of us has been given a gift from God to use to glorify His name.

"And you were dead in the trespasses and sins in which you once walked, following the course of this world, following the prince of the power of the air, the spirit that is now at work in the sons of disobedience-among whom we all once lived in the passions of our flesh, carrying out the desires of the body and the mind, and were by nature children of wrath, like the rest of mankind. But God, being rich in mercy, because of the great love with which he loved us, even when we were dead in our trespasses, made us alive together with Christ-by grace you have been saved- and raised us up with him and seated us with him in the heavenly places in Christ Jesus, so that in the coming ages he might show the immeasurable riches of his grace in kindness toward us in Christ Jesus. For by grace you have been saved through faith. And this is not your own doing; it is the gift of God, not a result of works, so that no one may boast. For we are his workmanship, created in Christ Jesus for good works, which God prepared beforehand, that we should walk in them." - Ephesians 2:1-10.

Notes:_____
_____
_____
_____
_____
_____
_____
_____
_____
_____
_____

Unity and Harmony

Unity and Harmony. There is very little unity or harmony found in our world today. Everyone seems divided over every single issue across the board. If you disagree with their position, you can no longer be friends, even if you agree on ninety-nine other topics. Division runs deep in our nation, and around the world, on things like politics, religion, race, human life and even sports. But Christianity doesn't seem any different than the rest of the unbelieving world. We have divided ourselves up into different groups and argue if someone believes differently than we do. Not a very good example for the unsaved to watch us bicker among ourselves.

We tend to all believe in the basic tenants of the faith: the big things of the Bible. But it's the minute things that we like to argue about with each other. Things like Bible versions, end times, and baptism timing. All things that don't make much of a difference to our eternal salvation, but things the devil likes to occupy our minds with.

The world is already the enemy of God's children, we should not add fuel to the fire by arguing among ourselves. As outsiders watch us bicker and divide up into different groups, the enemy cheers as we become less and less effective to the lost. How can we be inviting to the unbelieving world if we are so unattractive as we argue with one another? People want to see something different about us than the world they are already living in. They want to see harmony and unity in believers.

"May the God of endurance and encouragement grant you to live in such harmony with one another, in accord with Christ Jesus, that together you may with one voice glorify the God and Father of our Lord Jesus Christ." - Romans 15:5-6.

"Behold, how good and pleasant it is when brothers dwell in unity!" - Psalm 133:1.

"Finally, all of you, have unity of mind, sympathy, brotherly love, a tender heart, and a humble mind. Do not repay evil for evil or reviling for reviling, but on the contrary, bless, for to this you were called, that you may obtain a blessing." - 1 Peter 3:8-9.

If someone is blatantly wrong in their theology, correct them in private, not on social media. If you can't correct them privately, keep your comments to yourself and pray for them. Let us edify one another instead of tearing one another down over trivial things.

Notes:_____
_____
_____
_____
_____

Wrong Place, Wrong Time

Wrong place. Wrong time. Twice! The last two times I have been in the Charlotte airport, I have sat at the same gate waiting for my flight. Both times it has not been the gate my flight was going out of, just an empty gate with all the seats open. So, both times I sat and did some work and sent emails while I waited to go to the gate my flight was leaving from. For the second straight time, at the same exact gate, a service dog decided to stop right in front of that gate and relieve itself right on the floor.

Talk about sitting in the wrong place at the wrong time, how about doing it twice! And they say lightning doesn't strike in the same place twice, but obviously dogs do! I do not think I will be sitting at that gate any longer waiting for my flight and doing work, but could it really happen three times? I'm not going to test it.

It made me think of people in the Bible who happened just to be at the wrong place at the wrong time. My mind automatically went to the story of Jonah and those poor gentlemen that happened to be on the boat with him when the storm came. The storm came because Jonah was running from God and He was trying to get Jonah's attention. Those sailors knew that the storm was a punishment from God even though they didn't know Him personally.

"But the LORD hurled a great wind upon the sea, and there was a mighty tempest on the sea, so that the ship threatened to break up.
Then the mariners were afraid, and each cried out to his god. And they hurled the cargo that was in the ship into the sea to lighten it for them. But Jonah had gone down into the inner part of the ship and had lain down and was fast asleep." - Jonah 1:4-5.

"Then the men were exceedingly afraid and said to him, "What is this that you have done!" For the men knew that he was fleeing from the presence of the LORD, because he had told them." - Jonah 1:10. Who is getting caught in the repercussions of you fleeing from the will of God? Who in your life might be suffering from being in the wrong place at the wrong time because you are not being obedient to God's voice?

Notes:_____
_____
_____
_____
_____
_____
_____
_____
_____
_____

Hungry

Hungry. Ever have those days where you just feel hungry all day? Even after you eat, you still feel like you can eat again a couple hours later. That's been the feeling I've had all day today. I skipped breakfast at the hotel and didn't have anything all the way until lunch, once lunch came around, I ate pretty well. But just two hours later, I was ready for dinner but had to wait.

The there are other days, like on the weekends, where I may go all the way until mid-afternoon before I feel hungry for lunch because I have been working outside in the yard all morning. What makes our bodies have different levels of appetites on different days like that? I'm not a nutritionist so I won't try to answer that question. However, I think the same thing happens to us spiritually too.

I know there are days where prayer happens multiple times throughout the day as I am led by the Holy Spirit, and then there are days where I might go all day without the prompting to pray. Same goes with reading the Bible and subjects to post on this blog. I might get two or three ideas in a day and then some days I struggle to come up with a topic all day and then it just hits me. Why are our appetites for the things of God different on a daily basis?

""Blessed are those who hunger and thirst for righteousness, for they shall be satisfied." - Matthew 5:6. On days where we don't "feel" spiritual, we have to hunger and thirst for God's righteous. We must seek after God even when we don't feel His presence. We must hunger for His Word even when we don't feel like it. Every day is not a day of room service in the Christian life, there are days we have to go and pick it up ourselves.

There is a future day when we will not have to worry about being spiritually hungry anymore, "They shall hunger no more, neither thirst anymore; the sun shall not strike them, nor any scorching heat. For the Lamb in the midst of the throne will be their shepherd, and he will guide them to springs of living water, and God will wipe away every tear from their eyes." - Revelation 7:16-17.

Notes:_____
_____
_____
_____
_____
_____
_____
_____
_____
_____
_____

August 29

Rules

Rules. They are like a fence; some rules are to keep us within certain boundaries and some rules are to keep harmful things out. Sometimes rules protect us from others and sometimes they protect us from ourselves. There are times that we don't always like the rules and there are times we just don't obey them. We disobey them by mistake and we disobey them on purpose.

I disobeyed the rules by mistake (somewhat) today. I was on the plane and the stewardess asked me to stop doing something because it was against the rules. It actually wasn't against the rules they had outlined, but as much as I travel, I didn't want to get on any lists as being a disobedient flier. I didn't actually break the letter of the law, but I broke the spirit of the law.

We do the same thing with God's Law. We know what the spirit of God's Word says, but then we say, "what I'm doing isn't exactly what God's Word says!" And so, we go on breaking God's rules because we feel that God really didn't mean it that way. Or we think we are somehow above the Law of God. Of course, there are some that will say, "we don't live under the Law, we live under grace!" True, but that doesn't allow us to break God's commandments.

"What shall we say then? Are we to continue in sin that grace may abound? By no means! How can we who died to sin still live in it? Do you not know that all of us who have been baptized into Christ Jesus were baptized into his death? We were buried therefore with him by baptism into death, in order that, just as Christ was raised from the dead by the glory of the Father, we too might walk in newness of life." - Romans 6:1-4.

We follow God's commandments, not out of fear of being punished, but out of love for what He did for us through Christ. God's laws, statutes and commandments are just like that fence I mentioned earlier. They are there to protect us from others and from ourselves.

If you want to read a great chapter about God's rules, statues and commandments, take a moment to read through Psalm 119. Read as the psalmist praises God for His law. Let us play by the rules God has established for us, not out of fear, but out of love.

Notes:_____
_____
_____
_____
_____
_____
_____

August 30

House Hunting

House hunting. We spent the evening shopping for a new house. We went and saw three different houses all within about a five mile radius of each other. All three had their good points and all three had their shortcomings. We left the three houses narrowing it down to just two. We are torn between the two that we liked and we are having a tough time picking one we like better than the other.

We have spent the last fifteen years doing major renovations to our current house to get it exactly how we want it, but it's time to move on to something else. It's hard to leave a home that is the first home you bought, the house you brought your bride home to and the house your two children came home to from the hospital. Memories are hard to move away from.

"For everything there is a season, and a time for every matter under heaven: a time to be born, and a time to die; a time to plant, and a time to pluck up what is planted; a time to kill, and a time to heal; a time to break down, and a time to build up; a time to weep, and a time to laugh; a time to mourn, and a time to dance; a time to cast away stones, and a time to gather stones together; a time to embrace, and a time to refrain from embracing; a time to seek, and a time to lose; a time to keep, and a time to cast away; a time to tear, and a time to sew; a time to keep silence, and a time to speak; a time to love, and a time to hate; a time for war, and a time for peace." - Ecclesiastes 3:1-8.

Change happens throughout our lives: relationships, jobs, cities we live and even homes. We never lose the memories we have at the places we've lived, and we always have opportunities to make new memories the places we are going. We have to trust in the mighty hand of God that He will direct our paths and open doors for us to walk through. We have to trust that He will also close doors He does not want us to go through. "In all your ways acknowledge him, and he will make straight your paths." - Proverbs 3:6.

Notes:_____
_____
_____
_____
_____
_____
_____
_____
_____
_____
_____
_____
_____
_____

Bouncy House

Bouncy house. My son had a birthday party he was invited to today for a friend of his he plays soccer with. The party was in an auxiliary gym at a church by our house and when we got to the church there was a bouncy house set up for the kids to play in. My little guy had never been in one before because he had been too intimidated by the amount of kids that were in them other places, we had been that had one. But today there was a smaller number of kids that were his size and he tried it for the first time.

He loved it. He jumped in there and then slid down the slide for the longest time. When the other kids stopped to play other games, he stayed right in there and had the whole bouncy house to himself. When it was time to go, some tears were shed as he had to get out of the bouncy house. I had to assure him that there would be another bouncy house somewhere in his future.

The joy he had today was clearly evident as he bounced and bounced and bounced his little heart out. It's was a joy that he had never experienced before today. It was a joy that we as adults sometimes long for, but we are too old and weigh too much to find it in a bouncy house. That doesn't stop us from looking for joy in the things of this world. But with every new experience, the joy we thought we'd find, disappears like a vapor and we are left looking for joy in the next experience.

The Bible tells us that our joy is not found in the things of this world, but only in Christ Jesus. "Though you have not seen him, you love him. Though you do not now see him, you believe in him and rejoice with joy that is inexpressible and filled with glory, obtaining the outcome of your faith, the salvation of your souls." - 1 Peter 1:8-9.

Joy is different from happiness. Happiness is based upon current happenings, but joy is a feeling that is not dependent on the things that are happening in our lives. Joy is based upon the knowledge of know where our future lies, in Christ.

Notes:_____
_____
_____
_____
_____
_____
_____
_____
_____
_____
_____
_____

September 1

Faith

Faith. We had an awesome sermon today at church about walking on water. Pastor Phillip spoke on Peter being the only disciple that had the faith to step out of the boat and walk on the water to meet Christ amidst the storm. I've been thinking all afternoon about the faith that Peter showed to take that first step. Even though the storm raged all around them and the Savior was doing something they had never seen Him do before, Peter still left the security of the boat and followed Jesus' command to "Come!"

It made me question my own faith and if Christ called out to me to "come", would I go or would I be like the other eleven and stay in the security of the boat? What if Christ called me to go somewhere else in the world to share His message of salvation, would I leave the comfort of my current life and go? I guess the true answer would only come when He calls. We can say we would, but we don't really know until that call actually comes.

Peter showed no hesitation in getting out of the boat. We don't know how far away Christ was from the boat, but it really didn't matter, Peter showed faith in the command of Christ and in the person of Christ. It didn't matter that no one else was going with him or that the storm was swirling all around him, he knew who called. I pray that I have that same faith if Christ calls.

"And Peter answered him, "Lord, if it is you, command me to come to you on the water." He said, "Come." So, Peter got out of the boat and walked on the water and came to Jesus. But when he saw the wind, he was afraid, and beginning to sink he cried out, "Lord, save me." Jesus immediately reached out his hand and took hold of him, saying to him, "O you of little faith, why did you doubt?" And when they got into the boat, the wind ceased. And those in the boat worshiped him, saying, "Truly you are the Son of God.""- Matthew 14:28-33.

Notes:_____
_____
_____
_____
_____
_____
_____
_____
_____
_____
_____
_____
_____
_____

September 2

Labor Day

Labor Day. As Americans celebrate the unofficial end of summer today, there are some people that still had to work today as the rest of us had the day off. Certain professions never get a holiday, some employees may get the day off, but not because of the holiday. I think about our military, our police officers, firefighters, first responders and doctors and nurses, just to name a few.

As I enjoyed the day off from work, it didn't mean I completely had the day off from working. I finished off some work in the yard that I didn't get completed on Saturday and I washed my wife's car for her. I don't think we ever really have a time where there isn't some work, we can be doing. Whether it's in the yard or in the house, work can always be found to do. The Bible instructs is not to be idle, "Slothfulness casts into a deep sleep, and an idle person will suffer hunger." - Proverbs 19:15.

The Bible also instructs us about our work and our labor, "Whatever you do, work heartily, as for the Lord and not for men, knowing that from the Lord you will receive the inheritance as your reward. You are serving the Lord Christ." - Colossians 3:23-24.

And "For even when we were with you, we would give you this command: If anyone is not willing to work, let him not eat. For we hear that some among you walk in idleness, not busy at work, but busybodies. Now such persons we command and encourage in the Lord Jesus Christ to do their work quietly and to earn their own living." - 2 Thessalonians 3:10-12.

God created the first man and woman to work in the Garden of Eden. That work got harder when they sinned and got kicked out of paradise. We labor for the things that we have so that at the end of the day we can say that we received what we worked for.

"And he said to them, "The harvest is plentiful, but the laborers are few. Therefore, pray earnestly to the Lord of the harvest to send out laborers into his harvest.""- Luke 10:2. If we don't have work to do for an employer, we always have work to do for the Lord. The harvest is ready, are we ready to work?

Notes:_____
_____
_____
_____
_____
_____
_____
_____
_____
_____

September 3

Negotiations

Negotiations. As we have started going through the process of buying a new home, the art of the negotiation has become a major aspect of the dance called home buying. Making an offer, having someone else make an offer at the same time, receiving a request to make our best offer, making a new offer and then being requested for something else. I have to be honest; this isn't fun in the least. It is nerve wracking and frustrating at times. But, if we want a new house with more room, it's something we are going to have to wade through.

Negotiating on a house is much different than our everyday negotiating because there is definitely more at stake. We negotiate in different ways every day; we negotiate with our spouses and our kids and we negotiate at work. But, is everything negotiable? The answer to that, in a spiritual sense, is "no".

We are given this life by God to make the most important decision about our eternal life. We have a choice to either accept the death, burial and resurrection of Jesus Christ or deny Him and accept the punishment we deserve instead of accepting that He paid the punishment of our sins. That is what this life comes down to: accept or deny Christ. That decision seals our eternal destination; either heaven or hell.

Many people are under the impression that they will somehow be able to negotiate with God when they stand before Him, making their case as to how good of a person they were. The issue is that their standard of "good" has to stand up to God's standard of "good". "As it is written: "None is righteous, no, not one; no one understands; no one seeks for God. All have turned aside; together they have become worthless; no one does good, not even one."" - Romans 3:10-12.

The Bible says that those who do not accept Christ in this life, will be resurrected to stand before God in judgement. God will judge the works of unsaved men and women. "And I saw the dead, great and small, standing before the throne, and books were opened. Then another book was opened, which is the book of life. And the dead were judged by what was written in the books, according to what they had done." - Revelation 20:12. Everyone's name who is not found in the Lamb's Book of Life will be thrown into the lake of fire.

Notes:_____
_____
_____
_____
_____
_____
_____

Training

Training. We had a day of training at work today that everyone in my department took part in. Some of my coworkers did a portion of the training sessions and then our boss followed up with some additional training. I find it interesting to train on my profession whether that is internal or external in nature. To be able to take a day and learn new techniques and processes that work well for other members of our team and incorporate them into our own practices is so important.

Training spiritually is even more important. When we become Christians, we do not become fully in shape on that very first day. Actually, we will be in training to grow more and more like Christ for the rest of our lives. The Bible gives us so much instruction on training others, like our children, and training ourselves.

"Train up a child in the way he should go; even when he is old, he will not depart from it." - Proverbs 22:6.

"Have nothing to do with irreverent, silly myths. Rather train yourself for godliness; for while bodily training is of some value, godliness is of value in every way, as it holds promise for the present life and also for the life to come." - 1 Timothy 4:7-8.

"For the grace of God has appeared, bringing salvation for all people, training us to renounce ungodliness and worldly passions, and to live self-controlled, upright, and godly lives in the present age, waiting for our blessed hope, the appearing of the glory of our great God and Savior Jesus Christ, who gave himself for us to redeem us from all lawlessness and to purify for himself a people for his own possession who are zealous for good works." - Titus 2:11-14.

What if some of us trained spiritually as much as we train physically? How much of a stronger Christian could we be? Something to think about.

Notes:_____
_____
_____
_____
_____
_____
_____
_____
_____
_____
_____
_____

Hope

Hope. It does more than just float! I was flipping through the channels the other night and saw the movie Hope Floats was on. I stopped and watched it for a few minutes because I hadn't seen it in many years. The main character gets embarrassed by her friend on national television when it's revealed that her friend was having an affair with her husband. She packs up her daughter and heads back to her hometown to start over. There, she meets up with an old friend who helps get her back on her feet and find love.

People use the word "hope" all the time, like I hope it doesn't rain, or I hope I have a better day today than yesterday. We use the word hope like it's a wish, like we are throwing a penny in a wishing well and "hoping" for a dream to come true. But that isn't the hope that the Bible talks about. The world has a "hope so hope" while the Bible projects a "know so hope".

I think about the story of Abraham when he was told in his old age that he and his wife Sarah would have a promised child in which many nations would come from. He could have walked away from that promise and said, "I hope so". However, he walked away from the promise of God with a "know so hope". "In hope he believed against hope, that he should become the father of many nations, as he had been told, 'So shall your offspring be.'" - Romans 4:18. In "hope" (know so hope) he believed against "hope" (hope so hope).

"For in this hope we were saved. Now hope that is seen is not hope. For who hopes for what he sees? But if we hope for what we do not see, we wait for it with patience." - Romans 8:24-25. Our hope is in Jesus Christ and what He has done on the Cross for us. None of were alive to see it, so we believe in faith and put our hope in the promise of His future return. We hope that He will return soon. It's not a "hope so hope" but a "know so hope". We can have that kind of hope in God's Word because of the multitude of examples in which He has made a promise and kept it. That's where our hope comes from.

"For to this end we toil and strive, because we have our hope set on the living God, who is the Savior of all people, especially of those who believe." - 1 Timothy 4:10.

Notes:_____
_____
_____
_____
_____
_____
_____
_____
_____
_____

September 6

Encouragement

Encouragement. It's is so easy to encourage others in their walk, whatever that walk may look like. I know there is a radio station that is promoting being an encourager for the whole month of September. They are asking Christians to try to encourage one other person each day this month. I think that is an awesome idea and shouldn't stop when the month comes to an end. I've tried to increase my encouragement of others over the last few weeks because we all need encouragement along the way.

We should be encouraging other believers in their walk with Christ. We should be encouraging those small business owners who are trying so hard to get their business off the ground or to the next level. We should be encouraging those single moms and dads who are working so hard to raise their children, all on their own, without anyone else's help. There are so many people out there that just needs to know that someone believes in them and sees what they're doing and is willing to offer them a positive word.

Social media has made it so much easier to tear people down and offer our opinions on how they can do something better. We never know all the facts behind someone's struggle in life, so why do we feel our opinions are worth anything to them when they don't ask us for them. What people need is someone to just say, "nice job, I like what you're doing!" It's that simple and it goes a long way.

"Therefore encourage one another and build one another up, just as you are doing." - 1 Thessalonians 5:11.

"That we may be mutually encouraged by each other's faith, both yours and mine." - Romans 1:12

Notes:_____

_____
_____
_____
_____
_____
_____
_____
_____
_____
_____
_____
_____
_____
_____

Inspection

Inspection. One part of this whole home buying process is the inspection of homes. When you buy a new home, you make sure you get someone to perform a home inspection on your behalf to make sure everything is sound with the home. Most of us are not well versed enough to do it on our own so we pay someone else that does inspections for a living to do it for us. We make every effort to make sure that what we are putting an investment into is sound and not going to fall apart when we buy it.

We should put just as much effort into inspecting our own lives like we do our homes. The great thing is that we are experts on our lives because nobody knows us better than we do, except God. We don't have to hire and expert to inspect our lives, God gave us His Word to use to inspect how we are living according to what He seeks from us.

"But if we judged ourselves truly, we would not be judged." - 1 Corinthians 11:31. The Bible instructs is to judge ourselves, to inspect our own lives, so that we can see where we fall short of God's commands and then ask Him to change our hearts to match His. If we judge ourselves in that way, God will not have to pronounce judgement on us later.

"If we say we have no sin, we deceive ourselves, and the truth is not in us." - 1 John 1:8. The worse thing we can do is pretend we have no sin. We are all sinners by nature and God still loves us. We need to be honest with ourselves and inspect our own lives frequently. We don't need to worry about inspecting the lives of others, we have enough to worry about in our own house. Take time to regularly inspect your private lives like you would if you were inspecting a home. Your life is so much more valuable than a home will ever be.

Notes:_____
_____
_____
_____
_____
_____
_____
_____
_____
_____
_____
_____
_____
_____
_____
_____
_____
_____

Life is Short

Life is short. I bet I heard that phrase about a dozen times this week in general conversations with people at work. I've even seen that phrase posted on Facebook a couple of times this week. I agree and I disagree with that statement. I agree that life is short, shorter for some than it is for others. I disagree that life ends after we die. The Bible is clear that life is short, "Come now, you who say, 'Today or tomorrow we will go into such and such a town and spend a year there and trade and make a profit' - yet you do not know what tomorrow will bring. What is your life? For you are a mist that appears for a little time and then vanishes." - James 4:13-14.

What we call "life" is but merely a blip on the entire spectrum of time. We show up, and if we are lucky, live somewhere around 70 years. Some people have their lives cut shorter and even others surpass that amount of time by decades. "The years of our life are seventy, or even by reason of strength eighty; yet their span is but toil and trouble; they are soon gone, and we fly away." - Psalm 90:10.

So what is the purpose of our assumed 70 years on this earth? Without purpose, what are we really here for? We are created by God to glorify and praise Him, but we cannot do that until we find Him through His Son Jesus Christ. It is once we find Him that we begin to know what our purpose is here on His earth. Some people become Christians at a very young age and get to have years of praising Him and doing His work. Others don't find Christ until later on in life.

So, even though life is relatively short, like a vapor, what we do with our lives is eternally important. We will spend eternity in one of two places: Heaven or Hell. The decision we make in this life will have an effect on our eternity. "Whoever believes in the Son has eternal life; whoever does not obey the Son shall not see life, but the wrath of God remains on him." - John 3:36. That wrath of God will last for all of eternity as well. Those that reject Christ do not cease to exist, they spend eternity paying for their rejection of the free gift through the death, burial and resurrection of Jesus Christ. "For God has not destined us for wrath, but to obtain salvation through our Lord Jesus Christ, who died for us so that whether we are awake or asleep we might live with him." - 1 Thessalonians 5:9-10.

Notes:_____
_____
_____
_____
_____
_____
_____
_____
_____

September 9

Chaos

Chaos. When everything in our lives seems to be out of our control, we feel like chaos has taken over. Most of us, by nature, like things to be within our control. We like to have a daily routine; we like to be the ones who are in control of decisions that affect our day or our lives. When we lose that control and daily routine, we feel like our lives have been turned inside out. We tend to over exaggerated and say that our lives are in total and complete chaos. My wife and I have felt that way the last week or so as we are dealing with housing decisions.

However, when you really take a step back from all of the events that we feel are causing chaos in our lives, it's never usually as bad as it may seem. What happens is that we usually want to play God ourselves and have complete control over all things, but in reality, we are never truly in control of most of the things in our lives. We decided to end the chaos by turning all of it over to God and allowing Him to see it through. It was like a thousand pound weight was lifted from the situation.

When we turn our chaos over to God who already knows the outcome, we leave it in the most capable hands possible. He takes our chaos and gives us His peace. "Peace I leave with you; my peace I give to you. Not as the world gives do, I give to you. Let not your hearts be troubled, neither let them be afraid." - John 14:27. The devil wants us to live in constant chaos and to take our eyes off of Jesus and sometimes we all fall for that lie. But the Word says that we should not let our hearts be troubled.

"I have said these things to you, that in me you may have peace. In the world you will have tribulation. But take heart; I have overcome the world." - John 16:33. We will face chaos in this world and in our lives, but Christ has overcome this world so that we can have peace in Him. Have you gone to Him for peace?

Notes:_____

_____

_____

_____

_____

_____

_____

_____

_____

_____

_____

_____

_____

_____

September 10

Character vs. Reputation

Character vs. reputation. Have you ever thought about what the difference is between your character and your reputation? It's something that has been quoted by greats like Thomas Paine (below), John Wooden and Abraham Lincoln. The definition walks a thin line between the two. So, what is the more important trait to have: character or reputation.

As the statement by Thomas Paine says, our character is who we truly are and no one knows us better than God Himself. There is no hiding our true identities from the One who created us. I believe the Bible is also very clear that the spiritual realm, demons and angels, are all around us, just hidden to the human eye. So, it makes sense that the omniscience God and the hidden spiritual world of angels would know who we really are.

Our reputation is based upon what we allow others to see of us. Our true selves are masked from the eyes of others as we sometimes put on a facade in their presence. This is where we get the word "hypocrite" from. It was a mask used in plays to hide the true identities of the actors. We have a tendency to do this in our own lives because we either want to portray something we are not or have to maintain something that people have become accustomed to believing in us.

A former football coach once made the statement, "your character is who you are in the dark." I've also heard it said your character is who you are when no one is around. Both of those pretty much mean the same thing. Our concern should not be about our reputation because people are going to form opinions about us no matter what we do. Our concern should be what God knows about us because we will ultimately answer to Him for our actions. "So, then each of us will give an account of himself to God." - Romans 14:12.

Notes:_____
_____
_____
_____
_____
_____
_____
_____
_____
_____
_____
_____
_____
_____

Hatred

Hatred. That's the word I think of this day each year as we remember the events of 9/11 that occurred on American soil. Hatred that a small group of people had in their hearts for a nation and group of people that they were willing to forcefully take control of four airplanes full of unsuspecting passengers and attack our country. The events that took place in New York City, Washington DC and a field in Pennsylvania, will never leave my memory for the rest of my life. I remember watching the events unfold in my classroom like it was yesterday and calling friends and family back home in NY to check on their safety.

To be completely honest, I had hatred in my heart that day as the news unfolded on who the alleged attackers were, where they came from and what their religious beliefs were. At the point in my life, I was not a Christian. I had no real care in the world about anything surrounding the religious beliefs of anyone. I didn't believe in a God, but I did know that what was done that day was not right, no matter what you believe.

Since that day in history, I have given my life to Christ and see this world and the events that take place with a complete different world view. I see the world through the eyes of God's Holy Word. The hatred I had that day has changed, not that I don't hate what happened, but I don't hate those that are lost. "You have heard that it was said, 'You shall love your neighbor and hate your enemy.' But I say to you, love your enemies and pray for those who persecute you, so that you may be sons of your Father who is in heaven. For he makes his sun rise on the evil and on the good and sends rain on the just and on the unjust." - Matthew 5:43-45.

"For everyone who does wicked things hates the light and does not come to the light, lest his works should be exposed. But whoever does what is true comes to the light, so that it may be clearly seen that his works have been carried out in God." - John 3:20-21.

Notes:_____
_____
_____
_____
_____
_____
_____
_____
_____
_____
_____
_____
_____

Love and Unity

Love and unity. As much hatred as I had for the events of 9/11, they were changed the next day by the response of love and unity by my fellow Americans on 9/12. People made their way to the destruction to look for survivors and try to help the first responders. Others lined up at blood banks to donate blood for the wounded and injured. Politicians no longer cared what party they were from as they stood united on the Capitol steps. American flags flew from every location: house, bridges and anywhere else a place could be found. 9/12 was a great day in American history. What happened?

That feeling slowly faded over time as people went back to their normal lives and slowly the news stopped covering the event 24/7. People slowly went back to the divide we find our country in today. We are divided by politics, race, gender, sexual orientation and any other grouping you want to add in there. We are no longer just "Americans" we have some hyphenated word before it. The church is not immune from the same division. We divide ourselves up under the names Lutheran, Catholic, Presbyterian, Baptist and on and on, not daring to set foot in a church of another denomination. What happened?

This isn't how the church started. "And they devoted themselves to the apostles' teaching and the fellowship, to the breaking of bread and the prayers. And awe came upon every soul, and many wonders and signs were being done through the apostles. And all who believed were together and had all things in common. And they were selling their possessions and belongings and distributing the proceeds to all, as any had need. And day by day, attending the temple together and breaking bread in their homes, they received their food with glad and generous hearts,
praising God and having favor with all the people. And the Lord added to their number day by day those who were being saved." - Acts 2:42-47. Time has caused a division in God's Holy Church.

I long for the love and unity in our country on 9/12 to return, but I don't believe it will happen before the return of Christ. Let us, as Christians, not be the reason for the division we find in the country. Christ gave us a simple command, "And he answered, 'You shall love the Lord your God with all your heart and with all your soul and with all your strength and with all your mind, and your neighbor as yourself.'" - Luke 10:27.

Notes:_____
_____
_____
_____
_____
_____
_____

September 13

Comfortable

Comfortable. We all like to be comfortable, whether it's the clothes we are wearing, or a big oversized chair we get to sit in or maybe snuggled up under the covers in the morning not wanting to get out of bed. By nature, we like to be comfortable in bigger life events too. We like the comfort of our jobs, our relationships and where we live. When something disrupts that comfort, we become uneasy about life.

One of my fellow project managers at work celebrated his last day with our company today. He really pushed himself out of his comfort zone. I know the feeling of changing jobs and how uncomfortable that is, but he is changing jobs, changing the industry he works in and changing states. He took a new job that will move him and his family from the southeast to the Great Lakes area. Now that is a comfort zone change.

Why would we rather stay in our comfort zone instead of moving on to something bigger and better, and maybe something God is directing us too? Because we are just like the Israelites when they had fled Egypt and were wandering in the wilderness - we want to go back to the known routine (even if it is a worse situation). "Now the rabble that was among them had a strong craving. And the people of Israel also wept again and said, 'Oh that we had meat to eat! We remember the fish we ate in Egypt that cost nothing, the cucumbers, the melons, the leeks, the onions, and the garlic. But now our strength is dried up, and there is nothing at all but this manna to look at.'" - Numbers 11:4-6.

They were slaves in Egypt, being worked to death, but all they can think of was how good they thought they had it. We tend to overlook the possible ruts we've gotten ourselves into and just focus on the things we think are good. They may be good things, but God may have better things ahead for us if we just give them up. The promise land was Israel's final destination with a land flowing with milk and honey, but Israel wanted to go back. We do the same thing, when times get hard leaving our comfort zone, we want to go back to what we felt was comfortable.

Has God been pushing you out is your comfort zone but you want to stay or maybe even go back? God has something better for you on the other side of the wilderness. Trust Him in the journey and the promise, "I will never leave you nor forsake you." - Hebrews 13:5b.

Notes:_____
_____
_____
_____
_____
_____

Networking

Networking. With the rise of social media in the last decade or so, staying in touch with old friends and making new "friends" has become easier than it has ever been. Sites like Facebook, Instagram, LinkedIn and so many others allows us to network with people for many different reasons. We can connect with people from all over the world to share common interests, to make business connections or just to build up our following.

Before the internet era came on the scene, you used to have to meet people face-to-face and trade business cards or write your contact information on a napkin. Now it's only a click away and an acceptance and you're networking. Although how we go about networking has changed in the past decade, the idea of networking has been around for ages.

As I look at the Bible, I think one of the best networkers was the Apostle Paul. I have read the he mentions over 75 different people in his letters that were sent to the various churches. He frequently sent greeting to those he had met on past trips or people he had met somewhere along his journeys that were now relocated. In the letter to the Romans, he mentions the names of 27 different people alone in the last chapter. This was a church Paul had never visited and they only knew him by name, so he uses the end of his letter to make connections with those he did not know through those he did.

Although we will not find the word "networking" anywhere in the Bible, it doesn't mean that it didn't occur. Paul used the people he knew to bridge relationships to the people he didn't know so that he could prepare them for the message he was about to deliver. When we network with people, is it for our benefit or the benefit of sharing the Gospel of Jesus Christ?

"I planted, Apollos watered, but God gave the growth. So, neither he who plants nor he who waters is anything, but only God who gives the growth. He who plants and he who waters are one, and each will receive his wages according to his labor. For we are God's fellow workers. You are God's field, God's building." - 1 Corinthians 3:6-9.

Notes:_____

_____
_____
_____
_____
_____
_____
_____
_____
_____
_____

Mess

Mess. Last night my wife made chocolate brownies and iced them with some homemade chocolate icing. I have to say they are one of my favorite deserts. My little guy likes them pretty well too. While we were all doing something, my little guy decided he was going to help himself to the brownies but just focus on the icing part. When I caught him in the kitchen, his face, his hands and his pajama shirt was absolutely covered in chocolate icing. Down the entire length of the brownies were his finger marks where he ran his fingers to get the icing off. He was a mess.

After he got a little of the "what-for" for being disobedient for getting into the brownies he was told to stay out of, we cleaned him up from the chocolate explosion all over his face, hands and clothes. He was back to where he was before he started; the brownies: not so much. It made me think of the story of the prodigal son found in Luke 15. A young man that found himself and his life in a total mess. The Bible says that he reached a point where he finally "came to himself". He realized how bad it had become and he needed to turn back to where he once was.

I find the most interesting part of that story is that he did not say, "I need to find a job, get myself back on my feet and cleaned up, and then I'll go back to my father." Instead, he said, "I'm a mess, my father is my only way out and I'm going back just as I am: smelling like pig slop, dirty and with nothing to offer." I hear so many people say that as soon as they get their life straightened out, they'll come back to church or accept Christ. Christ wants you as the mess you are. "Come to me, all who labor and are heavy laden, and I will give you rest. Take my yoke upon you, and learn from me, for I am gentle and lowly in heart, and you will find rest for your souls. For my yoke is easy, and my burden is light." - Matthew 11:28-30.

Just like the father of the prodigal son who didn't care that his some was filthy and smelled like pigs, he took his son back just as he was. God doesn't want you to clean yourself up before coming to Him, He just wants you to "come to yourself" and turn back to Him. He will clean you up just like the prodigal's father did when he returned.

Notes:_____
_____
_____
_____
_____
_____
_____
_____
_____
_____
_____

September 16

Tomorrow

Tomorrow. Why do we put so much faith in tomorrow? Why do we put of things we should do today and things we should say today off until tomorrow? What's so special about tomorrow that we have to leave such important tasks for just one day? I don't know about you, but I'm guilty of depending on tomorrow way too much. Whether it's work related or personal, tomorrow seems to be our best friend. What happens if tomorrow doesn't come?

The Bible makes it very clear that we are not promised another tomorrow, "Come now, you who say, 'Today or tomorrow we will go into such and such a town and spend a year there and trade and make a profit' - yet you do not know what tomorrow will bring. What is your life? For you are a mist that appears for a little time and then vanishes." - James 4:13-14. I think about those that will go to bed tonight with plans of doing something important tomorrow yet will not wake up to see it through.

Life is precious, life short, and life is unpromised. Our lives could end at any time, either by death or the Lord's return (I pray it's the second one). We should take better advantage of today; to do and say the things we promise we'll do tomorrow. "Do not boast about tomorrow, for you do not know what a day may bring." - Proverbs 27:1. Is there something you should do today before it's too late? Is there something you should tell someone today before it's too late? Only you can answer that.

Notes:_____
_____
_____
_____
_____
_____
_____
_____
_____
_____
_____
_____
_____
_____
_____
_____
_____
_____
_____
_____
_____

September 17

Yesterday

Yesterday. Yesterday I posted about tomorrow and today I'm posting about yesterday, are you confused yet? The Beatles had a big hit called "Yesterday" and a movie by the same name was even made recently. Yesterday can be a two-edged sword; the memories of yesterday can haunt us, but the lessons from yesterday can guide us. Our yesterday's make up who we are today. However, we cannot spend too much time in yesterday or else it could have an adverse effect on our today.

Some of you might be a lot like me having some things in our yesterday that we are not very proud of. You may be struggling with the loss of a loved one that keeps you in yesterday and makes today feel insurmountable, and tomorrow something you can't even face. There is nothing we can really do about yesterday; it's gone and can't be recovered. But we can take the lessons of yesterday and apply them to what we are going through today.

I'm reminded of what the Apostle Paul told the believers in Philippi, "Brothers, I do not consider that I have made it my own. But one thing I do: forgetting what lies behind and straining forward to what lies ahead, I press on toward the goal for the prize of the upward call of God in Christ Jesus." - Philippians 3:13-14. If anyone had a past, they would like to forget, it was Paul, the approver of the death of Stephen.

Brothers and sisters, is there something in your yesterday that is holding you back? Something you believe God can never forgive you for. Don't believe the lies of Satan, God is able and willing to forgive you of any sins from yesterday, all you have to do is ask. Forget what is behind you and strive on towards the goal that is set before you.

Notes:_____
_____
_____
_____
_____
_____
_____
_____
_____
_____
_____
_____
_____
_____
_____
_____
_____
_____

Speechless

Speechless. Ever had a moment where something was said or something happened that completely left you speechless? I was on a conference call this morning and someone asked a question of one of my colleagues, who is never short on words, and there was absolute silence on the line as we waited for him to answer. At first, we thought maybe he was on mute and forgot to take it off when he started talking, but after a few seconds we knew that wasn't it. After a couple of jokes about him being left speechless, we realized he must have lost connection and dropped of the call. Within a few moments he had dialed back in and we were on our way again.

That brief little moment of silence and the thought of being speechless made me think about that moment when our eyes will get to see Christ. There are examples of Biblical men and women seeing God, Christ and angels, where that event left them completely speechless. I think of the men traveling with Saul on the road to Damascus, as they heard a voice but saw no one and it left them speechless (Acts 9:3-7).

There will be two groups of people that are speechless on that day they stand before God. There will by those that have accepted Christ as their Savior and they will stand there speechless and in awe at what Christ had done for them, how He took their place in paying for the punishment of their sins. There will also be a group that stand speechless before God as they will have no argument for the punishment they will receive. They will understand that they missed their chance at salvation here on earth and there are no arguments or good works that will gain them entry in Heaven. They will stand speechless and condemned.

I don't know which group those who are reading this post will be in, but I pray that we will all be in the group that is speechless at what Christ has done for us. If you don't know what group you will be in, repent of your sins and accept Jesus Christ as your Savior by faith. Admit you are a sinner in need of a Savior and that the only way to a relationship with God is by accepting what Christ did in your place by taking the penalty for your sins on the Cross at Calvary. Contact me if you have questions or need to know more. I'd be glad to help you understand your need for Jesus.

Notes:_____

_____

_____

_____

_____

_____

_____

_____

Risks

Risks. Are you a risk taker? Do you see something that looks exciting and just go for it instead of thinking it through and analyzing all the pros and cons? I was driving to work this morning in the normal amount of traffic and all of a sudden, this guy on a motorcycle comes flying through traffic like we were all standing still. He was going between cars, passing on entrance ramps and weaving between lanes like he was in some sort of race. I thought to myself, "this kid is going to get killed if someone changes lanes and don't see him". He was taking some terrible risks with his life.

Most of us probably would never participate in something as risky as what this guy was doing, but we all take different levels of risks through your lives. What we consider risky may not be risky at all to someone else, we all see risk differently based upon the possible outcome. There are people that over analyze everything and will never take a risk in their lives. There are other people that won't think twice about doing something and just go, worrying about the consequences later.

There are times in our lives when God leads us to take risks, or have faith, that what He is leading us to do is what is best for us. We may fully trust God and just go for it, or we may over analyze and miss out on the blessings of God. Not all risks are from God, it is our job, through the Holy Spirit, to make sure that what we are being asked to risk is truly from God. "Beloved, do not believe every spirit, but test the spirits to see whether they are from God, for many false prophets have gone out into the world." - 1 John 4:1.

God may ask you to witness to someone while you are standing in line waiting for a coffee. That may be risky for some people because they are shy. God may ask you to leave a profession and go into the ministry. That may be risky for some people because they have worked hard for the job they have. God may ask you to leave the country and become a missionary in another part of the world. That may be risky for some people because all their family and friends are here. Risk varies from person to person.

Know this, God will not ask you to take a risk that He has not already planned out for you ahead of time. He wants you to listen and obey in faith and take the risk to show others His glory.

Notes:_____
_____
_____
_____
_____
_____
_____

September 20

Voicemail

Voicemail. Does anyone still leave messages on voicemail anymore? If you call someone and they do not answer, do you leave a message or just hang up? I was trying to call a company today to make some changes to my account and the call went all the way to voicemail the first three times I called. I didn't leave a message because I didn't know if it would be checked or not, so I just kept calling back until they answered. I finally got through on the fourth try and made the changes that needed to be made.

Why are we hesitant to leave a voicemail when someone doesn't answer our call? Is it because we don't know if our voicemail will ever be heard and we will have to call back again anyway? It made me think of our prayer life as Christians. When we pray, do we have the fear that maybe God is not listening and will not answer our prayers fast enough, so we keep calling back until we get an answer? God hears our prayers if we are in fellowship with Him and if our request aligns with His will. "And this is the confidence that we have toward him, that if we ask anything according to his will, he hears us. And if we know that he hears us in whatever we ask, we know that we have the requests that we have asked of him." - 1 John 5:14-15.

Our fellowship with God is strengthened through our prayer life with Him. First, by repenting and asking for forgiveness of our sin. Second, by our seeking His will in our life instead of seeking to align God's will with our desires. Finally, our relationship with God is strengthened when we go to Him in prayer for the needs of others before ourselves. "You also must help us by prayer, so that many will give thanks on our behalf for the blessing granted us through the prayers of many." - 2 Corinthians 1:11.

God does not have a voicemail, He hears every one of our prayers as Christians if we go to Him with a clean heart and by faith. "And whatever you ask in prayer, you will receive, if you have faith." - Matthew 21:22.

Notes:_____
_____
_____
_____
_____
_____
_____
_____
_____
_____
_____
_____
_____

September 21

Doubt

Doubt. It's hard to believe everything you hear and read in this day and age, especially if it's on the news or social media. Yet, so many people are so quick to share stories that come out without giving it a chance to reveal all the evidence of the event. How many recent articles have had to be retracted because what was reported was not the full truth? It makes it very hard not to doubt almost every story that comes out anymore.

We all have different levels of doubt during the course of our lives. Even as Christians, we may go through seasons of doubt about our own faith and what we believe. Sometimes we are faced with difficulties in our lives that cause us to doubt if God really is who He says He is. We may come across questions that we cannot explain that may cause us to doubt what we believe. Doubt is a natural occurrence when we have to live by faith and not by sight.

The Word of God has been doubted for centuries. Even one of Jesus' own disciples had an issue with doubt, and he was living in the very presence of the Savior. How much easier is it for us to have doubts living almost two millennia removed from Christ walking this earth? I don't think doubt is something only felt by non-believers. I think it is something even we as Christians face at some point during our lives.

But what about those that doubt the truth of the Bible, can their doubt be overcome by the Holy Spirit? Yes, because I am living proof of that. Almost weekly, a new story comes out confirming the accuracy of God's Holy Word. New evidence is found about locations in the Bible that seemed to never have existed, only to be discovered by archeologists during their digs. Biblical leaders who have been questioned as to whether they have even lived or not have been confirmed in recent years. All things that help erase doubt that what the Biblical writers wrote is true.

"They will say, 'Where is the promise of his coming? For ever since the fathers fell asleep, all things are continuing as they were from the beginning of creation.' For they deliberately overlook this fact, that the heavens existed long ago, and the earth was formed out of water and through water by the word of God,
and that by means of these the world that then existed was deluged with water and perished. But by the same word the heavens and earth that now exist are stored up for fire, being kept until the day of judgment and destruction of the ungodly." - 2 Peter 3:4-7.

Notes:_____
_____
_____
_____
_____

Hide and Seek

Hide and seek. That was always a staple game growing up in our neighborhood, except we didn't call it hide and seek, we called it "ghost in the graveyard". It's the opposite of hide and seek. Instead of one person counting and everyone else going to hide, one person hid and the rest of the kids tried to find them. We used to have about 25 kids playing in our neighborhood each night during the summer and one game could last all the way until it was time to go home.

The game sort of went like this: one person would hide somewhere in the neighborhood and the rest of the kids would go looking for them. There was a set location that was considered home base. If one of the searchers saw the person hiding, they would yell "ghost in the graveyard" and everyone would run back to home base trying not to get tagged. As you could imagine, there were lots of false alarm calls and the group would have to start all over. It's some of the best memories I have growing up in my neighborhood as a kid.

We try to play hide and seek with God sometimes in our lives too. Definitely before we became Christians and even sometimes after we have. It is nothing new for God, and there is never a time we can actually hide from Him. Adam and Eve tried it in the Garden and were unsuccessful. "And they heard the sound of the LORD God walking in the garden in the cool of the day, and the man and his wife hid themselves from the presence of the LORD God among the trees of the garden. But the LORD God called to the man and said to him, "Where are you?" And he said, "I heard the sound of you in the garden, and I was afraid, because I was naked, and I hid myself." - Genesis 3:8-10. God didn't ask Adam where he was because He didn't know, He asked so that Adam would admit he was hiding because of his sin.

I remember how hard I used to seek after those that were hiding somewhere in my neighborhood. God wants us to seek Him with just as much diligence. "I love those who love me, and those who seek me diligently find me. " - Proverbs 8:17. We seek after God in our prayer lives, we seek after Him by studying His Word and we seek after Him by being around other likeminded people. "But seek first the kingdom of God and his righteousness, and all these things will be added to you." - Matthew 6:33.

Notes:_____
_____
_____
_____
_____
_____
_____
_____
_____

September 23

Appointments

Appointments. Our calendars are filled with appointments. We have work appointments for meetings and conference calls, we have personal appointments for sports practices and date nights, and we may have church appointments around committees we may be on. One thing is for sure, our calendars are full in comparison to what they were 50 years ago. But, do we make time for unscheduled appointments? Appointments set up by God for us to be a part of: Divine appointments!

I remember, pretty clearly, one such occasion in my life about fifteen years, or so, ago. I was sitting in a parking lot waiting for the time of my next scheduled appointment and someone came up to the side of my car asking if I could spare some money for them to get something to eat. I was sitting with the window down because it was the middle of summer, so he didn't have to knock. He startled me a bit because I didn't see him coming. As was normal, I didn't have any cash on me because I never carry cash. I told him that I couldn't help him because I didn't have anything to give. He said "thanks" and walked away.

As he left, I could feel the Holy Spirit convict me that I had not done what I needed to do during that divine appointment. I quickly thought to myself, "I have time before my appointment. I can drive him somewhere and get him something to eat." I got out of my car to flag him down and he was nowhere to be seen. It had only been 10 seconds at the longest; there was no way he got out of the parking lot that fast because I was parked squarely in the middle. I stood there looking around the entire parking lot for him, but he was gone! Instantly, the following verse popped into my head, "Do not neglect to show hospitality to strangers, for thereby some have entertained angels unawares." - Hebrews 13:2.

The rest of that day, my head raced through scenarios of what I could have done differently, so that I would never allow something like that to happen again. "The steps of a man are established by the LORD, when he delights in his way" - Psalm 37:23. I don't know if God established the steps of that man to my car that day to test my faithfulness to the Word of God, but I know I failed Him, and that stranger. I am prepared for the next time that ever happens to me. Have you ever had a divine appointment with someone and not know it until it had passed?

Notes:_____
_____
_____
_____
_____
_____
_____

Praise

Praise. We all like to be praised, to some extent, for the good things we have accomplished. Whether it's at work, or on the athletic field or even within our own home by our spouse, we have a need to be praised and acknowledged. We have taken the idea of praise to a somewhat dangerous place by praising people for every little thing that they do. We see that in parents praising their children for doing something that should be expected of them. We give out participation trophies to make sure that no one's feeling are hurt. Are we over-praising this generation of people today?

There is nothing wrong with praising those that deserve it, those that have gone above and beyond expectations in what they accomplished. But, with that praise, we also have to make sure that people aren't put on a pedestal and worshipped. Movie stars, athletes, singers and politicians should never be worshipped, that belongs to God, and God alone. We can praise those groups of people if they are deserving of praise, but never worship them. We will be thoroughly disappointed when they fall off of that pedestal, we, as a society or individual, put them on.

Praise belongs to God because He is worthy of our praise. "I will give to the LORD the thanks due to his righteousness, and I will sing praise to the name of the LORD, the Most High." - Psalm 7:17. "I call upon the LORD, who is worthy to be praised, and I am saved from my enemies." - Psalm 18:3. God offered up His only Son to save His creation from paying the punishment of their own sins, that is praise-worthy.

"Praise the LORD! Praise God in his sanctuary; praise him in his mighty heavens! Praise him for his mighty deeds; praise him according to his excellent greatness! Praise him with trumpet sound; praise him with lute and harp!
Praise him with tambourine and dance; praise him with strings and pipe! Praise him with sounding cymbals; praise him with loud clashing cymbals! Let everything that has breath praise the LORD! Praise the LORD!" - Psalms 150.

Notes:_____

_____
_____
_____
_____
_____
_____
_____
_____
_____
_____
_____

September 25

Drive Thru

Drive thru. As I was making my way through two different drive-thru windows for dinner tonight I thought about all the options we have for fast food. As I pulled up to the menu at the first stop, I looked at how many different options there were to choose from. I pulled up to the second establishment and their menu had just as many options as the first. You have options to order just single items or if you were real hungry you could make it a meal, and if you were starving you could super-size it!

It got me thinking about how we sometimes like to pick and choose what we follow in the Bible based upon how we feel we want to live our lives. We pick this and say, "we'll, that's not a problem for me to follow, so I guess I'll follow that one". But when God's Word pierces our hearts about some sin in our lives, we like to say, "that was meant for the people of that time and it doesn't mean anything in the society we live in today". The Bible is not a drive-thru menu that we can pick and choose what parts of it we want to follow and which ones we don't. True, some of the Bible was written for a specific time and to a specific people that were under the Law.

"For the word of God is living and active, sharper than any two-edged sword, piercing to the division of soul and of spirit, of joints and of marrow, and discerning the thoughts and intentions of the heart." - Hebrews 4:12. We live under the grace of God, but that does not give us the right to sin however we want to. If we read our Bibles, God will stick His finger right to the very heart of our sin and point it out to us. Many people stay away from God's Word just for that very reason.

"What shall we say then? Are we to continue in sin that grace may abound? By no means! How can we who died to sin still live in it? Do you not know that all of us who have been baptized into Christ Jesus were baptized into his death? We were buried therefore with him by baptism into death, in order that, just as Christ was raised from the dead by the glory of the Father, we too might walk in newness of life." - Romans 6:1-4.

Our society lives in this drive-thru world of picking and choosing what moral guidelines they want to follow, but we've been called out to be different than society. Do our lives show that we are different? Do our words show that we have a unique moral standard? Our lives and decisions should be based upon the Word of God, not our opinions and feelings.

Notes:_____
_____
_____
_____
_____
_____

Bus Stop

Bus stop. Some mornings, on my way to work, if I leave a few minutes late, I get stuck behind a school bus starting its morning route. I live in a rural area that doesn't have many places to pass because most of the roads are very windy. Also, because it is a rural area, the kids don't all meet at a common bus stop, the bus stops out in front of each house that has a student. So, as you can imagine, there are frequent stops along the route.

I noticed something this morning as I waited behind the bus at each stop, the younger the kid, the more excited they were to get on the bus. I watched as little ones, probably first or second graders, came running from the front porch and down the driveway (some went right through the lawn) and right up the steps of the waiting bus. You could tell they were excited to get to school.

Then, on the other hand, came the fifth and sixth graders, not so happy to be making their way to school. The bus came to a stop and there was no one to be seen for what felt like an eternity, and then all of a sudden, out came the student from the front door walking as slow as they possibly could as all of the cars behind the bus just had to sit there. You could tell by their body language that they were nowhere near as excited as the little ones.

I remember when I first became a Christian, there was such an excitement inside of me to learn and to study. I remember getting a copy of Our Daily Bread and using it every day. I had started halfway through the three month period that it covers, so I backtracked to make sure I caught up. I had such a thirst for all things Christ. I was just like that little first or second grader excited to get on that school bus.

Now I find myself, at times, more like that sixth grader and not always as excited about all things Jesus. Don't get me wrong, I love my Savior, but my excitement isn't the same as it once was. I'm sure some of you can relate, but some of you might be new to Christianity and still have that excitement - awesome! The Apostle John, in Revelation had a message from Jesus to the church in Ephesus, "But I have this against you, that you have abandoned the love you had at first. Remember therefore from where you have fallen; repent and do the works you did at first. If not, I will come to you and remove your lampstand from its place, unless you repent." - Revelation 2:4-5. I have to remind myself at times to remember that first love I had when Christ was new and exciting to me and return to that feeling once again. Have you ever experienced that same thing?

Notes:_____
_____
_____
_____
_____

September 27

Light Bulb

Light bulb. How many jokes are there out there about how many people it takes to change a light bulb? My guess is that there are thousands, all with the same premise: that there is nothing easier than changing a light bulb. I was changing out some old light bulbs tonight. Sounds easy for an adult to do right? Not if you drop one trying to get it out and it hits the bathroom sink faucet below it and shatters into a million bazillion pieces.

Not a big deal if I wasn't standing in the bathroom with bare feet now surrounded by broken glass shards. So, I had to carefully tip-toe my way out of the bathroom, making sure I didn't step on any tiny pieces. My little guy came running to see what that big noise was and I had to fend him off from running into the bathroom with his bare feet.

The funny things is, all the light bulbs worked, they just didn't match one another and I wanted to fix that. I set in to cleaning up all the glass pieces and running the small handheld vacuum over the entire area to make sure I got it all. Once I got it all cleaned up, I thought to myself, "why was I so intent in replacing light bulbs that worked with more light bulbs that worked"? I guess because I wanted all the bulbs to match.

I think we all like things to match, whether it's light bulbs or even our socks (maybe). We like order in our world. But do our lives match what we proclaim to be? Do our words match what we profess to believe? God wants our lives to match our hearts. If we profess to know and love Him, He wants our actions to show that we do. God likes things to match as well.

"They profess to know God, but they deny him by their works. They are detestable, disobedient, unfit for any good work." - Titus 1:16. God does not want empty professions that do not match our works. To Him that is detestable. "If we say we have fellowship with him while we walk in darkness, we lie and do not practice the truth." - 1 John 1:6. What we say and what we do are two different things and it is usually the reason unbelievers call Christians "hypocrites".

Do you match? Like all the light bulbs having to match in my bathroom, God wants our profession of Him to match our works. How do those two match up in your life? Do they match, or not quite? Would people be surprised you are a Christian because they don't see it in your life?

Notes:_____
_____
_____
_____
_____
_____

September 28

Stressed

Stressed. That has been our situation over the last forty-eight hours or so. We listed our house for sale late Monday night. Had three showings on Tuesday and three more on Wednesday. That was followed by two more on Thursday. Around lunch time Thursday we got our first offer on the house which we accepted Thursday evening. So, we spent today looking at house to buy so that we cannot go homeless for too long. We found one today and made an offer of our own, now we are just awaiting an answer from the homeowner. Stressed!!!!

It's natural to go through stressful situations, but as Christians, we should not stay in that state for very long. My wife and I have been in constant prayer this entire week. First, that God would send the right person to our house, someone that would fall in love with it and make and offer; prayers answered. Praise God! Second, that we would find a house that we would fall in love with that would meet our family's needs and be in our price range; again, prayers answered. Praise God!

Now our prayers continue, that our house will go through all of the due diligence and we can close at the end of October. Also, that our offer on our house will be accepted and it, too, will go through without issues. I know that God is in control of the entire thing and if something happens that we aren't praying for, it's because He knows something that we do not. We trust that what He does is what is best for His children.

"Come to me, all who labor and are heavy laden, and I will give you rest." - Matthew 11:28.

"Casting all your anxieties on him, because he cares for you." - 1 Peter 5:7.

"If you then, who are evil, know how to give good gifts to your children, how much more will your Father who is in heaven give good things to those who ask him!" - Matthew 7:11.

I know that God hears our prayers and answers those that are according to His will. We will continue to pray for God's guidance in all of these things dealing with our home. I will praise Him no matter the outcome because He is worthy to be praised!

Notes:_____
_____
_____
_____
_____
_____
_____
_____

September 29

Bicycle Race

Bicycle race. This past weekend there was a bicycle race that took place along most of the back roads of our little North Carolina county. There were hundreds of riders dressed in their team jerseys racing across the countryside. We had an appointment Saturday morning and didn't realize the race was taking place, so we got caught behind all of these racers as we were trying to make our way there. We had to drive really slow behind large groups of riders until there was a safe area to pass them using the opposite lane. As you can imagine, it took us a lot longer to get to our destination than originally planned.

It was an extreme test of patience as we drove only 5 miles per hour at times waiting to get around them. There were differently colored signs all along the roadsides showing different routes that the riders were to take to complete the race. We weren't sure if the different colors represented different laps or if they represented different courses for certain groups. The race took place over two days: Saturday and Sunday. I'm not sure who ended up winning the race but I'm sure someone is celebrating this evening for finishing first.

It got me thinking about what the Apostle Paul wrote to the Corinthians, "Do you not know that in a race all the runners run, but only one receives the prize? So, run that you may obtain it. Every athlete exercises self-control in all things. They do it to receive a perishable wreath, but we can imperishable." ~ 1 Corinthians 9:24-25. All of those bicyclists left off Saturday morning with the hopes of winning the race, but by Sunday only one of them realized that dream. I'm sure whoever won received some sort of prize, whether it was a trophy or some other prize.

Years from now that trophy or prize will become dusty and old, no longer having the luster it had when they received it today. We have an eternal prize waiting for us, as Christians, one day in heaven; one that will never lose its luster. "Do not lay up for yourselves treasures on earth, where moth and rust destroy and where thieves break in and steal, but lay up for yourselves treasures in heaven, where neither moth nor rust destroys and where thieves do not break in and steal. For where your treasure is, there your heart will be also." ~ Matthew 6:19-21.

Notes:_____

_____
_____
_____
_____
_____
_____
_____
_____

Library Books

Library books. My family made a trip to the local library this morning to pick out some new books. When I got home from work this evening, my little guy had to show me his eight new library books. Almost all of them centered around "Fall" and the sights and sounds and smells that surround it. After dinner was over, we climbed into the recliner and read all eight of them. It was so awesome just to sit there and have him holding onto my arm listening to me read to him. It's those little things that make my day.

I heard on the radio this morning that recent studies show that we spend a total of thirty-seven minutes a day in what we would consider quality time with our family. THIRTY-SEVEN MINUTES!!!! It didn't say what actually constituted "quality time", but I would assume that it would be time in meaningful activities that don't involve technology of any sort. I have to admit, and I bet we all can to some extent, that I have been guilty of this myself.

If we only spend thirty-seven minutes of quality time with our family, how much quality time do we spend with our Heavenly Father throughout the day? I have to admit, once again, it's not as much as it should be. God wants us to communicate with Him through everything we do. He wants to be the center of all that we do. He wants us to talk to Him not only as His friend, but as our Father. "Rejoice in hope, be patient in tribulation, be constant in prayer." ~ Romans 12:12.

"Do not be anxious about anything, but in everything by prayer and supplication with thanksgiving let your requests be made known to God." - Philippians 4:6. God longs for you to come to Him with your prayers. Even though He knows all things about you, He still wants you to seek Him in all things. How is your quality time with your family? Better yet, how is your quality time with God?

Notes:_____
_____
_____
_____
_____
_____
_____
_____
_____
_____
_____
_____
_____
_____

October 1

Stain

Stain. With us selling our house, we have been doing little projects before the inspector comes out to perform his inspection and dings us for the little things we can fix now. So, the other day, I replaced two pieces of decking that had rotted on one end of the plank. I ripped them out, cleaned up the area and nailed down two new replacement planks in their place. This afternoon I stained them to match the rest of the planks that were originally there. By the time I was done, I had stain all over the side of my right hand where it had hit the rim of the paint can. I was stained too.

The Bible tells us that our sins are stains that God sees when He looks at us before we accept Christ. It was a description that was used in both the Old Testament and the New Testament. "Though you wash yourself with lye and use much soap, the stain of your guilt is still before me, declares the Lord GOD." - Jeremiah 2:22. As much as we try to hide our sins and clean ourselves up with "good works", our sins are a stain on our lives. The guilt of being sinful men and women stand before God uncovered until they are nailed to the Cross with Christ.

"And have mercy on those who doubt; save others by snatching them out of the fire; to others show mercy with fear, hating even the garment stained by the flesh." - Jude 1:22-23. Our stains are a natural part of our fleshly nature. Our flesh wants to rebel against God and that rebellion stains our souls. Those of us who have accepted Christ as our Savior, have had our stains removed, not covered, removed! They were taken away by the death of Jesus Christ. "For our sake he made him to be sin who knew no sin, so that in him we might become the righteousness of God." - 2 Corinthians 5:21.

Have you had your sinful, stained soul forever cleansed by the death, burial and resurrection of Jesus Christ? He is waiting for you to come to Him in repentance and ask for forgiveness. "Come now, let us reason together, says the LORD: though your sins are like scarlet, they shall be as white as snow; though they are red like crimson, they shall become like wool." - Isaiah 1:18.

Notes:_____
_____
_____
_____
_____
_____
_____
_____
_____
_____

October 2

Potholes

Potholes. On my way to work this morning, as I was going around a turn, I got a little too close to the shoulder of the road and I hit a pothole with my tire. I hit it hard. Hard enough to think that I may have popped the tire. I pulled over a little further down the road just to make sure I didn't hear any air leaking from the tire. No issues with the tire going flat but it did drive a little funny after that.

But isn't that a lot like life thought, we are cruising right along with no issues and then out of nowhere we hit a pothole. Maybe it's a financial pothole, or a health pothole or maybe even a relationship pothole. And all of a sudden things no longer feel right. We aren't on the side of the road broken down, but things are no longer running like they once did.

There will be potholes throughout our entire lives. Things that catch us by surprise. Some potholes may be bigger than others and some potholes may do more damage than others. But life goes on. We make the necessary repairs and continue down the road. As Christians, we've never been promised a smooth road, in fact, just the opposite is true. "I have said these things to you, that in me you may have peace. In the world you will have tribulation. But take heart; I have overcome the world." - John 16:33.

Potholes will come, there's no doubt about it. Make the repairs and keep on your journey to becoming more and more like Christ.

Notes:_____

_____
_____
_____
_____
_____
_____
_____
_____
_____
_____
_____
_____
_____
_____
_____
_____
_____
_____
_____
_____
_____

October 3

Justice and Mercy

Justice and mercy. It was never more evident than in the courtroom yesterday. A former cop shot a killed a man that she thought was inside her apartment. The problem was that it wasn't her apartment, she was on the wrong floor. She went to trial and was found guilty of murder and was sentenced to ten years in prison yesterday. Justice was served.

But an amazing thing happened after the sentencing was over: mercy showed up. The brother of the victim offered forgiveness to the lady that shot and killed his brother. He spoke from the witness stand saying that he didn't want bad things for her life, he wanted her to find grace in the person of Jesus Christ. He got up from the witness stand and went down to the young lady and hugged her as an outward sign of his mercy and grace towards her.

It wasn't only the brother of the victim that came down to show mercy to the recently sentenced ex-cop. The judge rose from her bench and came down to hug the accused, as well as, the mother of the victim. The judge gave the young lady a copy of her personal Bible that she kept at her bench and instructed her to take the time she was sentenced to, to read it.

I can't count the number of times that I have heard God spoken of in one of two ways: as a ruthless judge looking to condemn people to hell, or a God of love that would never send anyone to hell. Both descriptions are not fully accurate of who God is. God is a Holy and Righteous God who cannot be in the presence of sin, because of that He must judge sin and those that commit sin. God is love. He loves His creation so much He sent His only Son to die on the Cross in our place. Just like a coin has two sides, so does God.

There is no better example of justice and mercy than the Cross of Calvary. Justice needed to be carried out for the sin of man because God demands justice. But mercy showed up in the form of Jesus Christ who went to the Cross to pay for our sins; that's love. "For our sake he made Him to be sin who knew no sin, so that in Him we might become the righteousness of God." - 2 Corinthians 5:21. Justice was carried out that day on Jesus Christ so that we who put our faith in Him may receive the mercy of God, just like what happened in that courtroom yesterday.

Notes:_____

_____

_____

_____

_____

_____

_____

October 4

Burn the Ships

Burn the ships. That seems like an odd topic for a post about Christianity doesn't it? Actually, it comes from a newly released song that is out on the radio. The first time that I heard it, I didn't understand what burning ships had to do with God. But, the more that I listened to the song, the more it made sense in the context of the rest of the song. The concept of burning the ships relates to forgetting our past and moving on with our future.

I don't know about you, but there are many things in my past that I regret, both before I became a Christian and after I became one. The one thing about our past is that we can't change it, it's gone, and we can't do anything about it. All we can do is learn from what we did and apply those lessons to the rest of our lives to make sure that we do not commit the same mistakes in the future.

I think of all of the people in the Bible that had either a sketchy past, or a downright sinful past, that God still used. People that had committed murder, people that were harlots, and people that were the least respected in the culture of their time. God forgot about their past and was more concerned about their future. The Apostle Paul comes to mind. He approved of the stoning death of Stephen and was the hunter of people of the Way. God met him along the road to Damascus and forever changed his future.

"Brothers, I do not consider that I have made it my own. But one thing I do: forgetting what lies behind and straining forward to what lies ahead, I press on toward the goal for the prize of the upward call of God in Christ Jesus." - Philippians 3:13-14. There may be things in your past that keep you from moving forward with life, from doing the things that God has called you to do. We need to forget what lies behind because God has - "as far as the east is from the west, so far does he remove our transgressions from us." - Psalm 103:12.

Don't worry about your past, there is nothing you can do to change it and if Satan wants to bring it up, tell him that it has already been nailed to the Cross. Forget what lies behind and keep pushing forward towards the mark.

Notes:_____
_____
_____
_____
_____
_____
_____
_____
_____
_____

October 5

Turn Around

Turn around. I was on my way to a yearly event tonight by myself as my family stayed at home. As I was making my way to the event, the Holy Spirit spoke to me to turn around and go back home and spend the evening with my family. I'm going to be doing some traveling soon and will be away from them during that time, I didn't need to be away from them tonight. I tried to argue with the Holy Spirit that I only do this event once a year, but He wasn't having it. So, I turned around and came back home. I'm glad I did. We had dinner and then a family movie.

God wants us to "turn around" too; it's called repentance. To repent means to realize the path you are traveling down is the wrong path, so you turn around and head back towards the direction you left. The wrong path is the path that leads away from God, so to turn around, or repent, means to turn back towards the direction of God. It's not a ninety degree turn, it's a one hundred and eighty degree turn.

"Just so, I tell you, there will be more joy in heaven over one sinner who repents than over ninety-nine righteous persons who need no repentance." - Luke 15:7.

"Repent therefore, and turn back, that your sins may be blotted out, that times of refreshing may come from the presence of the Lord, and that he may send the Christ appointed for you, Jesus." - Acts 3:19-20.

"For godly grief produces a repentance that leads to salvation without regret, whereas worldly grief produces death." - 2 Corinthians 7:10.

I am glad that I turned back tonight and came home to my family. But more importantly, I'm glad I turned back one day about seventeen years ago and came home to my Heavenly Father. He greeted me with open arms, just like the father of the prodigal son, and said, "Welcome home my child, I've been waiting for you!"

Notes:_____
_____
_____
_____
_____
_____
_____
_____
_____
_____
_____
_____

October 6

Balance

Balance. Have you ever just lost your balance because you've gotten your foot caught unexpectedly? It hasn't happened to me often. About ten years ago I got my foot caught in a book bag strap and dislocated all my fingers in my right hand. This morning, on the way to church, I got my foot caught in between the car door and the porch and lost my balance. I didn't fall hard, but I did do enough to twist my knee. I don't know if it was more about being embarrassed than being hurt, but I jumped back to my feet as quickly as I could.

Life works the same way, we are occasionally knocked off balance by unexpected events in life. Those events are different for each of us, some may be facing health issues that knock us off balance, some may be facing family issues and others may be facing work or school issues. Life knocks us down and we have two decisions to make: stay down and sulk or get up and keep going.

I think about the prodigal son, when he came to the end of his money and he had to hire himself out as a pig farmer, living in the mud with pigs. He could have just stayed in the slop and decided that it was his lot in life, but he didn't. He came to his sense and said that working for his father was better than what he was doing at that point. "I will arise and go to my father, and I will say to him, "Father, I have sinned against heaven and before you. I am no longer worthy to be called your son. Treat me as one of your hired servants."" - Luke 15:18-19.

He decided to get up from the pig pen and go back home admitting that he had sinned. "And the son said to him, 'Father, I have sinned against heaven and before you. I am no longer worthy to be called your son.'" - Luke 15:21. When we break our fellowship with God, we need to go back to the Father admitting that what we had done was sin in His eyes. And just like the father of the prodigal son, our Heavenly Father will welcome us home with open arms. "And he arose and came to his father. But while he was still a long way off, his father saw him and felt compassion, and ran and embraced him and kissed him." - Luke 15:20.

Have you fallen in your walk with God recently? Are you far from Him and don't know how to go back? It's easy; come to your sense and head back to God and admit to Him that you had sinned. He'll welcome you back without hesitation.

Notes:

October 7

Homecoming

Homecoming. It's that time of year again. I've seen tons of pictures of my high school friends who have kids that are now in high school and all the homecoming dance pictures from this weekend. Everyone was all dressed up and looking pretty in their dress and handsome in their suits and ties. My alma mater had their homecoming weekend this past weekend with my former college having an alumni soccer game as part of the celebration. Too bad I live about 700 miles away or I would have loved to go back and catch up with old friends and teammates.

There have been some awesome stories in the news the past couple of weeks where high school student bodies selected classmates, that would otherwise be left out, as their kings and queens. Kids with special needs being honored by their classmates by being crowned to homecoming courts. One story told of a girl who had been shot a few years ago, and recovered, being chosen as the homecoming queen. All feel good stories that bring a tear to your eye. Kids that normally aren't considered the popular crowd being given the spotlight of their school for one special night. I congratulate their classmates for doing such an honorable thing.

Jesus taught His disciples the same principle about honoring those that may be considered less fortunate or not the most popular people. "He said also to the man who had invited him, 'When you give a dinner or a banquet, do not invite your friends or your brothers or your relatives or rich neighbors, lest they also invite you in return and you be repaid. But when you give a feast, invite the poor, the crippled, the lame, the blind, and you will be blessed, because they cannot repay you. For you will be repaid at the resurrection of the just.'" - Luke 14:12-14.

We are blessed when we bless those who cannot provide us anything in return. Those that are not able to repay you for what you have done receive a greater blessing than those that can give back to you what you have given to them. There will always be people more fortunate than we are, and there will always be people that are less fortunate. God commands us to reach down and help those that we can without needing to be repaid for what we've done.

Notes:_____
_____
_____
_____
_____
_____
_____
_____

October 8

Bad News

Bad news. We've all gotten it at some point in our lives. Maybe it was the unexpected loss of a loved one, or maybe your company was downsizing and they were letting you go, or maybe a doctor's visit didn't go how you had planned. Bad news comes in all shapes and sizes and doesn't care about your social status, age or race. Most of us will not, and probably have not, received bad news only once in our lives. If you're reading this today, you have survived 100% of the bad news you have been given so far in life.

So what do we do when bad news comes knocking at our doors as Christians? What should our response be? The Bible is pretty clear on what our course of action should be when the time comes: pray. First and foremost, we should personally pray to God for our own situation. We should go to Him with our fears, our weaknesses and our questions. God is big enough to handle all of them. I think of the life of David between when he was anointed king and he actually became king. The trials and tribulations (bad news) he endured during those times that give us so much of the Book of Psalms. "I sought the LORD, and he answered me and delivered me from all my fears." - Psalm 34:4.

Second, we should confide in our closest circle the need for them to pray with us and for us. Our closest and dearest friends and family will always seek the Lord on our behalf in whatever bad news we may be facing making supplications for our needs. "Therefore, confess your sins to one another and pray for one another, that you may be healed. The prayer of a righteous person has great power as it is working." - James 5:16. We know from God's Word that where two or three are gathered together in His name, He is there. When we ask for His will to be done, He hears our prayers.

Lastly, when we are done praying, we are to pray some more, seeking God's intervention. "Ask, and it will be given to you; seek, and you will find; knock, and it will be opened to you. For everyone who asks receives, and the one who seeks finds, and to the one who knocks it will be opened." - Matthew 7:7-8. God's answer may not always be what we think is the correct response, but it is always the right response in accordance to His Will. Even our Savior knew that, "And going a little farther he fell on his face and prayed, saying, 'My Father, if it be possible, let this cup pass from me; nevertheless, not as I will, but as you will.'" - Matthew 26:39.

Notes:_____
_____
_____
_____
_____
_____
_____

October 9

Good News

Good news. Sometimes in the midst of getting bad news over and over again, God breaks into your world and brings you a bit of good news. Even things that we feel have no way of turning out for the good, God answers prayers and shows up right on time and with just what you need. My wife and I have experienced this very thing just this week. When we felt everything was against us, God showed that He was for us. "What then shall we say to these things? If God is for us, who can be against us?" - Romans 8:31.

God shows up throughout the Bible in times of despair and hopelessness to bring good news. In the most evil of days, the days of Noah, when all the earth was doing what it felt was right in their own eyes, God showed up. He chose a man named Noah to bring the good news of His salvation. Noah preached that judgement was coming, that repentance was need and the only salvation from the coming judgement was an ark. In the end, only eight people accepted that good news and the rest perished in the flood.

Another time came when man was once again far from God, even though they thought they were as close as they could ever be. During that time, God sent the Good News of His one and only Son, Jesus Christ. And just as Noah preached, so too did John the Baptist and Christ Himself; repentance was needed and judgement was coming. The only way to escape the coming judgement was to accept the Good News of Jesus Christ.

The Good News has come and the promised judgement is coming too. Have you heard the Good News? Christ came into the world to save sinners and by believing in His death, burial and resurrection you can be saved from that coming judgement. Have you accepted Christ as you Savior? He wants you to accept His Good News.

Notes:_____
_____
_____
_____
_____
_____
_____
_____
_____
_____
_____
_____
_____
_____
_____
_____
_____
_____
_____

October 10

Suspenders

Suspenders. I ran across an older gentleman today waiting on my flight in the airport. He looked like we was a war veteran of some sort. He wasn't old enough to be a WWII veteran and looked like he may have been a Korean War vet. He had a Navy hat on and he reminded me of my grandfather because of a certain item of clothing he was wearing. I remember him always wearing a pair of suspenders. The guy I met today not only had on a pair of suspenders, but he had on a belt for extra security.

One of my former bosses used to always use that expression "belt and suspenders" when he discussed making sure we had all our bases covered. This gentleman was definitely a "belt and suspenders" kind of guy. It made me laugh and think about my grandfather. Some people are just programmed that way in their preparation and some people are not.

I've heard people explain our eternity the same way. That we can either be prepared for eternity (belts and suspenders) or just take our chances and see what happens. I have heard it said that "I would rather believe that the Bible is true and accept it by faith and put my trust in Christ only to find out after I die that it wasn't true, than to not believe it and find out too late that it is true."

"Not everyone who says to me, 'Lord, Lord,' will enter the kingdom of heaven, but the one who does the will of my Father who is in heaven. On that day many will say to me, 'Lord, Lord, did we not prophesy in your name, and cast out demons in your name, and do many mighty works in your name?' And then will I declare to them, 'I never knew you; depart from me, you workers of lawlessness.'" - Matthew 7:21-23.

Those will be awful words to hear. Being "religious" or "spiritual" won't save you. Having a relationship with Jesus Christ by accepting His work of salvation by faith is what saves you. Not going to church, not giving money, not singing in the choir or any other religious work will save you. Only Christ and Him alone.

Notes:_____
_____
_____
_____
_____
_____
_____
_____
_____
_____
_____

October 11

Fall

Fall. I have to admit this is my favorite time of year out of all of the seasons. No, it's not because of anything flavored with pumpkin or spice; I don't even drink coffee. I love the smell of fall. I love the cool mornings and the warm afternoons. I love the smell of burning leaves (weird, I know). I love sweatshirts. Fall brings back a lot of memories for me growing up in upstate New York. Fall isn't quite the same down here in North Carolina. Fall doesn't show up like it does in New York.

The changing of seasons remind me of the main theme of the Bible: death and rebirth. "Truly, truly, I say to you, unless a grain of wheat falls into the earth and dies, it remains alone; but if it dies, it bears much fruit." - John 12:24. You can't have a rebirth unless you first have a death. Living in farm country, it's easy to understand the saying of Christ. In order for the rebirth of the wheat, the seed has to be put in the ground to die so it can once again bear fruit.

"Jesus answered them, 'Destroy this temple, and in three days I will raise it up.'" - John 2:19. Jesus understood that for Him to be reborn into glory, He was first going to have to pay the penalty for sin and die a substitutionary death on the Cross. It would only be after His death that He could bear much fruit. That fruit is you and I when we accept Him as our Savior.

We are told that, we too, must die. Not physically, but spiritually. "He himself bore our sins in his body on the tree, that we might die to sin and live to righteousness. By his wounds you have been healed." - 1 Peter 2:24. We have to die to the sin nature we have and take on the righteousness of Christ. Have you died to sin? Have you been born again?

Notes:

Firsts

Firsts. Today was a day of firsts. We had a soccer game this morning with the U5 team my son plays on. We have eight players on the team and only three play at a time. All eight players were able to score a goal today, three of them scored a goal for the first time this year. Our best player, who could have scored twenty goals himself, was very unselfish by getting the ball to the goal and letting the other players score. I've never seen a four year old be so concerned about his teammates. It was an awesome show of putting others before yourself and a four year old helped us to remember that.

Then, this afternoon, the very first friend I ever had in my life posted pictures of one of her birthday parties and tagged me in the post. It was so awesome to go back to those days and remember first friends like that, especially when you haven't seen them in almost 30 years. We remember the things that happened in our lives that were "firsts". They tend to stand out so vividly in our minds. "Firsts" are important to us and they are to God.

"Honor the LORD with your wealth and with the firstfruits of all your produce" - Proverbs 3:9. God wants the best of what we have. He wants us to bring to Him the firstfruits of our lives. He doesn't want what is leftover, like an afterthought, He wants the best. He wants to be first and foremost in what we give to Him. He wants to know that we see Him as the most important part of our lives. When we give Him what we have left, we show Him that what we want is more important to us than what He has commanded us to give.

"Of his own will he brought us forth by the word of truth, that we should be a kind of firstfruits of his creatures." - James 1:18. The Bible describes believers as Christ's firstfruits. Christ, himself, is also described as the firstfruits of the Resurrection as a promise that we too will be resurrected when the time comes. "But in fact, Christ has been raised from the dead, the firstfruits of those who have fallen asleep." - 1 Corinthians 15:20.

Just like we remember the things in our lives that were "firsts", God wants to be first in all that we do and say.

Notes:_____
_____
_____
_____
_____
_____
_____
_____
_____
_____
_____
_____

October 13

Embarrassed

Embarrassed. Have you ever done something out in public that was embarrassing and you looked around to see if anyone else saw you do it? That happened to me tonight. I was at a hardware store and was loading the things I bought into the trunk of my car. I picked up one of the items that was extremely heavy and when I did the big metal cart that it was on rolled right into my shin. If you have ever been hit in the shin, you know that feeling of instant pain (even after playing soccer for 20 years, it still hurts).

So after I got all of the stuff in my trunk and limped my way over to where you return the carts in the parking lot, I made my way to my car. With my shin still stinging from getting hit, I decided I would pull up my pant leg to make sure I didn't cut myself. As I bent over to look at my leg, I opened the car door and the corner of the door hit me right in the forehead. There was no cut on my leg, but now I have a big cut across the left side of my forehead. After the sudden flood of pain that came from hitting my head, I realized I was in the middle of a parking lot, so I looked around to see if anyone caught this comedy show.

I didn't see anyone in their cars laughing hysterically, but they could have been doubled over in the passenger seat trying to catch their breath. Even though it didn't seem anyone witnessed that event, I was still embarrassed by the stupidity I had just taken part in. I got in the car really quick and found some napkins to stop the bleeding. The bleeding stopped before the feeling of being embarrassed did.

The Bible tells us of a group of people that will one day feel that same embarrassment as I did today, except to a much greater degree and with a more serious consequence. "Not everyone who says to me, 'Lord, Lord,' will enter the kingdom of heaven, but the one who does the will of my Father who is in heaven. On that day many will say to me, 'Lord, Lord, did we not prophesy in your name, and cast out demons in your name, and do many mighty works in your name?' And then will I declare to them, 'I never knew you; depart from me, you workers of lawlessness.'" - Matthew 7:21-23.

The embarrassment of thinking that you are a Christian because of your works will one day be exposed on that fateful day. Those that did not have a personal relationship with Jesus Christ will be turned away. Those that believed their "works" would be enough to save them will face the embarrassment of being not known by the Savior. There will be many in that day who had masqueraded as Christians only to be exposed that they truly were not. Don't be those people! Stop relying on your works to save you and give your life to Christ.

Notes:_____
_____
_____
_____

October 14

Hardships

Hardships. Have you ever wondered why God allows you to go through things that are hard in life; trials and tribulations you thought you would avoid once you became a Christian? Why do we suffer the same things that those that don't belong to Christ do? Shouldn't we have an "advocate" that protects us from these types of things? We go through divorce, financial issues, the death of loved ones, the loss of jobs just like the rest of the world does, but why?

One of my favorite section of verses in the Bible gives us insight as to why we go through trials and tribulations as Christians. "Blessed be the God and Father of our Lord Jesus Christ, the Father of mercies and God of all comfort, who comforts us in all our affliction, so that we may be able to comfort those who are in any affliction, with the comfort with which we ourselves are comforted by God. For as we share abundantly in Christ's sufferings, so through Christ we share abundantly in comfort too." - 2 Corinthians 1:3-5.

There are things in my life that I wish I never had to go through and I hope I never have to go through them again, Lord willing. But those trials and tribulations produced in me the ability to comfort those that go through it after me. How much easier is it to talk to someone who has lost a spouse if you have lost one too? Or how much can you comfort someone going through a divorce when you have already gone through one yourself?

Sometimes the trials and tribulations that we go through aren't always about us. How we handle those trials can serve as a witness to our faith in Christ to those watching who are not believers. It can also serve as an experience for a future event involving someone else that goes through the same trial. The Bible never promises us a trial free life, it actually promises the opposite, "I have said these things to you, that in me you may have peace. In the world you will have tribulation. But take heart; I have overcome the world." - John 16:33.

Are you going through trials and tribulations now brothers and sisters? What can you do to be a witness for Christ through the midst of it? What can you learn from it to support other who will go through the same thing later? "And we know that for those who love God all things work together for good, for those who are called according to his purpose. For those whom he foreknew he also predestined to be conformed to the image of his Son, in order that he might be the firstborn among many brothers."- Romans 8:28-29.

Notes:_____
_____
_____
_____
_____

Change

Change. I'm not talking about "the times they are a changin'" as Bob Dylan sang about, although I could. It's that time of the year where you see visible changes almost every day. The temperature has changed in the mornings. The leaves are changing colors. The amount of daylight is changing. We can all see a change in our world during this time of the year. We can feel it, we can smell it and we can taste it (if you're a pumpkin spice addict). What about you, can people see a change in you since you have become a Christian?

For the most part, when we put our faith in Jesus Christ as our personal Savior, there is no physical outside change that happens. You don't get this glow that appears around you, nor do you get a halo that shows up over your head. It may put a smile on the face of someone that was once always sad or grumpy, but other than that, nothing physically happens. The change that takes place is usually internal. "Therefore, if anyone is in Christ, he is a new creation. The old has passed away; behold, the new has come." - 2 Corinthians 5:17.

I think of the story of the Apostle Paul in the book of Acts. How he went around arresting people of "the Way" and putting them in prison because of their belief in Christ. But, when Christ showed up on the road to Damascus, a change occurred in Paul that would change the history of the world. There was an immediate change in him after those scales were removed from his eyes three days after meeting Christ. The change was so drastic, people had a hard time believing it was true. "And immediately he proclaimed Jesus in the synagogues, saying, 'He is the Son of God.' And all who heard him were amazed and said, 'Is not this the man who made havoc in Jerusalem of those who called upon this name? And has he not come here for this purpose, to bring them bound before the chief priests?'" - Acts 9:20-21.

Can you remember back to when you accepted Christ as your Savior, are you the same person you used to be, or has there been such a change in you that people are skeptical? We should see a change from who we once were, to who we are now. Our thoughts should be different, our words should be different and our lives should be different. Are you different now that you met Jesus? Have you changed?

Notes:_____

_____
_____
_____
_____
_____
_____
_____
_____

Packing

Packing. Well, we are now two weeks away from having to move out of our house. As you can imagine, it's getting a lot more serious now as we get closer to the closing date. The packing up of our stuff has begun and we have started moving it to a storage unit since we have about a week between moving out of the old house and moving into the new one. My wife has done most of the packing the past week and I couldn't be more grateful to her for doing it on her own while I'm at work.

You never really understand how much stuff you have, that you never use, until you start packing up your house. Along with packing the stuff we are taking with us; we have made some trips to the landfill to get rid of the stuff that we've held onto all these years for no reason. Neither one us are pack rats that hold on to thing for years, so it was kind of surprising that we actually had so much "junk". We've had to be selective of what we were going to bring and what we were going to get rid of.

When our time comes to leave this earth, either through death or the return of our Lord and Savior, there will be nothing physical that we will be taking with us to Heaven. I've heard it said many times, "you never see a U-Haul following behind a hearse". All that we own will be left to someone else to sort out when we are gone. However, there will be some things that we can bring to Heaven with us: other believers that came to Christ because of our witness.

"For what is our hope or joy or crown of boasting before our Lord Jesus at his coming? Is it not you? For you are our glory and joy." - 1 Thessalonians 2:19-20. When the Apostle Paul wrote to the Thessalonian believers, he called them his "crown" that he would be able to boast about when the Lord came back. He could boast because they would be in Heaven with him because of his sharing the Gospel with them and their acceptance of Christ. Paul wasn't worried about possessions he would take with him to Heaven, he was worried about souls that would be in Heaven because of his sharing the Gospel.

When you stand before Christ to give an account of your life, who will step forward on that day and say, "I am here because you shared the Gospel of Jesus Christ with me"? The most important thing we can pack for our trip to Heaven is the souls of others - friends and family. Have you started packing yet for your move?

Notes:_____
_____
_____
_____
_____
_____

So Good to Me

So good to me. In the midst of our everyday life, the complaining about various things like politics, the weather, our jobs and whatever else bothers us, do we ever stop and realize how good God has been to us? I don't mean in a material way like money or possessions; I mean in a spiritual way. Have you stopped and thought where your eternity would lie if God wasn't so good to us in sending His Son? Sometimes it just overwhelms me when I think about the fact that before time began, He thought about me and made a way for me to have a personal relationship with Him through Jesus Christ.

God has been so good to me even though I don't deserve it. His blessing doesn't have anything to do with what I have and has everything to do with where I am going. In all honesty, I've never gone hungry, I've never been homeless and I've never been without the things I need to survive; God has provided for all my needs. He is the Bread of Life, He is the Shelter in a time of storms and He's the Living Water. He meets all our spiritual needs.

"But for me it is good to be near God; I have made the Lord GOD my refuge, that I may tell of all your works." - Psalm 73:28.

"The LORD is good to all, and his mercy is over all that he has made." - Psalm 145:9.

"And Jesus said to him, 'Why do you call me good? No one is good except God alone.'" - Luke 18:19.

Have you paused recently to think about how good God has been to you? The fact that He loves you so much He sent His Son to pay for your sins. He loves you and wants what is good for you, more than you want what is good for yourself. Take time to praise Him for being so good to you.

Notes:_____

_____
_____
_____
_____
_____
_____
_____
_____
_____
_____
_____
_____

October 18

Rescue

Rescue. There was a story on the news and the internet the other day about a dog that had to be rescued from a hiking trip in the mountains. A 190 pound mastiff went hiking with its owner and about halfway through the trip became too tired to finish the hike back. Rescue crews had to be sent up to carry the huge dog back down the mountain. As you can imagine, the terrain isn't really suitable for hiking down a mountain carrying 190 pounds of dog! The story did end successfully and the dog was able to go back home with its owner.

I can't count the number of times that God has had to rescue me from things that I got myself into without thinking it all the way through. I'm sure, just like the rescuers of the dog, there had to be some times that God muttered under His breath, "what were you thinking?" But no matter the situation, God is a willing rescuer of those that need Him.

All those stories of David when he was anointed king but Saul was still on the throne. How he was hunted down and pursued by Saul and his men trying to kill him. "He rescued me from my strong enemy and from those who hated me, for they were too mighty for me." - Psalm 18:17. Once he became king, and his children were grown, he was still chased out of Jerusalem by his own son trying to kill him. In all those moments, God rescued him from his enemies. Most of the Psalms are about those trying times.

As Christians, we have a Rescuer too, that goes by the name of Jesus Christ. He rescues us from the penalty of our sins. He rescues us from times of trouble in our lives. And He rescues us from things we won't even know about until it's revealed to us in eternity. "The Lord will rescue me from every evil deed and bring me safely into his heavenly kingdom. To him be the glory forever and ever. Amen." - 2 Timothy 4:18.

More than anything, He wants to hear the words of the unsaved crying out to Him to be rescued from their sins. Just like the psalmist wrote, "In your righteousness deliver me and rescue me; incline your ear to me and save me!" - Psalm 71:2. He wants to save you from the penalty of your sins. Cry out to Him to rescue you and He will hear you and save you!

Notes:_____
_____
_____
_____
_____
_____
_____
_____
_____
_____

October 19

Late

Late. I hate being late to anything. I hate being late to work, I hate being late to events, I hate being late to church, I just hate that feeling of being behind schedule. I woke up a lot later than I normally do this morning and it just made me feel like I was behind schedule even though there were really no plans to be late for. I think I get it from my father, he always had to be somewhere thirty minutes before it was time. Being late doesn't bother some people at all, but it makes me edgy. Are you and early person or does the clock not matter to you?

God is never late! Have you ever thought about that? We seem to always want God to show up on our timing and not His own. We think that things have to be done according to our schedule not realizing that our schedule may be the wrong timing - ask Mary and Martha. The story of Lazarus' death reminds us that God's timing is always right on time. Jesus could have shown up while Lazarus was sick and healed him, but He had something better that needed to be done. So when He shows up four days after Lazarus had already been in the grave, He was met with some questions.

"Jesus said, 'Take away the stone.' Martha, the sister of the dead man, said to him, 'Lord, by this time there will be an odor, for he has been dead four days.' Jesus said to her, 'Did I not tell you that if you believed you would see the glory of God?' So they took away the stone. And Jesus lifted up his eyes and said, 'Father, I thank you that you have heard me. I knew that you always hear me, but I said this on account of the people standing around, that they may believe that you sent me.' When he had said these things, he cried out with a loud voice, 'Lazarus, come out.'" - John 11:39-43.

Are you waiting on God to show up in your life to deal with an issue you have? Do you feel like he has left you alone to deal with this on your own? Don't give up, God always shows up right on time, even when we think He is too late. God has something He wants to reveal to not only you, but maybe to others as well, so that He May be glorified.

Notes:_____

_____
_____
_____
_____
_____
_____
_____
_____
_____
_____
_____
_____
_____

Fantasy Football

Fantasy football. Maybe some of you play fantasy football in a league with your buddies from work, or from college or maybe from high school. Maybe some of you have spouses that play fantasy football and it drives you crazy the amount of time they spend worrying about it. I spend too much time worrying about it too and then get frustrated on Sundays when my "players" don't do well. And it's all make believe when it comes down to it, they're not "my" players and could care less about my score.

I've had people tell me that they think the Bible is all "fantasy". It's filled with nice fairy tales to make Christians feel good about themselves and unbelievers feel bad about themselves, they say. Maybe you have heard scoffers say something similar about their beliefs about the Word of God. If they don't believe the Bible is true and it's the Word of God, it is hard to reach them trying to use scripture because they don't believe it to begin with.

The Bible has been proven true over and over again that it is not fantasy. Extrabiblical accounts match up to historical events and people that are mentioned in the Bible to prove its authenticity. Archeological finds have proven that long believed errors in the Bible were actually true and just needed to be found to prove it. The writings of Luke have long believed to be completely inaccurate according to history, but more and more of his writings are becoming proven fact.

God even tells us that His Word is true and accurate, "All Scripture is breathed out by God and profitable for teaching, for reproof, for correction, and for training in righteousness, that the man of God may be complete, equipped for every good work." - 2 Timothy 3:16-17.

Even though the Bible was physically written by men, the content was given to them by inspiration of the Holy Spirit. "And we have the prophetic word more fully confirmed, to which you will do well to pay attention as to a lamp shining in a dark place, until the day dawns and the morning star rises in your hearts, knowing this first of all, that no prophecy of Scripture comes from someone's own interpretation. For no prophecy was ever produced by the will of man, but men spoke from God as they were carried along by the Holy Spirit." - 2 Peter 1:19-21.

Notes:_____
_____
_____
_____
_____
_____
_____

October 21

Bad Decisions

Bad decisions. I have to admit, I've made my share of bad decisions in my life, both before I became a Christian and after. I think we can all admit to making bad decisions in our lives at some point in time. Some of us may have made more than our fair share, but does making bad decisions make us a bad person? It's amazing how many good decisions you can make that no one pays any attention to but make one bad decision and that's all you are remembered for. Why do bad decisions seem to stick in people's minds but our good one's don't?

There are plenty of Biblical stories of "good" people making bad decisions that tends to be something they are remembered for. I think of King David and all the good that he had done for Israel when he became king and then he makes that bad decision involving Bathsheba. Because of that the child dies. Or what about Moses, he does all those great things to lead Israel out of bondage and then hits the rock twice for water when he had been instructed only to hit it once. Because of that he's not allowed to enter into the Promised Land.

I think of the Apostle Peter as well. After all he had done and seen with Jesus, he tells Him he would never deny Him. But, when the time came in the courtyard of Jesus' trial, he is accused of being one of Christ's disciples and he denies it, not once but three times. A bad decision made by a good person. It could have been the end of his story right there, but Christ restores him back to good standing.

"When they had finished breakfast, Jesus said to Simon Peter, "Simon, son of John, do you love me more than these?" He said to him, "Yes, Lord; you know that I love you." He said to him, "Feed my lambs." He said to him a second time, "Simon, son of John, do you love me?" He said to him, "Yes, Lord; you know that I love you." He said to him, "Tend my sheep." He said to him the third time, "Simon, son of John, do you love me?" Peter was grieved because he said to him the third time, "Do you love me?" and he said to him, "Lord, you know everything; you know that I love you." Jesus said to him, "Feed my sheep."- John 21:15-17.

Notes:_____
_____
_____
_____
_____
_____
_____
_____
_____
_____

Stone Walls

Stone walls. As I was driving through Connecticut this afternoon, I passed through a bunch of small towns as I went along some back country roads. You could tell these were old towns that had probably been around since shortly before or after the Revolutionary War. The style of the houses were just beautiful and in this one town there was a two foot stone wall around the outside of each of the properties. It was just awesome. I thought about how long ago those walls were built.

Not only were the walls built possibly hundreds of years ago, but they were still standing just like when they were first built. I'm sure that some maintenance has been done to them to repair places that may have come apart over the years. I also started thinking about the people who built those walls. These were probably men that had very few tools to construct these walls that still stood where they were built. I don't know who they were, whether they were masons by trade or the owners of the houses themselves, but whoever built them has left a legacy for many generations.

As Christians, we have legacies that we leave within our own families. I know my wife continues a legacy that started many generations before her. As for me, I am the starter of the legacy for my children from my side of the family. As I said before, I didn't grow up in a Christian family where a legacy had been established. The legacy from my side of the family starts with me. It is important to remember those that came before us and built upon those before them in establishing a Christian legacy in our families.

"A good man leaves an inheritance to his children's children" - Proverbs 13:22a.

What we teach our children about Christ and leading them to a personal relationship with Him, is the best inheritance we can leave them. That legacy is greater than all the gold and silver and jewels in the world because it is an eternal treasure. "Blessed be the God and Father of our Lord Jesus Christ! According to his great mercy, he has caused us to be born again to a living hope through the resurrection of Jesus Christ from the dead, to an inheritance that is imperishable, undefiled, and unfading, kept in heaven for you, who by God's power are being guarded through faith for a salvation ready to be revealed in the last time." - 1 Peter 1:3-5.

Notes:_____
_____
_____
_____
_____
_____
_____

October 23

First Class

First class. For the first time ever, I got to sit in first class today on one of the legs of my flight. Of course, it was the shortest leg, only a twenty minute flight, but it was still first class. Due to my recent travels, I have secured quite a few miles and have moved up in rank to get automatic upgrades. But, because I'm so new to the upgrades, they are usually filled by other people ahead of me before they ever get to my name. So, while I get the perks of automatic upgrades, I've never actually received the perk of sitting in first class; until today.

My original seat was all the way in the back of the plane, in row nineteen. I was sitting there and a lady came and sat at the window seat next to me and we started up the normal conversation with someone who sits next to you: heading home? where are you coming from? how long you been gone? - stuff like that. All of a sudden, the guy from the check-in counter was walking down the aisle looking for someone in a particular seat. He stopped at my seat and asked my name. When I told him, he said, "would you like to upgrade to first class?" I didn't hesitate in agreeing to the seat change.

As I walked from the back of the plane to the front, I'm sure people were watching to see where I was off to. The others that had been seated in first class sort of looked at me funny when I made my way into their protected territory. They were probably asking themselves why I was getting to move up to the empty first class seat. Some of them probably understood that I was next on the list for the upgrade, but it felt like I was looked at sort of funny for joining their group so late.

It made me think of church. When the invitation is given and people come from the back up to the altar, I think about when I did it for the first time. You wonder what people are thinking as you walk past them to the front. We tend to think the worst - that they're living in some sort of sin and are there to confess of their wrongdoing.

"'Judge not, that you be not judged. For with the judgment you pronounce you will be judged, and with the measure you use it will be measured to you. Why do you see the speck that is in your brother's eye, but do not notice the log that is in your own eye? Or how can you say to your brother, 'Let me take the speck out of your eye,' when there is the log in your own eye? You hypocrite, first take the log out of your own eye, and then you will see clearly to take the speck out of your brother's eye.'" - Matthew 7:1-5.

Notes:_____
_____
_____
_____
_____
_____

October 24

A View

A view. As I was flying back yesterday, I sat in the only seat in my row which happened to be a window seat. I usually always book an aisle seat when I travel because of the leg room I need with my bad knees. So, I don't usually get to look out the window while flying, but yesterday was different. As I flew the twenty minutes from one airport to the other, I watched the familiar terrain below us. I took a picture of the awesome view as I started to think about God's creation.

Because it was such a short flight, I think we only climbed to about 9000 feet, so you could still see the details of things below. I saw little towns; I saw farmlands and I saw larger cities. In between were the woods and rivers created by God. "And God said, 'Let the earth sprout vegetation, plants yielding seed, and fruit trees bearing fruit in which is their seed, each according to its kind, on the earth.' And it was so. The earth brought forth vegetation, plants yielding seed according to their own kinds, and trees bearing fruit in which is their seed, each according to its kind. And God saw that it was good. And there was evening and there was morning, the third day." - Genesis 1:11-13.

I couldn't help but think of God's creation as I looked down on it in amazement at how beautiful it was. I can't imagine how anyone could believe that all of creation appeared by happenstance. There is so much design in creation that it points to a Creator. "For his invisible attributes, namely, his eternal power and divine nature, have been clearly perceived, ever since the creation of the world, in the things that have been made. So, they are without excuse." - Romans 1:20.

Sometimes we need to stop and look at the creation that was made by God, knowing that what we see now is not what was originally made. We now live in a world under a curse that affects the real beauty of God's creation. "For we know that the whole creation has been groaning together in the pains of childbirth until now." - Romans 8:22.

Notes:_____
_____
_____
_____
_____
_____
_____
_____
_____
_____
_____
_____

Stuff

Stuff. You want to know how much stuff you've accumulated over the years - move! It's amazing how many things you have that you rarely use, that you didn't even know you had. Neither my wife nor I would consider ourselves hoarders in any way, yet here we are with more "stuff" than we need or want. As you can imagine, all of that stuff has resulted in trips to Goodwill and the landfill.

It made me think of the story of the rich young ruler found in the Bible. It was such an important story that Matthew, Mark and Luke included it in their Gospels. It's a story about how much of an affect "stuff" can have in our lives. I'm not talking about hoarding type "stuff", I mean the desire to have more things, things we could do without. Here's the story:

"And behold, a man came up to him, saying, 'Teacher, what good deed must I do to have eternal life?' And he said to him, 'Why do you ask me about what is good? There is only one who is good. If you would enter life, keep the commandments.' He said to him, 'Which ones?' And Jesus said, 'You shall not murder, you shall not commit adultery, you shall not steal, you shall not bear false witness, honor your father and mother, and, you shall love your neighbor as yourself.' The young man said to him, 'All these I have kept. What do I still lack?' Jesus said to him, 'If you would be perfect, go, sell what you possess and give to the poor, and you will have treasure in heaven; and come, follow me.' When the young man heard this, he went away sorrowful, for he had great possessions." - Matthew 19:16-22.

It wasn't the "stuff" that was keeping this young man out of Heaven, it was his faith in that "stuff". Jesus wanted him to put his faith in Him instead of his possessions, but the rich young man couldn't trust that what Jesus was offering was better than all that he had. Because of this, it said that the young man went away sorrowful because he was rich.

What you have is not as important as who you have! If you don't have Christ as your personal Savior, all your "stuff" means nothing. If you have Christ, you understand that all your "stuff" belongs to Him anyway and we are just stewards of it. We will be much more willing to let go of our stuff the sooner we understand that.

Notes:_____
_____
_____
_____
_____
_____
_____

Pause

Pause. I was flipping through the channels the other day to find something for the kids to watch while I was working on something else. I came across a family favorite, The Andy Griffith Show, so I stopped it there for them to watch. It was the episode about the guest preacher that had come to town and filled in at Mayberry's church. He preached on how fast paced their world had become (if he could only see it now) and how we needed to slow down and enjoy some down time.

It sort of went along with the post I shared earlier about the "pause" and how at certain times of our lives we should "pause", and when we "pause", we should pray. This world we live in now is definitely more fast paced than the time period of Andy Griffith, and if they thought they needed to slow down then, how much more do we need to do the same today. We want everything done now, we want our kids to participate in everything they can, and we want to fill our schedules until we don't understand why we don't have any time.

"Be still before the LORD and wait patiently for him; fret not yourself over the one who prospers in his way, over the man who carries out evil devices!" - Psalm 37:7. Be still, that's a novel idea. Wait patiently, there's another one. Why do we have to constantly have to be on the go?

"Be patient, therefore, brothers, until the coming of the Lord. See how the farmer waits for the precious fruit of the earth, being patient about it, until it receives the early and the late rains. You also, be patient. Establish your hearts, for the coming of the Lord is at hand." - James 5:7-8.

We need to spend more time being still so that God can speak to us. It's not in the busyness of our lives that He speaks to us, but in the stillness of our lives that we hear from Him. "And he said, "Go out and stand on the mount before the LORD." And behold, the LORD passed by, and a great and strong wind tore the mountains and broke in pieces the rocks before the LORD, but the LORD was not in the wind. And after the wind an earthquake, but the LORD was not in the earthquake. And after the earthquake a fire, but the LORD was not in the fire. And after the fire the sound of a low whisper." - 1 Kings 19:11-12.

Notes:_____
_____
_____
_____
_____
_____
_____

October 27

LEGOs

LEGOs. For the past two days, the kids have had all the LEGOs out in my little guy's room building all sorts of things. It's been a LEGO minefield trying to get from one side of the room to the other. They've built all different items but set out yesterday in building a house. By the end of the night they had themselves a nice house built from the LEGOs. Of course, there was some arguing along the way on how to go about building it, but when it was all said and done, they made a very nice house that they are still playing with tonight.

Luckily, my daughter has some understanding that my son has yet to figure out. He wanted to build the bottom smaller than he wanted to build the top. Of course, that's going to lead to a house that is not going to be very sturdy. My daughter understands that for the house to be built correctly it has to have a bigger and stronger base than the top of the house. It made me think of the teachings of Jesus on building a house.

"Everyone then who hears these words of mine and does them will be like a wise man who built his house on the rock. And the rain fell, and the floods came, and the winds blew and beat on that house, but it did not fall, because it had been founded on the rock. And everyone who hears these words of mine and does not do them will be like a foolish man who built his house on the sand. And the rain fell, and the floods came, and the winds blew and beat against that house, and it fell, and great was the fall of it." - Matthew 7:24-27.

When we build our house upon the Rock of God, the foundation is sturdy and can withstand any storm that may come, just like the house my daughter made out of the LEGOs. However, when we build our house on the sand of this world, when storms come the house falls because the foundation is not built on God and His Word, just like the house my son wanted to build.

What foundation have you built your life on? Have you designed and built it upon the promises of God found in the Bible or have you built it on the sand that this world wants you to believe in? Storms will come and your faith will be tested, but God is faithful to those who build upon Him.

Notes:_____

_____

_____

_____

_____

_____

_____

_____

_____

_____

October 28

Near to God

Near to God. As I flew recently, I sat by the window and looked out most of the way at the terrain some thirty-five thousand feet below. It's amazing what you can see from that far up that is probably hours' worth of driving to cover. As I sat there, I thought about how close I was to God being that far above the ground. And then I corrected myself that I was no closer to God in that airplane as I was before I took off. God is close to believers at all times because we have the third person of the Trinity living inside us.

Maybe it was the amazing view that got my mind confused about being closer to God at that moment, I don't know, but I liked the fact that being close to God came to my mind. As believers, there isn't anywhere we can go that God isn't near to us. "If I ascend to heaven, you are there! If I make my bed in Sheol, you are there! If I take the wings of the morning and dwell in the uttermost parts of the sea, even there your hand shall lead me, and your right hand shall hold me." - Psalm 139:8-10. The psalmist had it right, that no matter where we go, God is there.

We draw close to God when we seek Him in His Word and in prayer. God never has a need to draw close to us because He never moves, but we do and because of that we have to seek Him in order to draw closer. "But for me it is good to be near God; I have made the Lord GOD my refuge, that I may tell of all your works." - Psalm 73:28.

Have you found yourself feeling like you are no longer as near to God as you once were? Is there something in your life that has broken fellowship with God? Confess your sins and seek His face, draw near to Him and you will once again feel His presence. "Draw near to God, and he will draw near to you. Cleanse your hands, you sinners, and purify your hearts, you double-minded." - James 4:8.

Notes:_____

_____

_____

_____

_____

_____

_____

_____

_____

_____

_____

_____

_____

_____

October 29

Lost

Lost. Have you ever been somewhere that you are somewhat familiar with but not totally comfortable driving in and got lost? Happened to me today. I'm very comfortable driving from the airport to the hotel and to the plant but have me drive somewhere that I haven't been and I'm not feeling it. I got a bit lost this evening return from a restaurant to the hotel. I missed a turn and found myself on a back road I wasn't familiar with. I kept going straight until I came to a landmark I knew near the hotel and then I was back on track.

We can get lost in our spiritual walk sometimes as well. We go through the normal routine that we are familiar with sometimes just out of habit. We say our prayers the same time every day, we may read our Bibles each day, we go to church on a normal routine but then something happens we become lost. Not lost in a sense that we aren't saved, but lost in a sense that we can't hear or sense God in our lives.

We may end up wandering in that state for a while just staying straight on the road we are traveling until we find something in our lives that is familiar and we can get back on track. We may find ourselves so lost spiritually that we may need to stop and ask for directions from someone who is on the right path. It's okay to feel that way sometimes, I think we all go through it. The important thing is that we realize it as soon as possible and search to get back to God. "I have gone astray like a lost sheep; seek your servant, for I do not forget your commandments." - Psalm 119:176.

Maybe you are really lost and don't know if God is even in your life. God sent His Son to save those that are lost. "For the Son of Man came to seek and to save the lost." - Luke 19:10. He is waiting for you to put your trust and faith in the death, burial and resurrection of Jesus Christ. If you are lost, seek Him and He will find you.

Notes:_____
_____
_____
_____
_____
_____
_____
_____
_____
_____
_____
_____
_____

Wildfires

Wildfires. As I watch the news reports coming out of California about the wildfires, I think of our current customers that live and work in that area. I think about how their lives are now completely focused on the potential dangers at hand. I have heard that multiple major highways in the area have been shut down making it difficult and slow to get from one place to another. I think about how some have had to evacuate their homes, with all their possessions left behind, to seek safety in a different location. How they do not know if they will come back to their homes in the same condition that they left them?

I've never had to experience something like that and I pray that I never will. But that doesn't change my concern for them and their safety. Not only for their safety (people I hardly know that well other than work) but also the safety of their families. Being completely on the other side of the country leaves me in a position of not being able to help. The most I can do is pray for their safety and the safety of their families and their belongings. All belongings can be replaced, but lives can't.

What if our concern for the eternal safety of our friends and family matched up with our concern for their temporary safety? Would we live our lives with more purpose of spreading the Gospel and its eternal saving power if we knew the threat was as eminent? I'm not only posting this for you, but for myself as well. Am I doing what I need to do to bring Christ to others before it's eternally too late?

The Bible gives us a detailed description of what Hell is like and it's not a party like some think it's going to be. "The Son of Man will send his angels, and they will gather out of his kingdom all causes of sin and all law-breakers and throw them into the fiery furnace. In that place there will be weeping and gnashing of teeth." - Matthew 13:41-42.

""Then he will say to those on his left, 'Depart from me, you cursed, into the eternal fire prepared for the devil and his angels.'" - Matthew 25:41.

Eternity in a literal place called "Hell" is real and people who reject Christ will spend it there. What are we doing to spread the message of the saving grace of God to keep as many from going there as we can? If you are like me, the answer is "Not enough!"

Notes:_____

_____

_____

_____

_____

_____

_____

The Dash

The Dash. I've seen many people posting over the last few days about the loss of friends and loved ones. There have been those that were young that passed away and there were those that were old that passed away. I don't think death is easy, no matter what age a person is when they pass away. Death is something that none of us are going to avoid, unless Christ comes back to call home His bride. So how do we live our lives between those two dates that end up on our headstone? That dash that separates our birth date and our death date represents our lives, how are we going to live out "the dash"?

Now, you won't find anything in Scripture talking about "the dash" because headstones in a graveyard didn't exist during Biblical times; that is rather new to history. However, we will find many references in the Bible to living out our lives to the glory of God. "I appeal to you therefore, brothers, by the mercies of God, to present your bodies as a living sacrifice, holy and acceptable to God, which is your spiritual worship. Do not be conformed to this world, but be transformed by the renewal of your mind, that by testing you may discern what is the will of God, what is good and acceptable and perfect." - Romans 12:1-2.

God has given us breath and life for this particular day to use to bring honor and glory to Him. We are not promised tomorrow, so if we are given another day when we awake, we must use it to add to the kingdom of God. "Come now, you who say, 'Today or tomorrow we will go into such and such a town and spend a year there and trade and make a profit' - yet you do not know what tomorrow will bring. What is your life? For you are a mist that appears for a little time and then vanishes." - James 4:13-14.

What are you doing during "the dash"? How will people look at your life when it's over and describe to others what your "dash" meant to them? We may have been kind of slack so far in building our "dash", but if the Lord blesses us with another day tomorrow, it can be the first day of building our "dash".

Notes:_____
_____
_____
_____
_____
_____
_____
_____
_____
_____
_____
_____
_____
_____

This is Paradise

This is Paradise. We've all had those vacations, whether on a tropical island or a cabin in the mountains, where we thought to ourselves "this is paradise". We've also faced the disappointment of having to pack up and leave on that last day. Imagine the feeling Adam and Eve had that day they were kicked out of the Garden of Eden and access to the Tree of Life from was taken away and guarded by two angels with flaming swords. They were never going to be able to go back to their original state and could only turn around and move forward.

It's hard not to look back on times and things we once had and find comfort and joy in those things only to know we can never have them back. Lot's wife looked back at Sodom against God's command and lost her life. The nation of Israel wanted to go back to the pleasures of Egypt while they wandered through the wilderness, but God had better things for them up ahead in the Promised Land.

As Christians, we can't look back at our old lives and fall for the lies that this world has something better to offer us. As the Apostle Paul told the Philippians, and what we should do as Christians, "forgetting what lies behind and straining forward to what lies ahead".

Our Tree isn't back in the Garden, our Tree is up ahead in the New Jerusalem and it's there for our nourishment and healing.

Notes:_____

_____
_____
_____
_____
_____
_____
_____
_____
_____
_____
_____
_____
_____
_____
_____
_____
_____
_____
_____
_____

November 2

The Pleasures of Egypt

The Pleasures of Egypt. After more than 400 years of living in Egypt, the nation of Israel saw the miraculous power of God as He sent the ten plagues and then parted the Red Sea to save them from Pharaoh and the Egyptian army. Not long after, they lost their faith in the power of God as they wandered in the wilderness and times had gotten tough. They longed to go back to the pleasures of Egypt even though they were once in bondage there, but God had a better place ahead for them.

I completely understand their desire to go back to the familiar even though God has better plans for us up ahead. I didn't come to know Christ as my Savior until I was in my 30's and that time after becoming a Christian was hard. Just like Israel, I had spent so much of my life in "Egypt" it was hard to let go and I made some big mistakes early in my Christian life, but God had a better plan up ahead for me.

There's a difference in knowing Jesus Christ as our Savior and knowing Him as our Lord. It was many years after accepting Christ as my Savior that I made Him my Lord also and the difference was outstanding. Not only did I trust him with my soul, now I trust him with my life, this life I'm living between the Trees.

Maybe you're in the same position I was, you accepted Christ's saving power but haven't turned your life over to His lordship. Maybe you're wondering why this Christian life seems so hard and why you keep being drawn back to Egypt. Turn your life over to Him as Lord and see the difference it will make.

Notes:_____
_____
_____
_____
_____
_____
_____
_____
_____
_____
_____
_____
_____
_____
_____
_____
_____
_____
_____
_____

Satan Provides a Boat Too

Satan Provides a Boat too. Jonah, the prophet of God, was called to go to Nineveh to warn an evil generation that they were going to be judged. Jonah had a high disdain for them because they weren't Jews like him, but God called him to warn these people whether he liked it or not.

Jonah ran from God and made his way down to Joppa to find a boat that would get him to Tarshish. Satan made a ship available to him when he arrived and off, he went in the opposite direction from where God had called him to go.

As Christians we need to be careful when we pray for God to open doors for us that they are actually from God and not Satan. Satan will make things available to us that we have been praying for that in reality take us from where God wants us. The opportunity looks just like what we've been praying for but actually takes us further from God or the things God wants for us.

Maybe it's a new job or a new house or something else we've been praying for a long time. It looks great on the surface but if we really search the opportunity it's not from God at all. That new job may mean less time with your family or for church, maybe that new house takes away all your money to do the things your family loves or the money you used to tithe to church.

Searching for God's will in new opportunities will let you know if they are from Him or if they are meant to draw you away from Him. Let the Holy Spirit have the freedom to work in your life and trust those little nudges from Him that something may not be right. God will never put you in a position that takes you away from Him.

Jonah quickly learned that the ship heading for Tarshish was not God's will for his life (and so did the other sailors on that ship).

Notes:_____
_____
_____
_____
_____
_____
_____
_____
_____
_____
_____

November 4

A Second Chance God

A Second Chance God. Everyone knows the story of Jonah and the great fish, even unbelievers. However, Jonah being swallowed by the great fish isn't the point of the story, in fact, the great fish is only mentioned in 3 verse out of four chapters.

The point of the story is that God is a God of second chances. He gave Jonah a second chance to go Nineveh as he was commanded after he came to himself in the belly of the fish. (That phrase "came to himself" is the same phrase used with the prodigal son). God could have given up on Jonah and just let him die in the belly of that fish and sent someone else. But God had a plan for Jonah and He had a plan for the people of Nineveh.

Jonah isn't the only person in the story to receive a second chance, the people of Nineveh were about to get their opportunity at a second chance as well. In the end, both Jonah and Nineveh took advantage of the second chance God had provided them.

I don't know about you, but I am glad that my God is a God of second chances! If we are honest, most of us would probably admit that we are all far past just our second chance and have seen God give us more chances than we probably deserve.

Maybe you feel you have done too many things in your life for God to give you another chance; the Bible would prove that to be wrong. If you cry out to God, He'll hear you and give you another chance to follow His will for your life! We can't go back and change things we've done, but we can keep going forward looking toward that future Tree of Life awaiting us.

Notes:_____
_____
_____
_____
_____
_____
_____
_____
_____
_____
_____
_____
_____
_____
_____
_____
_____
_____

November 5

Rescue the Perishing

Rescue the Perishing. Even though Jonah is an Old Testament prophet, as Christians we can use his life as an example for our own. Jonah was full of religious pride feeling that the grace and salvation

of God should only be for his people, the Jews. However, God had a plan for the Gentiles that lives in Nineveh and Jonah wasn't happy about it.

We can learn three things from Jonah that sometimes cause us as Christians to keep the message of Jesus Christ and his work on the Cross for our sins to ourselves.

First, Jonah didn't have a Godly love for those in Nineveh that were perishing. Jonah thought God's forgiveness was only for the Jews and he didn't care that the people of Nineveh were going to be judged if he didn't share God's message. Do we look at people and think that God's forgiveness isn't for them because of how they are currently living or things they did in their past?

Second, Jonah wasn't right with God himself. He ran from God as far and as fast as he could not to share God's love. Do we find ourselves feeling unworthy of sharing the Gospel because we ourselves aren't in fellowship with God? Are we ashamed of what those we witness to might say about our own lives or be surprised we call ourselves Christians?

Finally, Jonah felt he had to have his own message to bring to the people of Nineveh when actually God just told him to "go" and he would provide the message when he obeyed. Do we feel inadequate because we don't know what message to share or we don't think we know enough about God's Word? It's not about our message, it's about God's message! The Holy Spirit will give us the words we need to share when we obey His call to do so.

Do you see people without Christ as perishing? Are we in fellowship with God ourselves and living right? Are we ready to share God's message and not our own?

Notes:_____
_____
_____
_____
_____
_____
_____
_____
_____
_____

November 6

A Love that's Multiplied

A Love that's Multiplied. When I first became a father to our daughter over ten years ago, I never thought I could ever love something more than I loved that little girl. We tried for years to have another child and thought maybe I was just too old and it wasn't in God's plan for our lives to have more than one child. We got to the point that we sold all the baby stuff we had held onto in hopes that another one may come along soon.

I now know that God has a great sense of humor because on Father's Day, after almost everything was sold, my wife told me she was pregnant and we were going to have another child. I couldn't tell you how excited I was to find out we were going to have a little boy to go along with our beautiful daughter.

In all honesty, I was quite scared as well. I had never experienced that type of love that you have when you become a parent for the first time and realize through God's grace you created another human being. Now I was going to have to share that love with another child. It scared me that one child may receive more love than the other and that my love for both of them would now have to be divided.

When our son was born, I learned a great lesson; my love for my two children was not divided, but it was multiplied. God's love for us works the same way. As people accept Christ as their Savior, God's love for His family is not divided but it is multiplied. What a great Truth we have about the love of God! Don't be afraid to share the message of Christ because in doing so, and making converts, God's love is multiplied into the lives of the new believer.

Notes:_____

_____

_____

_____

_____

_____

_____

_____

_____

_____

_____

_____

_____

_____

_____

_____

_____

What happened to our Parents?

What happened to our parents? The same people who ruled over us with an iron fist, that kicked us under the table, pinched us on the arm or leg, or gave us that death stare straight from Satan himself when we misbehaved. All of a sudden, they became grandparents and all rules seemed to go out the window.

It amazes me the things that our kids get away with at our parent's house that we wouldn't even imagine doing when we were young. Now our kids are allowed to jump on the furniture and eat chocolate whenever they want it. What happened to the response "your legs aren't broken" when we asked them to get us something? Now when the grandkids ask for something, they jump off the chair like it was spring loaded.

Why couldn't they be our grandparents when we were growing up instead of our parents? They're much more laid back now than they used to be but I guess they thought the same thing about their parents when we were little.

As Christians, sometimes we expect God to act like our grandfather instead of our father. We hope that He will just shrug off our sins or look the other way. When we willingly choose not to obey Him and instead choose to sin, we can expect consequences for our actions. If we have accepted Christ as our Savior, the consequences won't be eternal, but there will be consequences for our actions here on earth.

God has no grandchildren, only sons and daughters, so we need to stop thinking that God will treat us like our parents treat our kids. We have a Heavenly Father and not a Heavenly Grandfather.

Notes:_____

_____
_____
_____
_____
_____
_____
_____
_____
_____
_____
_____
_____
_____
_____
_____

Been There, Done That

Been There, Done That. This guy is walking down the street when he falls in a hole. The walls are so steep he can't get out.

A doctor passes by and the guy shouts up, "Hey you. Can you help me out?" The doctor writes out a prescription and throws it down in the hole and moves on.

Then a priest walks by and the guy shouts up, "Father, I'm down in this hole, can you help me out?" The priest writes out a prayer, throws it down in the hole and moves on.

Then a friend walks by, "Hey Joe, it's me can you help me out?" And the friend jumps in the hole. Our guy says, "Are you stupid? Now we're both down here."

The friend says, "Yeah, but I've been down here before and I know the way out."

We go through various things in our lives that God allows us to go through, good or bad. Sometimes those things are to discipline us, sharpen us like iron or maybe refine us like precious metal. Other times the things we go through may not even be for our benefit but for the benefit of someone else that has yet to go through it.

The Apostle Paul told the Corinthian church in his second letter to them, that we serve a God of mercy that comforts us in our affliction so that we may comfort others going through that same affliction in a manner similar to how God has comforted us.

Who's going through something in their lives right now that you have already been through and know the way out? Reach out to them and comfort them through these difficult times.

Notes:_____

_____
_____
_____
_____
_____
_____
_____
_____
_____
_____
_____
_____
_____
_____
_____

November 9

Hide and seek

Hide and Seek. I find it funny to watch little children try to hide something that they did wrong. Having a two year old allows me to watch firsthand how far a little guy will go to try to hide something that he knows he did wrong.

It amazes me to see the depth of their knowledge as to what is right and what is wrong. Some of it is learned from past experiences but a lot of it is intrinsic to their nature. We are all born with that sin nature and leaning to break the rules before we learn to follow them.

It's no different when we grow up and learn to better hide our sins as teenagers. We think we have become masters at keeping things from our parents but as I've gotten older, I have learned that my parents knew more about what I used to do than I thought they did. As adults, we continue to work hard to hide certain sins in our lives and other sins are now labeled as our "personality".

The events of Calvary show us two main things. First, it shows how far man is willing to go to protect his sins. Second, Calvary shows how far God is willing to go to save man from his sins.

Jesus, the perfect Son of God, who committed no sin, was willing to sacrifice His own life to pay for the sins of the world. Man was willing to crucify Christ in order to satisfy their own pride as religiously superior.

Are you holding on to your own pride so hard that you are willing to sacrifice the love of God, and what He did for you through Jesus Christ on Cavalry, or are you willing to humble yourself and call out to God for salvation? It's the most important decision you will ever make; eternity depends on it.

Notes:_____
_____
_____
_____
_____
_____
_____
_____
_____
_____
_____
_____
_____
_____

My Story - Part 1

What's your story? Everybody has one. We have stories about all sorts of things that have happened in our lives: becoming parents, buying a car or a house, going through a divorce, battling addiction, the loss of a loved one and so on. We have a story of our lives only we can tell and personal stories have a deep impact on those who hear it because it somehow draws them in and connects you to them.

Over the next series of posts I'm going to tell you "my story" of how I came to know Christ and accept Him as my Savior. Each one of us who are Christians have a different story on how we have received the grace of God and it's your story that only you can tell. The advantage of sharing your story is that no one can argue with your personal experience. Here goes!

I wasn't born into a family that would be considered a Christian family. I would say it was more of a moral family. We were taught the difference between right and wrong; we were taught how to be respectful and how to be the best people we could be. But there was no Bible in our house, we didn't bow our heads in prayer and thank God for His blessings on us or our food, and we weren't drug to church every Sunday.

I don't know if it was because of my grandparents urging or because of the fact that friends of my parents were doing it with their kids, but we went to Sunday School every once in a while at the local Catholic Church in our hometown. We went through all of the ceremonial practices of the Church: first communion and confirmation. I would even go to mass sometimes after Sunday school after begging my parents to come back and get me an hour later because some of my other friends happened to be going that Sunday. Most of the mass we just messed around in the pew and didn't pay a bit of attention.

After I made my confirmation in eighth grade, I would say I maybe went occasionally on Easter and Christmas (usually because a girl was going too). Religion was not a big part of my life and it wasn't something I was interested in. Looking back, I don't remember it ever being a topic of conversation amongst any of my friends nor did I ever remember my parent's friends talking about church. It was something that was very private to people.

In my next post I'll share my story of my college experience at a Catholic school.

Notes:_____
_____
_____
_____
_____
_____

My Story - Part 2

I told you about my childhood and teen years in yesterday's post and how I grew up in a moral home but not a Christian home. I'll continue my story with my experience in college.

I ended up going to a Catholic college in Albany, NY called the College of Saint Rose. I didn't go because of its religious affiliation but because it was a school that offered me a chance to play both soccer and baseball at the collegiate level. It also had a nationally recognized art program that I was able to get into.

More than 50% of my college professors outside of my art classes were nuns. I had professors that went by the names of Sister Tess and Sister Agnes Rose. The school used to be an all-girl school until the late 70's or early 80's.

For three of the four years that I went to college there, I lived within 200 yards of the Catholic church on the corner. There were students that went to church regularly, but I was not one of them. I did not step foot in that church one time in my four years there and really had no interest in anything "religious" at all. I went to school there for art, sports and girls (probably in reverse order).

The nuns that I mentioned, Sister Tess and Sister Agnes Rose, we're both huge sports fans. They came to the soccer games, the basketball games and the baseball games and would talk to me about games I played in that they attended. However, they never once asked me about going to church or my religious beliefs. Looking back, I find that kind of odd that my spiritual well-being wasn't as important to them as my athletic well-being.

After four years of college, I received my degree in elementary education and moved back home. After a year of teaching I got an opportunity to interview for a teaching position in North Carolina.

I'll continue my story tomorrow about my move to the Bible Belt.

Notes:_____
_____
_____
_____
_____
_____
_____
_____
_____
_____
_____

My Story - Part 3

I got a phone call late one Tuesday night. I had spent all summer sending applications down to NC and heard nothing, and then all of a sudden, I got the call. I packed that night and left Wednesday morning. I interviewed on Thursday and start teaching first grade on Friday.

What a whirlwind that week was. From starting a fill-in teaching job in Massachusetts Tuesday morning to leaving on Wednesday and teaching in North Carolina on Friday. I left with only my clothes and my car.

I was in a strange new world with people I had a hard time understanding what the heck they were saying. Looking back now, my new teaching partners were some of the nicest people I have ever met. They took in this northern boy right from day one, but I soon realized I was living in a whole new world.

I can't tell you how many times in the first few weeks of moving here that I was asked if I had found a place to go to church or if I would like to go to church with someone. As I told you in my last post, people didn't do that in NY. Your religious life was your personal life and you didn't ask people if they went to church or if they wanted to go to church with you.

This concept of being asked to church pushed me even further away from wanting to go. I did try a couple times just to be nice but it never "stuck".

When I started teaching at the high school the invitations changed from other teachers asking me, to now my students were asking me to go or where I was currently going. I used to make fun of them for asking me. I was downright mean sometimes. I remember one girl in my class witnessing to me about my spiritual condition and I made fun of her that I must be better than she was because she was the one that had to go to church three times a week and not me. Oh, how I feel for that girl now and how I treated her, and she was one of the sweetest students I ever had. She was just concerned about me and I must have made her feel horrible. I've never had a chance to apologize to her for that, but if I see her again that will be the first thing I do. I was going on with my life in my own little happy world until it was turned upside down. As most stories go.......I met a girl.

Notes:_____
_____
_____
_____
_____
_____
_____
_____

My Story - Part 4

Yadkin Plaza Restaurant! Who would have ever thought that would be where love would start? This is where a young lady first caught my eye and later stole my heart. It was a teacher workday and I had been going through some rough events in my life and was not looking for a relationship of any sort. I walked into the restaurant and saw her across the room. She was sitting with my former teaching partners so I had an instant "in". I went over to their table and was introduced to Jennifer, my future bride. After we left the restaurant I immediately called over to the school to talk to the teacher she was doing her student teaching under to find out about her relationship status; she was single.

We went on our very first date the next day and I also met her parents that day when I went to pick her up. We went to lunch and a little shopping because school was closed due to snow. We've been together ever since that first date. She was a lot different than I was. Her and her family were very much involved in the church and I was as far away from the church as one could possibly be. But Jennifer and her family accepted me just as I was with no pressure whatsoever to change or conform to their standards. They just accepted and loved on me.

I remember meeting them at their house for lunch on Sunday afternoon after they had gone to church and I had not. Still no pressure from them to join them but I saw something different in her family that I had never experienced before. It was a love that I just couldn't put my finger on. The more my relationship grew with Jennifer, the more time I wanted to spend with her and that meant church. I started meeting them at church on Sunday morning services only. Then it progressed to Sunday School before service too. Then it was Sunday night service and finally Wednesday night service as well. Still I was never pressured by Jennifer or her family to go but the more often I went the more my eyes were opened to my need for a Savior.

I don't remember the exact day, but it was during the Christmas season, and I was laying in my bed one night and it hit me like a ton of bricks. If I were to die tonight, I would have to spend my eternity paying for my own sins in a place called hell. That night I got "saved". All I had to do was put my faith in what He did and that it was sufficient for my sins (it is!). Praise God my eternity is sealed in heaven. I was now saved and a born-again Christian, but that didn't mean life automatically became perfect. I'll tell you about my rough start to this thing called Christianity tomorrow.

Notes:_____
_____
_____
_____
_____

My Story - Part 5

Failure. Fake. Fraud. All thing I felt like after I made a major mistake in my life. I was a new Christian and an even newer husband. How could I let something like this happen to me? Had I really become a Christian or was I just playing a game?

All these questions went through my mind after making a major mistake in my life, an almost catastrophic mistake. My whole life was falling apart and I was questioning my new faith in Christ. Was it real? How was I going to get through this?

It was hard, I'm not going to lie. I lost people that were in my life that I thought were friends but they were just acquaintances. My wife showed me what it meant to be a Christian and so did her family and a handful of friends (they know who they are) as they stood right beside me during this difficult time.

It changed my life. It changed my relationships. It change my relationship with Christ. I had accepted Him as my Savior and I knew that I was saved, but I had never turned my life over to Him as Lord, to use it as He saw fit. I wanted to still hold on to my old life (that life in Egypt I wrote about), but still try to live this new life as a Christian.

It doesn't work and I found that out the hard way. I don't think I'm the only Christian that has gone through this, especially living so long not being a Christian and now starting this new life that was foreign to me. It was this event in my life that really made me look at what being a Christian meant. I think a lot of people get saved and then that's it. They have their security blanket that they are going to heaven and they are fine with just that, but they never really go to the next step - that was me.

There came a point in time that I finally gave my entire life to the Lord and submitted to His will and not my own. Once I did that, my life really changed. My marriage changed. My priorities changed. My goals changed. I don't live like I used to because I'm no longer the person I used to be.

Notes:_____
_____
_____
_____
_____
_____
_____
_____
_____
_____
_____
_____

November 15

That's My Story

"That's my story and I'm sticking to it!" is what country artist Collin Raye sang back in the 90's. Many of you have been following along as I shared my story. I didn't tell you all of my story but just enough for you to understand how God was in control of the whole thing even if I wasn't interested in Him. It's so much easier to see now looking back over my life.

That's the great thing about sharing your own story; people can't argue what you went through and what you experienced. They can argue your interpretation of the Bible, they can argue your doctrine and they can argue your theology. But they cannot (and will not by the way) argue your story of how God changed your life. People listen to your story as was evident by how many people started following this little page since I started telling my story.

Your story creates a connection with people because they see themselves in parts of our story and they can relate. They become part of the story and they start to feel what you felt. Have you ever been scared to share the Gospel of Jesus Christ with people because you felt you didn't know enough about the Bible? Share your story! People don't want to be preached to; they want to know how it will change their lives.

What's your story? Have you ever just sat down and thought through how God changed your life? How He was there when you needed Him most that people would see how God worked in your life. Our story should never focus on our triumphs but should focus on God's glory. We use our story to point others to His story. This life isn't about our story it's about His and it's a pretty simple story.

Man was separated from God because of our sin. God wanted to restore that relationship but needed someone to pay for our sins. Jesus Christ was born of the Virgin Mary and lived a sinless life. He was crucified, died and rose again as payment for our sins to satisfy the wrath of God. If we put our faith in Christ that he is the Son of God and He took our place on the Cross, we can be saved from our sins. It's that simple. No rules, no works, just faith and the grace of God.

Message me if you want to know more. If you think my story would bless your church, or your Sunday School class, or your group, I would love to come speak for you; just message me.

Notes:_____
_____
_____
_____
_____

Change

CHANGE!!! This word has been on my mind so much this past week as I've been sharing my story. As I wrote each post, I notice how many changes took place in my life through each part of the story. Change is not always easy and not always clear in which direction to go.

Change usually comes about in two ways: either we make the choice to change something in our lives or circumstances force us into the change. The first one seems easier because we feel we are in control of the decision while the second one seems scary because we have no control. The fact is that both can be scary. "Did I make the right decision to change?" Or, "why is this happening to me?"

Sometimes God wants us to change but we are reluctant to follow his calling because we are too frightened to leave our current state of familiarity. God may patiently wait on us to finally trust him and make the change on our own or He may cause events to happen in our lives to make us change.

It reminds me of the story of the prophet Elijah in 1 Kings 17. He had just given King Ahab the bad news that God was going to cause a drought on Israel because of their idolatry. God instructed Elijah to go to a brook called Cherith and the ravens would bring him food daily and he could drink from the brook.

Elijah must have felt that life was great. He was safe, well fed and well-watered. He was content with his current location and lifestyle. But God had more work for him to do so that the idolatrous nation of Israel would know the power and glory of God, so He dried up that brook forcing Elijah to move on out of his comfort zone.

God has work for each of us to do. He doesn't want us to stay in our comfort zones for long periods of time. Sure, there are times He allows us to rest but He doesn't expect us to believe our jobs are done here. There are no retired Christians. What has He been calling you to CHANGE?

Notes:_____

_____

_____

_____

_____

_____

_____

_____

Run Your Own Race

"Run your own race!" Or as my sister tells my nephew all the time, "Drive your own bus!" We spend too much of our time comparing our lives and the things we have to others around us. We try to "keep up with the Joneses" or what the world tells us we should be doing, what we should own or what we should look like.

Jennifer and I had the opportunity a few weekends ago to run in the Rugged Maniac mud run in Greensboro with a great group of friends. It was cold and wet and extremely muddy. We had been preparing to complete this 5k and 25 obstacle course for quite a few months, but there was really no preparing for this.

We left off with a large group of people of all shapes and sizes, of all ages and of all different physical abilities. An hour and a half later, our group of 11 runners finished the race together. We stuck with one another and made sure everyone made it through each obstacle. We cheered each other on and we lent a helping hand when needed.

As we were about halfway through the course, I started noticing that groups of runners that were released in heats after ours were starting to pass us. I realized that some of the runners were not running just to finish like we were, they were running to compete against a time or a personal best. We were just trying to finish with no injuries!!!

My competitive spirit from long ago started to rise up inside of me and I started to think "I need to run this again some time and just try to do my best." Then reality came back to me and I said, "I'm 46 years old and I don't need to show my long lost athletic ability any longer!" I was worried about the other racers and not my own race.

As Christians, we need to worry about our own race. We need to concentrate on what God has called us to do and not compare our Christian walk with someone else's. God doesn't want us to race someone else's race, He wants us to run oar's

Our race contains obstacles and trials that are meant for us. Some of us go through cancer, some go through divorce, others go through death of a child or a spouse or a parent. That is our race and those are the obstacles that God has for us to overcome. We look at other people and usually have no idea what obstacles they have overcome in their lives or what obstacles they are currently tackling. We shouldn't judge our lives to others and we shouldn't judge their lives to ours.

Notes:_____
_____
_____
_____

November 18

No One Sees the Wizard

"No one gets in to see the Wizard. Not nobody. Not no how." As we drove from North Carolina towards New York yesterday, the kids were watching videos on the DVD player and our daughter watched the Wizard of Oz. I could only hear the movie as I was driving and this part of the movie really stuck out to me as I listened to the interaction between the Wizard and Dorothy and her friends.

After they finally got in to see him because of Dorothy's ruby red slippers, they all make their plea to the Wizard to get the things that they were missing in their lives. Dorothy wanted to go home to Kansas. The Scarecrow wanted a brain. The Tin Man wanted a heart. And the Cowardly Lion wanted courage. The Wizard sends them out to bring back the broom of the wicked Witch of the West and he would grant them their wishes.

The world, and sometimes Christians, see God in the same way. They feel that if they complete some task or some set of works that God will be pleased with them and finally accept them and give them their hearts desires. Unfortunately, God doesn't work that way. There is nothing we can do within our own strength or anything we can complete that would make us acceptable to God. Even all the works that Mother Teresa did are considered dirty rags in the sight of God.

We can never "do" enough to earn access or favor with God, the Bible makes that clear. We can only come to God in faith and belief in what His Son, Jesus Christ, did on the Cross of Calvary.

The Apostle Paul told the Ephesians that "by grace we have been saved through faith. And this is not of your own doing; it is the gift of God, not a result of works, so that no one can boast." Heaven would be hell if we had to spend all of eternity listening to how many good deeds everyone had done to get there. Instead, everyone will have the same story, they got there because of the shed blood of Jesus Christ and that's it. All praise will go to God and not ourselves. Oh, what a day!!!

Notes:_____
_____
_____
_____
_____
_____
_____
_____
_____
_____
_____

Why Does God Allow Evil?

Why Does God Allow Evil? Traveling almost 700 miles over two days from North Carolina to New York for the Thanksgiving holiday will really show you the good and evil in people. Watching how people drive and interact with other drivers will show you the evil in people's hearts. God forbid you pull out in front of someone to get out from behind a tractor trailer or if you happen to be going a bit slower than they want to be going.

It got me to thinking, "Why does God allow evil into the world when He could just get rid of it so easily?" I mean you watch the news and that's all that they show. People killing other people, people hating each other and because they believe something different, or just the fury of nature with the fires in California. Couldn't He just fix all of this?

Of course He could. But God created us with free will which allows us to choose between good and evil. If God wanted there to be no evil in the world, He would have had to create us like robots that are programmed just to do as they're told. God didn't want robots, He wanted His creation to actively choose to follow Him and by doing such, He gave mankind free will to choose.

However, with free will, man has the ability to choose evil instead of good. Even the created angelic beings have the free will to choose to serve God or not to. Satan and a third of the angelic host chose not to follow God and instead revolted against Him and were ultimately cast out of heaven. If angels, who served God directly and had access to Him, were able to freely choose evil over good, so man, who hasn't seen God directly, can also choose the same path.

Evil exists because God loves us and wants us to choose to have a relationship with Him. How weird would your relationship be with your spouse if they were forced to love you instead of choosing to do so. I don't believe that would be a relationship worth being in and that's not the relationship God wants to be in with us. He wants us to actively pursue and love Him just like He actively pursues and loves us.

This free will has a negative consequence called evil. Evil exists not because God can't get rid of it or cannot control its existence, it exists because God loves us so much, He wants us to freely choose good (Him) over evil (Satan). What, or who, have you chosen?

Notes:_____
_____
_____
_____
_____
_____

The Narrow Road

The Narrow Road. "Those are some seriously narrow roads!" I have never realized how narrow some of the roads are in the middle of town in my hometown in New York. I was remind yesterday as we drove through. My wife mentioned how nerve wracking it was to drive through that short stretch.

The road is barely wide enough for two cars to park along the curbs and then two more cars to pass each other on the street, especially if one of those vehicles is a tractor trailer. The locals don't seem to even think twice about it and neither did I growing up; it was all I ever knew. But now coming back only once a year it really drew my attention. I'm sure that truck drivers try to avoid this section of road whenever they can.

It got me thinking about what the Bible says about the narrow way. "Enter by the narrow gate. For the gate is wide and the way is easy that leads to destruction, and those who enter by it are many. For the gate is narrow and the way is hard that leads to life, and those who find it are few." This Christian life isn't easy and the way can be hard at times but the reward is great. The road the world wants you to follow is wide and easy to follow and the world just follows along but the path leads to destruction.

When I wasn't a Christian, I really never thought about the road I was on; it was all I ever knew and the same road everyone else was traveling as well. But now that I have been away from that life for quite a while, it stands out rather dramatically as I look back, just like the narrow roads in my hometown. Sometimes it just takes a different perspective and some time to see things how they really are. I never knew I was on the wrong road until I got off and looked back at it from the correct road; the narrow road.

What road are you traveling in life? The wide one that everyone else is on that ultimately leads to destruction. Or the narrow road that is hard and not as well traveled but leads to eternal life? The choice is yours. You need to decide today.

Notes:_____
_____
_____
_____
_____
_____
_____
_____
_____
_____
_____
_____

November 21

Be the One

Be the one!!! Be that one person that stands out from the rest as being a person that is thankful and grateful for all the things you have in your life. It doesn't matter if the things or events that occur in your life are great things or if they are just small events; be thankful and grateful for them.

Luke 17 tells us a story of ten lepers that were living apart from all of society because the Law of Moses forced them to. They were in a community filled with only other people just like them, sick with not possibility of being cured. They were pretty much sentenced to a slow death among others that were slowly dying as well. But by God's grace, Jesus passed through that area.

As you can imagine, they called out to Him, asking Jesus for His mercy on them. They knew that He was the only answer to their death penalty. He went to them and healed them of the terrible disease. As they went away so extremely happy to have their lives back and able to go back to their families and society in general, only one turned and went back to Jesus to thank Him for what He had done. Only one!

Be the one! Be thankful for all that God has done for you and all that He has blessed you with. We have so much to be thankful for!

I'm thankful for my family: my beautiful wife and kids, my family in New York and my family in North Carolina, my friends in both places and my brothers and sister in Christ. But most of all, I'm thankful for my Savior Jesus Christ, that took the penalty of this sinner and accepted me into the family of God even though He knows me better than anyone. He still thought I was worth dying for. Thank you, Jesus!!!!

Notes:_____

_____
_____
_____
_____
_____
_____
_____
_____
_____
_____
_____
_____
_____

November 22

Adoption

Adoption. November is National Adoption Month. I'm not an adopted child, my parents are my biological mother and father, but I have had the opportunity over the years to know people who have adopted and who are adopted. I was a teenager when one of our close family friends adopted a small boy from the Midwest, and years later another boy. I remember them bringing him home and getting to meet him. His adopted parents were so excited to have him in their family since they couldn't have their own biological children. It was an exciting time for our family too as we welcomed in a new member to our extended family.

I know that there are people that are probably reading this post that were adopted as small children or maybe have adopted children of their own. Stories vary from person to person on the effects that an adoption had on their lives. Some stories involve children taken out of some very bad situations and brought into warm and loving homes. For every one hundred of those stories, there are stories of adoption not working out as well. I want to focus on the positive changes that adoption has had on so many lives. The future of some of these children have changed forever because of the love of people who adopt and provide a better life.

Spiritually, if you have put your faith in Christ, you are adopted as well. God's Word talks a lot about being adopted into the family of God. The Apostle Paul talked often about adoption. "But when the fullness of time had come, God sent forth his Son, born of woman, born under the law, to redeem those who were under the law, so that we might receive adoption as sons. And because you are sons, God has sent the Spirit of his Son into our hearts, crying, 'Abba! Father!' So, you are no longer a slave, but a son, and if a son, then an heir through God." - Galatians 4:4-7.

For those of you who have been adopted by earthly parents, happy National Adoption Month. For those of us who have been adopted by God when we put our faith and trust in the death, burial and resurrection of His Son, Jesus Christ; happy eternal adoption. I can't wait to meet each of you in eternity.

Notes:_____
_____
_____
_____
_____
_____
_____
_____
_____
_____
_____

Black Friday Deal

Best. Deal. Ever. That's what all the advertisements will try to sell you on today. Black Friday: the biggest shopping day of the year. Everyone out shopping for deals for all of their Christmas presents. The roads are packed, traffic is terrible, you can't find a parking spot and the checkout lines are a mile long. All for that advertised deal to save some money.

We are currently on our way back to North Carolina from New York and celebrating Thanksgiving with my family. We pick this day every year to travel back in hopes that most people will be shopping and not on the interstate. That's what I think is a good deal.

If you think that the Black Friday deals are good, I have the best deal ever for you. Imagine if someone would take the penalty on themselves for all of the bad things you have done in your entire life. Imagine being sentenced before a judge for some crime you had committed and all of a sudden someone you don't know says, "I'll serve the punishment for him/her." What would you do? Would you argue with them and tell them that wasn't necessary and that you will serve the time yourself?

About 2000 years ago, on a Black Friday, Jesus Christ did just that for you. He hung on the Cross as payment for your sins and not His own. He was willing to take your punishment even though He had not committed the crime. But man is so hard hearted that he is unwilling to take the gift. Instead of accepting the free gift of Christ, man is more willing to say "no thank you" instead of humbling himself and accepting the free gift of Christ.

What is keeping you from that free gift? Is it pride? Is it that you don't believe that it could be that easy? Or maybe you have never heard this Good News. Please message me if you want to know more. I would love to explain to you the free gift of accepting Jesus Christ.

If you have already accepted Christ as your Savior; AMEN! I look forward to spending eternity with you in the presence of God.

Notes:_____

_____
_____
_____
_____
_____
_____
_____
_____
_____
_____
_____

The Way of the Cross

"The way of the Cross leads home!" That old hymn came to mind yesterday as we drove back to North Carolina from New York. When you come into the state of Virginia on Interstate 81 after leaving West Virginia, there is a huge iron cross on the property of a church right along the highway. It has to be five stories high and looks like scaffolding. It is painted white and is lit up at night for all to see.

As we kept traveling south, about thirty minutes after that first large cross, there are three huge wooden crosses up on a hill that can once again be seen from the highway (the picture shows these three crosses).

I was further reminded that we were back in the Bible Belt as church after church could be seen along the side of the highway as we continued traveling south through Virginia towards home. As we were traveling, that old hymn came to mind, "The Way of the Cross Leads Home", and I've been singing it ever since (and I'm not a good singer):

I must needs go home by the way of the cross,
There's no other way but this;
I shall ne'er get sight of the gates of light,
If the way of the cross I miss.

Chorus:
The way of the cross leads home, (leads home,)
The way of the cross leads home; (leads home;)
It is sweet to know as I onward go,
The way of cross leads home.

I must needs go on in the blood sprinkled way,
The path that the Savior trod,
If I ever climb to the heights sublime,
Where the soul is at home with God. [Chorus]

Then I bid farewell to the way of the world,
To walk in it nevermore,
For the Lord says, "Come," and I seek my home
Where He waits at the open door. [Chorus]

Notes:_____
_____
_____
_____
_____

Stuck in Traffic

Stuck in Traffic. There is nothing worse than being stuck in traffic when you are trying to get home after being away all week. We had just left the hotel and we hadn't been on the highway for more than five miles when we hit the first accident and came to a dead stop.

After about three more accidents along the way and inching along behind tractor trailers, we finally reached our destination. But it was definitely frustrating having to just sit and wait. It was pouring rain outside and being stuck behind the tractor trailers; you couldn't see anything that was going on up in front of you. You just had to WAIT!

So it is in life! Sometimes we feel as if we are just stuck; sitting in life and feeling like we are not making any progress. We live in an age where we want everything done quickly. We want our food quickly, we want our coffee quickly and sometimes we want answers in our life quicker.

Maybe it's a job or a relationship; whatever it might be, we want things done quicker. We hate to have to wait. We want a microwave God; one that answers our prayers on our timing. We don't have time to wait!

But God wants us to wait on Him. He wants us to trust Him and His timing. You may be waiting because there is something up ahead that He wants you to avoid. He may be having you wait to teach you to be patient and trust Him. Being stuck may be for our benefit.

You may be stuck because there is something in your life that is keep you back from moving forward. God may be keeping you where you are because you are not ready to move yet. Whatever it may be, be patient during this time of waiting and trust that God will have you move when the time is right. Keep praying. Keep trusting. And keep being patient.

Notes:_____
_____
_____
_____
_____
_____
_____
_____
_____
_____
_____
_____
_____

White Knuckles

White knuckle driving. I had my hands wrapped around the steering wheel so tight that the knuckles on my hands were white and cramped. The rain was coming down so hard and the spray from the tires of all cars and tractor trailers made visibility almost zero. Of course, that didn't matter to some drivers as they weaved in and out at eighty miles per hour.

I admit, I was pretty nervous driving in those conditions. I had a lot of valuable items in the minivan: my wife and two kids. I was watching what was going on in front of me, on all sides of me, and behind me with intense scrutiny to make sure we were safe.

As we were driving through this mess, I looked in the rear view mirror and there was my daughter on her iPad and my son watching a movie. They did not have a single concern of what we were traveling through. They completely trusted me that I was going to do everything in my power to get them to their destination safely: home!

They never once told me how to drive, never told me what lane I should be in, never told me that I was going too fast or too slow, and they didn't give me any instructions on what exits to take. They trusted me to do what was best for them.

Do we trust God the same way my kids trusted me? Do we live life fully knowing that He is doing everything in His power to get us safely to our final destination: Heaven!

Or do we constantly offer our suggestions on how He should be doing things, or what lane we think He should have us in, or maybe that He has things going too slow for our liking, or maybe even telling Him what exits we think we should be getting off?

God has our best interests in mind. He created us and knows every hair on our heads. He knows our past and already knows our future. If we can trust our eternity to Him, why can't we trust our present to Him as well? Trust that He knows what's best for you and let Him be God.

Notes:_____

_____

_____

_____

_____

_____

_____

_____

_____

_____

_____

November 27

Too Young to Die

Too Young to Die. It's hard to believe it's been 12 years already since my father passed away. I remember getting the news and I was devastated. My dad was much too young to have died this early. The thing is, we never know when our time here on earth will come to an end.

My dad was always a great man in my eyes. He was a high school athlete in football, basketball and baseball. He was a military man that served his country in the Vietnam War. He received the Purple Heart and Silver Star for his injuries and valor. He was a loving husband, father and grandfather. He loved to joke and pick with the people he loved and cherished as friends.

His service to our country is what ultimately cost him his life. He contracted leukemia from his exposure to Agent Orange and fought the good fight all the way to the end. It had gotten so aggressive that they were trying experimental drugs on him to see if they could slow it down. In the end, the disease won and he passed away.

I miss my dad dearly every day and wish he was around for his advice and to just talk about life and baseball. Life is precious and we need to love our family and friends while we still have the opportunity to do so.

I pray that you share with your family and friends that death isn't the end. We have all of eternity to spend in one of two places: heaven or hell. Make sure your loved ones know that the only way to heaven is by accepting the saving work of Jesus Christ on the cross of Calvary. God loves you so much He sent His Son to die in your place so that He could spend eternity with you in His presence. If you don't know Christ as your Savior, contact me and I would love to share with you how you can be saved.

Notes:_____
_____
_____
_____
_____
_____
_____
_____
_____
_____
_____
_____
_____

November 28

Walking the Walk

Walking the Walk. If you're going to talk the talk, you better walk the walk! How many times have you heard that phrase before? It could never be more true than in the Christian life. The way you live your life better match up with the message of the Good News of Jesus Christ when you share it.

The story of Naaman in 2 Kings 5 reminded me of this truth when I taught it this past Sunday at church. Just the first five verses show us how important our walk is when we want to share about God.

Naaman was the main commander of the Syrian army and the text emphasizes how great a man he was. But he was dying from leprosy with no cure for this disease at that time.

In the same text is a young Jewish girl that was a servant, or maiden, to Naaman's wife. She was probably captured during one of Naaman's military events and she was made a servant in his household. She was evidently privy to conversations between Naaman and his wife about his disease. This maiden tells her master that she wishes he was in her homeland of Samaria because there was a man of God there (Elisha) that could heal him of his disease. This must have been relayed to Naaman because he goes to the king of Syria asking for permission to go to Samaria to find Elisha. This is what made me think of walking the walk and talking the talk.

Why would this commander, the second most powerful man in Syria, take the advice from this little Jewish servant girl? It had to be because they had seen the life she lived under their roof. I assume she did all she was asked to do and probably some things she wasn't asked to as well. She lived a life of service to the God of Israel that Naaman and his wife did not worship.

When it was time for her to speak up, her life gave additional credence to the words she spoke. They saw in her a faith in God that had an effect on these two non-believers. So much so that they were willing to take her advice and seek after Elisha. Naaman found Elisha and he gave him instructions to be healed. By faith Naaman followed the instructions and was healed of his leprosy. All because a little servant girl lived a life faithful to God and was willing to speak up when the opportunity showed itself.

Notes:_____
_____
_____
_____
_____
_____

Celebrate Good Times

"Celebrate good times, come on!" (I bet you'll be singing that song for the next hour now). It's that time of year once again to get together with friends and family to celebrate the holidays. It starts with Thanksgiving and then moves to Hanukkah or Christmas or Kwanza or even Festivus (whatever you celebrate), and it comes to an end on New Year's Eve. All these man-made holidays give us a reason to celebrate.

We have so many other things to celebrate throughout the year: little things that deserve celebrating. These events can even be daily accomplishments that need to be celebrated. Things like losing that last pound of weight you've been trying to get rid of for the longest time. That promotion you've deserved for years. The daily victory of overcoming some addiction you've been battling all your life whether it's food or alcohol or drugs or something else. Celebrate those little things, those little victories that keep us going for the next day.

By celebrating those milestones, we open our hearts to joy and thankfulness for the small things in our lives. The Apostle Paul told the believers in Philippi to "rejoice in the Lord always; and again, I say, rejoice!" Celebrate all things and praise God for the things He allows in your life.

As Christians, we have things to celebrate every day: our salvation first and foremost, and the fact that we are one day closer to the return of the Lord to take us with Him so that "we shall forever be with the Lord". If you can't celebrate at least those two things every day, then you better check yourself.

Notes:_____
_____
_____
_____
_____
_____
_____
_____
_____
_____
_____
_____
_____
_____
_____
_____
_____

Close Talker

Are you a close talker? Do you know a close talker? I think everyone has come across someone that has been a little too close to us while we were in a conversation with them. The TV sitcom "Seinfeld" had a whole half hour show about a close talker.

What makes us so uncomfortable about someone being right up in our face like that? Is it the possibility that we might smell their breath and what they just had to eat? Or is it that we feel we may not have enough time to dodge a sneeze if it was to happen? I don't know about you, but I just don't feel comfortable with someone that close up to me unless it's my beautiful bride or kids.

I do know someone that loves close talkers: God. When we pray to God it's almost as if we are face to face with Him and there is no one else in the world but us and Him. Picture your prayer life as being a close talker with God. Like you are right there; nose to nose with Him telling Him all things as He intently listens. He has no concerns with you being that close; in fact, He loves it. The closer the better.

I have to be honest; I wish my prayer life was better sometimes. You could probably say the same thing about your own prayer life at times. What I do know, is that when my prayer life is where it's supposed to be, I feel like I'm closer to God. I feel like I am in step with everything He wants me to do. But when my prayer life is lacking it feels like I'm miles away. I know He hasn't moved; it's me.

I need to do a better job talking with God, how about you? Let us all work on be close talkers with God. Let's get face to face with Him on a more regular basis.

"Rejoice in hope, be patient in tribulation, be constant in prayer." Romans 12:12

Notes:_____
_____
_____
_____
_____
_____
_____
_____
_____
_____
_____
_____

December 1

Relationships

Relationships. We all love being in relationships. We develop relationships our whole life. Relationships come in all different shapes and sizes: family relationships, intimate relationships, friendships, relationships with coworkers, etc. Our first relationship comes as children with our parents. Not long after that our children form relationships with their siblings, grandparents and aunts and uncles. Then our friendship circle gets larger until we find the one! And then we start a relationship that trumps all others.

Why are we so desperate for that relationship bond with others? It's because we are created to have relationships. We are relationship-oriented people. We were all created by God who desires relationships.

God has always existed, from eternity past, in three persons: The Father, the Son and the Holy Spirit, yet he created man so that He could have a relationship with him. That original relationship was not corrupted by sin. Adam and Eve communed with God face to face. Then the sin of Adam and Eve marred that relationship.

Ever since that day, God has been working to resume that relationship with man once again. In the Old Testament that relationship hinges on the sacrificial system. In the New Testament it hinges on Christ. For some, sin keeps that relationship with God from happening. God desires a relationship with His creation. He wants to commune with us once again.

There is a God shaped hole in man's heart that can only be filled by a relationship to Him. Man tries to fill that hole with many other things: money, fame, drugs, alcohol, sex and so on. But only He can fulfill that missing relationship.

Do you have a relationship with Him? He wants one with you. He created you and knows how to fill that hole in your heart. Does it feel like something is missing in your life? It's Him, He's what's missing. If you need help finding Him, let me know, I'd love to introduce you to Him.

Notes:_____
_____
_____
_____
_____
_____
_____
_____
_____

December 2

Fishing

Fishing. I miss fishing when I was younger. My godfather Chris used to take me fishing all the time when I was a kid. He would take me to different locations and we would spend the day together fishing. I may have fished a handful of times since then. I miss it and wonder if I should take it up once again.

I don't think it's as much about catching fish (I don't eat fish), but more about the wonderful time spent with others that you take fishing, like your children. To be able to spend a couple of hours just out there by a pond or river with your kids away from the distractions of the television or tablets seems rewarding in itself.

More importantly than catching fish, as Christians we should be fishing for men. Jesus Christ summoned Peter and Andrew away from their profession of fishing to follow Him as disciples. He told them "follow Me and I will make you fishers of men". He calls us to do the same thing when we become believers.

Don't let your argument be that you haven't been called to the ministry or to the mission field. Your world is your mission field and your life is your ministry. Are you casting your nets in the waters you live in? First of all, are you casting your nets in your own house? Are you making sure your family is following Christ? Second, are you casting your nets at work, where you spend most of your day? Just like Jesus mentioned that the harvest was ready, so are the fishing holes. People are starving for truth and if you know Christ, you have the truth to give.

Notes:_____
_____
_____
_____
_____
_____
_____
_____
_____
_____
_____
_____
_____
_____
_____
_____
_____
_____

December 3

Traffic Jams

Traffic Jams. There have to be few things in the world that rank above traffic jams as the worst things to deal with. I hate having to sit in traffic and it looks like that is going to be my lot in life for at least the next 18 months. My main route to work has been shut down for road work, serious road work, like tear up the whole road and redesign it kind of road work.

Because of this road work, hundreds if not thousands of people have to find new routes to work and it makes things a mess. All of these detours are causing traffic jams all throughout the city. Everyone just ends up sitting bumper to bumper waiting. Have I said that I hate waiting in traffic jams?

I have taken multiple detours trying to find a route that causes me the least amount of pain. My choices are either take the highway with everyone else and just sit and wait until we move or take the backroads through the city and hit a couple of dozen stoplights. I have been taking the backroads and find it the safest route even though it might not be the fastest.

Has God ever thrown traffic jams in your life? Things that seem to get in the way of where you want to get to? They always seem to come up just when you think everything is going along smoothly, then all of a sudden BAM! It ends up being a total shock to the system.

Maybe the detours come in the form of a divorce, or health issues or the loss of a job. All things that can really throw you for a loop and feel like a major traffic jam in your life. You know - things that cause life to all of a sudden come to a drastic stop. How do we deal with these things as Christians when they happen?

We keep moving forward no matter how slow the pace may be. We have a destination that God is leading us to and our job is to trust him and just keep moving forward. There may be detours he wants us to travel because the original road may have been leading towards something dangerous. Trust Him because He sees things well ahead of what we do. He is not limited by time like we are, He sees all things throughout time.

Traffic jams while driving, just like traffic jams in life, can be frustrating and test our patience, but we just need to remember that reaching our destination safely is more important than reaching it quickly.

Notes:_____
_____
_____
_____
_____

Money or Meaning

Money or meaning? Pay the bills or find joy in what you do? I had a wonderful woman ask me those questions at church Sunday night. Her dilemma was to stay in a job to be able to help pay the bills or take a job that brings her joy and is more meaningful. I think at one time or another we have all been in that situation. Some people are lucky enough to find joy and meaning in their work that also pays the bills.

I didn't have the answer to that question for her and I don't have that answer for you. Every situation is different for every person and there is not a cookie cutter response that I can give. However, there are some questions I asked her and you can ask yourself. "How do you know that the job that will bring you joy and meaning also won't pay the bills?" "What can you do to reduce your debt so that you don't have to worry about the lost income?"

Money is an important part of our lives that is needed to make ends meet, but money should not be the top priority in our lives. God does bless some with wonderful incomes and some He does not. God knows who is capable of managing His money and who cannot. "To whom much is given, much is also required." All things are given by God and also belongs to Him. So, in actuality, what He blesses us with should be used to then bring Him glory by how we use it.

The Bible says "For the love of money is the root of all evil." Many people get that wrong; that money is evil, but that is not what the text says. It says that the "LOVE" of money is the root of all kinds of evil. It's the greed of wanting more money that leads to all other type of evil things. Having money is not evil. Loving money over all other things is what is evil.

Do you control your money or does your money control you? That is one of the most important questions that Dave Ramsey asks in his book "Total Money Makeover". We live in a world that pushes us to have more, want more and buy more by selling us on the lie that we will be happier. Don't drink the Kool-Aid!

Notes:_____
_____
_____
_____
_____
_____
_____
_____
_____
_____
_____
_____

December 5

Past, Present and Future

Past, present and future. No, I'm not talking about verb tenses for all my English teacher friends out there. I'm talking about life like I always do. It is something that every single one of us has in common with one another. We all have a past; good or bad or even both. We are all currently in the present. And we all have a future.

A few weeks ago I shared with you "my story" and how I came to know Christ as my personal Savior. When I share my story at churches, I always bring it back to Scripture and how my story (and your story) relates to the Bible. This is what makes the Word of God real in people's lives. The Scripture I use is my favorite part of the Bible: Ephesians 2:1-10.

The first seven verses of Ephesians 2 gives us a Biblical look at who we were, who we are and who we will be.

Verses 1 through the first half of verse 5 tells us who we once were. The Apostle Paul uses phrases like dead in our trespasses and sins, sons of disobedience, following the passions of our flesh, following the desires of our body and mind, and children of wrath. We all have those things in common no matter how we grew up. God still sees most of the people in the world this way unless they have accepted His Son.

The second half of verse 5 through verse 6 God tells us of our present standing if we have been saved. We are made alive in Christ and are no longer dead, He has raised us up and He has seated us in heavenly places. All of these things are done by Him and are not of works that we can do. Thank God He is in control.

Verse 7 gives us a hint of our future. He has saved us so that in the coming ages He is going to show His children immeasurable riches of His grace and kindness toward us because of what Christ Jesus has done in our place. Oh, happy day! If that doesn't make the hair on your arms stand up you better check and see if you have a pulse. Or maybe you better check your spiritual standing with God.

I don't know if there are many better passages in Scripture for the Christian, but if you have one, I would love for you to share it in the comments section below and tell me why it means so much to you.

Notes:_____
_____
_____
_____
_____

December 6

Buttinsky

Buttinsky. Be honest: are you a buttinsky? Well, are you? Can you not let someone finish their sentence without trying to finish it for them? What if someone is having a conversation and you aren't involved, do you have to join in with your thoughts? If you answered yes to either of those two questions, you are a buttinsky!

I have to admit, sometimes I'm a buttinsky. My name is Paul, and I'm a buttinsky. That feels good to get that off my chest. You should try it too if you're a buttinsky. I butt in more than I should sometimes, especially with my wife and I want to publicly apologize for doing that to you baby doll!

What is it about not being able to just be patient and letting the person finish their thought before we have to bust in with an answer or solution? Why do we feel we have to take part in everybody else's conversation when we haven't been invited in? I think it's because we want to show other people how much we know about whatever subject is being discussed.

Yesterday I shared my favorite section of Scripture and how it relates to every person that has a past, present and future. I left out the very best part of Ephesians 2 because I wanted to cover it today all by itself. After the first three verses tell us about how separated from God we were, the start of verse 4 has the two best words in the Bible: BUT GOD!

No matter how evil we have acted and how separated we are from God, He still loves us enough to "butt" into our lives when we are at our farthest from Him. When we are dead in our trespasses and sins, God butts in! When we follow the course of this world, He butts in! When we are disobedient and children of wrath, God butts in!

Has God "butted" into your life yet? Is there a moment in time where you can say, "God butted into my life right here and thank God He did?" God wants to be a buttinsky, but not for the reasons we do, He wants to butt in because He wants your life to be radically changed. Let today be the day He "butts" in.

Notes:_____
_____
_____
_____
_____
_____
_____
_____
_____
_____

December 7

Storm Warning

Storm warning. If you live in the south and the western part of North Carolina, you have been watching the forecast over the past few days and know that they are forecasting a big storm to come through this weekend. It started as a forecast of four to six inches and then quickly changed to eight to ten inches. Now they are predicting possibly over a foot of snow. I know that's not a big deal in some places, they deal with it all the time, but here in North Carolina, a storm like that can cripple us for a week.

We've already had two hurricanes come through the state this fall, so now we are adding a major snowstorm to the mix this month. The good thing about all three of these major storms is that they have been predicted, we have known they were all coming about a week or so in advance. That gives us ample time to prepare for what might lie ahead.

That doesn't always happen in life. We don't always get a chance to prepare for storms that show up in our lives. They tend to be more like tornadoes than they are hurricanes or snowstorms. They show up with little to no warning and they can sometimes leave a wake of damage in their paths. It could be a relationship storm, a financial storm or storm caused by the sudden death of a loved one.

Even though their timing may come as a surprise to us, the fact that storms are coming should not be. Jesus warned us, "I have said these things to you, that in me you may have peace. In the world you will have tribulation. But take heart; I have overcome the world." – John 16:33. Christ warned us that this life, even as Christians, was not going to be easy, there will be times of storms, but we have a Comforter to get us through those stormy times in our lives; His name is Jesus.

Notes:_____

_____
_____
_____
_____
_____
_____
_____
_____
_____
_____
_____
_____
_____
_____
_____
_____

Bread of Life

Bread of Life. Well, it's the morning of the big storm coming through western North Carolina and by now the store shelves must be empty. I'm not sure why everyone rushes to the grocery store before storms, everyone must build up a huge appetite from all the shoveling. The bread shelves are empty, the milk cooler is down to just coffee creamer and the egg area is wiped out. Makes me wonder if everyone eats French toast during snowstorms.

I have to admit, my wife went to the grocery store this week too, but it was her normal weekly trip and we didn't get anything out of the ordinary because of the storm. From what I hear this trend of emptying out grocery store shelves is also starting to move to other parts of the country.

Although the grocery store shelves may be empty of bread by now, Jesus says that "He is the bread of life and whoever comes to Him shall not hunger." We may constantly have to go back to the grocery store for physical bread as it runs out or turns bad, we never have to worry about the spiritual bread turning bad or ever running out.

The nation of Israel wandered through the wilderness for 40 years as they were being punished for their lack of faith in God. But God did not leave them out there to perish, He provided fresh manna for them daily to meet the needs they had for just that day (and twice on Friday). They did nothing to earn that grace from God, but because of His love for His people, He provided for them.

Just like God continued to provide for the nation of Israel with heavenly manna while they wandered through the wilderness for 40 years, God will continually provide for His children with the bread of life; Jesus Christ.

Notes:_____
_____
_____
_____
_____
_____
_____
_____
_____
_____
_____
_____
_____

December 9

White Out Conditions

White Out Conditions. It was snowing so hard yesterday that I could not see the road in front of my house nor the road behind my house and both of them are not more than 100 yards away. It was a "white out" at times during the day. I went out early to shovel off the side porch and brush off the cars but the effort was futile. We probably got another six to eight inches after that.

The snow does make everything look so clean and pure in comparison to what it looked like the day before. On Saturday everything out there was dead and brown and just looked dirty like fall usually looks, but when I woke up Sunday morning everything looked clean and new. I started to think about what the Bible says in Isaiah 1, "though your sins be like scarlet, they shall be as white as snow".

The sin in our lives makes us like the deadness of fall, but the blood of Jesus Christ cleanses us from our sins and makes us as white as snow and alive again. "If we confess our sins, He is faithful and just to forgive us of our sins and cleanse us from all unrighteousness" (1 John 1:9). We have that access to God because of the death, burial and resurrection of Jesus Christ.

I am thankful that the "white out" I experienced today brought me back to God's Word so that I could praise Him in this storm and thank Him for what He has done for a sinner like me. That because of Christ, He has "whited out" my sins and erased them from all record and declared me to be righteous. It was nothing I have done but all what Christ has done in my place. Have your sins been "whited out"?

Notes:_____
_____
_____
_____
_____
_____
_____
_____
_____
_____
_____
_____
_____
_____
_____
_____
_____
_____

December 10

I Quit

I quit. I did, I quit Facebook because I was tired of all the negative posts and the arguing and bickering between friends that have been friends for so long. I got tired of the constant division between groups based upon their opinions and beliefs. If you didn't agree with someone, you were labeled with some term that ended in "-ist". People constantly sharing their opinion as if their opinion was the only correct way of looking at a particular topic. There was, and still is, such a lack of respect anymore on social media. Things you would never say to a person face-to-face has become so easy to type out behind a screen. So, I got tired of it and left Facebook for a while.

But, when you quit something like that, you miss all of the positive things that are going on in people's lives. You miss celebrating birthdays and anniversaries with people you know. You miss pictures of family and big announcements. Things were going on in our lives that were being shared on Facebook and I wasn't able to take part in those big life events. So, after about four months, I decided it was time to come back to Facebook and see what I had been missing. But I made a deal with myself before coming back.

First, I was not going to post anything negative on Facebook that would cause division or allow an argument to start. Second, I was not going to share anyone's post that could possibly lead to division or argument. And third, I was not going to comment in a negative way on anyone else's post as to start an argument. I had made up my mind that I was only going to use social media in a positive way.

Along with all the things I was "not" going to do, I decide that I was going to do something daily that would be positive in nature, and that is how the page Between Two Trees started out on Facebook. And now, a whole year later, God has open the door for all of those posts to become a book that you are reading.

"Let no corrupt talk come out of your mouth, but only such as is good for building up, as fits the occasion, that it may give grace to those who hear." – Ephesians 4:29.

Notes:_____

_____
_____
_____
_____
_____
_____
_____
_____
_____
_____
_____
_____

December 11

Seasons

Seasons. I have to admit that winter is not my favorite season. I highly dislike the cold weather and the snow that it brings. It is one of the main reasons I looked to leave New York and relocate in the south. Even though our winter season is much shorter and milder than it is in the north, it still brings back bad memories of all the snow shoveling I had to do as a kid.

If I had to choose, I would say that autumn is my favorite season followed by summer and spring. I like the warm days and cool mornings/evenings. I like the smell in the air, the colors of the trees and the memories of soccer seasons gone by. It may be one of the oddest things you hear all day, but I love the smell of burning leaves! Crazy right?

Even though I dislike the winter season, I have a great appreciation for it because I know that it was instituted by God. There is a reason for the four seasons most of the world goes through. It is a reminder of the cycle of life: birth, maturity and death. The book of Ecclesiastes tells us that there is a time for all things.

"For everything there is a season, and a time for every matter under heaven:
a time to be born, and a time to die; a time to plant, and a time to pluck up what is planted;
a time to kill, and a time to heal; a time to break down, and a time to build up;
a time to weep, and a time to laugh; a time to mourn, and a time to dance;" - Ecclesiastes
3:1-4

Life brings us through all seasons and so does our lives as Christians. There are times when we feel reborn with a new zest for life and the things of God. But there are also times when we feel spiritual dead, times when God feels distant and our Christian lives feel like they are in a rut. Be encouraged that it is just a season. It's not the end and just like the four seasons that we experience, there is a time when your current season will come to an end and a new season will begin.

Notes:_____
_____
_____
_____
_____
_____
_____
_____
_____
_____
_____
_____

December 12

Giving

Giving. "It is better to give than to receive." How many times have you heard that in your life? As a kid I thought that was the stupidest thing ever said. How can it be better to give than it is to receive? Now that I'm older, I find that statement to be one of the truest things I have ever heard. What a difference age and wisdom makes.

It's that time of year when we give each other gifts, things we wouldn't normally buy for ourselves but would love to have someone else give us for a gift. We get caught up in the spirit of giving, especially to our children, to bring them happiness, only to have those gifts lose their luster a couple of weeks later.

In the past week or so, there have been at least three instances of famous rich people paying off items on layaway at various Walmart locations across the country. Names like Tyler Perry, Kid Rock and the owner of Jimmy Johns have made the news for paying off hundreds of thousands of dollars' worth of layaway items. I think it is wonderful that they use their financial blessings to bless others that may be in need.

I don't know about you, but I don't have hundreds of thousands of dollars to pay off layaways at Walmart. But I do have the means to pay for someone's lunch behind me in the drive thru or someone's coffee at the gas station or maybe all I can afford is a warm smile and a "hello". We all have opportunities this holiday season to give back just a little bit to brighten someone else's day. It may not seem like much to us in comparison to the amounts given by others, but it may mean the world to the one we bless.

"For God so loved the world, He GAVE His only begotten Son that whosoever believes in Him shall not perish but have eternal life." That is the ultimate act of giving, when God gave us His Son, in the form of a baby, that would grow up to live a sinless life and die on the cross of Calvary in our place so that we can be given the gift of forgiveness of our sins. There is no better gift ever given in the history of the world than Jesus Christ.

I hope you have accepted God's gift. It's a gift, meaning it's free, all you have to do is accept it.

Notes:_____
_____
_____
_____
_____
_____
_____
_____

December 13

Black Ice

Black Ice. Probably more dangerous than driving in the snow itself. At least with the snow you can see it. Black ice just comes out of nowhere when you least expect it. The longer we drive in winter conditions, the more wisdom we gain where the black ice might be around curves, under tree-lined areas and so forth. But sometimes you just aren't expecting it.

It happened to me this morning driving in to work. Having driven the same route all week, I knew where the tricky spots were going to be, but I got too comfortable with my driving. I was driving along and came to a bridge that had not been icy all week and when I hit that area my truck went almost completely sideways. Luckily there was no one else around me and I was able to quickly get it back under control.

Life happens the same way sometimes. We have an understanding where the tricky spots in our lives are and we take precautions with them, but sometimes we get way too comfortable with life. We just end up going through the motions out of routine and then all of a sudden, what we should have been prepared for and on the lookout for, catches us off guard and sends us spinning. Sometimes we gain control back right away and other times it may send us into the snowbank and needing help from others to get out.

The Bible warns us multiple times to "be ready" and to "be alert". God wants us to understand that the devil and his demons are going to do anything they can to trip us up. They know that if we fall into some sort of sin that it will ruin our testimony to others. As Christians, we are instructed to always be ready and always be on alert so that we can avoid the dangers and pitfalls that may be in our path.

However, that does not mean we are to live our lives in fear! The Bible also encourages us to "fear not"! That phrase, fear not, occurs 365 times in the Bible; one occurrence for every day of the year as a daily reminder that God doesn't want us to live in fear. Being alert and being fearful are two different thing. The Word of God tells us to be ready but not to be scared.

Keep your eyes out for black ice this winter and keep your eyes out for the "slippery slopes" in your life as well.

Notes:_____
_____
_____
_____
_____
_____
_____

Work

Work. I was doing a little work during the recent snowstorm, clearing out the fallen snow before the storm had stopped to make the final shoveling less heavy. It had snowed about ten inches already and it was the wet, heavy snow, so I didn't want to break my back trying to do it all at once. Although it is twice the work to shovel now and then again later, it is worth not having to kill myself when the storm is over.

The idea got me thinking about the concept of work. The Bible talks about two different types of work; the work we do before we become Christians and the work we do after we become Christians. The work we do before we become Christians is all for naught because there is nothing good we can do that will put us in good standing with God. Other religions stress the importance of works as a way to earn your way into the next life, but Christianity isn't about works, it's about a relationship. We only have that relationship with God through accepting what His Son, Jesus Christ, did for us on the Cross of Calvary.

The second concept of work come after we become Christians. We don't work for God in order to keep good standing with Him, we work for God as an appreciation of what He has done for us. Our works are an outward showing of the grace that God has given us through Christ. "But someone will say, 'You have faith and I have works.' Show me your faith apart from your works, and I will show you my faith by my works." – James 2:18.

Our Christian works do not save us, our Christian works show others our faith in God. Our work as Christians should never be about our own glory, but, instead, should be all about God receiving the glory He so richly deserves. Any work we do as Christians for our own glory will be burned up when we stand before God as would hay, wood and straw. But, if our works are done to God's glory, they will pass through the fire like precious jewels. (1 Corinthians 3:12-15)

Notes:_____

_____
_____
_____
_____
_____
_____
_____
_____
_____
_____
_____
_____
_____
_____

Truth About Christmas - Part 1

The truth about Christmas. Over the next couple of posts, we will use the Gospels of Luke and Matthew to piece together the actual events that surround the birth of Jesus Christ. During this time of year, we see a lot of representations of what happened that first Christmas, but are they accurate? Movies, television shows, Christmas carols and nativity scenes all try to give us an understanding of what happened, but we will look to the truth of God's Word to find the answers.

The first thing we will look at is when was Jesus really born. Was He born during the month of December? Was it cold and snowy when He arrived? The answer to both of those questions is "no". Jesus Christ was probably born sometime in the spring between March and May.

We know from Luke 2:1-15 that the shepherds were watching their flocks at night. Under normal circumstances the shepherds would have put their flocks in a sheep fold and been done with them for the night and would have gotten some sleep. But the fact that they were watching their sheep means there was some extenuating circumstances: the sheep were pregnant and about the have their lambs. This would have kept the shepherds on high alert and some of them would have been awake while the others slept; taking turns on watch during the night.

So, it turns out that as these shepherds were watching their sheep that night awaiting the birth of the lambs while the birth of the Lamb of God was about to take place a short distance away from the fields outside of Bethlehem were these shepherds were.

So why do we celebrate the birth of the Savior on the 25th of December every year? It was instituted by Pope Julius I in 385 AD to challenge the celebration of the pagan and immoral Roman god Saturn called Saturnalia. Festivities included the exchanging of gifts, gambling, sacrifices to Saturn and societal role reversals. Pope Julius felt that celebrating the birth of Christ shortly after the celebration of Saturn would challenge the Roman belief system of multiple gods.

Tomorrow we will look at the announcement of the arrival of the Savior to the shepherds by the angelic host and the response of those shepherds.

Notes:_____

_____

_____

_____

_____

_____

December 16

Truth About Christmas - Part 2

Imagine the darkness of night being interrupted by the bright glow of an angelic being that you have never seen before. When I talk about darkness of night, I mean pitch dark, not living in the suburbs dark. It was out in the country dark, nothing but light from the moon and the stars. And then all of a sudden..... BAM! This angelic being that you have never before witnessed shows up out of nowhere. They may have heard of angels, but they had obviously never seen one.

These lowly shepherds were so frightened by the appearance of this angel that even the angel of God had to start out by reassuring them to "fear not". I'm sure that the shepherds didn't automatically just go, "Oh, okay, we're good now."

The angel of God gave them a message of utmost importance; the Savior, that the entire nation of Israel had been waiting for, has now arrived. The angel gave them specific instructions of where to find the baby and in what condition they would find him in. As soon as the announcement was made, the entire sky was lit up with the angelic host of heaven giving praises to God. If the shepherds were afraid at the appearance of just one angel, I wonder what their fear level was raised to when this happened?

I have always wondered why the God of Creation chose the lowest class of society, shepherds, to receive the announcement of the birth of the long awaited Christ. Why wasn't it announced to the royalty of the times or the religious leaders of the day? The answer is simple, God chose to announce the birth of the Savior to those that were going to be just like Jesus Christ, a shepherd. John the Baptist announced, "Behold, the Lamb of God who takes away the sins of the world." Christ himself said, "I am the good Shepherd. The good Shepherd lays down his life for his sheep."

Christ was the Shepherd King and those that first proclaimed the birth of the Savior were the shepherds. Luke 2:20 says "the shepherds returned and glorified and praised God for all they had heard and seen." Besides the angelic announcement to them, the shepherds became the first to spread the Good News of the Savior's birth. The lives of these men were changed and they couldn't do anything but share what they had seen.

Tomorrow we will look at the movement of Jesus and His family to fulfill the Law after His birth.

Notes:_____
_____
_____
_____
_____

Truth About Christmas - Part 3

They needed to follow the Law. Now that Jesus had been born to Mary and Joseph, His parents were under strict requirements to follow the Law of Moses. Mary and Joseph were both decedents of David, meaning they were Jewish and had to follow the Law.

Found in Leviticus 2:2-8, the Law said that any woman that bore a male child was ceremoniously unclean for seven days. Then on the eighth day, according to the Law, Jesus was brought to a rabbi in Bethlehem and circumcised. Mary would then have to go through another thirty-three days of purification to be considered completely clean.

So after a total of forty-one days, Mary, Joseph and Jesus leave Bethlehem and travel to Jerusalem according, once again, to the Law. The Law stated they were to present the first born male child to the Lord and offer a sacrifice. The sacrifice of two turtle doves shows just how poor Joseph and his family was because that was the minimum sacrifice that could be made.

Luke 2:39 tells us that after the sacrifice was made in Jerusalem, that Mary, Joseph and Jesus left Jerusalem and went home to Nazareth. They did not go back to Bethlehem. They went home, not to the inn. This means within the first two months of Jesus being born they are back home in Nazareth. This will have significant importance when we look at the wise men and their introduction into the story tomorrow.

Notes:_____
_____
_____
_____
_____
_____
_____
_____
_____
_____
_____
_____
_____
_____
_____
_____
_____
_____
_____
_____
_____
_____

Truth About Christmas - Part 4

Beautiful star of Bethlehem. At the same time that Luke's version of the birth of Christ is taking place and the angels are informing the shepherds of the birth of the Savior, Matthew is telling about additional events taking place hundreds of miles away that same night. As the angelic host lit up the sky around the shepherds, a beautiful star was over Bethlehem for all the world to see and it caught the attention of wise men in the East.

Chapter two of the Gospel of Matthew gives us further insight into the events that took place on that fabulous night. Wise men, probably astronomers, noticed something different in the sky that evening. The East probably meant somewhere around Babylon, present day Iraq.

Because they were "wise men" they searched for a meaning to why this magnificent star appeared in the night sky on this specific occasion. This led them to the scriptures of the Old Testament and possibly directly to Numbers 24:17 that the star had come from Jacob and the scepter from Israel.

It would have taken a considerable amount of time from the appearance of the star until they made their way to the location of the star they saw that night. First, they had to find out what the star meant, then they would have prepared for such a journey and finally they would have made the 600-800 mile journey by land. In all, it probably would have been between eighteen to twenty-four months before they made it to Israel.

Tomorrow we will look at what happened when the wise men finally made it to King Herod to inquire of the appearance of the star.

Notes:_____

_____

_____

_____

_____

_____

_____

_____

_____

_____

_____

_____

_____

_____

_____

_____

December 19

Truth About Christmas - Part 5

The wise men finally made it to Jerusalem. After about almost two years from the appearance of the star, the wise men finally made it to where they would find the answer to the meaning of the star. We can assume that it took nearly two years to get there because in Matthew 2:16, King Herod orders all the male children ages two years old and younger be killed. If the star had only been a couple of months earlier, why kill children as old as two?

Not knowing where to go and who to go to for information about the appearance of the star, they decide to go to the king to find out about the King of the Jews. Not knowing the answers to the questions of the wise men, King Herod inquires of them when the star appeared and then sent the scribes and chief priests to learn more information. The king's scholars point the wise men in the direction of Bethlehem because of the prophecy in Micah 5:2 and the wise men leave to find the baby.

At some point from their journey from Jerusalem to Bethlehem, the star appears once again over where they would find the baby. The star lead them to Jesus, not to Bethlehem, but to where Jesus was. Bethlehem is never mentioned again after King Herod sent them in that direction other than killing the male children there and the surrounding areas. If Jesus was still in Bethlehem, the appearance of the star would not have been necessary. But Jesus wasn't in Bethlehem.

When the wise men arrived, Jesus was no longer a baby. It said the child was with His mother. This means he was independent of her or else it would have said the mother was with the child. The wise men found them in a house and not in a stable, another way we know they were no longer in Bethlehem. Finally, the wise men offered their gifts directly to Jesus showing that He was old enough to accept them Himself.

The text of Matthew never says that there were three wise men, only that the wise men gave three gifts: gold, frankincense and myrrh. There could have been four, five or six wise men, we don't know but we always assume three.

Tomorrow we will look at the final part of the Christmas story.

Notes:_____

_____
_____
_____
_____
_____
_____
_____

Truth About Christmas - Part 6

Dreams, angels and one furious king. After the wise men had delivered their gifts and worshipped the child King of the Jews, they received a message by the way of a dream telling them they were not to go back to King Herod as requested. Herod had instructed them to return and tell him the whereabouts of the child so he could go and worship him. If he really wanted to worship Jesus, he would have went along with the wise men.

The wickedness inside of Herod's heart didn't want to worship the One who would take his place, he wanted to get rid of him. When the wise men did not return, he was furious and decreed that all the male children of Bethlehem and the surrounding areas be killed in hopes this would eliminate the threat to his throne.

Knowing the heart of Herod, God sent an angel of the Lord to Joseph telling him to flee with his family to Egypt to escape the slaughter of innocent boys. After Herod had died, the same angel appeared to Joseph once again, this time in a dream, telling him it was safe to return to his hometown of Nazareth.

Luke tells us that Jesus increased in wisdom and in stature and in favor with God and man. All of these events happened exactly the way they did so that the fulfillment of prophecy could prove that this child, Jesus Christ, was the long promised Messiah that Israel had been waiting for.

Notes:_____

_____
_____
_____
_____
_____
_____
_____
_____
_____
_____
_____
_____
_____
_____
_____
_____
_____
_____
_____
_____

Thank You

Thank you. It's something that isn't said much anymore in our society. Have you ever held a door open for someone and they walk right past and don't say a word to you; not a "thank you" or an "I appreciate that"? I recently stopped to help someone pick stuff up off the floor that they had dropped and not one word was mentioned of me stopping to help. What type of society have we become where we can't even thank people for going out of their way to help us? It's not a hard thing to do, say "thank you", but it has become less and less prominent in the day we live.

So, I wanted to stop today and say, "thank you"! I want everyone to know how thankful I am as we come upon the Christmas season. I want to say thank you to the people that followed the Between Two Trees blog from day 1. For those of you who liked and loved the posts, for those of you who commented that the post was exactly what you needed to hear that day, and for those of you who shared the post on a daily basis with the people who follow you so that they could read the post as well. A great big "thank you" goes out to all of you for making the page grow over the year.

Thank you to those who verbally encouraged me to continue to write a post every day. Thank you to my family; my wife and children, for putting up with the time I invested in this blog that has become a book. Thank you to my family who was the basis for most of the activity I ended writing about. Thank you for those couple of people that gave me the idea to turn my blog posts into a daily devotional, this is the work of your speaking up as I believe God led you to do so.

But, most of all, during this time we celebrate the birth of our Savior, I want to thank God for thinking so much of me that He sent His only begotten Son into this world to ultimately die a horrible and painful death in my place so that I may have access and a relationship with Him. That is the purpose of the season; the birth of our Savior. God leaving the glory of heaven to become a baby, to grow up living a sinless life and going to the Cross of Calvary to pay for my sins, and your sins; sins He didn't commit.

Are you thankful?

Notes:_____

_____

_____

_____

_____

_____

_____

_____

_____

December 22

Swaddling Clothes

Swaddling Clothes. "You will find a baby wrapped in swaddling clothes and lying in a manger." That was going to be the sign to the shepherds to show that what the angel said about the birth of the Savior was true. Such an innocent line in Luke but filled with so much meaning when put in its context.

It is believed that these shepherds outside of Bethlehem weren't just average, everyday shepherds, they were temple shepherds caring for sheep that were ready to deliver lambs for the sacrifices. When these lambs were born and inspected to make sure they had no spot or blemish, that they were perfect lambs, they were wrapped in swaddling cloth to make sure that they did not become flawed in any way. These lambs were needed for the temple sacrifices and these shepherds would make their living from the birth of these lambs.

So when the Angel of the Lord told them that the sign that the Savior was born was that they would find him wrapped in swaddling clothes, this would have had a completely different meaning to them than it does to us. See, they would have automatically associated this to mean that the baby Jesus was truly the Lamb of God, perfect and spotless. They may not have known what the full meaning was and that He was going to be the perfect sacrifice, but they knew He was born spotless and pure.

The cousin of Jesus, John the Baptist, had this understanding about the Christ. When Jesus came on the scene at the Jordan River where John was baptizing Jews, he stopped and said, "Behold, the Lamb of God who takes away the sins of the world."

The One who started off in this world wrapped in swaddling clothes, ended up being the perfect sacrifice for our sins. Born amongst the new lambs, God's Lamb was treated just like the sacrificial lambs born to the shepherds in the fields outside of Bethlehem. The major difference was the animal sacrifices only covered the sin of the people, while the sacrifice of the Lamb of God removed their sins, as far as the east is from the west.

Notes:_____

_____
_____
_____
_____
_____
_____
_____
_____
_____
_____
_____

December 23

Prophecy of the Christ

The birth of the Savior was found in the prophecy of the Old Testament.

Isaiah 7:14 - "Therefore the Lord Himself will give you a sign. Behold, the virgin shall conceive and bear a son, and shall call His name Emmanuel."

Psalm 72:9-10 - "May desert tribes bow down before him.....May the kings of Tarshish and of the coastlands render him tribute; May the kings of Sheba and Seba bring gifts!"

Numbers 24:17 - "I see him, but not now; I behold him, but not near: a star shall come out of Jacob, and a scepter shall rise out of Israel."

Jeremiah 23:5 - "Behold, the days are coming, declares the Lord, when I will raise up for David a righteous branch, and he shall reign as king and deal wisely, and shall execute justice and righteousness in the land."

Micah 34:23 - "But you, O Bethlehem Ephrathah, who are too little to be among the clans of Judah, from you shall come forth for me one who is to be ruler in Israel, whose coming forth is from old, from ancient days."

Ezekiel 34:23 - "And I will set up over them one shepherd, my servant David, and he shall feed them: he shall feed them and be their shepherd."

Isaiah 60:6 - "They shall bring gold and frankincense, and shall bring good news, the praises of the Lord."

Hosea 11:1 - "When Israel was a child, I loved him, and out of Egypt I called my son."

Isaiah 9:6 - "For unto us a child is born, to us a sin is given; and the government shall be upon his shoulder, and his name shall be called Wonderful Counselor, Mighty God, Everlasting Father, Prince of Peace."

There are no prophecies about Muhammad (Islam), Joseph Smith (Mormonism), Charles Russell (Jehovah's Witness) or Siddhartha (Buddhism). The only one who was promised and came was the Savior, Jesus Christ.

Notes:_____
_____
_____
_____
_____

December 24

The Word Became Flesh

Christmas Eve. For the past week we have looked at the truth about Christmas and the birth of the Savior from the Gospels of Matthew and Luke. We looked at the purpose of His Incarnation, His Crucifixion, our Salvation and God's Glorification. We looked at the meaning of the swaddling clothes and the Old Testament prophecy of His birth.

We sometimes celebrate His birth with the misunderstanding that this was the beginning of His existence, but it was not. The Gospel of John tell us that He has always existed. In the beginning was the Word (Jesus), and the Word was with God, and the Word was God. Christ always existed from eternity past and was with God and the Holy Spirit before the creation of anything that existed (1:1). His death on the Cross was not the end of His existence either; He lives today!

"And the Word became flesh and dwelt among us, and we have seen his glory, glory as of the only Son from the Father, full of grace and truth." (John 1:14). It's hard to grasp that God was willing to leave the throne of heaven to become like His own creation so that He could save us from our sins. While on earth, He was still fully God as well as being fully human. He still knew all things but still got hungry and tired.

That baby in the manger that we celebrate at Christmas became the man that was despised and crucified on the Cross. "He came unto His own and His own received Him not" (John 1:11). There is no Christmas without Jesus Christ! He is THE reason for the season.

Notes:_____

_____
_____
_____
_____
_____
_____
_____
_____
_____
_____
_____
_____
_____
_____
_____
_____
_____
_____

The Purpose of Christmas

Merry Christmas. My prayer for you is that you are celebrating the birth of our Savior with all of your family and friends this year. Have you ever stopped and wondered what the purpose of Christmas is? It is not about Santa Claus, trees, presents or parties. It's about the birth of the Savior of the world. It's about Jesus Christ leaving His throne in heaven to become a mortal baby, still fully possessing His divine nature while also taking on the nature of His creation.

The purpose of Christmas is the incarnation of God in human form. The birth of the coming Messiah was forecast all the way back in the third chapter of the book of Genesis. The coming of the Messiah was spoken of by the prophets of the Old Testament. The Gospel accounts give us a narrative of the incarnation of God among His creation. If we do not have the incarnation of God, we have no possibility of salvation.

The whole purpose of the incarnation was to lead Christ to the crucifixion. Without the incarnation of Christ, there is no possibility of His crucifixion. The crucifixion of Christ is the debt payment that God required for the sins of the world. Christ wasn't paying for His own sins on the Cross, He was paying for my sins on the Cross, and He was paying for your sins on the Cross. That was the purpose of the crucifixion.

The purpose of the crucifixion was to lead to the resurrection of Christ from the grave. If Christ wasn't crucified and died, there would be no opportunity for the resurrection of our Savior. The resurrection of Jesus Christ from the sealed tomb after three days was to show that God was satisfied with the payment for our sins by the death of His Son. If Christ wasn't resurrected, then God was not satisfied and we are still accountable to Him for our sins. But now, when we place our faith in Jesus Christ, that We accept His death in our place for the payment of our sins, we are saved from having to pay the punishment for our own sins because Christ has already paid it.

And that, my brothers and sisters in Christ, is the purpose of Christmas.

I hope you have a Merry Christmas and a wonderful New Year!

Notes:_____
_____
_____
_____
_____
_____
_____
_____
_____
_____
_____

December 26

Christmas Letdown

Oh, the letdown! The day after Christmas, sometimes starting Christmas evening, is such a letdown. Since Thanksgiving, everything has been geared toward the celebration of Christmas. The shopping started, travel reservations may have been made, deciding what to cook and so on and so on. And then it's over in a blink of an eye!

Some of us may have had to head back to work today and that made Christmas night all the less enjoyable. Some of us may be heading to the landfill to throw away bags of wrapping paper and loads of Amazon boxes. Even more may be heading back to one of the stores to exchange that gift that makes you wonder if people even know who you are and what you like!

It got me thinking about Mary and Joseph and the day after the birth of the promised Savior. They had all the shepherds show up that first night to welcome the newborn King, offering praises and stories of the news from the angels out in the fields. That very first night was an exciting time and then the next day everyone was gone and it was just the three of them. The gift of God had arrived and it was celebrated and now it was back to the normal life, somewhat.

Now that the celebration of Christmas is gone and we head back to our normal lives for another year, we still have reasons to celebrate Christ. Just like Mary and Joseph, life goes on the same as it was, but completely different than it was, because the Savior was born. The Gospel of Luke tells us that Jesus grew and became strong, filled with wisdom. And the favor of God was upon him (2:40).

We should strive to do the same: grow spiritually, become stronger in our faith and be filled with wisdom of God's Word. The results will be that the favor of God will also be upon us. Don't let today be a letdown, our work has just begun.

Notes:_____
_____
_____
_____
_____
_____
_____
_____
_____
_____
_____
_____

December 27

Finish Strong

Finish Strong. This time of year, can be very hard on those that have lost loved ones this past year. I saw many posts on Christmas of friends and family mentioning that this year was different than the last year because someone in their lives were missing. It makes my heart hurt for them because I know how they feel to miss loved ones.

I've also seen where some people have passed away over the last couple of days, people I know and people I have never met. Life is fragile and we never know when the end will come for each of us. We do know that it will come at some point unless the Lord comes back again soon. So, the question is: how are we living in light of that fact?

Unlike a race that has a finish line where you know how much further you have before completing the race, life doesn't give us that option. It can be hours, days, months or years. We just need to keep running until that time comes. I don't know about you but I want to finish strong!

The Apostle Paul told Timothy that he had fought the good fight and he had finished his race. That which the Lord had placed in front of him to accomplish had been completed and Paul finished strong. We have that same opportunity to finish strong or we can give up and quit the race that God has placed before us.

It reminded me of a sermon I heard a couple months ago up in Christiansburg, VA preached from the book of Philemon. The focus was on the last four people mentioned in the letter: Epaphras, Mark, Aristarchus and Demas. Of those four men, three finished strong but Demas did not. We know from Paul's second letter to Timothy that Demas abandoned Paul and chased after the love of the world. He didn't finish strong. He lost sight of the race and chased after the lies the world has to offer.

As we come to the end of this year, let us make it a priority to finish 2018 strong. And let us make it a priority in our lives, not knowing when it will end, to finish strong. To complete the race that God has placed in front of us so that on that day, we can stand before God and hear those words that every believer longs to hear, "Well done good and faithful servant."

Notes:_____
_____
_____
_____
_____
_____

December 28

Power of Prayer

The power of prayer. As you can imagine, a lot of prayer requests come in to Between Two Trees for different needs that people have in their lives. Sometime the requests come in and I am asked to share them publicly because those making the request know that the power of the prayers of God's saints is powerful and effective. At other times, the requests come in and they do not want them to be shared publicly, and that is fine too. I've been able to see the prayer requests turn out like people had prayed for, and I've seen God not answer the prayer in the way that we had hoped.

It is hard sometimes when God does not answer our prayer the way that we hope He will. But we have to understand that God knows so much more about the situation and the future than we ever will. God is not bound by time so He understands things that we have yet to understand. God specifically says in His Word, "For my thoughts are not your thoughts, neither are your ways my ways, declares the Lord. For as the heavens are higher than the earth, so are my ways higher than your ways and my thoughts than your thoughts." Isaiah 55:8-9.

The good thing is that we know from God's Word that He hears our prayers when we call out to Him. We may not always understand the outcome of why our prayers are not answered the way we want, but we have to put our trust in God and that His ways are perfect. It still hurts when things don't go the way we want, but we also have a God that will comfort us in our times of pain and sorrow.

I am sure that you have been through things in your life that you wish God had done differently, I know I have, but we can be assured that the God we serve is not a vengeful God, but a loving God that wants better for us than we do ourselves. Those things that we go through are meant to help us being comforters to others that experience the same issues.

"Blessed be the God and Father of our Lord Jesus Christ, the Father of mercies and the God of all comfort, who comforts us in all of our afflictions, so that we may be able to comfort those who are in any affliction, with the comfort with which we ourselves are comforted by God." – 2 Corinthians 1:3-4.

Notes:_____
_____
_____
_____
_____
_____
_____
_____
_____

December 29

Be Positive

Be positive! If you can be anything in this world, choose to be nice. I've seen that meme on Facebook quite often. I would say, be nice, but also be positive. There is so much negativity in this world it is hard sometimes to be positive. Admittedly, I get caught up in the negative things of this world and it's hard to always be positive, but as Christians, we have so much to be positive about.

I mentioned in my video yesterday that I gave up Facebook for a while because of all the negative things I was getting caught up in and decided to come back to make a positive page that I could share every day. But I made three promises to myself that I would stick to when I came back. First, I wouldn't share any posts that were political or would cause division. Second, I would no longer comment on any of the negative posts and if someone wanted to argue I would not respond. Last, I would start Between Two Trees so that I could share Biblical truths and positive words on a daily basis.

Some people might wonder, "Isn't sharing your faith a possible cause for division?" Yes, but it's different because it's not based upon my opinion, it's based upon the Truth of God's Word. That makes it automatically divisive right there. The difference is that it's God's Truth verses Satan's lies, it's light verses darkness and it's the holy verses the unholy.

The author of the Book of Hebrews wrote, "For the word of God is living and active, sharper than any two-edged sword, piercing to the division of soul and of spirit, of joints and of marrow, and discerning the thoughts and intentions of the heart." - Hebrews 4:12. I share the Word of God because it pierces the heart and soul of those that hear it. People aren't going to hear the Truth unless somebody shares His Truth.

Be positive in this negative world. Be a light in the darkness of this world. And be Holy in this world that celebrates the unholy. Share the Gospel of Jesus Christ, not to divide, but to reconcile.

Notes:_____

_____
_____
_____
_____
_____
_____
_____
_____
_____
_____

December 30

Rejection Hurts

Rejection hurts! It is something all of us deal with throughout our lives, some are rejected more than others, but we have all faced rejection. We may be rejected as children by our parents because we are unwanted. Or maybe we are rejected from sports teams because we are not athletic enough. We face rejection from the opposite sex as we grow up and want to start dating. Colleges reject us because we aren't intelligent enough to meet their requirements. Or we may face rejection from employers because we don't have enough experience. Whatever the situation, we all face rejection.

Most of us are strong enough to face rejection and move on in life, whether it is finding a new hobby, a new relationship or a new job. We make it and still thrive in whatever new endeavors we move on to.

However, there is a future date in everyone's life where if you are rejected there is no further opportunity. The Bible tells us that we will all stand before God one day and give an account of our lives. Those that accepted Christ's saving actions on the Cross will be accepted because of their position in Christ. But there is going to be another group that didn't accept Christ's free gift of salvation and they will be rejected. They will hear the most horrible five words spoken in the Bible, "Depart, I never knew you."

That final rejection seals their eternal destiny in a place called hell. A place created for Satan and his demons and not for man. People will ask, how could a loving God send people to hell? God doesn't send anyone to hell but the devil and his demons, everyone else chooses to go there by not accepting Christ as their Savior here on earth. That decision needs to be made now because you won't get that opportunity when you stand before God, your fate will have already been sealed. I pray you bow your knee and confess Jesus Christ as your Savior now because you will either do it know on your own or you will do it before Him later, but it will be too late.

Notes:_____
_____
_____
_____
_____
_____
_____
_____
_____
_____
_____
_____
_____
_____

December 31

New Year's Eve

It's almost over! This year comes to an end tonight at midnight. Tomorrow starts a whole new year. Does it really make that big of a difference? I've never been that into the big deal of a new year. It just means I'll struggle for the next couple of months to remember to write '19 on things instead of '18. I'm sure I'll be crossing the wrong date out for a while.

The beginning of a new year is usually a good time to start over and do the things this year that we promised ourselves we would start doing last year. We'll get in better shape, we'll lose weight, we'll save more money, read more books, and so on and so on. This week will start one of the busiest sign up times at gyms across the country only to be abandoned by March. Why do we do this? Because our will power just doesn't match the effort needed to fulfill the promises, we make to ourselves. As the old saying goes, "our eyes are bigger than our bellies!"

This transfers to the Christian life as well. We say we'll attend church more regularly, we'll read our Bibles more, we'll do a better job praying or we will share the Gospel with others every chance we get. All great things to strive for as a Christian, and I wish you all the success of accomplishing them this year if they are your goals. But we can't do any of them in our own strength, we must let the Holy Spirit work in us to convict us to follow through on them. As Jesus told his disciples in the Garden of Gethsemane, "the spirit is willing, but the flesh is week.

Spend time today praying that God will show you what He wants you to let the Spirit work on this year in you. "Ask, and it will be given to you; seek, and you will find; knock, and it will be opened to you." Luke 11:9.

Notes:_____
_____
_____
_____
_____
_____
_____
_____
_____
_____
_____
_____
_____
_____
_____
_____
_____

Made in the USA
Coppell, TX
04 January 2020